The Peloponnese

David Willett

LONELY PLANET PUBLICATIONS
Melbourne • Oakland • London • Paris

GREECE

Evia

Gulf
of
Evia

Sterea
Ellada

THE ACROPOLIS
The most famous monument
of the ancient world

DIAKOFTO – KALAVRYTA RAILWAY
An unforgettable ride through the spectacular Vouraïkos Gorge

ANCIENT CORINTH
Explore the ruins of ancient Greece's richest city

ANCIENT MYCENAE
Mythology and history are inextricably linked in this magnificent city

ANCIENT OLYMPIA
Pay homage to the birthplace of the Olympic Games

KARITENA
Leave the medieval village behind by mountain bike

Livadia

Thiva (Thebes)

Attica

ATHENS
Piraeus
Eleﬁna
Megara
Agios Theodoi
E94
Loutraki
Isthmia
Corinth
Ancient Corinth
Kato Almyri
Kehries
Hiliomodi
Sofﬁko
Derveni
Xylokastro
Kiato
Vasiliko
Zemeno
Stimaga
Nemea
Arﬁa Kloutra
Dervenakia
Mycenae
Neo Ireo
Agia Triada
Argos
Kafalari
Ellniko
Karia
Mt Artemisio (1771m)
Kiveri
Neo Kios
Naﬂio
Tolo
Astros

Corinthian Gulf
Derveni
Akrata
Diakofto
Zahlorou
Kalavryta
Cave of the Lakes
Kastria
Mt Helmos (2130m)
Stemnitsa
Steno
Mt Kilini (2374m)
Mt Pharmakas (1615m)

Salamis
Saronic Gulf
Aegina
Anﬁstri

Argolis
Corinthia

Ancient Olympia
Olympia
Pyrgos
Zacharo

Nea Manolada
Andravida
Lehena
Amaliada
Efira
Kato Ahaïa
Patras
Rio
Antirio
Nafpaktos

Achaïa
Mt Panahaïko (1924m)
Mt Erymanthos (2224m)
Mt Lambia (1791m)
Lambia
Mt Aphrodisio (1445m)
Dafni
Ilia
Kalithea
Figalia
Andritsena

Arcadia
Tripolis
E65
E55

Karitena
Megalopoli
Mt Lykaio (1420m)
Mt Tetrazio (1389m)

Kyparissia Gulf
Cape Tripiti
Katakolo
Kastro
Gastouni
Kyllini
Lake Kotihi

Patras Gulf

Methana
Poros
Galatas
Troizina
Mt Didimo (1121m)
Driopi
Iraﬁa
Trahia
Palea Epidavros
Mt Arahneo (1197m)
Lygourio
Asklepion Epidavros
Dimena
Nea Epidavros
Kortos
Kehries Bay

Gulf of Hydra
Hydra
Krandi
Porto Heli
Frachthi Cave
Ermioni
Kamezorka
Iria
Kandia

Gulf of Tolo
Aghios Andreas
Eleohori

HYDRA
Relax on this beautiful, tranquil island where there are no private motor vehicles

LEONIDIO
Attractive white-washed village set at the mouth of the dramatic Badron Gorge

MONEMVASIA
Cross the causeway to reach the Gibraltar of Greece

KYTHIRA
Tranquil villages and some of the cleanest beaches in Greece

STOUPA
Dance like Zorba or dream away on the golden beach where the real-life original may have strolled

KALAMATA
Eat your fill of olives without having them shipped to you

FINIKOUNDA
A pretty fishing village with glorious beaches

IONIAN SEA

MIRTOO SEA

MEDITERRANEAN SEA

Lakonian Gulf

Messinian Gulf

Messinia

Lakonia

Taygetos Mountains

Mt Profitis Ilias (2404m)

Mt Parnon (1839m)

Parnon Mountains

Langada Pass

River Pamisos

Mt Likodimo (960m)

Cape Akritas

Methoni Peninsula

Pilos Bay

Navarino Bay

Kythira

Spetsopoula

Leonidio
Pouliitra
Kyparissi
Kosmas
Geraki
Molai
Skala
Gythio
Elea
Pitra
Geráki
Gefyra
Monemvasia
Neapoli
Elafonisi
Elafonisi
Kotronas
Porto Kagio
Gerolimenas
Lakonian Mani
Dhiros Caves
Areopoli
Langada
Stoupa
Kardamyli
Messinian Mani
Krokees
Sparta
Mystras
Kalamata
Messini
Petalidi
Koroni
Finikounda
Methoni
Pilos
Gialova
Hora
Gargaliani
Filiatra
Mavromati
Proti
Sapientza
Venetiko
Schiza

Agia Pelagia
Diakofto
Kapsali
Hora

86
86
39
39
E961
7
82
9

ELEVATION
2000m
1500m
1000m
500m
0

0   15   30km
0   10   20miles

The Peloponnese
1st edition – March 2003

Published by
Lonely Planet Publications Pty Ltd ABN 36 005 607 983
90 Maribyrnong St, Footscray, Victoria 3011, Australia

Lonely Planet Offices
Australia Locked Bag 1, Footscray, Victoria 3011
USA 150 Linden St, Oakland, CA 94607
UK 10a Spring Place, London NW5 3BH
France 1 rue du Dahomey, 75011 Paris

Photographs
Many of the images in this guide are available for licensing from
Lonely Planet Images.
w www.lonelyplanetimages.com

Front cover photograph
Temple of Apollo, Ancient Corinth (George Tsafos)

ISBN 1 74059 014 7

Printed through Colorcraft Ltd, Hong Kong
Printed in China

Contents – Text

Contents – Maps

The Author

David Willett

David is a freelance journalist based near Bellingen on the mid-north coast of New South Wales, Australia. He grew up in Hampshire, England, and wound up in Australia in 1980 after stints working on newspapers in Iran and Bahrain. He spent two years working as a subeditor at the Melbourne *Sun* newspaper before trading a steady job for the warmer climate of northern NSW.

Between jobs, David has travelled extensively in Europe, the Middle East and Asia. He is a regular visitor to the Peloponnese as coordinator of Lonely Planet's *Greece* guidebook and is also the coordinator of the *Athens* and *Greek Islands* guides. David also wrote Lonely Planet's *Tunisia* guide, and has contributed to various other titles, including *Africa, Australia, Indonesia, Southeast Asia on a shoestring, Mediterranean Europe* and *Western Europe*.

FROM THE AUTHOR

I'd like to thank all the friends who have contributed so much to my understanding of Greece over the years, especially Maria Economou from the Greek National Tourism Office; the Kanakis family; Ana Kamais; Matt Barrett; Tolis Houtzoumis; Petros and Dimitris in Nafplio; Yiannis in Sparti; the irrepressible Voula in Gythio; Bob Barrow from Stoupa; the Dimitreas family from Kardamyli; and Andreas the magician from Patras.

This Book

David Willett researched and wrote this first edition of *The Peloponnese*.

FROM THE PUBLISHER

This first edition of *Peloponnese* was produced in Lonely Planet's Melbourne office. Editing was coordinated by Susan Keogh, with invaluable assistance from Hilary Ericksen and Kim Hutchins. Melanie Dankel stepped in to help at the last minute. Barbara Benson drew the maps, with help from Joelene Kowalski and Jacqueline Nguyen. Climate charts were in the safe hands of Csanad Csutoros. Quentin Frayne compiled the Language chapter and Nina Rousseau whipped up the index.

The book was designed and laid out by Barbara Benson, who also selected the images. Thanks to Pepi Bluck for assistance with illustrations, and to Lonely Planet Images for the photographs. Maria Vallianos designed the cover.

Commissioning Editor Michala Green and Project Manager Bridget Blair streamlined the whole process.

Special thanks to Gina Tsarouhas for all things Greek.

Stin igiá mus!

Foreword

ABOUT LONELY PLANET GUIDEBOOKS

The story begins with a classic travel adventure: Tony and Maureen Wheeler's 1972 journey across Europe and Asia to Australia. There was no useful information about the overland trail then, so Tony and Maureen published the first Lonely Planet guidebook to meet a growing need.

From a kitchen table, Lonely Planet has grown to become the largest independent travel publisher in the world, with offices in Melbourne (Australia), Oakland (USA), London (UK) and Paris (France).

Today Lonely Planet guidebooks cover the globe. There is an ever-growing list of books and information in a variety of media. Some things haven't changed. The main aim is still to make it possible for adventurous travellers to get out there – to explore and better understand the world.

At Lonely Planet we believe travellers can make a positive contribution to the countries they visit – if they respect their host communities and spend their money wisely. Since 1986 a percentage of the income from each book has been donated to aid projects and human rights campaigns, and, more recently, to wildlife conservation.

> Although inclusion in a guidebook usually implies a recommendation we cannot list every good place. Exclusion does not necessarily imply criticism. In fact there are a number of reasons why we might exclude a place _ sometimes it is simply inappropriate to encourage an influx of travellers.

UPDATES & READER FEEDBACK

Things change – prices go up, schedules change, good places go bad and bad places go bankrupt. Nothing stays the same. So, if you find things better or worse, recently opened or long-since closed, please tell us and help make the next edition even more accurate and useful.

Lonely Planet thoroughly updates each guidebook as often as possible – usually every two years, although for some destinations the gap can be longer. Between editions, up-to-date information is available in our free, monthly email bulletin *Comet* (w www.lonelyplanet.com/newsletters). You can also check out the *Thorn Tree* bulletin board and *Postcards* section of our website, which carry unverified, but fascinating, reports from travellers.

Tell us about it! We genuinely value your feedback. A well-travelled team at Lonely Planet reads and acknowledges every email and letter we receive and ensures that every morsel of information finds its way to the relevant authors, editors and cartographers.

Everyone who writes to us will find their name listed in the next edition of the appropriate guidebook. The very best contributions will be rewarded with a free guidebook.

We may edit, reproduce and incorporate your comments in Lonely Planet products such as guidebooks, websites and digital products, so let us know if you don't want your comments reproduced or your name acknowledged.

How to contact Lonely Planet:
Online: e talk2us@lonelyplanet.com.au, w www.lonelyplanet.com
Australia: Locked Bag 1, Footscray, Victoria 3011
UK: 10a Spring Place, London NW5 3BH
USA: 150 Linden St, Oakland, CA 94607

Introduction

The gods of Ancient Greece may have listed the frosty summit of far-off Mt Olympus as their official residence, but they spent much of their time visiting the Peloponnese in pursuit of their duties.

Doubtless, like so many of today's visitors, they were drawn by the sheer magic of the landscapes. It's a region of outstanding natural beauty: of fertile plains backed by lofty, snowcapped mountains; of golden beaches and rocky coves; of hidden valleys of citrus groves and cypress trees; of cool springs and mountain streams.

This was the heartland of the ancient Greek world, and the setting for many of mythology's epic tales: history and mythology are so closely intertwined that it's hard to separate fact from fiction in the Peloponnese. Heracles, first of the superheroes, performed many of his labours here. It was the home of King Agamemnon and wise King Nestor, whose exploits in the *Iliad* and the *Odyssey* were thought to be figments of Homer's epic imagination until archaeologists made their remarkable discoveries at Mycenae and Pylos. And it was the home of mighty Sparta, whose rigorously disciplined armies dominated Greece in classical times.

The region is a veritable treasure trove for archaeology enthusiasts. Reminders of the past are everywhere. The landscape is dotted with the legacies of the many civilisations that have come and gone: Mycenaean palaces; classical Greek temples; crumbling Byzantine cities; Frankish and Venetian fortresses; converted mosques and ornate Turkish fountains.

The biggest crowd pullers are Mycenae, once centre of the mighty Mycenaean civilisation, and Ancient Olympia, spiritual home of the Olympic Games. Other important sites include the celebrated Theatre of Epidavros, with its remarkable acoustics; Roman Corinth, where St Paul preached in vain to the loose-living locals; and Mystras, where the Byzantine civilisation enjoyed a late but spectacular revival in the 14th century.

The old Venetian towns of Monemvasia and Nafplio qualify as two of Greece's romantic destinations.

Nafplio, first capital of independent Greece, is a town that occupies a special place in the hearts of all Greeks. Nestled below the ancient fortress of Akronafplia, its narrow streets are lined with reminders of its colourful past. Ornate Turkish fountains stand alongside fine Venetian houses and elegant neoclassical mansions. It boasts some of the finest accommodation in the Peloponnese, as well as a busy nightlife.

Monemvasia, an island fortress hidden away off the Lakonian coast, is a living museum, its maze of cobbled streets and stone mansions created by the Venetians at the beginning of the 17th century.

The Peloponnese is a destination for all seasons. Springtime is the perfect time to go trekking in the mountains of Arcadia, or in the Mani, where the hillsides bristle with the remains of fortified tower houses built from the 17th century onwards. The Mani is also famous for its wildflowers, which carpet the region's otherwise barren hills in March and April.

Summer in the Peloponnese means it's time to head for the beach: the beaches of Messinia in the southwest are among the finest in Greece, while Finikounda is a favourite destination for windsurfers. Winter means it's time to head for the ski fields at Mt Helmos and Mt Menalo.

THE PELOPONNESE

Facts about the Peloponnese

HISTORY
Stone Age
Human activity in the Peloponnese can be traced back at least 25,000 years.

Excavations at the Frachti Cave, in south-west Argolis, have revealed a history of continuous occupation from Upper Paleolithic to Late Neolithic times (25,000 BC to 3000 BC), making it one of the most important early sites in Europe.

Until 7000 BC, the cave's residents existed as hunter gatherers; the move to a pastoral existence came during Neolithic times (7000–3000 BC). The people grew barley and wheat, and bred sheep and goats. They used clay to produce pots, vases and simple statuettes of the Great Mother (the earth goddess), whom they worshipped.

By 3000 BC, people were living in settlements complete with streets, squares and mud-brick houses.

Bronze Age
Around 3000 BC, Indo-European migrants introduced bronze (an alloy of copper and tin), launching three remarkable civilisations: the Cycladic, Minoan and Mycenaean.

Initially it was the islands that flourished. Crete's Minoan civilisation was the first advanced civilisation to emerge in Europe, drawing its inspiration from two great Middle Eastern civilisations: the Mesopotamian and the Egyptian. Archaeologists divide the Minoan civilisation into three phases: Early (3000–2100 BC), Middle (2100–1500 BC) and Late (1500–1100 BC). The Minoan civilisation reached its peak during the Middle period, producing pottery and metalwork of remarkable beauty and with a high degree of imagination and skill.

The Cycladic civilisation, centred on the Cyclades Islands, developed at the same time and is also divided into three periods: Early (3000–2000 BC), Middle (2000–1500 BC) and Late (1500–1100 BC). Its most impressive legacy is the statuettes carved from Parian marble – the famous Cycladic figurines. Like statuettes from Neolithic times, they depicted images of the Great Mother.

In the Peloponnese meanwhile, the Neolithic inhabitants had retreated to the mountains of Arcadia in the face of a wave of migration of Ionian and Aetolian peoples from the north. They brought with them a new style of pottery and a new style of building. These newcomers also established trading contacts with their more sophisticated neighbours in the Aegean, laying the foundations for the subsequent rise of the Mycenaean civilisation (1900–1100 BC).

The Mycenaean civilisation reached its peak between 1500 and 1200 BC. Named after the ancient city of Mycenae, where the German archaeologist Heinrich Schliemann made his celebrated finds in 1876, it is also known as the Achaean civilisation.

Unlike Minoan society, where the lack of city walls seems to indicate relative peace under some form of central authority, Mycenaean civilisation was characterised by independent city-states such as Corinth, Pylos, Tiryns and – the most powerful of them all – Mycenae. They were ruled by kings who inhabited palaces enclosed within massive walls on easily defensible hilltops.

The Mycenaeans' most impressive legacy is their magnificent gold jewellery and ornaments, the best of which can be seen in the National Archaeological Museum in Athens. The Mycenaeans wrote in what is called Linear B, a script which has been deciphered and is an early form of Greek, unrelated to the Linear A script developed in Crete. The gods they worshipped were precursors of the later Greek gods.

Examples of Linear B have also been found on Crete, suggesting that Mycenaean invaders may have conquered the island, perhaps around 1500 BC, when many Minoan palaces were destroyed. Mycenaean influence stretched farther than Crete: the Mycenaean city-states banded together to defeat Troy (Ilium) and protect their trade routes to the Black Sea. Archaeologists have unearthed Mycenaean artefacts as far away as Egypt, Mesopotamia and Italy.

The glories of the Mycenaean civilisation came to an end during the 12th century BC when the Peloponnese was overrun by the Dorians.

Geometric Age
The origins of the Dorians remain uncertain. They are generally thought to have

come from Epiros or northern Macedonia, but some historians argue that they only arrived from there because they had been driven out of Doris, in central Greece, by the Mycenaeans. Their arrival triggered a series of further migrations, with the vanquished Ionians moving east to the Cyclades and then to the coast of Asia Minor (now southwestern Turkey).

The Dorians brought a traumatic break with the past, and the next 400 years are often referred to as Greece's 'dark age'. Very little is known about this period, except that the Dorians brought iron with them and developed a new style of pottery, decorated with striking geometrical designs (although art historians are still debating whether the Dorians merely copied the designs perfected by Ionians in Attica). The Dorians worshipped male gods instead of fertility goddesses and adopted the Mycenaean gods of Poseidon, Zeus and Apollo, paving the way for the later Greek religious pantheon.

Archaic Age

By about 800 BC, life had begun to settle down again. The Dorians had developed into a class of land-holding aristocrats, and the Peloponnese had been divided into a series of city-states. The most important of these were Argos, Corinth, Elis, Sikyon and Sparta.

Most city-states were built to a similar plan, surrounding a fortified acropolis (the highest point of a city). The acropolis contained the cities' temples and treasury, and served as a refuge during invasions. Outside the acropolis was the *agora* (market), a bustling commercial quarter, and beyond it the residential areas.

The city-states were autonomous, free to pursue their own interests as they saw fit. Most city-states abolished monarchic rule in favour of an aristocratic form of government, usually headed by an *arhon* (chief magistrate).

The people of the various city-states were unified by the development of a Greek alphabet (of Phoenician origin, though the Greeks introduced vowels), the epic poetry of Homer (which created a sense of a shared Mycenaean past), the establishment of the Olympic Games at Olympia (which brought all the city-states together under truce), and the setting up of central sanctuaries such as

Delphi (a neutral meeting ground for lively negotiations), giving Greeks, for the first time, a sense of national identity. This period is known as the Archaic, or Middle, Age.

Aristocrats were often disliked by the population because of their inherited privileges, and some city-states fell to the rule of tyrants after Kypselos started the practice in Corinth in about 650 BC. Tyrants seized their position rather than inheriting it. These days they've got an image problem, but in ancient times they were often seen as being on the side of ordinary citizens.

Peacetime also brought a rapid increase in population. With good agricultural land at a premium, many city-states sought to solve the problem by sending their surplus citizens off to found new colonies across the seas. The Corinthians were the pacesetters, taking over Corfu in 734 BC as a stepping stone to a string of colonies in southern Italy and Sicily.

The Rise of Sparta

Sparta was responsible for just one colony, Taras (Tarentum) in southern Italy. It preferred to solve its land problem by conquering neighbouring Messinia. Beginning in about 730 BC, the two fought a succession of wars before Sparta assumed complete control in about 600 BC. The vanquished Messinians headed off to found the city of Messina in Sicily, while Sparta turned its attentions north to Arcadia and the city of Argos.

The main obstacle in Arcadia was the city of Tegea, won over by alliance after a series of inconclusive battles at the beginning of the 6th century BC.

Argos was defeated at Thyrea, near modern Astros, in 544 BC. The encounter was known as the Battle of the Champions after it was agreed that each side would select 300 of its finest warriors to fight the battle. It proved inconclusive, so both sides threw their full armies into the fray. Victory, and a series of subsequent alliances, left Sparta as the leader of what has become known as the Peloponnesian League.

The Spartans were now powerful enough to impose their will on Athens, which they attacked in 508 BC to depose the tyrant Hippias. Any thought of further conflict between the two was put on the back burner with the arrival of the Persians.

The Persian Wars

The Persian drive to destroy Athens was sparked by the city's support for a rebellion in the Persian colonies on the coast of Asia Minor. Emperor Darius spent five years suppressing the revolt, and emerged hell-bent on revenge. He appealed to Sparta to attack Athens from behind, but the Spartans threw his envoy in a well and Darius was left to do the job alone.

A 25,000-strong Persian army reached Attica in 490 BC, but suffered a humiliating defeat when outmanoeuvred by an Athenian force of 10,000 at the Battle of Marathon. Sparta, in a belated show of Greek solidarity, sent a contingent of 2000 men to fight on the Athenian side – but it arrived after the battle. Sparta was to play a much more important role in subsequent campaigns.

Darius died in 485 BC before he could mount another assault, so it was left to his son Xerxes to fulfil his father's ambition of conquering Greece. In 480 BC Xerxes gathered men from every nation of his far-flung empire and launched a coordinated invasion by army and navy, the size of which the world had never seen. The historian Herodotus estimated that there were five million Persian soldiers. No doubt this was a gross exaggeration, but it was obvious Xerxes intended to give the Greeks more than a bloody nose.

Some 30 city-states from the Peloponnese and Central Greece met in Corinth to devise a common defence (others, including Delphi, sided with the Persians). They agreed on a combined army and navy under Spartan command, with the Athenian leader Themistocles providing the strategy. The Spartan king Leonidas led the army to Thermopylae, near present-day Lamia in Central Greece, to block the main passage into central Greece from the north. This narrow pass was easy to defend, and although the Greeks were greatly outnumbered they held it until a traitor showed the Persians a path over the mountains. The Greeks were forced to retreat, but Leonidas, along with 300 of his elite Spartan troops, fought to the death. The fleet, which held off the Persian navy north of Euboea (Evia), had no choice but to retreat as well.

The Spartans and their Peloponnesian allies fell back on their second line of defence (an earthen wall across the Isthmus of Corinth), while the Persians advanced upon Athens. Themistocles ordered his people to flee the city: the women and children to the island of Salamis, and the men to sea with the Athenian fleet. The Persians razed Attica and burned Athens to the ground.

Things did not go so well for the Persian navy. By skilful manoeuvring, the Greek navy trapped the larger Persian ships in the narrow waters off Salamis, where they became easy pickings for the more mobile Greek vessels. Xerxes, who watched the defeat of his mighty fleet from the shore, returned to Persia in disgust, leaving his general Mardonius and the army to subdue Greece. The result was quite the reverse. A year later the Greeks, under the Spartan general Pausanias, obliterated the Persian army at the Battle of Plataea, about 50km northeast of Athens. The Athenian navy then sailed to Asia Minor and destroyed what was left of the Persian fleet at Mykale, freeing the Ionian city-states there from Persian rule.

Classical Age

After defeating the Persians, the disciplined Spartans retreated to their Peloponnesian 'fortress', while Athens basked in its role as liberator and embarked on a policy of blatant imperialism. In 477 BC it founded the Delian League, so called because the treasury was kept on the sacred island of Delos. The league consisted of almost every state with a navy, no matter how small, including many of the Aegean islands and some of the Ionian city-states in Asia Minor.

Ostensibly its purpose was twofold: to create a naval force to liberate the city-states that were still occupied by Persia and to protect against another Persian attack. The swearing of allegiance to Athens and an annual contribution of ships (later just money) were mandatory. The league, in effect, became an Athenian empire.

Indeed, when Pericles became leader of Athens in 461 BC, he moved the treasury from Delos to the Acropolis and used its contents to begin a building programme in which no expense was spared. His first objectives were to rebuild the temple complex of the Acropolis that had been destroyed by the Persians, and to link Athens to its lifeline, the port of Piraeus, with fortified walls designed to withstand any future siege.

Under Pericles' leadership (461–429 BC), Athens experienced a golden age of unprecedented cultural, artistic and scientific achievement. With the Aegean Sea safely under its wing, Athens began to look westwards for further expansion, bringing it into conflict with the city-states of the mainland. It also encroached on the trade area of Corinth, which belonged to the Sparta-dominated Peloponnesian League. A series of skirmishes and provocations led to the Peloponnesian Wars.

First Peloponnesian War One of the major triggers of the first Peloponnesian War (431–421 BC) was the Corcyra incident, in which Athens supported Corcyra (present-day Kerkyra or Corfu) in a war with its mother city, Corinth. Corinth called on Sparta for help, and it rallied to the cause.

Athens knew it couldn't defeat Sparta on land, so it abandoned Attica to the Spartans and withdrew behind its mighty walls, opting to rely on its navy to put pressure on Sparta by blockading the Peloponnese. Athens suffered badly during the siege. Plague broke out in the overcrowded city, killing a third of the population – including Pericles – but the defences held firm. The blockade of the Peloponnese eventually began to hurt, and the two reached an uneasy truce.

The Sicilian Adventure Throughout the war Athens had maintained an interest in Sicily and its grain, which the soil in Attica was too poor to produce. The Greek colonies there mirrored the city-states in Greece, the most powerful being Syracuse, a Corinthian colony that had remained neutral during the war.

In 416 BC, the Sicilian city of Segesta asked Athens to intervene in a squabble it was having with Selinus, an ally of Syracuse. A hot-headed second cousin of Pericles, Alcibiades, convinced the Athenian assembly to send a flotilla to Sicily; it would go on the pretext of helping Segesta, and then attack Syracuse.

The flotilla, under the joint leadership of Alcibiades, Nicias and Lamachos, was ill fated from the outset. Nicias' health suffered and Lamachos, the most adept of the three, was killed. After laying siege to Syracuse for over three years, Alcibiades was called back to Athens on blasphemy charges arising from a drinking binge during which he had knocked the heads off a few sacred statues. Enraged, he travelled not to Athens but to Sparta and persuaded the surprised Spartans to go to the aid of Syracuse. Sparta followed Alcibiades' advice and broke the siege in 413 BC, destroying the Athenian fleet and army.

Second Peloponnesian War Athens was now depleted of troops, money and ships; its subject states were ripe for revolt and Sparta was there to lend them a hand. In 413 BC the Spartans occupied Decelea in northern Attica and used it as a base to harass the region's farmers. Athens, deprived of its Sicilian grain supplies, soon began to feel the pinch. Its prospects grew even bleaker when Darius II of Persia, who had been keeping a close eye on events in Sicily and Greece, offered Sparta money to build a navy in return for a promise to restore the Ionian cities of Asia Minor to Persia.

Athens went on the attack and even gained the upper hand for a while under the leadership of the reinstated Alcibiades, but its days were numbered once Persia entered the fray in Asia Minor and Sparta regained its composure under the outstanding general Lysander. Athens surrendered to Sparta in 404 BC.

Corinth urged the total destruction of Athens but the Spartan admiral Lysander felt honour-bound to spare the city that had saved Greece from the Persians. Instead he crippled it by confiscating its fleet, abolishing the Delian League and tearing down the walls between the city and Piraeus.

Spartan Rule The Peloponnesian Wars had exhausted the city-states, leaving only Sparta in a position of any strength. During the wars, Sparta had promised to restore liberty to the city-states that had turned against Athens, but Lysander now changed his mind and installed oligarchies (governments run by a small group) supervised by Spartan garrisons. Soon there was widespread dissatisfaction.

Sparta found it had bitten off more than it could chew when it began a campaign to reclaim the cities of Asia Minor from Persian rule. This brought the Persians back into Greek affairs, where they found willing clients in Athens and increasingly powerful Thebes. Meanwhile, Athens regained some of its former power at the head of a new league of Aegean states known as the Second Confederacy – this time aimed against Sparta rather than Persia.

The rivalry culminated in the decisive Battle of Leuctra in 371 BC, where Thebes, under the leadership of the remarkable statesman and general Epaminondas, inflicted Sparta's first defeat in a pitched battle. Spartan influence collapsed and Thebes filled the vacuum. Epaminondas moved quickly to ensure against future Spartan expansion by founding Messini as the main town of independent Messinia, and Megalopolis in Arcadia to the north.

In a surprise about-turn, Athens now allied itself with Sparta. Their combined forces met the Theban army at Mantinea in the Peloponnese in 362 BC. The battle was won by Thebes but Epaminondas was killed. Without him, Theban power soon crumbled but neither Athens nor Sparta was able to take advantage of the situation.

The city-states were now spent forces and a new power was rising in the north: Macedon.

The Rise of Macedon

While the Greeks engineered their own decline through the Peloponnesian Wars, Macedon (geographically the modern province of Macedonia) was gathering strength. Macedon had long been regarded as a bit of a backwater, a loose assembly of primitive hill tribes nominally ruled by a king. The Greeks considered the people to be barbarians (those whose speech sounded like 'bar-bar', which meant anyone who didn't speak Greek).

The man who turned them into a force to be reckoned with was Philip II. In 338 BC he defeated a combined army of Athenians and Thebans at the Battle of Khaironeia (338 BC). Philip took care to cultivate good relations with the Peloponnese. By promising to lead a campaign against Persia, he persuaded the city-states (with the exception of Sparta) to form the League of Corinth and to swear allegiance to Macedonia. In return, the city-states were guaranteed their autonomy and his protection.

Philip's ambition to tackle Persia never materialised. In 336 BC he was assassinated and his son, the 20-year-old Alexander, became king.

MARTIN HARRIS

Alexander the Great

Alexander the Great Alexander, highly educated (he had been tutored by Aristotle), fearless and ambitious, was an astute politician and intent upon finishing what his father had begun. Philip II's death had been the signal for rebellions throughout the budding empire and Alexander wasted no time in crushing them. After restoring order he headed to Corinth to be proclaimed as leader of the war against Persia before marching off to Asia Minor in 334 BC at the head of an army of 40,000 men.

After a few bloody battles with the Persians, most notably at Issus (333 BC), Alexander succeeded in conquering Syria, Palestine and Egypt – where he was proclaimed pharaoh and founded the city of Alexandria. Intent on sitting on the Persian throne, he then began hunting down the Persian king, Darius III, defeating his army in Mesopotamia in 331 BC.

Alexander continued east into what is now known as Uzbekistan, Afghanistan and northern India. His ambition was now to conquer the world, which he believed ended at the sea beyond India. But his soldiers grew weary and in 324 BC forced him to return to Mesopotamia. The next year he fell ill suddenly and died, heirless, at the age of 33. His empire soon fell apart.

Macedon struggled to maintain its grip on the Peloponnese despite a campaign in

303 BC by Demetrios Poliorcetes that briefly revived the League of Corinth. Most of the city-states abandoned the Macedonians for the Achaean League in 280 BC, a sort of declaration of independence that Macedon disputed with occasional military campaigns. On one such campaign in 221 BC, they fought their way right down to the southern tip of the Mani Peninsula, becoming the first foreign army to set foot in Sparta in the city's history. The result of the fighting was that neither Macedon nor the Achaean League was in much condition to contest the arrival of the Romans.

Roman Rule

While Alexander the Great was forging his empire in the east, the Romans had been expanding theirs to their west. Now they were keen to start making inroads into Greece. Several wars were needed to subjugate Macedon, but in 168 BC Macedon lost the decisive Battle of Pydnaa, north of Mt Olympus.

The Achaean League was defeated in 146 BC, and the Roman consul Mummius made an example of the rebellious Corinthians by completely destroying their beautiful city, massacring the men and selling the women and children into slavery.

For the next 400 years, the Peloponnese became part of the Roman province of Achaea, governed from Corinth. The Romans had always venerated Greek art, literature and philosophy (aristocratic Romans sent their offspring to schools in Athens) but they were also hard taskmasters who taxed the local populace to the hilt.

Sparta, which helped Octavian (later Augustus Caesar) to defeat the forces of Antony and Cleopatra in 31 BC, was the only city to be spared from the harsher side of Roman rule.

Christianity & the Byzantine Empire

The period of peace known as the Pax Romana came to an abrupt end in 267 AD when the Goths crossed the Isthmus of Corinth and swept through the Peloponnese, sacking the cities of Corinth, Argos, Tegea and Sparta before departing. They were the first of a succession of invaders spurred on by the 'great migrations' in northern and eastern Europe. They were

followed in 395 by the Visigoths, who raided as far south as Sparta, and then in 465 by the Vandals, who switched their attentions to Zakynthos after they were prevented from landing on the Mani Peninsula.

Christianity, meantime, had emerged as the country's new religion. St Paul had made several visits to Greece in the 1st century AD, including an extended stay in Corinth. The definitive boost to the spread of Christianity in this part of the world came with the conversion of the Roman emperors and the rise of the Byzantine Empire, which blended Hellenistic culture with Christianity.

In 324 Emperor Constantine I (also known as Constantine the Great), a Christian convert, transferred the capital of the empire from Rome to Byzantium, a city on the western shore of the Bosphorus, which was renamed Constantinople (present-day İstanbul). This was as much due to insecurity in Italy itself as to the growing importance of the wealthy eastern regions of the empire.

By the end of the 4th century, the Roman Empire was formally divided into a western and an eastern half. While Rome went into terminal decline, the eastern capital grew in wealth and strength, long outliving its western counterpart (the Byzantine Empire lasted until the capture of Constantinople by the Turks in 1453). Emperor Theodosius I made Christianity the official religion in 394 and outlawed the worship of Greek and Roman gods, now branded as pagan.

The Emperor Justinian, who ruled from 527 to 565, provided the Peloponnese with some protection from the threat of land invasion by building a mighty defensive wall, known as the Hexamilion, across the Isthmus of Corinth.

In 610 the Peloponnese became a Byzantine province in its own right, again ruled from Corinth. Corinth, now specialising in the production of silk, became one of the most important cities in the empire and a major trading centre.

Disaster struck in the middle of the 8th century when the population was devastated by the plague, which spread from the port of Monemvasia – introduced by sailors trading with Asian Minor. Many areas were repopulated with Slavic people encouraged to relocate by Emperor Constantine V.

The Crusades

It is one of the ironies of history that the demise of the Byzantine Empire was accelerated not by invasions of infidels from the east or barbarians from the north but by fellow Christians from the west – the Frankish crusaders.

The stated mission of the crusades was to liberate the Holy Land from the Muslims but in reality they were driven as much by greed as by religious fervour. By the time the First Crusade was launched in 1095, the Franks had already made substantial gains in Italy at the empire's expense and the rulers of Constantinople were understandably nervous about giving the crusaders safe passage on their way to Jerusalem. The first three crusades passed by without incident, but the fourth proved that the fear was justified.

The Venetians, whose fleet provided the transport between Europe and the Holy Land, were able to persuade the crusaders that Constantinople presented richer pickings than Jerusalem. Constantinople was sacked in 1204 and much of the Byzantine Empire was partitioned into feudal states ruled by self-styled 'Latin' (mostly Frankish) princes.

The Peloponnese became the Principality of Achaea, ruled by Geoffrey de Villehardouin from Andreville (now the small regional town of Andravida in Elia). De Villehardouin set about remodelling the region in the manner of his native Champagne district in France, dividing the Peloponnese into 12 feudal baronies. The island fortress of Monemvasia was the only town that remained in Byzantine hands, and it fell in 1248 to Guillaume de Villehardouin, who had succeeded Geoffrey two years earlier.

Despite this, Byzantium was not yet dead. After the fall of Constantinople the Byzantine court had retreated to Nicaea, south of Constantinople, to set about regaining its lost possessions. In 1259 the Byzantine emperor Michael VIII Palaeologos captured De Villehardouin at the Battle of Pelagonia (in northwestern Greece). He was held captive for three years before being freed in exchange for the castles at Monemvasia and Mystras. Michael VIII managed to reclaim Constantinople in 1261, but by this time Byzantium was a shadow of its former self. The empire was to enjoy one last burst of glory at Mystras.

Mystras grew steadily despite opposition from the Franks, whose influence was now confined largely to the northwest corner of the Peloponnese. Its pre-eminent position was confirmed in 1348 when the Emperor John VI Katakouzenos chose it as the capital of the new Despotate of the Morea, headed by his son Manuel. The despotate passed into the hands of the Palaiologou family in 1384 after a palace coup in Constantinople.

The Venetians

The Venetians had quietly established themselves as one of the leading players in the Peloponnese. They had gained their first foothold in 1082, when they were granted Methoni by the Byzantines in return for helping to fight off the Normans. (Based in Sicily, they spent much of the 11th century terrorising the Mediterranean coast in search of further conquests.)

The Venetians were required to hand Methoni over to the Franks in 1204, but grabbed it back three years later together with Koroni. These two key ports became known as the 'eyes of Venice', and played a key role in Venice's push to dominate the eastern Mediterranean. Nafplio (1389) and Monemvasia (1464) were added to the fold before the arrival of the Turks.

The Ottoman Empire

The Seljuk Turks, a tribe from central Asia, had first appeared on the eastern fringes of the Byzantine Empire in the middle of the 11th century. They established themselves on the Anatolian plain by defeating a Byzantine army at Manzikert in 1071. The threat looked to have been contained, especially when the Seljuks were themselves overrun by the Mongols. By the time Mongol power began to wane, the Seljuks had been supplanted as the dominant Turkish tribe by the Ottomans – the followers of Osman, who ruled from 1289 to 1326. The Muslim Ottomans rapidly expanded the areas under their control and by the mid-15th century were harassing the Byzantine Empire on all sides.

They ventured into the Peloponnese for the first time in 1423, breaking through the Hexamilion Wall and sacking Mystras before withdrawing. The wall was hastily reinforced but proved little obstacle when the

Turkish armies returned in 1446, withdrawing only after the payment of tribute. Constantinople fell in 1453, marking the formal end of the Byzantine Empire. Mystras fell shortly afterwards but was returned to the Palaiologou family by Sultan Mohammed II. It remained in Palaiologou hands until 1460, when the last despot of Morea handed the town back to the sultan.

Turks vs Venetians

The Venetians, who still held Koroni, Methoni, Monemvasia and Nafplio, were now the main threat to Turkish control of the Peloponnese.

The rivalry between the two was to lead to numerous conflicts over the next 250 years. The first round was fought between 1463 and 1479, when the Venetians won back much of the Peloponnese with the help of local forces before making a separate peace deal with the Turks. The deal gave them control of Navarino Bay (Pylos) in addition to their previous holdings, whereupon the Venetians withdrew – leaving the locals at the mercy of Turkish reprisals.

Not surprisingly, the Venetians found zero local support when the Turks campaigned to seize first Koroni, Methoni and Navarino (1499–1502), then Monemvasia and Nafplio (1537–40). After 1540 Nafplio became the capital of the Ottoman *sanjak* (province) of Morea. Ottoman power was now at its zenith. Under Sultan Süleyman the Magnificent (ruled 1520–66), the empire expanded north through the Balkans and Hungary to the gates of Vienna.

Realising that the Turks held all the aces on land, Venice took to harassing the Ottomans by sea. Its ships played a key role in the destruction of the Turkish fleet at the Battle of Lepanto, fought off the port of Naufpaktos in Central Greece in 1571.

The Venetians waited until 1684 to launch their next campaign on land. With their Mediterranean trading empire in decline, Venice was keen to reassert itself in the Peloponnese. The campaign was entrusted to its most celebrated general, Francisco Morosini. By the end of 1687 all of the Peloponnese was in Venetian hands except Monemvasia, and Morosini's troops had advanced as far as Athens. The Parthenon was destroyed during the fighting when a shell struck a store of Turkish gunpowder.

Monemvasia fell in 1690 and Venice poured a lot of energy into fortifying its new possessions. It was all for nothing when the Turks returned in 1715, recapturing all their lost territory in less than a year.

Despite this success, Ottoman power was in decline, and it was to be the Russians who next stepped up to challenge the sultans for control of Greece.

Russian Involvement

Russia's link with Greece went back to Byzantine times, when the Russians had been converted to Christianity by Byzantine missionaries. The church hierarchies in Constantinople and Kiev (later in Moscow) soon went their separate ways, but when Constantinople fell to the Turks, the metropolitan (head) of the Russian Church declared Moscow the 'third Rome', the true heir of Christianity, and campaigned for the liberation of its fellow Christians. This fitted in nicely with Russia's efforts to expand into Ottoman territory – perhaps even to turn the Ottoman Empire back into a Byzantine Empire dependent on Russia.

The first indication of Russian involvement in Greek affairs came with the abortive Orloff uprising in 1770. Promised troops and guns by agents of Catherine the Great, rebels quickly seized the fortresses at Koroni, Methoni and Pylos and advanced on Mystras – only for the uprising to fizzle out when it emerged that the Russian assistance amounted a mere handful of men. Many people fled to the nearby Ionian and Saronic Gulf islands to escape the savage reprisals.

The next phase of the struggle against the Ottomans began in the town of Odessa, on the Black Sea, in 1814 with the founding of the first Greek independence party, the Filiki Eteria (Friendly Society). It believed that armed force was the only effective means of liberation and made generous monetary contributions to the freedom fighters. The society's message spread quickly and found plenty of supporters in the Peloponnese.

The War of Independence

Officially, the War of Independence began on 25 March 1821, when Bishop Germanos of Patras hoisted the Greek flag at the monastery of Agias Lavras, near Kalavryta. Unofficially, the fighting had begun several days earlier when the Maniot chieftain Theodore Kolokotronis marched north from Areopoli to seize Kalamata.

Either way, the raising of the flag marked the start of all-out war, with fighting erupting almost simultaneously across most of Greece and the occupied islands. The Greeks made big early gains, particularly in the Peloponnese. Kolokotronis marched north from Kalamata into Arcadia, defeating the Turks at Valtetsi before capturing Tripolis.

The fighting was savage, with atrocities committed on both sides. After the capture of Tripolis, its 12,000 Turkish inhabitants were put to the sword, while Maniot freedom fighters razed the homes of thousands of Turks. The Turks retaliated with massacres in Asia Minor, most notoriously on the island of Chios where 25,000 civilians were killed.

The fighting continued to spread and within a year the Greeks had captured the fortresses of Monemvasia, Navarino and Nafplio, as well as Messolongi, Athens and Thiva (Thebes) in Central Greece. Greek independence was proclaimed at Nea Epidavros on 13 January 1822.

The cause was not lacking in leaders; what was lacking was unity of objectives and strategy. Internal disagreements twice escalated into civil war, the worst in the Peloponnese in 1824. The sultan took advantage of this and called in Egyptian reinforcements. Led by Ali Pasha, Egyptian troops landed at Methoni and set about reconquering the Peloponnese.

The western powers were reluctant to intervene, fearing the consequences of creating a power vacuum in southeastern Europe, where the Turks still controlled much territory. Help came from the philhellenes (literally, lovers of Greece and Greek culture) – aristocratic young men, recipients of a classical education, who saw themselves as the inheritors of a glorious civilisation and were willing to fight to liberate its oppressed descendants. The philhellenes included Shelley, Goethe, Schiller, Victor Hugo, Alfred de Musset and Lord Byron.

At last the western powers intervened and a combined Russian, French and British fleet destroyed the Turkish-Egyptian fleet in the Bay of Navarino in October 1827. Sultan Mahmud II proclaimed a holy war, prompting Russia to send troops into the Balkans to engage the Ottoman army. Fighting continued until 1829 when, with Russian troops at the gates of Constantinople, the sultan accepted Greek independence by the Treaty of Adrianople.

Birth of the Greek Nation

The Greeks busied themselves with organising the independent state they had proclaimed several years earlier. Nafplio was chosen as the capital and in April 1827 they elected Ioannis Kapodistrias as their first president. He was a Corfiot who had been the foreign minister of Tsar Alexander I.

With his Russian past, Kapodistrias believed in a strong, centralised government. While he was good at enlisting foreign support, his autocratic manner at home was unacceptable to many of the leaders of the War of Independence, particularly the Maniot chieftains who had always been a law unto themselves. He was assassinated in 1831.

European powers stepped in again, declaring that Greece should become a monarchy. In January 1833 Otto of Bavaria was installed as king. His ambition, called the Great Idea, was to unite all the lands of the Greek people to the Greek motherland. In 1862 he was peacefully ousted and the Greeks chose George I, a Danish prince, as king.

In WWI Prime Minister Venizelos allied Greece with France and Britain. King Constantine (George's son), who was married to the Kaiser's sister Sophia, disputed this and left the country.

Smyrna & WWII

After the war Venizelos resurrected the Great Idea. Underestimating the new-found power of Turkey under the leadership of Atatürk, he sent forces to occupy Smyrna (now the Turkish port of İzmir) which had a large Greek population. The army was repulsed and many Greeks were slaughtered. This led to a brutal population exchange between the two countries in 1923.

In 1930 George II, Constantine's son, was reinstated as king and he appointed the dictator General Metaxas as prime minister. Metaxas' grandiose ambition was to take the best from Greece's ancient and Byzantine past to create a Third Greek Civilisation. What he actually created was a Greek version of the Third Reich. His chief claim to fame is his celebrated *okhi* (no) to Mussolini's request to allow Italian troops into Greece in 1940 at the outset of WWII.

Despite Allied help, Greece fell to Germany in 1941. Resistance movements polarised into royalist and communist factions, leading to a bloody civil war that lasted until 1949. The country was left in chaos. More people were killed in the civil war than in WWII, and 250,000 people were left homeless. The sense of despair became the trigger for a mass exodus. Almost a million Greeks headed off in search of a better life elsewhere, primarily to Australia, Canada and the USA. Villages – whole islands even – were abandoned as people gambled on a new start in cities such as Melbourne, Toronto, Chicago and New York. While some have drifted back, the majority have stayed away.

The Colonels
Continuing political instability led to the colonels' coup d'etat in 1967. King Constantine (son of King Paul, who succeeded George II) staged an unsuccessful countercoup, then fled the country. The colonels' junta distinguished itself by inflicting appalling brutality, repression and political incompetence upon the people. In 1974 they attempted to assassinate Cyprus' leader, Archbishop Makarios. When Makarios escaped, the junta replaced him with the extremist Nikos Samson, prompting Turkey to occupy Northern Cyprus. The continued occupation remains one of the most contentious issues in Greek politics. The junta, now discredited, had little choice but to hand back power to civilians. In November 1974 a plebiscite voted against restoration of the monarchy and Greece became a republic. An election brought the right-wing New Democracy (ND) party into power.

The Socialist 1980s
In 1981 Greece entered the then EC (European Community, now the European Union, or EU). Andreas Papandreou's Panhellenic Socialist Movement (PASOK) won the next election, giving Greece its first socialist government. PASOK promised removal of US air bases and withdrawal from NATO, which Greece had joined in 1951. It did neither and instead Papandreou presided over seven years of rising unemployment and spiralling debt.

He was forced to step aside in 1989 while an unprecedented conservative and communist coalition took over to investigate a scandal involving the Bank of Crete. Papandreou and four ministers were ordered to stand trial and the coalition ordered fresh elections for October 1990.

The 1990s
The elections brought New Democracy back to power with a majority of two, but tough economic reforms introduced by Prime Minister Konstantinos Mitsotakis soon made his government deeply unpopular. By late 1992 allegations began to emerge about the same sort of corruption and dirty tricks that had brought Papandreou unstuck. Mitsotakis himself was accused of having a secret horde of Minoan art, and he was forced to call an election in October 1993.

Greeks again turned to PASOK and the ailing Papandreou, who eventually had been cleared of all charges. He had little option but to continue with the austerity programme begun by Mitsotakis, quickly making his government equally unpopular.

Papandreou was forced to step down in January 1996 after a lengthy spell in hospital. His departure produced a dramatic change of direction for PASOK, with the party abandoning its leftist policies and electing experienced economist and lawyer Costas Simitis as its new leader. Cashing in on his reputation as the Mr Clean of Greek politics, Simitis romped to a comfortable majority at a snap poll called in October 1996.

His government has since focused almost exclusively on the push for further integration with Europe. His prime goal of admission to the euro club was achieved at the beginning of 2001 and Greece adopted the euro as its currency in 2002.

Simitis was rewarded with a further four-year mandate in April 2000 but was suffering a serious mid-term popularity slump at the time of research. Newspaper polls in May 2002 showed PASOK trailing the opposition New Democracy party by more than 7%. The next election is due before April 2004.

Recent Foreign Policy
Greece's foreign policy is dominated by its extremely sensitive relationship with Turkey, its giant Muslim neighbour to the east.

After decades of constant antagonism, these two uneasy NATO allies were jolted to their senses (literally) by the massive earthquake which devastated the İzmir area of western Turkey in August 1999. According to geologists, the quake moved Turkey 1.5m closer to Greece. It had the same effect on the Greek people, who urged their government to join the rescue effort. Greek teams were among the first on the scene, where they were greeted as heroes. The Turks were quick to return the favour after the Athens quake of 7 September 1999. The relationship has continued to blossom, despite the occasional hiccup, and at the time of research the two countries were contemplating mounting a joint bid to stage the 2008 European football championship.

While Turkey remains the top priority, Greece has also had its hands full in recent years coping with events to the north precipitated by the break-up of former Yugoslavia and the collapse of the communist regimes in Albania and Romania.

The first issue to surface was the attempt by the former Yugoslav republic of Macedonia to become independent Macedonia. This prompted an emotional outburst from Greece, which argued that the name 'was, is, and always will be' Greek. Greece was able to persuade its EU partners to recognise Macedonia only if it changed its name, which is how the independent acronym of FYROM (Former Yugoslav Republic of Macedonia) came into being.

The wars in Croatia and Bosnia had little political impact on Greece, but the country found itself in an impossible position during the 1999 NATO conflict with Serbia over Kosovo. The Greek public, already strongly sympathetic towards their fellow Orthodox Christian Serbs in the battle against the Muslim Albanian Kosovars, was outraged when the NATO bombing began. The Americans bore the brunt of anti-NATO demonstrations, violent at first, that lasted throughout the war.

Although Thessaloniki was used as a shipment point for NATO equipment, Greece played no active part in the war.

GEOGRAPHY

The Peloponnese represents the southern extremity of the Balkan Peninsula. Shaped like a giant three-fingered hand, it is linked to the rest of mainland Greece only by the narrow Isthmus of Corinth in the northeast. That link was severed in 1896 with the completion of the Corinth Canal, so that road and rail bridges are now the only connections to the mainland.

Otherwise the Peloponnese is very much the *nisos* (island) suggested by its name, 'Island of Pelops'. West of the isthmus, it is divided from Central Greece by the Gulf of Corinth, which becomes the Gulf of Patras beyond the Rio Straits. The west coast is washed by the Ionian Sea, while the south is divided into the Messinian and Lakonian gulfs by the central Mani Peninsula. Most of the east coast is bounded by the Myrtoo Sea, which becomes the Argolic Gulf further north in the lee of the Argolid Peninsula. The waters northeast of the Argolid are known as the Saronic Gulf.

The Peloponnese occupies a land mass of 21,440 sq km. Roughly two-thirds of the land is mountainous, much of it more than 700m above sea level. The mountains are the southern extension of the Dinaric Alps, which run the length of the Balkan Peninsula. The highest peak is Mt Profitis Ilias (2404m) in the Taygetos Mountains of the south; in the north, Mt Killini (2374m) just takes the honours from nearby Mt Helmos (2338m).

The biggest river is the Alphios, which rises in the mountains of Central Arcadia and flows into the Ionian Sea south of Pyrgos. Just north of the Alphios is the Pinios, which rises on Mt Erymanthos. Once diverted by Heracles to cleanse the stables of King Augeas, the Pinios has now been dammed to create Lake Pinios, the largest water storage in the Peloponnese. Other important river systems include the Evrotas in Lakonia and the Pamissos in Messinia.

GEOLOGY

The Peloponnese lies at the heart of one of the most seismically active regions in the world and earthquakes have occurred regularly throughout history.

Hundreds of quakes are recorded every year. Fortunately, most of them are so minor that they are detectable only by sensitive seismic monitoring equipment. The reason for all this activity is that the Eastern Mediterranean lies at the meeting point of three continental plates: the Eurasian, African and Arabian. The three grind away at each other constantly, generating countless earthquakes as the land surface reacts to the intense activity beneath the earth's crust.

The system has two main fault lines. The most active is the North Aegean Fault, which starts as a volcano-dotted rift between Greece and Turkey, snakes under Central Greece and the Peloponnese and then runs north up the Ionian and Adriatic coasts. The earthquake that struck Athens on 7 September 1999, leaving 139 dead and 100,000 homeless, was caused by this fault.

Less active but more dramatic is the North Anatolian fault that runs across Turkey, renowned for major tremors like the 7.4 (Richter-scale) monster that struck Turkey on 17 August 1999, leaving more than 40,000 dead. Seismologists maintain that activity along the two fault lines is not related.

CLIMATE

The Peloponnese can be divided into a number of main climatic regions.

The east coast is typically Mediterranean with very hot, dry summers and mild winters; while temperatures on the west coast are less extreme in summer. The west coast is also the region with the highest rainfall.

Conditions in the mountains of Arcadia are more Balkan than Mediterranean, with hot, humid summers followed with freezing winters. The higher peaks are blanketed in snow from November to March, with cover persisting until May in some places.

A feature of summer on the east coast is the *meltemi*, a strong northerly wind caused by air pressure differences between North Africa and the Balkans. The wind is a mixed blessing: it reduces humidity but plays havoc with everything from washing to ferry schedules. It's at its fiercest in July and August, when it can blow for days on end. The west coast is cooled by the *maistros*, a light to moderate northwesterly wind that rises in the afternoon.

The rains start in mid-October in most areas, and the weather stays cold and wet until February – although there are also occasional winter days with clear blue skies and sunshine.

ECOLOGY & ENVIRONMENT

Greece is belatedly becoming environmentally conscious; regrettably, it is often a case of closing the gate after the horse has bolted. Deforestation and soil erosion are problems that go back thousands of years. Olive cultivation (see the boxed text 'The Evil Olive', p20) and goats have been the main culprits, but firewood gathering, shipbuilding, housing and industry have all taken their toll.

Forest fires are also a major problem, with an estimated 25,000 hectares destroyed every year. The 2000 season was one of the worst on record, particularly in the Peloponnese. This loss of forest cover has been accompanied by serious soil erosion. The problem is finally being addressed with the start of a long overdue reafforestation programme.

General environmental awareness remains at a very low level, especially where litter is concerned. The problem is particularly bad in rural areas, where roadsides are strewn with soft-drink cans and plastic packaging hurled from passing cars. Environmental education has begun in schools, but it will be some time before community attitudes change.

FLORA & FAUNA
Flora

The Peloponnese is famous for its wildflowers, which continue to thrive because most of the land is too poor for intensive agriculture and has escaped the ravages of manufactured fertilisers. More than 6000 species have been identified in Greece and

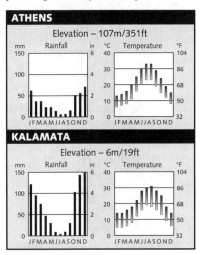

The Evil Olive

It is a sad irony that the tree most revered by the Greeks is responsible for the country's worst ecological disaster. The tree is the olive. It was the money tree of the early Mediterranean civilisations, providing an abundance of oil that not only tasted great but could also be used for everything from lighting to lubrication. The ancient Greeks thought it was too good to be true and concluded it must be a gift from the gods.

In their eagerness to make the most of this gift, native forest was cleared on a massive scale to make way for the olive. Landowners were urged on by decrees such as those issued in the 6th century BC by the *arhon* (chief magistrate) of Athens, Solon, who banned the export of all agricultural produce other than olive oil and made cutting down an olive tree punishable by death.

Much of the land planted with olives was unsuitable hill country. Without the surface roots of the native forest to bind it, the topsoil of the hills was rapidly washed away. The olive tree could do nothing to help. It has no surface root system, depending entirely on its impressive tap root.

Thus, the lush countryside so cherished by the ancient Greeks was transformed into the harsh, rocky landscape that greets the modern visitor.

most are to be found in the Peloponnese. The otherwise barren Mani Peninsula is particularly famous for its spring displays.

Trees begin to blossom as early as the end of February in warmer coastal areas, and the wild flowers start to appear in March. During spring the hillsides are carpeted with flowers, which seem to sprout even from the rocks. Spring flowers include anemones, white cyclamens, irises, lilies, poppies, gladioli, tulips, countless varieties of daisies and many more. By summer, the flowers have disappeared from all but the northern mountainous regions. Autumn brings flowers too, especially crocuses.

The forests that once covered the region have been decimated by thousands of years of clearing for agriculture, boat building and housing, but large areas of pine forest survive in the mountains.

The Cyprus plane (*Platanus orientalis insularis*) is another common species, which thrives wherever there is ample water. It seems as if every village has a plane tree shading its central square – and a Taverna Platanos.

Australian eucalypts were widely used in tree-planting programmes from the 1920s onwards, particularly along roadsides and railway lines.

Fauna

The Peloponnese also has a large range of fauna, but you won't encounter much of interest unless you venture out into the prime habitat areas.

Bird-watchers have more chance of coming across something unusual than animal spotters. The region has all the usual Mediterranean small birds – wagtails, tits, warblers, bee-eaters, larks, swallows, flycatchers, thrushes and chats – as well as some more distinctive species such as the hoopoe. A large number of migratory birds, most of which are merely passing by on their way from winter feeding sites in north Africa to summer nesting grounds in Eastern Europe, can also be seen.

The wetlands at Gialova, near Pylos, and at the mouth of the River Evrotas, east of Gythio, are important breeding grounds for large numbers of water birds.

The brown bear and the grey wolf disappeared from the Peloponnese long ago, but

The hoopoe, part of the kingfisher family

wild boar are still found in reasonable numbers in the mountains and are a favourite target for hunters. Squirrels, rabbits, hares, foxes and weasels are all fairly common.

Reptiles are well represented. The snakes include several poisonous viper species. For more information on snakes in Greece, see the Health section in the Facts for the Visitor chapter. You're more likely to see lizards, all of which are harmless.

Tortoises are also common, despite the huge numbers that end up squashed on the roads. The main species is the marginated tortoise, which can grow as large as 8kg.

Dolphins are frequent visitors to the waters around the Peloponnese, and can often be seen from the shore. Although there are many dolphins in the Mediterranean, the striped dolphin has recently been the victim of murbilivirus – a sickness that affects the immune system. Research into the virus is being carried out in the Netherlands. You can get more information about dolphins from the **Greek Society for the Protection & Study of Dolphins & Cetaceans** (☎/fax 21-0422 3305; e delphis@hol.gr; Pylis 75-79, Piraeus 185 33).

Endangered Species
The sandy beaches of the west coast and at the head of the Lakonian Gulf are important nesting grounds for the threatened loggerhead turtle (Careta careta).

The **Sea Turtle Protection Society of Greece** (☎/fax 21-0523 1342; e stps@compulink.gr; Solomou 57, Athens 104 32) runs monitoring programmes and is always looking for volunteers in the Peloponnese as well as on the Ionian island of Zakynthos – home to the last large sea-turtle colony in Europe. The society runs an information stall by the ferry quay in Gythio during summer.

GOVERNMENT & POLITICS
Since 1975 democratic Greece has been a parliamentary republic with a president as head of state. The president and parliament, which has 300 deputies, have joint legislative power. The PASOK party of Prime Minister Simitis holds 163 seats in the current parliament. Greek governments traditionally name very large cabinets – Simitis fronts a team of 43, with 19 ministries. Papandreou had 52 in his last cabinet!

For administrative purposes, the Peloponnese is divided into the prefectures (nomoi in Greek) of Achaïa, Arcadia, Argolis, Corinthia, Elia, Lakonia and Messinia – all based on historical regions.

ECONOMY
The economy of the Peloponnese remains predominantly agricultural, defying a national trend that has seen the importance of agriculture decline rapidly since WWII.

Accurate statistics on the percentage of the workface engaged in agriculture are unobtainable because so many people work the land as a second job, but doubtless it is much higher than the national figure of 22% (contributing 15% of GNP). Industry is very low key: the only cities with industrial zones of any significance are Corinth, Kalamata and Patras.

Tourism, domestic and international, is the biggest single contributor to the local economy.

On a national level, the economic future looks brighter now than for many years – although Greece has the second-lowest per capita income of all the EU countries (after Portugal). Tough austerity measures imposed by successive governments have finally banished the country's reputation for financial irresponsibility, enabling Greece to join the euro club at the beginning of 2001.

The investment climate remains healthy, despite the bursting of the stock market bubble in 2000 after several years of boom. Many Greeks lost a fortune in the crash after a buying frenzy had pushed the stock index to an insupportable high of almost 11,000 points. At the time of research, it was hovering around a more realistic 6000.

POPULATION & PEOPLE
A census taken in early 2001 found that the total population of Greece was 10,939,771, a 6.6% increase from the previous census in 1991. It is unlikely, however, that the Peloponnese population has grown much in the intervening 10 years – largely because of continued migration to Athens. The 1991 figures showed that the Peloponnese was home to just over one million people. Patras was by far the largest city with a population of 153,300. It was followed by Kalamata (44,000), Pyrgos (28,900) and Corinth (27,400).

These figures were part of a national population of 10.3 million, of whom 3.1 million lived in the greater Athens area. The latest census is expected to reveal that the capital's population has grown to at least 3.7 million.

The ethnic composition of the Peloponnese has changed constantly over the millennia.

The inhabitants before 3000 BC, according to Herodotus, were Pelasgians, who are thought to have originated from what is now northwestern Greece. They were replaced by Ionians and Aetolians, and then by the Dorians – who made up the bulk of the population in classical times.

The Dorians formed the basis of the region's 'Greek' stock until the middle of the 8th century, when the population was decimated by bubonic plague. The Byzantines then repopulated by encouraging the arrival of large numbers of Slavic people. It is estimated that more than half the place names in the Peloponnese are of Slav origin.

More recently, the collapse of the communist regimes in Albania and Romania produced a wave of economic refugees across Greece's poorly guarded northern borders, with an estimated 300,000 arriving from Albania alone. Many have settled in the Peloponnese, where they have become a vital source of cheap labour for the agricultural sector; fruit and vegetable prices have actually gone down as a result of their contribution. Albanians also have a reputation as fine stone masons, and their influence can be seen everywhere.

EDUCATION
Education is free at all levels of the state system, from kindergarten to tertiary. Primary schooling begins at the age of six, but most children attend a state-run kindergarten from the age of five. Private kindergartens are popular with those who can afford them. Primary school classes tend to be larger than those in most European countries – usually 30 to 35 children. Primary school hours are short (8am to 1pm), but children get a lot of homework.

At 12, children enter the *gymnasio*, and at 15 they may leave school, or enter the *lykeio*, from where they take university-entrance examinations. Although literacy levels are high, many parents and pupils are dissatisfied with the education system, especially beyond primary level. The private sector therefore flourishes, and even relatively poor parents struggle to send their children to one of the country's 5000 *frontistiria* (intensive coaching colleges) to prepare them for the very competitive university-entrance exams. Parents complain that the education system is badly underfunded. The main complaint is about the lack of modern teaching aids in both *gymnasio* and *lykeio*.

Grievances reached a peak in 1991, when *lykeio* students staged a series of sit-ins in schools throughout the country and organised protest marches. In 1992 *gymnasio* pupils followed suit and the government responded by making proposals that called for stricter discipline and a more demanding curriculum. More sit-ins followed, and in the end the government changed its plans and is still reassessing the situation.

ARTS
Architecture
Of all the ancient Greek arts, it is architecture that perhaps has had the greatest influence on Western thinking. Greek temples, seen throughout history as symbols of civilisation, have been the inspiration for architectural movements such as the Italian Renaissance and the British Greek Revival.

Architecture in the Peloponnese begins with the Mycenaeans, who used their advanced engineering skills to create mighty citadels fortified by immense walls. The finest examples are the walls of the ancient citadels at Mycenae and Tiryns. The famous Lion Gate at Mycenae is the oldest monumental gate in Europe.

The next great advance came with the building of the first monumental stone temples in the Archaic and classical periods. From this time, temples were characterised by the famous orders of columns, particularly the Doric, Ionic and Corinthian.

Doric columns feature cushion capitals, fluted shafts and no bases. The most famous Doric temple in Greece is, of course, the Parthenon, which graces the Acropolis in Athens. Others include the Temple of Hera at Olympia and the Temple of Apollo at Corinth.

The shaft of the Ionic column has a base in several tiers and has more flutes. Unlike the austere Doric style, its capital has an ornamented necking. In all, the Ionic order is

Know your columns: (from left to right) Doric, the simplest in design; Ionic, featuring ornamental 'necking'; and Corinthian, with its characteristic rows of acanthus leaves

less massive than the Doric, and is generally more graceful. The little temple of Athena Nike by the entrance to the Athenian Acropolis, and the Erechtheion, opposite the Parthenon, are two famous Ionic temples.

The distinct and ornate Corinthian column features a single or double row of leafy scrolls (usually acanthus). This order was introduced at the end of the classical period and was subsequently used by the Romans in many of their buildings. The Temple of Olympian Zeus in Athens is a good example.

Theatre design was also a hallmark of the classical period. The finest example is the Theatre of Epidavros, famous for its remarkable acoustics. Like the smaller Theatre of Herodes Atticus in Athens, it's still used for summer festivals. Other theatres dating from this period are those at Megalopoli and Argos.

The Roman period saw Corinth become an important Roman city, with excavations revealing fountains, baths and gymnasia surrounding the ancient forum where St Paul once preached in vain. Athens also obtained a new commercial agora (now known as the Roman Agora) in the time of Augustus.

During the Byzantine period the Parthenon was converted into a church and other churches were built throughout Greece. These early churches usually featured a central dome supported by four arches on piers and flanked by vaults, with smaller domes at the four corners and three apses to the east.

After the sack of Constantinople by the Crusaders in 1204, the Peloponnese was claimed by the Franks, who were responsible many of the splendid old castles that dot the landscape, including those at Hlemoutsi in Elia, Kalamata and Mystras.

There is very little architecture of the Ottoman period surviving in Greece.

After the War of Independence, Greece continued the neoclassical style that had been dominant in Western European architecture and sculpture from 1760 to 1820, thus providing a sense of continuity with its ancient past. Nafplio's old town has some wonderful buildings dating from its brief reign as capital of Greece.

Sculpture

Taking pride of place in the collections of the great museums of the world, the sculptures of ancient Greece have extraordinary visual power and beauty.

The prehistoric art of Greece has been discovered only recently, most notably in the Cyclades. The pared-down sculptures of this period were carved from high-quality marble in the middle of the 3rd millennium BC. Their primitive and powerful forms have inspired many artists since.

The Mycenaean period was notable for the production of small terracotta figurines of women with a circular body or with arms upraised. These are known to modern scholars as phi (φ) and psi (ψ) figurines from their resemblance to these letters of the Greek alphabet.

Displaying an obvious debt to Egyptian sculpture, the marble sculptures of the Archaic period are the true precursors of the famed Greek sculpture of the classical period. The artists of this period began to represent figures that were true to nature, rather than flat and stylised. Seeking to master the depiction of the naked body, sculptors of the period focused on figures of naked youths *(kouroi)*, with their set symmetrical stance and enigmatic smiles. The sculpture of the classical period shows an obsession with the human figure and with drapery. At first the classical style was rather severe, as can be seen in the sculptures from the temple at Olympia. Later, as sculptors sought ideal proportions for the human figure, it became more animated.

Unfortunately, little original work of the classical period survives. Most freestanding classical sculpture described by ancient writers was made of bronze and survives only as marble copies made by the Romans. Fortunately, a few classical bronzes, lost at sea in antiquity, have been recovered. These include the statue of a youth (c. 350–330 BC) found off Antikythira, now on display at the National Archaeological Museum, Athens.

The sculpture of the Hellenistic period (c. 330–146 BC) continued the quest to attain total naturalism. Works of this period were animated, almost theatrical, in contrast to their serene Archaic and classical predecessors. The focus was on realism. Just how successful the artists of this period were is shown in the way they were revered by later artists, such as Michelangelo.

The end of the Hellenistic age signalled the decline of Greek sculpture's preeminent position in the history of the art form. The torch was handed to the Romans, who proved worthy successors.

Pottery

Say the words 'Greek art' and many people immediately visualise a painted terracotta pot. Represented in museums and galleries worldwide, the pots of ancient Greece have a high profile for a number of reasons, chief among these being that there are lots of them around! The excavation of these pots, buried throughout Greece over millennia, has enabled us to appreciate in small measure the tradition of ancient pictorial art. Quite simply, in the absence of significant examples of Greek painting, pots are all we've got!

Practised from the Stone Age on, pottery is one of the most ancient arts. At first, vases were built with coils and wads of clay, but the art of throwing on the wheel was introduced in about 2000 BC and was then practised with great skill by Mycenaean artists.

Mycenaean pottery shapes include a long-stemmed goblet and a globular vase with handles resembling a pair of stirrups. They were decorated with flowing designs with spiral or marine and plant motifs.

The 10th century BC saw the introduction of the Protogeometric style, with its substantial pots decorated with blackish-brown horizontal lines around the circumference, hatched triangles and compass-drawn concentric circles. This was followed by the new vase shape and more crowded decoration of the pots of the Geometric period. By the early 8th century, figures were introduced, marking the introduction of the most fundamental element in the later tradition of classical art – the representation of gods, humans and animals.

By the 7th century BC, Corinth was producing pottery with added white and purple-red clay slip. These pots often featured friezes of lions, goats and swans with a background fill of rosettes. In 6th-century Athens, artists used red clay with a high iron content. A thick glaze made from this clay produced a glossy black surface that contrasted with the red and was enlivened with added white and purple-red. Attic pots, famed for their high quality, were exported throughout the Greek empire during this time. Many of these exports are the pots that grace the collections of international museums today.

Painting

The lack of any comprehensive archaeological record of ancient Greek painting has forced art historians to rely largely on the evidence of pottery decoration to trace the early development of this art form. There are a few exceptions, such as the Cycladic frescoes now in the collection of the National Archaeological Museum in Athens.

Greek painting came into its own during the Byzantine period. Byzantine churches were usually decorated with frescoes on a dark blue ground with a bust of Christ in the dome, the four Gospel writers in the pendentives (triangular sections) supporting the dome and the Virgin and Child in the apse. They also featured scenes from the life of Christ and figures of the saints.

Painting after the Byzantine period became more secular in nature, with 19th-century Greek painters specialising in portraits, nautical themes and representations of the War of Independence. Major 19th-century painters included Dionysios Tsokos and Andreas Kriezis.

From the first decades of the 20th century, artists such as Konstantinos Parthenis, Konstantinos Kaleas and, later, George Bouzianis were able to use the heritage of the past and at the same time assimilate various developments in modern art. These works of these artists are best appreciated in the National Art Gallery in Athens.

Dance

Music and dancing have played an important role in Greek social life since the dawn of Hellenism. You may even think at times that Greeks live solely for the chance to sing and dance. You wouldn't be that wrong. Whether it be at a traditional wedding, a night club or a simple village *kafeneio*, a song and a dance are not far from people's minds.

The style of dancing often reflects the climate or disposition of the participants. The graceful *kalamatianos* circle dance, where dancers stand in a row with their hands on one another's shoulders, reflects years of proud Peloponnese tradition. Originally from Kalamata in the Peloponnese, this dance can be seen everywhere, most commonly on festive occasions.

The so-called 'Zorba's dance' or *syrtaki* is a stylised dance for two or three men or women with linked arms on shoulders, while the often-spectacular solo male *zeïmbekikos* with its whirling improvisations has its roots

in the Greek blues of the hashish dens and prisons of prewar times. The women counterpoint this self-indulgent and showy male display with their own sensuous *tsifteteli*, a svelte, sinewy show of femininity evolved from Middle Eastern belly dancing.

The folk dances of today derive from the ritual dances performed in ancient Greek temples. The syrtos is one of these dances, and is depicted on ancient Greek vases. There are also references to dances in Homer's works. Many Greek folk dances, including the syrtos, are performed in a circular formation; in ancient times, dancers formed a circle in order to seal themselves off from evil influences.

Music

Music has been integral to life since ancient times, and musical styles are as widely divergent as Greek dancing. Cycladic figurines holding musical instruments resembling harps and flutes date back to 2000 BC. Musical instruments of ancient Greece included the lyre, lute, *piktis* (pipes), *kroupeza* (a percussion instrument), *kithara* (a stringed instrument), *aulos* (a wind instrument), *barbitos* (similar to a cello) and the *magadio* (similar to a harp).

If ancient Greeks did not have a musical instrument to accompany their songs, they imitated the sound of one. It is believed that unaccompanied Byzantine choral singing derived from this custom.

The ubiquitous stringed *bouzouki*, (right) which you hear everywhere in Greece, is a relative newcomer to the game. It is a mandolin-like instrument similar to the Turkish *saz* and *baglama*.

MARTIN HARRIS

The plucked strings of the bulbous *outi* (oud), the strident sound of the Cretan *lyra* (lyre) and the staccato rap of the *toumberleki* (lap drum) bear witness to a rich range of musical instruments that share many common characteristics with instruments all over the Middle East.

The *bouzouki* is one of the main instruments of *rembetika* music – the Greek equivalent of the American Blues. The name *rembetika* may come from the Turkish word *rembet*, which means outlaw. Opinions differ as to the origins of *rembetika*, but it is probably a hybrid of several different types of music. One source was the music that emerged in the 1870s in the 'low life' cafes, called *tekedes* (hashish dens), in urban areas and especially around ports. Another source was the Arabo-Persian music played in sophisticated Middle Eastern music cafes *(amanedes)* in the 19th century. *Rembetika* was popularised in Greece by the refugees from Asia Minor.

The songs which emerged from the *tekedes* had themes concerning hashish, prison life, gambling, knife fights etc, whereas cafe *aman* music had themes which centred around erotic love. These all came together in the music of the refugees, from which a subculture of rebels, called *manges*, emerged. The *manges* wore showy clothes even though they lived in extreme poverty. They worked long hours in menial jobs, and spent their evenings in the *tekedes*, smoking hashish and singing and dancing. Although hashish was illegal, the law was rarely enforced until Metaxas did his clean-up job in 1936. It was in a *tekes* in Piraeus that Markos Vamvakaris, now acknowledged as the greatest *rembetis*, was discovered by a recording company in the 1930s.

Metaxas' censorship meant that themes of hashish, gambling and the like disappeared from recordings of *rembetika* in the late 1930s, but continued clandestinely in some *tekedes*. This polarised the music, and the recordings, stripped of their 'meaty' themes and language, became insipid and bourgeois; recorded *rembetika* even adopted another name – *Laïko tragoudi* – to disassociate it from its illegal roots. Although WWII brought a halt to recording, a number of composers emerged at this time. They included Apostolos Kaldaras, Yiannis Papaïoanou, Georgos Mitsakis and Manolis Hiotis; one of the greatest female *rembetika* singers, Sotiria Bellou, also appeared at this time.

During the 1950s and 1960s *rembetika* became increasingly popular, but less and less authentic. Much of the music was glitzy and commercialised, although the period also produced two outstanding composers of popular music (including *rembetika*) in Mikis Theodorakis and Manos Hatzidakis. The best of Theodorakis' work is the music which he set to the poetry of Seferis, Elytis and Ritsos.

During the junta years many *rembetika* clubs were closed down, but interest in genuine *rembetika* revived in the 1980s – particularly among students and intellectuals. There are now a number of *rembetika* clubs in Athens.

Other musical forms in Greece include *dimotika* – poetry sung and more often than not accompanied by the *klarino* (clarinet) and *defi* (tambourine) – and the widely popular middle-of-the-road *elafrolaïka*, best exemplified by the songs of Giannis Parios. The unaccompanied, polyphonic *pogonisia* songs of northern Epiros and southern Albania are spine-chilling examples of a musical genre that owes its origins to Byzantium. At the lesser end of the scale, the curiously popular *skyladika* or 'dog songs' – presumably because they resemble a whining dog – are hugely popular in clubs known as *bouzouxidika* where the *bouzouki* reigns supreme, but where musical taste sometimes takes a back seat.

Since independence, Greece has followed mainstream developments in classical music. The Athens Concert Hall has performances by both national and international musicians.

Comparatively few Greek performers have hit it big on the international scene. The best known is Nana Mouskouri. Others include Demis Roussos, the larger-than-life singer who spent the 1980s strutting the world stage clad in his kaftan, and the US-based techno wizard Yanni.

You'll also find all the main forms of Western pop music. Rock, particularly heavy metal, seems to have struck a chord with young urban Greeks, and Athens has a lively local scene as well as playing host to big international names. The biggest local bands are *Xylina Spathia* (Wooden Swords) and *Tripes* (Holes).

Literature

The first, and greatest, ancient Greek writer was Homer, author of the *Iliad* and *Odyssey*. Nothing is known of Homer's life: where or when he lived, or whether, as it is alleged, he was blind. The historian Herodotus thought Homer lived in the 9th century BC and no scholar since has proved or disproved this.

Herodotus (5th century BC) was the author of the first historical work about Western civilisation. His highly subjective account of the Persian Wars has, however, led him to be regarded as the 'father of lies' as well as the 'father of history'. The historian Thucydides (5th century BC) was more objective in his approach but took a high moral stance. He wrote an account of the Peloponnesian Wars and also the famous *Melian Dialogue*, which chronicles the talks between the Athenians and Melians prior to the Athenian siege of Melos.

Pindar (c. 518–438 BC) is regarded as the pre-eminent lyric poet of ancient Greece. He was commissioned to recite his odes at the Olympic Games. The greatest writers of love poetry were Sappho (6th century BC) and Alcaeus (5th century BC), both of whom lived on Lesvos. Sappho's poetic descriptions of her affections for other women gave rise to the term 'lesbian'.

Dionysios Solomos (1798–1857) and Andreas Kalvos (1796–1869), who were both born on Zakynthos, are regarded as the first modern Greek poets. Solomos' work was heavily nationalistic and his *Hymn to Freedom* became the Greek national anthem.

The best-known 20th-century poets are George Seferis (1900–71), who won the Nobel Prize for literature in 1963, and Odysseus Elytis (1911–96), who won the same prize in 1979. Seferis drew his inspiration from mythology, whereas Elytis' work is surreal.

The most important novelist of the 20th century is Nikos Kazantzakis (1883–1957), whose unorthodox religious views created a stir in the 1920s. See the Books section in the Facts for the Visitor chapter for a commentary on his works.

Nikos Dimou is a modern writer who has created a similar stir with his controversial observations on Greek society. His book *I Dystihia tou na Eisai Ellinas (The Misery of Being Greek)* has sold more than 100,000 copies. His work isn't available in English, but that may change. He has a English-language website (W www.ndimou.gr).

Apostolis Doxiadis achieved international fame in 2000 with his unusual novel *Uncle Petros and Goldbach's Conjecture*. He's better known at home as a film director.

Drama

Drama in Greece can be dated back to the contests staged at the Ancient Theatre of Dionysos in Athens during the 6th century BC for the annual Dionysia festival. During one of these competitions, Thespis left the ensemble and took centre stage for a solo performance regarded as the first true dramatic performance. The term 'thespian' for actor derives from this event.

Aeschylus (525–456 BC) is the so-called 'father of tragedy'; his best-known work is the *Oresteia* trilogy. Sophocles (c. 496–406 BC) is regarded as the greatest tragedian. He is thought to have written over 100 plays, of which only seven major works survive. These include *Ajax*, *Antigone*, *Electra*, *Trachiniae* and, his most famous play, *Oedipus Rex*. His plays dealt mainly with tales from mythology and had complex plots. Sophocles won first prize 18 times at the Dionysia festival, beating Aeschylus in 468 BC, whereupon Aeschylus went off to Sicily in a huff.

Euripides (c. 485–406 BC) was another famous tragedian, more popular than either Aeschylus or Sophocles because his plots were considered more exciting. He wrote 80 plays of which 19 survive (although one, *Rhesus*, is disputed). His most famous works are *Medea*, *Andromache*, *Orestias* and *Bacchae*. Aristophanes (c. 427–387 BC) wrote comedies – often ribald – which dealt with topical issues. His play *The Wasps* ridicules Athenians who resorted to litigation over trivialities; *The Birds* pokes fun at Athenian gullibility; and *Plutus* deals with the unfair distribution of wealth.

You can see plays by the ancient Greek playwrights at the Hellenic Festival in Athens and Epidavros (see the Athens and Argolis chapters), and at various other festivals around the country.

Drama continues to feature prominently on the domestic arts scene, although activity is largely confined to Athens and Thessaloniki. The first couple of the modern

Ancient Greek Mythology

Mythology was an integral part of life in ancient times. The myths of ancient Greece are the most familiar to us, for they are deeply entrenched in the consciousness of Western civilisation. They are accounts of the lives of the deities whom the Greeks worshipped and of the heroes they idolised.

The myths are all things to all people – a ripping good yarn, expressions of deep psychological insights, words of spine-tingling poetic beauty and food for the imagination. They have inspired great literature, art and music – as well as the odd TV show.

The myths we know are thought to be a blend of Dorian and Mycenaean mythology. Most accounts derive from the works of the poets Hesiod and Homer, produced in about 900 BC. The original myths have been chopped and changed countless times – dramatised, moralised and even adapted for ancient political propaganda, so numerous versions exist.

The Greek Myths by Robert Graves is regarded as being the ultimate book on the subject. It can be heavy going, though. *A Layman's Guide to the Greek Gods* by Maureen and Alan Carter makes more entertaining reading.

Olympian Creation Myth

According to mythology, the world was formed from a great shapeless mass called Chaos. From Chaos came forth **Gaea**, the earth goddess. She bore a son, **Uranus**, the Firmament, and their subsequent union produced three 100-handed giants and three one-eyed **Cyclopes**. Gaea dearly loved her hideous offspring, but not so Uranus, who hurled them back into Tartarus (the underworld).

The couple then produced the seven **Titans**, but Gaea still grieved for her other children. She asked the Titans to take vengeance upon their father, and free the 100-handed giants and the Cyclopes. The Titans did as they were requested, castrating the hapless Uranus, but **Cronos** (the head Titan), after setting eyes on Gaea's hideous offspring, hurled them back into Tartarus, whereupon Gaea foretold that Cronos would be usurped by one of his own offspring.

Cronos married his sister **Rhea**, but wary of his mother's warning, he swallowed every child Rhea bore him. When Rhea bore her sixth child, **Zeus**, she gave Cronos a stone in place of the child, which he duly swallowed. Most versions of mythology state that Rhea took the baby Zeus to Crete, where he was raised in the Dikteon Cave in the care of three nymphs. The Arcadians, however, believed that he was taken to Mt Lykeio, while the Messinians believed that he was reared on Mt Ithomi.

On reaching manhood, Zeus, determined to avenge his swallowed siblings, became Cronos' cupbearer and filled his cup with poison. Cronos drank from the cup, then disgorged first the stone and then his children **Hestia**, **Demeter**, **Hera**, **Poseidon** and **Hades**, all of whom were none the worse for their ordeal. Zeus, aided by his regurgitated brothers and sisters, deposed Cronos, and went to war against the Titans who wouldn't acknowledge him as chief god. Gaea, who still hadn't forgotten her beloved offspring, told Zeus he would only be victorious with the help of the Cyclopes and the 100-handed giants, so he released them from Tartarus.

The Cyclopes gave Zeus a thunderbolt, and the three 100-handed giants threw rocks at the Titans, who eventually retreated. Zeus banished Cronos, as well as all of the Titans except **Atlas** (Cronos' deputy), to a far-off land. Atlas was ordered to hold up the sky.

Mt Olympus became home-sweet-home for Zeus and his unruly and incestuous family. Zeus, taking a fancy to Hera, turned himself into a dishevelled cuckoo whom the unsuspecting Hera held to her bosom, whereupon Zeus violated her, and Hera reluctantly agreed to marry him. They had three children: **Ares**, **Hephaestus** and **Hebe**.

The Twelve Deities

The main characters of the myths are the 12 deities, who lived on Mt Olympus.

The supreme deity was **Zeus**, who was also god of the heavens. His job was to make laws and keep his unruly family in order by brandishing his thunderbolt. He was also the possessor of an astonishing libido and vented his lust on just about everyone he came across, including his own mother. Mythology is littered with his offspring.

Ancient Greek Mythology

Zeus was married to his sister **Hera**, the protector of women and the family. Hera was able to renew her virginity each year by bathing in a spring.

Ares, god of war, was the embodiment of everything warlike. Strong and brave, he was definitely someone to have on your side in a fight – but he was also hot-tempered and violent, liking nothing better than a good massacre. Athenians, who fought only for such noble ideals as liberty, thought that Ares must be a Thracian – a people whom they regarded as bloodthirsty barbarians.

Hephaestus was worshipped for his matchless skills as a craftsman. When Zeus decided to punish mortals, he asked Hephaestus to make a woman. So Hephaestus created Pandora from clay and water, and, as everyone knows, she had a box, from which sprang all the evils afflicting humankind.

The next time you have a bowl of corn flakes, give thanks to **Demeter**, the goddess of earth and fertility. The English word 'cereal', for products of corn or edible grain, derives from the goddess' Roman name, Ceres. The Greek word for such products is *demetriaka*.

The goddess of love (and lust) was the beautiful **Aphrodite**. Her *tour de force* was her magic girdle which made everyone fall in love with its wearer. The girdle meant she was constantly pursued by both gods and goddesses – the gods because they wanted to make love to her, the goddesses because they wanted to borrow the girdle. Zeus became so fed up with her promiscuity that he married her off to Hephaestus, the ugliest of the gods.

Athena, the powerful goddess of wisdom and guardian of Athens, is said to have been born (complete with helmet, armour and spear) from Zeus' head, with Hephaestus acting as midwife. Unlike Ares, she derived no pleasure from fighting, preferring to use her wisdom to settle disputes peacefully. If need be, however, she went valiantly into battle.

RICARDO BUSTOS

Poseidon, the brother of Zeus, was god of the sea and preferred his sumptuous palace in the depths of the Aegean to Mt Olympus. When he was angry (which was often) he would use his trident to create massive waves and floods. His moods could also trigger earthquakes and volcanic eruptions. He was always on the lookout for some real estate on dry land and challenged Dionysos for Naxos, Hera for Argos and Athena for Athens.

Apollo, god of light, was the son of Zeus by the nymph Leto. He was the sort of person everybody wanted to have around. The ancients Greeks associated sunshine with spiritual and intellectual illumination. Apollo was also worshipped as the god of music and song, which the ancients believed were heard only where there was light and security.

Apollo's twin sister, **Artemis**, seems to have been a bit confused by her portfolio. She was worshipped as the goddess of childbirth, yet she asked Zeus to grant her eternal virginity; she was also the protector of suckling animals, but loved hunting!

Hermes, messenger of the gods, was another son of Zeus – this time by Maia, daughter of Atlas. He was a colourful character who smooth-talked his way into the top ranks of the Greek pantheon. Convicted of rustling Apollo's cattle while still in his cradle, he emerged from the case as the guardian of all divine property. Zeus then made Hermes his messenger, and fitted him out with a pair of winged golden sandals to speed him on his way. His job included responsibility for commerce, treaties and the safety of travellers. He remained, however, the patron of thieves.

Hermes completes the first XI – the gods whose position in the pantheon is agreed by everyone. The final berth is normally reserved for **Hestia**, goddess of the hearth. She was as pure as driven snow, a symbol of security, happiness and hospitality. She spurned disputes and wars and swore to be a virgin forever.

Ancient Greek Mythology

She was a bit too virtuous for some, who relegated her to the ranks of the Lesser Gods and promoted the fun-loving **Dionysos**, god of wine, in her place. Dionysos was a son of Zeus by another of the supreme deity's dalliances. He had the job of touring the world with an entourage of fellow revellers spreading the word about the vine and wine.

Lesser Gods

After his brothers Zeus and Poseidon had taken the heavens and seas, **Hades** was left with the underworld (the earth was common ground). This vast and mysterious region was thought by the Greeks to be as far beneath the earth as the sky was above it. The underworld was divided into three regions: the Elysian Fields for the virtuous, Tartarus for sinners and the Asphodel Meadows for those who fitted neither category. Hades was also the god of wealth, in the form of the precious stones and metals found deep in the earth.

Pan, the son of Hermes, was the god of the shepherds and an important figure in Peloponnesian folklore. Born with horns, beard, tail and goat legs, his ugliness so amused the other gods that eventually he fled to Arcadia where he danced, played his famous pipes and watched over the pastures, shepherds and herds.

RICARDO BUSTOS

Other gods included **Asclepius**, the god of healing; **Eros**, the god of love; **Hypnos**, the god of sleep; **Helios**, god of the sun; and **Selene**, goddess of the moon.

Mythical Heroes

Mythology's other major players were the superheroes, who were elevated almost to the ranks of the gods.

The best known of these was **Heracles**, yet another of Zeus' offspring, who was performing astonishing feats of strength before he had left the cradle. He features prominently in Peloponnese lore. Although originally from Central Greece, he was a resident of Tiryns at the time of the 12 labours for which he is famous. These labours were performed on behalf of King Eurystheus of Argos, whom Heracles had been sentenced to serve to atone for the murder of his own wife and children in a bout of madness.

Many of the labours were local jobs, such as dispatching the Lernaean Hydra. This fearsome beast, which had a body like a dog and multiple snakelike heads, lived in the wetlands around the modern village of Myli, just south of Argos.

The slaying of the Nemean Lion was an obvious priority, given that the rolling hills of Nemea, between Argos and Corinth, were producing great red wine even back in those days.

Lake Stymfalia, west of Nemea, remains a delightfully tranquil spot since Heracles scared off the man-eating Stymfalian birds.

He also travelled west to capture the giant Erymanthian boar, which roamed the pine forests of Mt Erymanthos, and to Elis to flush the foul stables of King Augeas. His mission to capture of Cerberus, the savage three-headed dog that guarded Tartarus, took Heracles south to Cape Tenaro at the tip of the Mani Peninsula, where a deep cave led to the Underworld.

Theseus was another local favourite. He was from the city of Troizen, on the Saronic Gulf coast of Argolis. His deeds included the slaying of the Minotaur at Knossos, and he later became king of Athens.

Other heroes include **Odysseus**, whose wanderings after the fall of Troy are recorded in Homer's *Odyssey*, and **Jason**, who led his Argonauts to recover the golden fleece from Colchis (in modern Georgia).

Xena, regrettably, does not feature anywhere. The strapping 'warrior princess' of TV fame is a scriptwriter's invention – not a myth!

Greek theatre are playwrights Thanasis Reppas and Mihailis Papathanasiou, also noted writers of screenplays and movie directors. Unfortunately, performances of their work are only in Greek.

Cinema

Greeks are avid cinema-goers, although most of the films they watch are North American or British. The Greek film industry has long been in the doldrums, largely due to inadequate funding. The problem is compounded by the type of films the Greeks produce, which are famously slow moving, loaded with symbolism and generally too avant-garde to have mass appeal.

The leader of this school is Theodoros Angelopoulos, winner of the Golden Palm award at the 1998 Cannes Film Festival for *An Eternity and One Day*. It tells the story of a terminally ill writer who spends his last day revisiting his youth in the company of a 10-year-old boy. His other films include *The Beekeeper*, *Alexander the Great* and *The Hesitant Step of the Stork*.

Although it produces no action films, the Greek cinema has shown in recent years that it does have a lighter side. The big hit at the time of research was *Safe Sex*, a light-hearted look at sexuality directed by Thanasis Reppas and Mihailis Papathanasiou.

SOCIETY & CONDUCT
Women in Society

Despite the positive role model provided by mythology, which filled its pantheon with equal numbers of gods and goddesses, women barely rate a mention in most histories of ancient Greece – unless they happened to have a face lovely enough to launch a thousand ships.

Women were denied the vote, and were excluded from such events as the Olympic Games – on pain of death. Their role was to give birth to warriors and look after the domestic realm.

That role remained virtually unchanged until very recently. Women finally got the vote in 1956, but had to wait until the 1980s for the formal abolishment of the dowry system. The 1983 Family Law Act, which also gave women equal property rights and legalised abortion, finally put an end to a system that had remained largely unchanged since Byzantine times.

The result is that young women growing up today enjoy freedoms and opportunities that were unimaginable only a generation ago. The transition has not been entirely straightforward in a society so accustomed to male domination, nor is it complete. Outside major cities like Athens, Thessaloniki and Patras, times – and attitudes – have hardly changed. Women fill no more than a handful of seats in the nation's 300-strong parliament.

Ironically, despite the built-in, systemic disadvantages of being female, many of the country's best-known personalities of modern times have been women. Gianna Angelopoulos-Daskalaki, the glamorous head of the 2004 Athens Olympic Committee, is the latest in a line that includes the singers Maria Callas and Nana Mouskouri, and cultural crusader Melina Mercouri.

The main women's organisations are the **Greek Union of Women** (☎ 21-0823 4937; *Aharnon 51, Athens 104 39*); the **Greek Federation of Women** (☎ 21-0362 9460; *Ippokratous 120, Athens 114 72*); and the **League for Women's Rights** (☎ 21-0361 6236; *Solonos 41, Athens 106 72*).

Traditional Culture

Greece is steeped in traditional customs. Name days (see the boxed text p32), weddings and funerals all have great significance. On someone's name day an open-house policy is adopted and refreshments are served to well-wishers who stop by to give gifts. Weddings are highly festive occasions, with dancing, feasting and drinking sometimes continuing for days.

Greeks tend to be more superstitious than other Europeans. Tuesday is considered an unlucky day because on that day the Byzantine Empire fell to the Ottomans. Many Greeks will not sign an important transaction, get married or begin a trip on a Tuesday. Greeks also believe in the 'evil eye', a superstition prevalent in many Middle Eastern countries. If someone is the victim of the evil eye, then bad luck will befall them. The bad luck is the result of someone's envy, so one should avoid being too complimentary about things of beauty, especially newborn babies. To ward off the evil eye, Greeks often wear a piece of blue glass, resembling an eye, on a chain around their necks.

Social Graces

The Greeks' reputation for hospitality is not a myth, although it's a bit harder to find these days. In rural areas, Greece is probably the only country in Europe where you may be invited into a stranger's home for coffee, a meal or even to spend the night. This can often lead to a feeling of uneasiness in the recipient if the host is poor, but to offer money is considered offensive. The most acceptable way of saying thank you is through a gift, perhaps to a child in the family. A similar situation arises if you go out for a meal with Greeks; the bill is not shared as in northern European countries but paid by the host.

When drinking wine it is the custom to only half-fill the glass. It is bad manners to empty the glass, so it must be constantly replenished. When visiting someone you will be offered coffee; again, it is bad manners to refuse. You will also be given a glass of water and perhaps a small serve of preserves. It is the custom to drink the water, then eat the preserves and then drink the coffee.

Personal questions are not considered rude in Greece, and if you react as if they are you will be the one causing offence. You will be inundated with queries about your age, salary, marital status etc.

If you go into a *kafeneio*, taverna or shop, it is the custom to greet the waiters or assistant with *'kalimera'* (good day) or *'kalispera'* (good evening) – likewise if you meet someone in the street.

You may have come to the Peloponnese for sun, sand and sea, but if you want to bare all, other than on a designated nude beach, remember that Greece is a traditional country, and take care not to offend the locals.

Treatment of Animals

The Greek attitude to animals depends on whether the animal is a cat or not. It's definitely cool to be a cat. Even the mangiest-looking stray can be assured of a warm welcome and a choice titbit on approaching the restaurant table of a Greek. Most other domestic animals are greeted with a certain indifference. You don't see many pet dogs, or pets of any sort for that matter.

The main threat to animal welfare is hunting. Greek hunters are notorious for blasting anything that moves, and millions of animals are killed each year during the long 'open' season, from 20 August to 10 March, which encompasses the bird migratory period. The **Hellenic Centre for the Rehabilitation of Wild Animals and Birds** (☎ 2297-028 367), on the island of Aegina, reports that 80% of the animals it treats have been shot.

Name Days

Name days, not birthdays, are celebrated in Greece. Great significance is attached to the name given to a child, and the process of choosing a name follows fairly rigid conventions. The idea of a child being given a name just because the parents like the sound of it is unknown in Greece. Even naming a child after someone as a mark of respect or admiration is unusual. That so many children were named Vyronis (the Greek form of Byron) was a measure of the tremendous gratitude the Greeks felt for the philhellene Lord Byron.

Children are never named after parents, but the eldest son in a family is often called after his paternal grandfather, and the eldest daughter after her paternal grandmother. Names are usually of religious origin. Each island or area in Greece has a patron saint, and people living in that area often name a child after its patron saint. The patron saint of Corfu is Agios Spyridon and it seems as if about half of the men who were born there are called Spyridon. Exceptions to this custom occur if a family is not religious – quite a rarity in Greece. A non-religious family will often give their offspring a name derived from ancient Greece or mythology. Socrates, Aristotle, Athena and Aphrodite are popular.

Each saint has a special feast day. A person's name day is the feast day of the saint after which they were named. On someone's name day, open house is held and a feast is laid on for the friends and neighbours who call. They will give a small gift to the person whose name day it is, but there is less emphasis on the giving of presents than there is in birthday celebrations.

If you meet someone in Greece on their name day, the customary greeting is *'chronia polla!'*, which means 'many years'.

RELIGION

About 98% of the Greek population belongs to the Greek Orthodox Church. Most of the remainder are either Roman Catholic, Jewish or Muslim.

The Greek Orthodox Church is closely related to the Russian Orthodox Church; together they form the third-largest branch of Christianity. Orthodox, meaning 'right belief', was founded in the 4th century in the time of Constantine the Great, who was converted to Christianity by a vision of the Cross.

By the 8th century, there were a number of differences of opinion, as well as increasing rivalry, between the pope in Rome and the patriarch of Constantinople. One dispute was over the wording of the Creed. The original Creed stated that the Holy Spirit proceeds 'from the Father', which the Orthodox Church adhered to, whereas Rome added 'and the Son'. Another bone of contention concerned the celibacy of the clergy. Rome decreed priests had to be celibate; in the Orthodox Church, a priest could marry before becoming ordained. There were also differences in fasting: in the Orthodox Church, not only was meat forbidden during Lent, but wine and oil also.

By the 11th century these differences had become irreconcilable, and in 1054 the pope and the patriarch excommunicated one another. Ever since, the two have gone their own ways as the (Greek/Russian) Orthodox Church and the (Roman) Catholic Church. The brief visit to Athens by Pope John Paul II in May 2001 was the first by a pontiff for more than 1300 years.

During Ottoman times membership of the Orthodox Church was one of the most important criteria in defining a Greek, regardless of where he or she lived. The church was the principal upholder of Greek culture and traditions.

Religion is still integral to life in Greece, and the Greek year is centred on the festivals of the church calendar. Most Greeks, when they have a problem, will go into a church and light a candle to the saint they feel is most likely to help them. You will see hundreds of tiny churches dotted around the countryside. Most have been built by individual families in the name of their selected patron saint as thanksgiving for God's protection.

If you wish to look around a church, you should always dress appropriately. Women should wear skirts that reach below the knees, and men should wear long trousers and have their arms covered. Regrettably, many churches are kept locked nowadays but it's usually easy enough to locate caretakers, who will be happy to open them up for you.

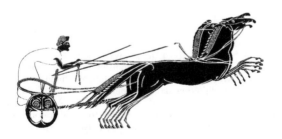

Facts for the Visitor

SUGGESTED ITINERARIES

One of the most difficult aspects of travel is organising an itinerary, especially if there is more than one person travelling! The following list provides a choice of itineraries for one week, two weeks and four weeks. (With your own transport, two weeks is sufficient to visit all of the major attractions. On public transport, allow at least three weeks, or be selective about your destinations.) The one-week itinerary is for people who want no more than a quick tour of the highlights, the two-week itinerary incorporates some of the harder-to-reach gems and the one-month tour is designed for people who really want to explore the full variety of the natural and ancient splendours on offer in the Peloponnese.

All the places featured in these itineraries are accessible by public transport, but you will have more fun – and more opportunities to explore – with your own vehicle. The itineraries assume that visitors will be travelling to the Peloponnese from Athens but it's just as easy to start from Patras.

One Week

Head from Athens to Corinth (one day) and visit ancient Corinth; continue to Nafplio (two days) and use it as a base for side trips to see the famous Theatre of Epidavros and Mycenae; go south to Sparta (one day) and check out the Byzantine city of Mystras; travel across the Taygetos Mountains to Kalamata and then up the west coast to Ancient Olympia (one day); visit the site early and continue north around the coast through Patras to Diakofto and ride the rack-and-pinion railway up to Kalavryta (one day); travel back to Diakofto and take the train back to Athens.

Two Weeks

Follow the above itinerary as far as Sparta/Mystras, and then head southeast to visit the romantic old Venetian town of Monemvasia (one day). From here, users of public transport will have to backtrack to Sparta in order to get to Gythio (one day); continue west to Aeropoli, main town of the Lakonian Mani, and use it as a base for a trip to the Diros Caves (one day); move

Highlights

- Roaming the wealth of ancient sites and antiquities

- Indulging in long lunches at harbourside restaurants

- Catching a Greek tragedy at one of the superb ancient theatres

- Walking among the wildflowers in the Mani in spring

- Trekking around Dimitsana and Kardamyli

- Relaxing on unspoilt beaches with crystal-clear water

- Skiing in the Peloponnesian mountains

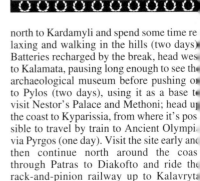

north to Kardamyli and spend some time relaxing and walking in the hills (two days). Batteries recharged by the break, head west to Kalamata, pausing long enough to see the archaeological museum before pushing on to Pylos (two days), using it as a base to visit Nestor's Palace and Methoni; head up the coast to Kyparissia, from where it's possible to travel by train to Ancient Olympia via Pyrgos (one day). Visit the site early and then continue north around the coast through Patras to Diakofto and ride the rack-and-pinion railway up to Kalavryta (one day); travel back to Diakofto and take the train back to Athens.

Four Weeks

Head from Athens to Corinth (two days) travel south via Nemea to Argos (one day) visit Mycenae (one day) and continue to Nafplio; spend some time exploring Nafplio and surrounds (two days); visit the Theatre of Epidavros and continue to Galatas to spend the night on Poros (one day); return to Nafplio and head to Tripolis (one day) travel to Sparta and visit Mystras (two days); move on to Monemvasia (one day) transfer to Gythio (one day); go south to Gerolimenas and visit some of the surrounding traditional Mani villages (two days); head to Aeropoli and visit the Diros Caves (one day); continue north to Kardamyli (two days); continue to Kalamata and visit ancient Messini (two days); go west to Pylos (two days); travel to Olympia (one day); backtrack to Pyrgos and travel to Andritsena – starting point for a visit to the Temple of Vasses (one day); continue east via Karitena to Dimitsana and use it as a base for walks in the beautiful Lousios Valley (two days). Bus travellers will need to go via Tripolis to get to Kalavryta (one day) – use Kalavryta as a base for walking in the Vouraïkos Gorge (one day); ride the rack-and-pinion railway down the gorge to Dikofto and take the train back to Athens.

PLANNING

When to Go

Spring and autumn are the best times to visit the Peloponnese. Most of the region's tourist infrastructure goes into hibernation from the end of November until the beginning of April – hotels and restaurants are closed at this time.

The cobwebs are dusted off in time for Easter, when the first tourists start to arrive. Conditions are perfect between Easter and mid-June, when the weather is pleasantly warm in most places but not too hot, beaches and ancient sites are relatively uncrowded, and accommodation is cheaper and easy to find.

Mid-June until the end of August is the high season. It's also very hot – in July and August the mercury can soar to 40°C (over 100°F) in the shade just about everywhere; the beaches are crowded, the ancient sites are swarming with tour groups and in many places accommodation is booked solid.

The season starts to wind down at the beginning of September and conditions are ideal once more until the shutdown at the end of November. Before you rule out a winter holiday entirely, it's worth considering going skiing (see Skiing under Activities later in this chapter, p57 for details).

Maps

Unless you are going to trek or drive, the free maps given out by the EOT (Ellinikos Organismos Tourismou, the Greek National Tourist Organization) will probably suffice, although they are not 100% accurate.

The best map you can get of the Peloponnese (1:250,000) is published by the Greek company Road Editions. Even the smallest roads and villages are clearly marked, and the distance indicators are spot-on – important when negotiating your way around the backblocks.

Freytag & Berndt also has good coverage of the Peloponnese, while Lonely Planet produces a handy city map of Athens.

What to Bring

Sturdy shoes are essential for clambering around ancient sites and wandering around historic towns and villages, which tend to have lots of steps and cobbled streets. Footwear with ankle support is preferable for trekking, although many visitors get by with trainers.

A day-pack is useful for the beach and for sightseeing or trekking. A compass is essential if you are going to trek in remote areas, as is a whistle, which you can use should you become lost or disoriented. A torch (flashlight) is useful for exploring caves and also comes in handy during occasional power cuts. If you like to fill a washbasin or bathtub (a rarity in Greece), bring a universal plug, as bathrooms rarely have plugs. A plastic food container, plate, cup, spoon, bottle opener, water container and all-purpose knife are useful for self-catering and picnicking.

Many camping grounds have covered areas where travellers without tents can sleep in summer, so you can get by with a lightweight sleeping bag and foam bedroll.

You will need only light clothing – preferably cotton – during the summer months. During spring and autumn you'll need a light sweater or jacket in the evening. In winter take a heavy jacket or coat, warm sweaters, winter shoes or boots, and an umbrella.

Sunscreen creams are expensive, as are moisturising and cleansing creams. Film is not expensive, especially in larger towns and tourist areas, but the stock tends to hang around for a while in remoter areas.

If you read a lot, it's a good idea to bring along a few disposable paperbacks to read and swap.

RESPONSIBLE TOURISM

Ideally, being a responsible traveller entails an effort to minimise the detrimental effects of travel – and maximise the benefits. This starts with such fundamental things as being polite and respectful.

The most irresponsible thing that a traveller can do is to 'souvenir' stones or small pieces of pottery from ancient sites. If every visitor picked up a stone from the Acropolis, there would soon be nothing left.

An easy way to be a responsible traveller is to economise on water use. Greece is a dry country and fresh water is a precious commodity, so turn the tap off while you're brushing your teeth and don't spend hours in the shower.

See Social Graces under Society & Conduct in the Facts about the Peloponnese chapter, p32, for tips about dress and how to avoid causing offence.

TOURIST OFFICES

Tourist information is handled by the Greek National Tourist Organization, known by the initials GNTO abroad and EOT (Ellinikos Organismos Tourismou) in Greece.

Local Tourist Offices

The head office of the **Greek National Tourist Organization** (*EOT;* ☎ *21-0331 0561/0562, fax 21-0325 2895;* **w** *www .gnto.gr; Amerikis 2, Athens 105 64*), is close to Plateia Syntagmatos (Syntagma Square). There is also an office at Athens international airport. In the Peloponnese, EOT operates regional offices in Gythio, Kalamata and Patras. All EOT staff speak English but they vary in their enthusiasm and helpfulness. Some offices, like that in Athens, have loads of useful local information but most have nothing more than glossy brochures, usually about other parts of the country.

In other towns, tourist information is handled by municipal tourist offices. They are often more helpful. There are municipal tourist offices in Olympia, Nafplio, Sparta and Tripolis.

Tourist Offices Abroad

Australia (☎ 02-9241 1663, fax 02-9235 2174) 51–57 Pitt St, Sydney, NSW 2000

Canada (☎ 416-968 2220, fax 514-968 6533) 91 Scollard St, Toronto, Ontario M5R 1G4; (☎ 514-871 1535) 1170, Place du Frere Andre, Montreal, Quebec H3B 3C6

France (☎ 1-42 60 65 75, fax 1-42 60 10 28) 3 Av de l'Opéra, Paris 75001

Germany (☎ 030-217 6262, fax 030-217 7965) Wittenbergplatz 3A, 10789 Berlin 30; (☎ 069-236 561, fax 069-236 576) Neue Mainzerstrasse 22, 60311 Frankfurt

(☎ 040-454 498, fax 040-454 404) Neurer Wall 18, 20254 Hamburg; (☎ 089-222 035, fax 089-297 058) Pacellistrasse 5, 2W 80333 Munich

Italy (☎ 06-474 4249, fax 06-488 3905, **w** www.ente-turismoellenico.com) Via L Bissolati 78-80, Rome 00187; (☎ 02-860 470, fax 02-7202 2589) Piazza Diaz 1, 20123 Milan

Japan (☎ 03-3505 5917, fax 03-3589 0467, **w** www.int-acc.or.jp/greece/) Fukuda Bldg West, 5th Floor 2-11-3 Akasaka, Minato-ku, Tokyo 107

UK (☎ 020-7734 5997, fax 020-7287 1369, **w** www.gnto.co.uk) 4 Conduit St, London W1R ODJ

USA (☎ 212-421 5777, fax 212-836 6940, **w** www.greektourism.com) Olympic Tower, 645 5th Ave, New York, NY 10022; (☎ 312-782 1084) Suite 160, 168 North Michigan Ave, Chicago, Illinois 60601; (☎ 213-626 6696) Suite 2198, 611 West 6th St, Los Angeles, California 92668

Tourist Police

The tourist police work in cooperation with the regular Greek police and EOT. Each tourist police office has at least one member of staff who speaks English. Hotels, restaurants, travel agencies, tourist shops, tourist guides, waiters, taxi drivers and bus drivers all come under the jurisdiction of the tourist police. If you think that you have been ripped off by any of these, report it to the tourist police and they will investigate. If you need to report a theft or loss of passport, then go to the tourist police first and they will act as interpreters between you and the regular police. The tourist police also fulfil the same functions as the EOT and municipal tourist offices, dispensing maps and brochures, and giving information on transport. They can often help you to find accommodation.

VISAS & DOCUMENTS
Passport

To enter Greece you need a valid passport, preferably with more than three months left until its expiry date, or, for EU nationals, travel documents (ID cards). You must produce your passport or EU travel document when you register in a hotel or pension in Greece. You will find that many accommodation proprietors will want to keep your passport during your stay. This is not a compulsory requirement; they need it only long enough to take down the details.

Visas

The countries whose nationals can stay in Greece for up to three months without a visa include Australia, Canada, all EU countries, Iceland, Israel, Japan, New Zealand, Norway, Switzerland and the USA. Other countries included are Cyprus, Malta, the European principalities of Monaco and San Marino and most South American countries. The list changes – contact Greek embassies for the full list. Those not included can expect to pay about US$20 for a three-month visa.

Northern Cyprus Greece will refuse entry to people whose passport indicates that, since November 1983, they have visited Turkish-occupied Northern Cyprus. This can be overcome if, upon entering Northern Cyprus, you ask the immigration officials to stamp a piece of paper (loose-leaf visa) rather than your passport. If you enter Northern Cyprus from the Greek Republic of Cyprus (only possible for a day visit), an exit stamp is not put into your passport.

Visa Extensions If you wish to stay in Greece for longer than three months, apply at a consulate abroad or at least 20 days in advance to the **Aliens Bureau** at the Athens **Central Police Station** (☎ 21-0770 5711; *Leoforos Alexandras 173; open 8am-1pm Mon-Fri*). Take along your passport and four passport photos. You may be asked for proof that you can support yourself financially, so keep all your bank exchange slips (or the equivalent from a post office). These slips are not always automatically given – you may have to ask for them. Elsewhere in Greece apply to the local police authority. You will be given a permit that will authorise you to stay in the country for a period of up to six months.

Most travellers get around this by visiting Bulgaria or Turkey and re-entering Greece.

Travel Insurance

A travel-insurance policy to cover theft, loss and medical problems is a good idea. The policies handled by STA Travel and other student-travel organisations are usually good value. There are a wide variety of policies available so check the small print.

Some policies specifically exclude 'dangerous activities', which can include scuba diving, motorcycling, even trekking. A locally acquired motorcycle licence is not valid under some policies.

You may prefer a policy that pays doctors or hospitals direct rather than you having to pay on the spot and claim later. If you have to claim later make sure you keep all documentation. Some policies ask you to call (reverse charges) a centre in your home country where an immediate assessment of your problem is made.

Check that the policy covers ambulances or an emergency flight home.

Driving Licence & Permits

Greece recognises all national driving licences, provided the licence has been held for at least one year. It also recognises an International Driving Permit, which should be obtained before you leave home. Travellers wishing to hire a motorbike or moped (anything above 500cc) need to have a licence that shows proficiency for the category of bike they wish to rent; British would-be bikers must have a Category A licence from the DVLA; a standard British driving licence won't be sufficient.

Hostel Cards

A Hostelling International (HI) card is of limited use. The only place you will be able to use it is at the Athens International Youth Hostel.

Student & Youth Cards

The most widely recognised form of student ID is the International Student Identity Card (ISIC). It qualifies you for half-price admission to museums and ancient sites. Aegean Airlines offers student discounts on some domestic flights but there are no discounts on buses, ferries or trains. Students will find some good deals on international air fares.

Several travel agencies in Athens can issue cards; see Travel Agents under Information in the Athens chapter, p84. You must show documents proving you are a student, provide a passport photo and cough up €7.35.

Seniors Cards

Card-carrying EU pensioners can claim a range of benefits such as reduced admission charges at museums and ancient sites and discounts on trains.

Copies

The hassles created by losing your passport, travellers cheques and other important documents can be reduced considerably if you take the precaution of taking photocopies. It is a good idea to have photocopies of the passport pages that cover personal details, issue and expiry date and the current entry stamp or visa. Other items worth photocopying are airline tickets, credit cards, driving licence and insurance details. You should also keep a record of the serial numbers of your travellers cheques, and cross them off as you cash them.

This emergency material should be kept separate from the originals, so that hopefully they won't both get lost (or stolen) at the same time. Leave an extra copy with someone at home just in case.

There is another option for storing details of your vital travel documents before you leave – Lonely Planet's online Travel Vault. Storing details of your important documents in the vault is safer than carrying photocopies. Your password-protected travel vault is accessible at any time. It's the best option if you travel in a country with easy Internet access. You can create your own travel vault for free at **W** www.ekno.lonelyplanet.com.

EMBASSIES & CONSULATES
Greek Embassies & Consulates

The following is a selection of Greek diplomatic missions abroad:

Australia (☎ 02-6273 3011, fax 02-6273 2620) 9 Turrana St, Yarralumla, Canberra, ACT 2600
Canada (☎ 613-238 6271, fax 613-238 5676) 76-80 Maclaren St, Ottawa, Ont K2P 0K6
France (☎ 01 47 23 72 28, fax 01 47 23 33 57, **W** www.amb-grece.fr/presse) 17 Rue Auguste Vaqueire, 75116 Paris
Germany (☎ 030-20 62 60, fax 030-20 62 64 44, **W** www.griechische-botschaft.de) 3rd floor, Jaegerstraasse 55, 10117 Berlin-Mitte
Italy (☎ 06-853 7551, fax 06-841 5927) Via S Mercadante 36, Rome 3906
Japan (☎ 03-3403 0871/2, fax 03-3402 4642, **W** www.greekemb.jp) 3-16-30 Nishi Ajabu, Minato-Ku, Tokyo 106-0031
New Zealand (☎ 04-473 7775, fax 04-473 7441) 5-7 Willeston St, Wellington
South Africa (☎ 12-430 7351/3, fax 12-430 4313) 1003 Church St, Hatfield, Pretoria 0028
Turkey (☎ 90312-4368 860/1/2, 90312-4365 240, fax 90312-4463 191) Ziya-ul-Rahman Caddesi 9-11, Gazi Osman Pasa 06700, Ankara

UK (☎ 020-7229 3850, fax 020-7229 7221, **W** www.greekembassy.org.uk) 1A Holland Park, London W11 3TP
USA (☎ 202-939 1300, fax 202-939 1324, **W** www.greekembassy.org) 2221 Massachusetts Ave NW, Washington, DC, 20008

Embassies & Consulates in Greece

All foreign embassies in Greece are in Athens and its suburbs. They include:

Australia (☎ 21 0645 0404) Dimitriou Soutsou 37, Athens 115 21
Canada (☎ 21 0727 3400) Genadiou 4, Athens 115 21
France (☎ 21 0361 1663) Leoforos Vasilissis Sofias 7, Athens 106 71
Germany (☎ 21 0728 5111) Dimitriou 3 & Karaoli, Kolonaki 106 75
Italy (☎ 21 0361 7260) Sekeri 2, Athens 106 74
Japan (☎ 21 0775 8101) Athens Tower, Leoforos Messogion 2–4, Athens 115 27
New Zealand (honorary consulate; ☎ 21 0687 4701) Kifissias 268, Halandri 152 32
South Africa (☎ 21 0680 6645) Kifissias 60, Maroussi, Athens 151 25
Turkey (☎ 21 0724 5915) Vasilissis Georgiou 8, Athens 106 74
UK (☎ 21 0723 6211) Ploutarhou 1, Athens 106 75
USA (☎ 21 0721 2951) Leoforos Vasilissis Sofias 91, Athens 115 21

Generally speaking, your own country's embassy won't be much help in emergencies if the trouble you're in is remotely your own fault. Remember that you are bound by Greek laws. Your embassy will not be sympathetic if you end up in jail after committing a crime locally, even if such actions are legal in your own country.

In genuine emergencies you might get some assistance, but only if other channels have been exhausted. For example, if you need to get home urgently, a free ticket home is exceedingly unlikely – the embassy would expect you to have insurance. If you have all your money and documents stolen, it might assist with getting a new passport, but a loan for onward travel is out of the question.

CUSTOMS

There are no longer duty-free restrictions within the EU. This does not mean that customs checks have been dispensed with: random searches are still made for drugs.

Upon entering the country from outside the EU, customs inspection is usually cursory for foreign tourists.

You may bring the following into Greece duty-free: 200 cigarettes or 50 cigars; 1L of spirits or 2L of wine; 50g of perfume; 250mL of eau de Cologne; one camera (still or video) and film; a pair of binoculars; a portable musical instrument; a portable radio or tape recorder; a typewriter; sports equipment; and dogs and cats (with a veterinary certificate).

Importation of works of art and antiquities is free but they must be declared on entry, so that they can be re-exported. Import regulations for medicines are strict; if you are taking medication, make sure you get a statement from your doctor before you leave home. It is illegal, for instance, to take codeine into Greece without an accompanying doctor's certificate.

An unlimited amount of foreign currency and travellers cheques may be brought into Greece. If you intend to leave the country with foreign banknotes in excess of US$1000, you must declare the sum upon entry.

It is strictly forbidden to export antiquities (anything over 100 years old) without an export permit. This crime is second only to drug smuggling in the penalties imposed. The place to apply for an export permit is the Antique Dealers & Private Collections Section, Archaeological Service, Polygnotou 13, Athens.

Vehicles

Cars can be brought into Greece for four months without a carnet; only a green card (international third party insurance) is required. Your vehicle will be registered in your passport when you enter Greece in order to prevent your leaving the country without it.

MONEY
Currency

Greece adopted the euro at the beginning of 2002 and the Greek drachma disappeared at the end of February that year after a two-month period of dual circulation.

The only place that will now convert outstanding drachma into euro is the National Bank of Greece and only at its central offices in major cities like Athens and Patras.

The Athens branch is at Panepistimiou 15, near Syntagma.

There are eight euro coins, in denominations of €2 and €1, then 50, 20, 10, five, two and one cents, and six notes: €5, €10, €20, €50, €100 and €200.

Exchange Rates

country	unit		euro
Albania	100 lekē	=	0.76
Australia	A$1	=	0.56
Bulgaria	1 lev	=	0.51
Canada	C$1	=	0.65
Japan	¥100	=	0.81
New Zealand	NZ$1	=	0.50
UK	UK£1	=	1.56
USA	US$1	=	1.00

Warning It's all but impossible to exchange Turkish lira in Greece. The only place you can change them is at the head office of the National Bank of Greece, Panepistimiou 15, Athens – and it'll give only about 75% of the going international rate.

Exchanging Money

Banks will exchange all other major currencies in either cash or travellers cheques. The best-known travellers cheques in Greece are Thomas Cook and American Express (AmEx). A passport is required to change travellers cheques, but not cash.

Commission charged on the exchange of banknotes and travellers cheques varies from bank to bank. It's less for cash than for travellers cheques. For travellers cheques, the commission can be as much as €4.40 for amounts under €100 and €5.90 for amounts over €100.

Post offices can exchange banknotes – but not travellers cheques – and charge less commission than banks. Many travel agencies and hotels will also change money and travellers cheques at bank rates, but their commission charges are higher.

If there is a chance that you may apply for a visa extension, make sure you receive, and keep hold of, a bank exchange slip after each transaction.

Cash Nothing beats cash for convenience – or for risk. If you lose cash, it's gone for good and very few travel insurers will come to your rescue. Those that will normally limit the amount to about US$300. It's best to carry no more cash than you need for the next few days, which means working out your likely needs whenever you change travellers cheques or withdraw cash from an ATM.

It's also a good idea to set aside a small amount of cash, say US$50, as an emergency stash.

Travellers Cheques The main reason to carry travellers cheques rather than cash is the protection they offer against theft. They are losing popularity as more and more travellers opt to put their money in a bank at home and withdraw it at ATMs as they go along.

AmEx, Visa and Thomas Cook cheques are all widely accepted and have efficient replacement policies. Maintaining a record of the cheque numbers and recording when you use them is vital when it comes to replacing lost cheques – keep this separate from the cheques themselves. Euros are a good currency to use.

ATMs Automatic teller machines are to be found in every town large enough to support a bank – and certainly in all the tourist areas. If you've got MasterCard or Visa/Access, there are plenty of places to withdraw money. Cirrus and Maestro users can make withdrawals in all major towns and tourist areas.

AFEMs (Automatic Foreign Exchange Machines) are common in major tourist areas. They take all the major European currencies, Australian and US dollars and Japanese yen, and are useful in an emergency. Note that they charge a hefty commission, though.

Credit Cards The great advantage of credit cards is that they allow you to pay for major items without carrying around great wads of cash. Credit cards are an accepted part of the commercial scene in Greece. They can be used to pay for a wide range of goods and services such as meals (in better restaurants) and accommodation, car hire and souvenir shopping.

If you are not familiar with the card options, ask your bank to explain the workings and relative merits of the various schemes: cash cards, charge cards and credit cards. Ask whether the card can be replaced in Greece if it is lost or stolen and check what fees are charged for purchases in foreign currencies and for withdrawals from overseas ATMs.

The main credit cards are MasterCard Visa (Access in the UK) and Eurocard, all of which are widely accepted in Greece They can also be used as cash cards to draw cash from the ATMs of affiliated Greek banks in the same way as at home. Daily withdrawal limits are set by the issuing bank. Cash advances are given in local currency only. Credit cards can be used to pay for accommodation in all the smarter hotels. Some C-class hotels will accept credit cards, but D- and E-class hotels rarely do.

The main charge cards are American Express (AmEx) and Diner's Club Card, which are widely accepted in tourist areas but unheard of elsewhere.

International Transfers If you run out of money or need more for whatever reason, you can instruct your bank back home to send you a draft. Specify the city and the bank as well as the branch that you want the money sent to. If you have the choice, select a large bank and ask for the international division. Money sent by electronic transfer should reach you within 24 hours.

Security

The safest way of carrying cash and valuables (passport, travellers cheques, credit cards etc) is a favourite topic of travel conversation. The simple answer is that there is no foolproof method. The general principle is to keep things out of sight. The front pouch belt, for example, presents an obvious target for a would-be thief – only marginally less inviting than a fat wallet bulging from your back pocket.

The best place is under your clothes in contact with your skin where, hopefully, you will be aware of an alien hand before it's too late. Most people opt for a money belt, while others prefer a leather pouch hung around the neck. Another possibility is to sew a secret stash pocket into the inside of your clothes. Whichever method you choose, put your valuables in a plastic bag first – otherwise they will get soaked in sweat as you wander around in the heat. After a few soakings, they will end up looking like they've been through the washing machine.

Costs

Greece is still a cheap country by Western European standards but it is no longer dirt-cheap. A rock-bottom daily budget would be €25. This would mean hitching, staying in youth hostels or camping, staying away from bars, and only occasionally eating in restaurants. Allow at least €50 per day if you want your own room and plan to eat out regularly as well as travelling about and seeing the sights. You will still need to do a fair bit of self-catering. If you really want a holiday – comfortable rooms and restaurants all the way – you will need closer to €100 per day. These budgets are for individuals travelling in high season (July/August). Couples sharing a double room can get by on less.

Your money will go a lot further if you travel in the quieter months. Accommodation, which eats up a large part of the daily budget, is generally about 25% cheaper outside high season. There are fewer tourists around and more opportunities to negotiate even better deals. All prices quoted in this book are for the high season.

Museums & Ancient Sites Admission to sites and museums is free for anyone under 18, and for card-carrying EU students, teachers and journalists. Students from outside the EU qualify for a 50% discount with an ISIC card, while pensioners (over 65) from EU countries also pay half price.

Museums and sites have free admission for everyone on Sundays from 1 November to the end of March, as well as on 6 March, 18 April, 18 May, 5 June and the last weekend in September.

Tipping & Bargaining

In restaurants the service charge is included in the bill but it is the custom to leave a small amount. The practice is often just to round off the bill. Likewise for taxis – a small amount is appreciated.

Bargaining is not as widespread in Greece as it is further east. Prices in most shops are clearly marked and non-negotiable. The same applies to restaurants and public transport. It is always worth bargaining over the price of hotel rooms or domatia (the Greek equivalent of the British B&B, minus the breakfast), especially if you are intending to stay a few days. You may get short shrift at the peak of the season, but prices can drop

dramatically in the off season. Souvenir shops and market stalls are other places where your negotiating skills will come in handy. If you feel uncomfortable about haggling, walking away can be just as effective – you can always go back.

Taxes & Refunds

The value-added tax (VAT) varies from 15% to 18%. A tax-rebate scheme applies at a restricted number of shops and stores; look for a 'Tax Free' sign in the window. You must fill in a form at the shop and present it with the receipt at the airport on departure. A cheque should be sent to your home address.

POST & COMMUNICATIONS

Post offices (tahydromio) are easily identifiable by means of the yellow signs outside. Regular postboxes are also yellow. The red boxes are for express mail only.

Postal Rates

The postal rate for postcards and airmail letters is €0.60 to all destinations. Mail to destinations within Europe takes five to eight days to arrive, and to the USA, Australia and New Zealand, nine to 11 days.

Express mail costs an extra €2 and should ensure delivery in three days within the EU – use the special red post boxes. Valuables should be sent registered post, which costs an extra €4.

Sending Mail

Do not wrap a parcel until it has been inspected at a post office. In Athens, take your parcel to the **Parcel Post Office** (☎ 21-0322 8940; in the arcade at Stadiou 4), and elsewhere to the parcel counter of a regular post office.

Receiving Mail

You can receive mail poste restante (general delivery) at any main post office. The service is free of charge but you are required to show your passport. Ask senders to write your family name in capital letters and underline it, and to mark the envelope 'poste restante'. It is a good idea to ask the post office clerk to check under your first name as well if letters you are expecting cannot be located. After one month uncollected mail is returned to the sender. If you are about to leave a town and expected mail hasn't arrived, ask at the post office to have it forwarded to your next destination, c/o poste restante. See Post & Communications under Information in the Athens chapter, p84, for information about poste restante mail in the capital.

Parcels are not delivered in Greece; they must be collected from the parcel counter of a post office – or, in Athens, from the Parcel Post Office.

Telephone

The Greek telephone service is maintained by the public corporation known as Organismos Tilepikoinonion Ellados, which is always referred to by the acronym OTE (pronounced O-tay).

The system is modern and reasonably well maintained. There are public telephones just about everywhere, including some unbelievably isolated spots. The phones are easy to operate and can be used for local, long distance and international calls. The 'i' at the top left of the push-button dialling panel brings up the operating instructions in English, French and German.

The biggest headache with the system is confusion over telephone numbers, which follows two changes to the numbering system in less than a year.

The changes were completed in November 2002 and involved converting all telephone numbers in Greece to 10 digits. This was achieved by incorporating the area code, followed by an extra 0, into the number. The initial 0 was then converted into a 2.

All the numbers listed in this book incorporate these changes but many brochures, business cards, websites and books have been unable to keep up.

All public phones use OTE phonecards, known as *telekarta*, not coins. The cards cost €2.95 for 1000 units, €5.60 for 2000 units, €12.35 for 5000 units, and €24.10 for 10,000 units. The 1000-unit cards are widely available at *periptera* (street kiosks), corner shops and tourist shops; the others can be bought at OTE offices. A local call uses 10 units for one minute.

It's also possible to use these phones using a growing range of discount card schemes, such as Kronokarta and Teledome, which involve dialling an access code and then punching in your card number. The cards come with instructions in

Useful Phone Numbers		
General		
International access code for Greece		☎ 30
International access code from within Greece		☎ 00
General telephone information		☎ 134
Numbers in Athens & Attica		☎ 131
Numbers elsewhere in Greece		☎ 132
International inquiries	☎ 161 or 162	
International telegrams		☎ 165
International dialling instructions in English, French & German		☎ 169
Domestic operator	☎ 151 or 152	
Wake-up service		☎ 182
Weather		☎ 149
Attica weather		☎ 148
Toll-free 24-hour emergency numbers		
Police		☎ 100
Tourist Police		☎ 171
Ambulance (Athens)		☎ 166
Fire Brigade		☎ 199
Roadside Assistance (ELPA)		☎ 104

Greek and English. They are easy to use and buy double the time.

Lonely Planet's ekno global communication service provides low-cost international calls – for local calls you're usually better off with a local phonecard. Ekno also offers free messaging services, email, travel information and an online travel vault, where you can securely store copies of all your important documents. You can join online at w www.ekno.lonelyplanet.com, where you will find the local-access numbers for the 24-hour customer-service centre. Once you have joined, always check the ekno website for the latest access numbers for each country and updates on new features.

It is no longer possible to use public phones to access other national card schemes, such as Telstra Australia's Telecard, for international calls. These calls can be made from private digital phones but the time you spend on the phone is also charged at local call rates. It's better to use Kronokarta or Teledome. You can use the ekno service but you must insert a phonecard first.

International calls can also be made from OTE offices. A counter clerk directs you to a cubicle equipped with a metered phone and payment is made afterwards. Villages and remote islands without OTE offices almost always have at least one metered phone for international and long-distance calls – usually in a shop, *kafeneio* (café) or taverna.

Another option is the *periptero*. Almost every *periptero* has a metered telephone which can be used for local, long distance and direct dial international calls. There is a small surcharge but it is less than that charged by hotels.

Reverse-charge (collect) calls can be made from an OTE office. The time you have to wait for a connection can vary considerably, from a few minutes to two hours. If you are using a private phone to make a reverse-charge call, dial the operator: domestic ☎ 151, international ☎ 161.

To call overseas direct from Greece, dial the Greek overseas access code ☎ 00, followed by the country code for the country you are calling, then the local area code (dropping the leading zero if there is one) and then the number. The charges vary between €0.29 and €0.67 per minute.

Off-peak rates are 25% cheaper. They are available to Africa, Europe, the Middle East and India between 10pm and 6am; to the Americas between 11pm and 8am; and to Asia and Oceania between 8pm and 5am.

Fax & Telegraph
Most post offices have fax machines; telegrams can be sent from any OTE office.

Email & Internet Access
Greece was slow to embrace the wonders of the Internet but is now striving to make up for lost time. There has been a huge increase in the number of hotels and businesses using email, and these addresses have been listed in this book where available.

Internet cafés are springing up everywhere, and are listed under Information in this book for cities and towns where appropriate. Some hotels catering for travellers also offer Internet access.

DIGITAL RESOURCES
Predictably enough, there has also been a huge increase in the number of websites providing information about Greece. A good place to start is the 500 Links to Greece site at Ⓦ www.viking1.com/corfu/link.htm. It has links to a huge range of sites on everything from accommodation to Zeus.

Mobile Phones

Few countries in the world have embraced the mobile phone with such enthusiasm as Greece. It has become the essential Greek accessory: everyone seems to have one.

Greece uses GSM 900/1800, which is compatible with the rest of Europe and Australia but not with the North American GSM 1900 or the totally different system in Japan (though some North Americans have GSM 1900/900 phones that do work here). If you have a GSM phone, check with your service provider about using it in Greece and beware of calls being routed internationally (very expensive for a 'local' call).

Greece's established mobile phone providers are Cosmote (GSM 1800), Vodafone-Panafon (GSM 900) and Telestet (GSM 900).

The address Ⓦ www.greektravel.com takes you to an assortment of interesting and informative sites on Greece by Matt Barrett. The Greek Ministry of Culture has put together an excellent site, Ⓦ www.culture.gr, with loads of information about museums and ancient sites. Other sites include Ⓦ www.gogreece.com/travel and Ⓦ www.agn.gr/main.html. You'll find more specialist websites listed through the book.

The Lonely Planet website (Ⓦ www.lonelyplanet.com) gives a succinct summary on travelling to Greece, postcards from other travellers and provides the Thorn Tree bulletin board, where you can ask questions before you go or dispense advice when you get back. The subwwway section links you to other useful travel resources on the Web.

BOOKS
Most books are published in different editions by different publishers in different countries. As a result, a book might be a hardcover rarity in one country while it's readily available in paperback in another. Fortunately, bookshops and libraries search by title or author, so your local bookshop or library is best placed to advise you on the availability of the following recommendations. (Some will not be available to buy.)

There are several specialist English-language bookshops in Athens, as well as shops selling books in French, German and Italian. All other major towns and tourist resorts have bookshops that sell some foreign-language books.

Imported books are expensive – normally two to three times the recommended retail price in the UK and the USA. Some hotels have small collections of second-hand books to read or swap.

Abroad, the best bookshop for new and second-hand books on Greece, written in both English and Greek, is the **Hellenic Book Service** (☎ 020-7267 9499, fax 7267 9498; e hellenicbooks@btinternet.com; w www .hellenicbookservice.com; 91 Fortress Rd, Kentish Town, London). It stocks many of the books recommended here.

Lonely Planet
The Lonely Planet guides *Mediterranean Europe* and *Western Europe* also include coverage of Greece and the Peloponnese, as does *Europe on a shoestring*. Other regional titles include *Greek Islands*, *Corfu & the Ionian Islands*, *Rhodes & the Dodecanese* and *Crete*. *Athens Condensed* is part of the popular pocket-guide series. The handy *Greek phrasebook* will help enrich your visit, while *World Food Greece* will help enrich your travel dining experiences.

Katherine Kizilos vividly evokes Greece's landscapes, people and politics in her book *The Olive Grove: Travels in Greece*. She explores the islands and borderlands of her father's homeland, and life in her family's village in the mountains of the Peloponnese. The book is part of the Journeys travel literature series.

These titles are available at the major English-language bookshops in Athens (see Bookshops under Information in the Athens chapter, p84, for details).

Guidebooks
The ancient Greek traveller Pausanias is acclaimed as the world's first travel writer. His *Guide to Greece* was written in the 2nd century AD during the reign of the emperor Hadrian. Umpteen editions later, it is now available in English in paperback. It includes detailed descriptions of all the major monuments of the Peloponnese, and historical and mythological background.

Travel
Patrick Leigh Fermor, well known for his exploits in rallying the Cretan resistance in WWII, now lives in Kardamyli in the Peloponnese. His highly acclaimed book *Mani: Travels in the Southern Peloponnese* is an account of his adventures in the Mani Peninsula during the 1950s.

Deep into Mani by Peter Greenhalgh & Edward Eliopoulis details a journey through the Mani some 25 years after Fermor's account.

Journey to the Morea by Nikos Kazantzakis is a highly readable account of the great writer's travels through the Peloponnese in the 1930s. The English painter and writer Edward Lear, of *The Owl and the Pussy-Cat* fame, visited the region during his extended trip to Greece in the mid-19th century and wrote about his experiences in *Journals of a Landscape Painter in Greece & Albania*.

The Colossus of Maroussi by Henry Miller is now regarded as a classic. It covers Miller's typically manic adventures in Athens, the Peloponnese and the Saronic Gulf Islands at the outbreak of WWII – related with feverish enthusiasm.

People & Society
You may only be able to find most of these books in libraries or second-hand, but they are worth the search. *Time, Religion & Social Experience in Rural Greece* by Laurie Kain Hart is a fascinating account of village traditions, many of which are alive and well beneath the tourist veneer.

Portrait of a Greek Mountain Village by Juliet du Boulay is in a similar vein, based on her experiences in an isolated village. *The Traveller's Journey is Done* and *An Affair of the Heart* (republished in 1999) by Dilys Powell, wife of archaeologist Humfry Payne, are very readable, affectionate insights into Peloponnese village life during the 1920s and 1930s.

Road to Rembetica: Music of a Greek Subculture – Songs of Love, Sorrow and Hashish by Gail Holst explores the intriguing subculture which emerged from the poverty and suffering of the refugees from Asia Minor.

History & Mythology
Traveller's History of Greece by Timothy Boatswain & Colin Nicolson gives the layperson a good general reference on the historical background of Greece, from Neolithic times to the present. *Modern*

Greece: A Short History by CM Woodhouse similarly provides good general background, although it has a right-wing bent. It covers the period from Constantine the Great to 1990.

Mythology was an intrinsic part of life in ancient Greece, and some knowledge of it will enhance your visit. One of the best publications on the subject is *The Greek Myths* by Robert Graves (two volumes) which relates and interprets the adventures of the gods and heroes worshipped by the ancient Greeks. *A Layman's Guide to the Greek Gods* and *A Layman's Guide to the Greek Heroes* by Maureen & Alan Carter present entertaining and accessible versions of the myths.

There are many translations around of Homer's *Iliad* and *Odyssey*, which tell the story of the Trojan War and the subsequent adventures of Odysseus (known as Ulysses in Latin). The translations by EV Rien are among the best, if you can find them.

The Greek publisher Malliaris-Paedia puts out a good series of books on the myths, retold in English for young readers by Aristides Kesopoulos. The titles are *The Gods of Olympus and the Lesser Gods*, *The Labours of Hercules*, *Theseus and the Voyage of the Argonauts*, *The Trojan War and the Wanderings of Odysseus* and *Heroes and Mythical Creatures*. Robin Lister's retelling of *The Odyssey* is aimed at slightly older readers (ages 10 to 12), but makes compelling listening for younger ones when read aloud.

Mistra: Byzantine Capital of the Peloponnese and *Byzantine Style and Civilisation* by Sir Steven Runciman (which you'll find most easily in libraries) and *Fourteen Byzantine Rulers* by Michael Psellus are both good introductions to Greece's Byzantine Age.

The Jaguar by Alexander Kotzias is a moving story about the leftist resistance to the Nazi occupation of Greece. Although a novel, it is packed with historical facts.

General

The most well-known and widely read Greek author is the Cretan writer Nikos Kazantzakis, whose novels are full of drama and larger-than-life characters. His most famous works are *The Last Temptation*, *Zorba the Greek*, *Christ Recrucified* and *Freedom or Death*. The first two have been made into films.

Athenian writer Apostolos Doxiadis has charmed critics the world over with his latest novel, *Uncle Petros and Goldbach's Conjecture*. It's an unlikely blend of family drama and mathematical theory, although you don't need to be a mathematical genius to enjoy the book.

English writer Louis de Bernières has become almost a cult figure following the success of *Captain Corelli's Mandolin*, which tells the emotional story of a young Italian army officer sent to the island of Kefallonia during WWII.

The Australian journalists George Johnston and Charmian Clift wrote several books with Greek themes during their 19 years as expatriates, including Johnston's novel *The Sponge Divers*, set on Kalymnos, and Clift's autobiographical *A Mermaid Singing*, which is about the couple's experiences on Hydra.

Sappho: A New Translation by Mary Bernard is the best translation of this great ancient poet's works.

Collected Poems by George Seferis, *Selected Poems* by Odysseus Elytis and *Collected Poems* by Constantine Cavafy are all excellent translations of Greece's greatest modern poets.

Flowers of Greece & the Aegean by Anthony Huxley & William Taylor is the most comprehensive field guide. The Greek writer, naturalist and mountaineer George Sfikas has written many books on Greece's natural history. Among them are *Wild Flowers of Greece*, *Trees & Shrubs of Greece* and *Medicinal Plants of Greece*.

NEWSPAPERS & MAGAZINES

Greeks are great newspaper readers. There are 15 daily newspapers, of which the most widely read are *Ta Nea*, *Kathimerini* and *Eleftheros Typos*.

After almost 50 years as a daily newspaper, the *Athens News* (€1.50) has become a weekly. It appears on Friday with an assortment of news, local features and entertainment listings. The prime source of daily news is now the Athens edition of the *International Herald Tribune* (€1.60), which includes an eight-page English-language edition of the Greek daily *Kathimerini*. Both are widely available at newspaper stalls around the Peloponnese. You'll find the *Athens News* on the Web at w www.athensnews.gr, while *Kathimerini* is at w www.ekathimerini.com.

Foreign newspapers reach Athens (Syntagma) at 3pm on the day of publication on weekdays, and at 7pm on weekends. You'll find all the British and other major European dailies, as well as international magazines such as *Time*, *Newsweek* and the *Economist*. They reach the Peloponnese the following day and can be found in all major towns and popular tourist destinations.

RADIO & TV

Greece has two state-owned radio channels, ET 1 and ET 2. ET 1 runs three programmes; two are devoted to popular music and news, while the third plays mostly classical music. It has a news update in English at 7.30am from Monday to Saturday, and at 9pm from Monday to Friday. It can be heard on 91.6 MHz and 105.8 MHz on the FM band, and 729 KHz on the AM band. ET 2 broadcasts mainly popular music. Local radio stations abound, but most have a fairly small broadcast area – requiring constant retuning.

Greek TV is a prime example of quantity rather than quality. There are nine free channels, as well as various pay-TV possibilities. All of them screen a fair proportion of programmes in English. Movies are broadcast in the original language with Greek subtitles, so a bit of channel hopping will normally turn up something to watch. You'll also find Greek versions of 'reality' shows like *Big Brother* and *Survivor*, and a local production of the international quiz favourite, *Who Wants to Be a Millionaire*.

You'll find a daily TV guide in the *Kathimerini* supplement inside the *International Herald Tribune* newspaper.

VIDEO SYSTEMS

If you want to record or buy video tapes to play back home, you won't get a picture unless the image registration systems are the same. Greece uses PAL, which is incompatible with the North American and Japanese NTSC system. Australia and most of Europe use PAL.

PHOTOGRAPHY & VIDEO
Film & Equipment

Major brands of film are widely available, although they can be expensive in smaller towns. In Athens, expect to pay about €4.40 for a 36-exposure roll of Kodak Gold ISO 100; less for other brands. You'll find all the gear you need in the photography shops of Athens and major towns around the Peloponnese.

As elsewhere in the world, developing film is a competitive business. Most places charge around €9 to develop a roll of 36 colour prints.

Video cartridges are also readily available, but it's worth buying a few cartridges duty-free to start off your trip. Make sure you keep the batteries charged and have the necessary charger, plugs and transformer for the country you are visiting.

Technical Tips

Because of the brilliant sunlight in summer, you'll get better results using a polarising lens filter. Lonely Planet's full-colour *Travel Photography: A Guide to Taking Better Pictures*, written by internationally renowned travel photographer Richard I'Anson, is full of handy hints and is designed to take on the road.

Restrictions & Etiquette

Never photograph a military installation or anything else that has a sign forbidding photography. Fourteen British and Dutch plane-spotting enthusiasts were arrested at the Kalamata military airport and convicted in April 2002 of illegally obtaining national secrets. At the time of writing, they were appealing their sentences.

Flash photography is not allowed inside churches, and it's considered taboo to photograph the main altar.

Greeks usually love having their photos taken but always ask permission first. The same goes for video cameras, probably even more annoying and offensive for locals than a still camera.

TIME

Greece is two hours ahead of GMT/UTC and three hours ahead on daylight-saving time, which begins on the last Sunday in March, when clocks are put forward one hour. Daylight saving ends on the last Sunday in September.

So, when it is noon in Greece it is also noon in İstanbul, 10am in London, 11am in Rome, 2am in San Francisco, 5am in New York and Toronto, 8pm in Sydney and 10pm in Auckland.

ELECTRICITY

Electricity is 220V, 50 cycles. Plugs are the standard Continental type with two round pins. All hotel rooms have power points and most camping grounds have supply points.

WEIGHTS & MEASURES

Greece uses the metric system. Liquids – especially barrel wine – are often sold by weight rather than volume: 959g of wine, for example, is equivalent to 1000mL.

Like other Continental Europeans, Greeks indicate decimals with commas and thousands with points.

LAUNDRY

There are several laundrettes in Athens but Kalamata and Patras are the only towns in the Peloponnese where you will find one. Most charge about €8 to wash and dry a load. Hotel and room owners will usually provide you with a washtub if asked.

TOILETS

Most places have Western-style sit-down toilets, especially hotels and restaurants which cater for tourists. You'll occasionally come across squat toilets in older houses, *kafeneia* and public toilets.

Public toilets are a rarity, except at airports, and at bus and train stations. Cafés are the best option if you get caught short, but you'll be expected to buy something for the privilege.

One peculiarity of the Greek plumbing system is that it can't handle toilet paper; apparently the pipes are too narrow. Whatever the reason, anything larger than a postage stamp seems to cause a problem; flushing away tampons is guaranteed to block the system. Toilet paper etc should be placed in the small bin provided in every toilet.

HEALTH

Travel health depends on your predeparture preparations, your day-to-day health care while travelling and how you handle any medical problem or emergency that develops. While the list of potential dangers can seem quite frightening, few travellers experience more than upset stomachs.

Pharmacies can dispense medicines which are available only on prescription in most European countries, so you can consult a pharmacist for minor ailments. Emergency

Codeine Warning

Codeine, which is commonly found in headache preparations, is banned in Greece; check labels carefully, or risk prosecution. There are strict regulations applying to the importation of medicines into Greece, so obtain a certificate from your doctor which outlines any medication you may have to carry into the country with you.

treatment is free to all nationalities in public hospitals. In an emergency, dial ☎ 166.

Predeparture Planning

Immunisations Before you leave, find out from your doctor, a travel-health centre or an organisation such as the US-based **Centers for Disease Control and Prevention** (w *www.cdc.gov*) what the current recommendations are for travel to your destination. Remember to leave enough time so that you can get any vaccinations you need – six weeks before travel is ideal. Discuss your requirements with your doctor but generally it's a good idea to make sure your tetanus, diphtheria and polio vaccinations are up to date before travelling.

Although there is no risk of yellow fever in Europe, if you are arriving from a yellow-fever infected area (most of sub-Saharan Africa and parts of South America) you'll need proof of yellow fever vaccination before you will be allowed to enter Greece.

Health Insurance Make sure that you have adequate health insurance. See Travel Insurance under Visas & Documents earlier in this chapter for details, p37.

Free or reduced-cost emergency treatment is available in Europe to citizens of European Economic Area (EEA) countries (the 15 member states of the European Community plus Iceland, Liechtenstein and Norway) on presentation of an E111 form. Ask about the E111 at your local health services department or travel agency at least a few weeks before you travel. In the UK you can get the form free from post offices. Treatment in private hospitals is not covered and charges are also likely for medication, dental work and secondary examinations, including X-rays and laboratory tests.

Medical Kit Check List

Following is a list of items you should consider including in your medical kit – consult your pharmacist for brands available in your country.

☐ **Aspirin or paracetamol (acetaminophen in the USA)** – for pain or fever
☐ **Antihistamine** – for allergies, eg, hay fever; to ease the itch from insect bites or stings; and to prevent motion sickness
☐ **Multivitamins** – consider for long trips, when dietary vitamin intake may be inadequate
☐ **Loperamide or diphenoxylate** – 'blockers' for diarrhoea
☐ **Prochlorperazine or metaclopramide** – for nausea and vomiting
☐ **Rehydration mixture** – to prevent dehydration, which may occur, for example, during bouts of diarrhoea; particularly important when travelling with children
☐ **Insect repellent, sunscreen, lip balm and eye drops**
☐ **Calamine lotion, sting relief spray or aloe vera** – to ease irritation from sunburn and insect bites or stings
☐ **Antifungal cream or powder** – for fungal skin infections and thrush
☐ **Antiseptic (such as povidone-iodine)** – for cuts and grazes
☐ **Bandages, Band-Aids (plasters) and other wound dressings**
☐ **Water purification tablets or iodine**
☐ **Scissors, tweezers and a thermometer** – note that mercury thermometers are prohibited by airlines

Travel Health Guides *Travel with Children* from Lonely Planet includes advice on travel health for younger children.

There are also a number of excellent travel health sites on the Internet. From the Lonely Planet home page there are links at **w** www.lonelyplanet.com/subwwway to the World Health Organization and the US Centers for Disease Control and Prevention.

Other Preparations Make sure you're healthy before you start travelling. If you are going on a long trip make sure your teeth are OK. If you wear glasses take a spare pair and your prescription.

If you require a particular medication take an adequate supply, as it may not be available locally. Take the part of the packaging showing the generic name rather than the brand, which will make getting replacements easier. It's a good idea to have a legible prescription or letter from your doctor to show that you legally use the medication to avoid any problems.

Basic Rules

Care in what you eat and drink is the most important health rule; stomach upsets are the most likely travel health problem (between 30% and 50% of travellers in a two-week stay experience this) but the majority of these upsets will be relatively minor. Don't become paranoid; trying the local food is part of the experience of travel, after all.

Avoid climatic extremes: keep out of the sun when it's hot, dress warmly when it's cold. You can avoid insect bites by covering bare skin when insects are around, by screening windows or beds and by using insect repellents.

Seek local advice: if you're told the water is unsafe due to jellyfish or whatever, don't go in. In situations where there is no information, discretion is the better part of valour.

Food & Water Tap water is safe to drink in Greece, but mineral water is widely available if you prefer it. You might experience mild intestinal problems if you're not used to copious amounts of olive oil; you'll get used to it and, besides, current research says it's good for you.

If you don't vary your diet, are travelling hard and fast and missing meals, or simply lose your appetite, you can soon start to lose weight and place your health at risk. Fruit and vegetables are good sources of vitamins and Greece produces a greater variety of these than almost any other European country. Eat plenty of grains (including rice) and bread. If your diet isn't well balanced or if your food intake is insufficient, it's a good idea to take vitamin and iron pills.

In hot weather make sure you drink enough – don't rely on feeling thirsty to indicate when you should drink. Not needing to urinate or passing very dark yellow urine is a danger sign. Always carry a water bottle with you on long trips. Excessive sweating can lead to salt loss and then muscle cramping. Salt tablets are not a good idea as

Traveller's Thrombosis

Sitting inactive for long periods of time on any form of transport (bus, train or plane), especially if in cramped conditions, can give you swollen feet and ankles, and may increase the possibility of deep vein thrombosis (DVT). DVT is when a clot forms in the deep veins of your legs. DVT may be symptomless or you may get an uncomfortable ache and swelling of your calf. What makes DVT a concern is that in a minority of people, a small piece of the clot can break off and travel to the lungs to cause a pulmonary embolism, a very serious medical condition. To help prevent DVT during long-haul travel, you should move around as much as possible and while you are sitting you should flex your calf muscles and wriggle your toes every half-hour. It's also a good idea to drink plenty of water or juices during the journey to prevent dehydration, and, for the same reason, avoid drinking lots of alcohol or caffeine-containing drinks. In addition, you may want to consider wearing support stockings, especially if you have had leg swelling in the past or you are over 40. If you are prone to blood clotting or you are pregnant, you will need to discuss preventive measures with your doctor before you leave.

a preventative but, in places where salt is not used much, adding salt to food can help.

Medical Problems & Treatment

Self-diagnosis and treatment can be risky, so you should always seek medical help. An embassy, consulate or five-star hotel can usually recommend a local doctor or clinic. Although we do give drug dosages in this section, they are for emergency use only. Correct diagnosis is vital. In this section we have used the generic names for medications – check with a pharmacist for brands available locally.

Heat Exhaustion & Prickly Heat Dehydration and salt deficiency can cause heat exhaustion and can lead to severe heatstroke (see the following section). Take time to acclimatise to high temperatures, drink sufficient liquids such as tea and drinks rich in mineral salts (such as clear soups, and fruit and vegetable juices), and

do not do anything too physically demanding. Salt deficiency is characterised by fatigue, lethargy, headaches, giddiness and muscle cramps; salt tablets may help but adding extra salt to your food is better.

Prickly heat is an itchy rash caused by excessive perspiration trapped under the skin. It usually strikes people who have just arrived in a hot climate. Keeping cool, showering often, drying the skin and using a mild talcum or prickly heat powder, wearing loose cotton clothing, or resorting to air-conditioning may help.

Heatstroke This serious, sometimes fatal, condition can occur if the body's heat-regulating mechanism breaks down and the body temperature rises to dangerous levels. Long, continuous periods of exposure to high temperatures can leave you vulnerable to heatstroke. You should avoid excessive alcohol consumption or strenuous activity when you first arrive in a hot climate.

The symptoms are: feeling unwell, not sweating very much or at all, and a high body temperature (39° to 41°C or 102° to 106°F). Where sweating has ceased the skin becomes flushed and red. Severe, throbbing headaches and lack of coordination will also occur, and the sufferer may be confused or aggressive. Eventually the victim will become delirious or convulse. Hospitalisation is essential, but in the interim get the victim out of the sun, remove their clothing, cover them with a wet sheet or towel and then fan continually. Give fluids, if the victim is conscious.

Hypothermia Too much cold is just as dangerous as too much heat, particularly if it leads to hypothermia. Although everyone associates Greece with heat and sunshine, the mountainous regions can be cool, even in summer. There is snow on the mountains of the Peloponnese from November to April. Keeping warm while trekking in these regions in spring and autumn can be as much of a problem as keeping cool in summer.

Symptoms of hypothermia are: exhaustion, numb skin (particularly toes and fingers), shivering, slurred speech, irrational or violent behaviour, lethargy, stumbling, dizzy spells, muscle cramps and violent bursts of energy. Irrationality may take the form of sufferers claiming they are warm and trying to take off their clothes.

To treat mild hypothermia, first get the person out of the wind and/or rain, remove their clothing if it's wet and replace it with dry, warm clothing. Give them hot liquids – not alcohol – and some high-kilojoule, easily digestible food. Do not rub victims; instead allow them to slowly warm themselves. This should be enough to treat the early stages of hypothermia. The early recognition and treatment of mild hypothermia is the only way to prevent severe hypothermia, which is a critical condition.

Sunburn By far the biggest health risk in Greece comes from the intensity of the sun. You can get sunburnt surprisingly quickly, even through cloud. Use a sunscreen and take extra care to cover areas which don't normally see sun. A hat helps, as does zinc cream or some other barrier cream for your nose and lips. Calamine lotion is good for mild sunburn. Greeks claim that yogurt applied to sunburn is soothing. Protect your eyes with good-quality sunglasses.

Infectious Diseases

Diarrhoea Simple things like a change of water, food or climate can all cause a mild bout of diarrhoea but a few rushed toilet trips with no other symptoms is not indicative of a major problem.

Dehydration is the main danger with any diarrhoea, particularly in children or the elderly, as dehydration can occur quite quickly. Under all circumstances *fluid replacement* (at least equal to the volume being lost) is the most important thing to remember. Weak black tea with a little sugar, soda water, or soft drinks allowed to go flat and diluted 50% with clean water are all good.

Fungal Infections More frequent in hot weather, fungal infections are most likely to occur on the scalp, between the toes (athlete's foot) or fingers, in the groin and on the body (ringworm). You get ringworm (a fungal infection, not a worm) from infected animals or by walking on damp areas like shower floors.

To prevent fungal infections wear loose, comfortable clothes, avoid artificial fibres, wash frequently and dry carefully. If you do get an infection, wash the infected area daily with a disinfectant or medicated soap and water, and dry well. Apply an antifungal cream or powder (tolnaftate). Expose the infected area to air or sunlight as much as possible and wash all towels and underwear in hot water as well as changing them often.

Hepatitis Hepatitis is a general term for inflammation of the liver. The symptoms are similar in all forms of the illness and include fever, chills, headache, fatigue, feelings of weakness and aches and pains, followed by loss of appetite, nausea, vomiting, abdominal pain, dark urine, light-coloured faeces, jaundiced (yellow) skin and yellowing of the whites of the eyes. People who have had hepatitis should avoid alcohol for some time after the illness, as the liver needs time to recover.

Hepatitis A is transmitted by contaminated food and drinking water. You should seek medical advice but there is not much you can do apart from resting, drinking lots of fluids, eating lightly and avoiding fatty foods. Hepatitis E is transmitted in the same way as hepatitis A; it can be particularly serious in pregnant women.

Hepatitis B is spread through contact with infected blood, blood products or body fluids, for example through sexual contact, unsterilised needles and blood transfusions, or contact with blood via small breaks in the skin. Other risk situations include having a shave, tattoo or body piercing with contaminated equipment. The symptoms of hepatitis B may be more severe than type A and the disease can lead to long-term problems such as chronic liver damage, liver cancer or a long-term carrier state. Hepatitis C and D are spread in the same way as hepatitis B and can also lead to long-term complications.

HIV & AIDS Infection with the human immunodeficiency virus (HIV) may lead to acquired immune deficiency syndrome (AIDS), which is a fatal disease. Any exposure to blood, blood products or body fluids may put the individual at risk. The disease is often transmitted through sexual contact or dirty needles – vaccinations, acupuncture, tattooing and body piercing can be potentially as dangerous as intravenous drug use. HIV/AIDS can also be spread through infected blood transfusions; blood used for transfusions in European hospitals is screened for HIV and should be safe.

Rabies Rabies is a fatal viral infection and is caused by a bite or scratch by an infected animal. It's rare but it's found in Greece. Dogs are noted carriers, as are monkeys and cats. Any bite, scratch or even lick from a warm-blooded, furry animal should be cleaned immediately and thoroughly. Scrub with soap and running water, and then clean with an alcohol or iodine solution. If there is any possibility that the animal is infected medical help should be sought immediately. Even if the animal is not rabid, all bites should be treated seriously, as they can become infected or can result in tetanus. A rabies vaccination is now available and should be considered if you are in a high-risk category – eg, if you intend to explore caves (bat bites can be dangerous), work with animals, or travel so far off the beaten track that medical help is more than two days away.

Sexually Transmitted Infections (STIs)
HIV/AIDS and hepatitis B can be transmitted through sexual contact – see the relevant sections earlier for more details. Other STIs include gonorrhoea, herpes and syphilis; sores, blisters or rashes around the genitals and discharges or pain when urinating are common symptoms. In some STIs, such as wart virus or chlamydia, symptoms may be less marked or not observed at all, especially in women. Chlamydia infection can cause infertility in men and women before any symptoms have been noticed. Syphilis symptoms eventually disappear completely but the disease continues and can cause severe problems in later years. While abstinence from sexual contact is the only 100% effective prevention, using condoms is also effective.

Cuts, Bites & Stings
Skin punctures can easily become infected in hot climates and may be difficult to heal. Treat any cut with an antiseptic such as povidone-iodine. Where possible avoid band ages and Band-Aids, which can keep wounds wet.

Although there are a lot of bees and wasps in Greece, their stings are usually painful rather than dangerous. Calamine lotion or sting relief spray will give relief and ice packs will reduce the pain and swelling.

Bedbugs & Lice Bedbugs live in various places, but particularly in dirty mattresses and bedding. Spots of blood on bedclothes or on the wall around the bed can be read as a suggestion to find another hotel. Bedbugs leave itchy bites in neat rows. Calamine lotion or sting relief spray may help.

All lice cause itching and discomfort. They make themselves at home in your hair, your clothing or in your pubic hair. You catch lice through direct contact with infected people or by sharing combs, clothing and the like. Powder or shampoo treatment will kill the lice and infected clothing should then be washed in very hot water.

Jellyfish, Sea Urchins & Weever Fish
Watch out for sea urchins around rocky beaches; if you get some of their needles embedded in your skin, olive oil will help to loosen them. If they are not removed they will become infected. Be wary also of jellyfish, particularly during the months of September and October. Although they are not lethal in Greece, their stings can be painful. Dousing in vinegar will deactivate any stingers which have not 'fired'. Calamine lotion, antihistamines and analgesics may reduce the reaction and relieve the pain. Much more painful than either of these, but thankfully much rarer, is an encounter with the weever fish. It buries itself in the sand of the tidal zone with only its spines protruding, and injects a painful and powerful toxin if trodden on. Soaking your foot in very hot water (which breaks down the poison) should solve the problem. It can cause permanent local paralysis in the worst instance.

Leeches & Ticks Leeches may be present in damp conditions. They attach themselves to your skin to suck your blood. Trekkers often get them on their legs or in their boots. Salt or a lighted cigarette end will make them fall off. Do not pull them off, as the bite is then more likely to become infected. An insect repellent may keep them away.

You should always check your body if you have been walking through a potentially tick-infested area, as ticks can cause skin infections and other more serious diseases. If a tick is found attached, press down around the tick's head with tweezers, grab the head and gently pull upwards. Avoid pulling the rear of the body as this may squeeze the tick's gut contents through the attached mouth parts into the skin, increasing the risk of infection and disease. Smearing chemicals on the tick will not make it let go and is not recommended.

Pine Processionary Caterpillar The pine processionary caterpillar is a feature of springtime in the pine forests of the Peloponnese. The caterpillar hatches in a white, silken cocoon woven around the tips of pine branches, emerging in March/April to feast on the new growth. Their appetites sated, the caterpillars form up into single file to travel down the trunk of the tree to the ground. It's not uncommon to see trails of them stretching up to 5m. By this stage, the caterpillars are about 4cm long and covered in black hairs. Unfortunately, the hairs give off a fine dust that is very irritating to the skin, requiring a shower and a change of clothes. Most years they are hardly an issue, but every few years they occur in plague proportions.

Scorpions You may encounter scorpions in dry, rocky country. They are seldom seen because they hunt at night, but it's sensible to wear good footwear and to take care when lifting rocks.

Sheepdogs These dogs are trained to guard penned sheep, and they are often underfed and sometimes ill-treated by their owners. They are almost always all bark and no bite, but if you are going to trek into remote areas, you should consider having rabies injections (see Rabies under Infectious Diseases, p51). You are most likely to encounter these dogs in the mountainous regions of Arcadia. Wandering through a flock of sheep over which one of these dogs is vigilantly (and possibly discreetly) watching is simply asking for trouble.

Snakes Always wear boots, socks and long trousers when walking through undergrowth where snakes may be present. Don't put your hands into holes and crevices, and be careful when collecting firewood.

Snake bites do not cause instantaneous death and antivenenes are usually available. Keep the victim calm and still, wrap the bitten limb tightly, as you would for a sprain, and then attach a splint to immobilise it.

Then seek medical help, if possible with the dead snake for identification. Don't attempt to catch the snake if there is even a remote possibility of being bitten again. Tourniquets and sucking out the poison are now comprehensively discredited as treatments.

Women's Health
Antibiotic use, synthetic underwear, sweating and contraceptive pills can lead to fungal vaginal infections, especially when travelling in hot climates. Fungal infections are characterised by a rash, itch and discharge and can be treated with a vinegar or lemon-juice douche, or with yogurt. Nystatin, miconazole or clotrimazole pessaries or vaginal cream are the usual treatment. Maintaining good personal hygiene and wearing loose-fitting clothes and cotton underwear may help prevent these infections.

Sexually transmitted infections are a major cause of vaginal problems. Symptoms include a smelly discharge, painful intercourse and sometimes a burning sensation when urinating. Medical attention should be sought and male sexual partners must also be treated. For more details see Sexually Transmitted Infections under Infectious Diseases, p51. Apart from abstinence, the best thing is to practise safer sex using condoms.

Pregnancy Pregnant women should take extra care when travelling, particularly in the first three months of pregnancy. Discuss with your doctor, but generally, it's best to avoid all vaccinations in those first three months as there's a theoretical risk of harm to the foetus and miscarriage. The best time to travel is during the middle three months when the risk of complications is less, the pregnancy is relatively well established and your energy levels are getting back to normal. Many airlines won't allow women past 34 weeks of pregnancy to travel, as they'll have to land as soon as possible and get you to a hospital, if you go into labour in the air. Seek medical advice from your doctor before travelling.

Less-Common Diseases
The following pose a small risk to travellers, and so are only mentioned in passing. Seek medical advice if you think you may have any of these diseases.

Lyme Disease This disease is an infection transmitted by ticks which may be acquired throughout Europe. The illness usually begins with a spreading rash at the site of the bite and is accompanied by fever, headache, extreme fatigue, aching joints and muscles and mild neck stiffness. If untreated, these symptoms usually resolve over several weeks but over subsequent weeks or months disorders of the nervous system, heart and joints may develop. The response to treatment is best early in the illness. The longer the delay, the longer the recovery period.

Typhus Tick typhus is a problem from April to September in rural areas, particularly areas where animals congregate. Typhus begins with a fever, chills, headache and muscle pains, followed a few days later by a body rash. There is often a large painful sore at the site of the bite and nearby lymph nodes are swollen and painful. There is no vaccine available. The best protection is to check your skin carefully after walking in danger areas such as long grass and scrub. A strong insect repellent can help, and serious walkers in tick areas should consider having their boots and trousers impregnated with benzyl benzoate and dibutyl-phthalate. (See Cuts, Bites & Stings, p51, for information about ticks.)

WOMEN TRAVELLERS
Many women travel alone in Greece. The crime rate remains relatively low, and solo travel is probably safer than in most European countries. This does not mean that you should be lulled into complacency; bag snatching and rapes do occur, although violent offences are rare.

The biggest nuisance to foreign women travelling alone are the guys the Greeks have nicknamed *kamaki*. The word means 'fishing trident' and refers to the *kamaki*'s favourite pastime, 'fishing' for foreign women. You'll find them everywhere there are lots of tourists; young (for the most part), smooth-talking guys who aren't in the least bashful about sidling up to foreign women in the street. They can be very persistent but they are a hassle rather than a threat.

The majority of Greek men treat foreign women with respect, and are genuinely helpful.

GAY & LESBIAN TRAVELLERS
In a country where the church still plays a prominent role in shaping society's views on issues such as sexuality, it should come as no surprise that homosexuality is generally frowned upon – especially outside the major cities. While there is no legislation against homosexual activity, it pays to be discreet and to avoid open displays of togetherness.

This has not prevented Greece from becoming an extremely popular destination for gay travellers. Athens has a busy gay scene but most gay travellers head for the islands.

The *Spartacus International Gay Guide*, published by Bruno Gmünder (Berlin), is widely regarded as the leading authority on the gay travel scene. The Greece chapter has lots of information on gay venues around the country but next to nothing on the Peloponnese.

The Internet is another good source of information. **Roz Mov** (Ⓦ *www.geocities.com /WestHollywood/2225/index.html*) as pages on travel info, gay health, the gay press, organisations, events and legal issues – and links to lots more sites.

Gayscape (Ⓦ *www.gayscape.com/gay scape/menugreece.html*) has a useful site with lots of links.

DISABLED TRAVELLERS
Travelling in the Peloponnese is a major challenge for people with mobility problems. The hard fact is that most hotels, museums and ancient sites in Greece are not accessible by wheelchair. This is partly due to the uneven terrain of much of the country, which, with its abundance of stones, rocks and marble, presents a challenge even for able-bodied people.

If you are determined, then take heart in the knowledge that people with disabilities do come to Greece for holidays. But the trip needs careful planning, so get as much information as you can before you go. The British-based **Royal Association for Disability and Rehabilitation** (*RADAR;* ☎ 020-7250 3222, *fax* 7250 0212; Ⓔ *radar@ radar.org.uk; 12 City Forum, 250 City Road, London*) publishes a useful guide called *Holidays & Travel Abroad: A Guide for Disabled People*, which gives a good overview of facilities available to travellers with disabilities in Europe.

TRAVEL WITH CHILDREN

Greece is a safe and relatively easy place to travel with children. It's especially easy if you're staying by the beach or at a resort hotel. If you're travelling around, the main problem is a shortage of decent playgrounds and other recreational facilities.

Don't be afraid to take children to the ancient sites. Many parents are surprised by how much their children enjoy them.

Hotels and restaurants are very accommodating when it comes to meeting the needs of children, although highchairs are a rarity outside resorts. Service in restaurants is normally very quick, which is great when you've got hungry children on your hands.

Fresh milk is readily available in large towns and tourist areas but hard to find on the smaller islands. Supermarkets are the best place to look. Formula is available everywhere, as is condensed and heat-treated milk.

Mobility is an issue for parents with very small children. Strollers (pushchairs) aren't much use in Greece unless you're going to spend all your time in one of the few flat spots. They are hopeless on rough stone paths and up steps, and a curse when getting on or off buses and ferries. Backpacks or front pouches are best.

Travel on ferries and buses is free for children under four. They pay half fare up to the ages of 10 (ferries) and 12 (buses); full fares apply otherwise. On domestic flights, you'll pay 10% of the fare to have a child under two sitting on your knee. Kids aged two to 12 pay half fare.

Matt Barrett's website (w www.greece travel.com/kids/index.html) has lots of useful tips for parents, while Barrett's daughter Amarandi has put together some tips for kids (w www.greece4kids.com).

Lonely Planet's *Travel with Children* provides inspiration, handy tips and down-to-earth advice.

USEFUL ORGANISATIONS
Mountaineering Clubs

Ellinikos Orivatikos Syndesmos (EOS – Greek Alpine Club; ☎ 21-0321 2429/2355; Plateia Kapnikareas 2, Athens) is the largest and oldest Greek mountaineering and trekking organisation. Its headquarters are on Ermou, 500m west of Syntagma. The place is staffed by volunteers with day-time jobs, but if you call or visit between 7pm and 9pm on a weekday, there should be someone there.

The EOS also operates the following regional offices in the Peloponnese:

Kalavryta Alpine Club (☎ 2692 022 611/346)
    25 Martiou, Kalavryta 250 01
Sparta Alpine Club (☎ 2731-023 100)
    Gortsolgou 97, Sparta 231 00
Tripolis Alpine Club (☎ 271-023 2243)
    Agios Konstantinou 6, Tripolis 221 00

Automobile Associations

ELPA (☎ 21-0779 1615; Athens Tower, ground floor, Messogion 2-4, Athens), the Greek automobile club, offers reciprocal services to members of national automobile associations on production of a valid membership card. If your vehicle breaks down, dial ☎ 104.

DANGERS & ANNOYANCES

Crime, especially theft, is low in Greece but unfortunately it is on the increase. The worst area is around Omonia in central Athens – keep track of your valuables here, on the metro and at the Sunday flea market. The vast majority of thefts from tourists are still committed by other tourists; the biggest danger of theft is probably in dormitory rooms in hostels and at camp sites. So make sure you do not leave valuables unattended in such places. If you are staying in a hotel room, and the windows and door do not lock securely, ask for your valuables to be locked in the hotel safe – hotel proprietors are happy to do this.

Bar scams continue to be an unfortunate fact of life in Athens – for the full run-down on this and other problems see Information in the Athens chapter, pp84–5.

LEGAL MATTERS
Consumer Advice

The **Tourist Assistance Programme** (☎ 21-0330 0673, fax 21-0330 0591; main office, Valtetsiou 43-45, Athens; open 10am-2pm Mon-Fri) exists to help people who are having trouble with any tourism-related service. Free legal advice is available in English, French and German from 1 July to 30 September. It is represented in Patras by the **Consumers' Association of Patras** (☎ 261-027 2481; Korinthou 213B).

Drugs

Greek drug laws are the strictest in Europe. Greek courts make no distinction between possession and pushing. Possession of even a small amount of marijuana is likely to land you in jail.

BUSINESS HOURS

Banks are open 8am to 2pm Monday to Thursday, and 8am to 1.30pm Friday. Some banks in large towns and cities open between 3.30pm and 6.30pm in the afternoon and on Saturday morning.

Post offices are open 7.30am to 2pm Monday to Friday. In the major cities they stay open until 8pm and are open from 7.30am to 2pm Saturday.

The opening hours of OTE offices (for long-distance and overseas telephone calls) vary according to the size of the town. Most are open 7.30am to 3pm daily; the main offices in Athens and Patras are open 24 hours.

In summer, the usual opening hours for shops are 8am to 1.30pm and 5.30pm to 8.30pm on Tuesday, Thursday and Friday, and 8am to 2.30pm on Monday, Wednesday and Saturday. Shops open 30 minutes later in winter. These times are not always strictly adhered to; you may find some businesses closed between around 3pm and 5pm for a siesta. Many shops in tourist resorts are open seven days a week.

Department stores and supermarkets are open 8am to 8pm Monday to Friday, 8am to at least 3pm on Saturday and closed Sunday.

Periptera are open from early morning until late at night. They sell everything from bus tickets and cigarettes to hard-core pornography.

Museums & Ancient Sites

The bigger the attraction, the longer it stays open. Places like the Acropolis and the National Archaeological Museum (Athens), Mycenae, Mystras and Olympia are open 8am to 7pm daily during summer (1 April to 31 October). They close at 5pm during the rest of the year.

Most other sites and museums open at 8am or 8.30am, and close at around 2.30pm and 3pm. It's no coincidence that these are the standard Greek public service hours! It means that you need to get out and about early if you want to visit more than one site a day. Most places are closed on Monday.

Lots of minor sites are unenclosed – and therefore always open to the public.

PUBLIC HOLIDAYS & SPECIAL EVENTS

All banks and shops and most museums and ancient sites close on public holidays. National public holidays in Greece are

New Year's Day 1 January
Epiphany 6 January
First Sunday in Lent February
Greek Independence Day 25 March
Good Friday March/April
(Orthodox) Easter Sunday March/April
Spring Festival/Labour Day 1 May
Feast of the Assumption 15 August
Ohi Day 28 October
Christmas Day 25 December
St Stephen's Day 26 December

The Greek year is a succession of festivals and events, some of which are religious, some cultural, others an excuse for a good knees-up, and some a combination of all three. The following is by no means an exhaustive list but it covers the most important events, both national and regional. If you're in the right place at the right time, you'll certainly be invited to join the revelry.

January

Feast of Agios Vasilios (St Basil) The year kicks off with this festival on 1 January. A church ceremony is followed by the exchange of gifts, singing, dancing and feasting; the New Year pie (vasilopitta) is cut and the person who gets the slice containing a coin will supposedly have a lucky year.

Epiphany (the Blessing of the Waters) On 6 January Christ's baptism by St John is celebrated throughout Greece. Seas, lakes and rivers are blessed and crosses immersed in them. The largest ceremony occurs at Piraeus.

February–March

Carnival The Greek carnival season is the three weeks before the beginning of Lent (the 40-day period before Easter, which is traditionally a period of fasting). The carnivals are ostensibly Christian pre-Lenten celebrations but many derive from pagan festivals. There are many regional variations but fancy dress, feasting, traditional dancing and general merrymaking prevail. The Patras carnival is the largest and most exuberant, with elaborately decorated chariots parading through the streets.

Shrove Monday (Clean Monday) On the Monday before Ash Wednesday (the first day of Lent), people take to the hills throughout Greece to have picnics and fly kites.

March
Independence Day The anniversary of the hoisting of the Greek flag by Bishop Germanos at Moni Agias Lavras, near Kalavryta, is celebrated on 25 March with parades and dancing. Germanos' act of revolt marked the official start of the War of Independence. Independence Day coincides with the Feast of the Annunciation, so it is also a religious festival.

March–April
Easter Easter is the most important festival in the Greek Orthodox calendar. Emphasis is placed on the Resurrection rather than on the Crucifixion, so it is a joyous occasion. The festival begins on the evening of Good Friday when a shrouded bier (representing Christ's funeral bier) is carried through the streets to the local church. This moving candlelit procession can be seen in towns and villages throughout the country. From a spectator's viewpoint, the most impressive of these processions climbs Lykavittos Hill in Athens to the Chapel of Agios Georgios.

The Resurrection Mass starts at 11pm on Saturday night. At midnight, packed churches are plunged into darkness to represent Christ's passing through the underworld.

The ceremony of the lighting of candles which follows is the most significant moment in the Orthodox year, for it symbolises the Resurrection. Its poignancy and beauty are spellbinding. If you are in Greece at Easter you should endeavour to attend this ceremony, which ends with the setting off of fireworks and candlelit processions through the streets. The Lenten fast ends on Easter Sunday with the cracking of red-dyed Easter eggs and an outdoor feast of roast lamb followed by Greek dancing. The day's greeting is *'Hristos anesti'* (Christ is risen), to which the reply is *'Alithos anesti'* (Truly He is risen).

May
May Day On the first day of May there is a mass exodus from towns to the country. During picnics, wildflowers are gathered and made into wreaths to decorate houses.

June
Navy Week The festival celebrates the long relationship between the Greek and the sea with events in fishing villages and ports throughout the country. Hydra commemorates War of Independence hero Admiral Andreas Miaoulis, who was born on the island, with a re-enactment of one of his naval victories, accompanied by feasting and fireworks.

Feast of St John the Baptist Wreaths made on May Day are kept until this feast day (24 June), when they are burned on bonfires.

July
Feast of Profitis Ilias This feast day is celebrated on 20 July at hilltop churches and monasteries dedicated to the prophet.

August
Assumption Greeks celebrate Assumption Day (15 August) with family reunions. The whole population seems to be on the move either side of the big day, so it's a good time to avoid public transport.

September
Genesis tis Panagias (the Virgin's Birthday) This day is celebrated on 8 September with religious services and feasting.

Exaltation of the Cross This event is celebrated on 14 September with processions and hymns.

October
Ohi (No) Day Metaxas' refusal to allow Mussolini's troops free passage through Greece in WWII is commemorated on 28 October with remembrance services, military parades, folk dancing and feasting.

December
Christmas Day Although not as important as Easter, Christmas is still celebrated with religious services and feasting. Nowadays much 'Western' influence is apparent, including Christmas trees, decorations and presents.

Summer Festivals & Performances
The most important of the summer festivals is the Hellenic Festival, which features performances of drama, dance and music at the Theatre of Herodes Atticus in Athens, as well as performances of ancient Greek drama at the famous Theatre of Epidavros in the Peloponnese.

The Athens programme runs from mid June into September, while the Epidavros programme runs only during July and August. See the Athens and Argolis chapters pp86, 120–1, for more information.

ACTIVITIES
Windsurfing
Windsurfing is the most popular water sport in Greece, and you'll see people out on their sailboards just about everywhere there's water and a breeze. The best spot in the Peloponnese is Finikounda, at the south western tip of Messinia.

Sailboards can be imported freely from other EU countries but the import of boards from other destinations, such as Australia and the US, is subject to some quaint regulations. Theoretically, importers need a Greek national residing in Greece to guarantee that the board will be taken out again. Contact the **Hellenic Windsurfing Association** (☎ 21-0323 0330, fax 21-0322 3251; e ghiolman@ghiolman.com; Filellinon 7, Athens) for more information.

Snorkelling & Diving

Snorkelling is enjoyable just about everywhere around the coast of the Peloponnese, and flippers, masks and snorkels are readily available from local shops.

Diving is another matter. Any kind of underwater activity using breathing apparatus is strictly forbidden other than under the supervision of a diving school. This is to protect the many antiquities that lie in Greek waters. There are no diving schools in the Peloponnese but **Hydra Divers** (☎ 2298-053 900; e diveinst@x-treme.gr, w www.divingteam.gr) offers dives at a range of locations around the nearby Peloponnese coast.

Trekking

The Peloponnese is a veritable trekkers' paradise, particularly in springtime when the region's magnificent wildflowers are at their showiest.

Kardamyli, in the Messinian Mani, is a favourite destination. The well-organised locals maintain a number of colour-coded trails around the western foothills of the Taygetos Mountains. On the eastern side of the Taygetos, the climb from Mystras to Anavryti is one of the highlights of the E4 trail. Serious trekkers can continue from Anavryti to the summit of Mt Profitis Ilias, the highest mountain in the Peloponnese. Further south, Gerolimenas is a good base for treks around the villages of the Lakonian Mani.

Other popular trekking areas include the Lousios Valley, between Dimitsana and Karitena in Central Arcadia, and the Vouraïkos Gorge between Diakofto and Kalavryta.

Some of these walks follow *kalderimi*, ancient cobbled or flagstone paths that have connected remote villages since Byzantine times. Many have been bulldozed to make way for roads, but there are some good examples around Kardamyli.

A number of companies run organised treks, including Greece's biggest trekking operator, **Trekking Hellas** (☎ 21-0323 4548, fax 21-0325 1474; w www.trekking.gr; Filellinon 7, Athens). It runs treks to all the areas previously mentioned. Its eight-day trip to the Taygetos Mountains is especially designed for English-speaking visitors. It starts in Athens, taking in the main sites, before heading off for a series of treks around both Kardamyli and Mystras. Adventure specialist **Alpin Club** (☎ 21-0729 5486, fax 21-0721 2773; w www.alpinclub.gr; Mihalakopoulou 39, Athens) offers day treks in the Lousios Valley.

Rafting

Rafting enthusiasts should try to include a trip down the Lousios River on their holiday agenda. It isn't one of the great rafting rivers of the world, with only one rapid rated above Grade 2, but the scenery makes up for it. Thanks to the many permanent springs that feed the river, it is also the only place in Greece where rafting is possible year-round.

Alpin Club (see the preceding Trekking section for details) runs rafting trips down the Lousios every weekend from its base at Karitena. It also offers kayaking, hotdogging in inflatable canoes and canyoning.

Skiing

While sun, sand and sea generally come to mind when you picture a Greek holiday, the mountains of the Peloponnese actually offer some of the cheapest skiing in Europe. There are ski centres at Mt Helmos, 16km east of Kalavryta in the mountains of Achaï, and at Mt Menalo, 31km north of Tripolis in Arcadia. There are no foreign package holidays to these resorts, which are used almost exclusively by Greeks. They have all the necessary facilities and are a pleasant alternative to the glitzy resorts of Western Europe.

The season depends on snow conditions but runs approximately from January to the end of April. You'll find information about the latest snow conditions on the Internet at w www.snowreport.gr.

COURSES

There are no courses on offer in the Peloponnese.

WORK
Permits
EU nationals don't need a work permit but they do need a residency permit if they intend to stay longer than three months. Nationals of other countries are supposed to have a work permit.

English Tutoring
If you're looking for a permanent job, the most widely available option is to teach English. A TEFL (Teaching English as a Foreign Language) certificate or a university degree is an advantage but not essential. In the UK, look through the *Times Educational Supplement* or Tuesday's edition of the *Guardian* newspaper for opportunities – in other countries, contact the Greek embassy.

Another possibility is to find a job teaching English once you are in Greece. You will see language schools everywhere. Strictly speaking, you need a licence to teach in these schools but many will employ teachers without one. The best time to look around for such a job is late summer.

The notice board at the **Compendium bookshop** *(Nikis 28, Plaka)* in Athens sometimes has advertisements looking for private English lessons.

Volunteer Work
The **Sea Turtle Protection Society of Greece** *(☎/fax 21-0523 1342;* e *stps@compulink.gr; Solomou 57, Athens)* uses volunteers for its monitoring programmes in the Peloponnese.

Bar & Hostel Work
The hostels and travellers hotels in Athens employ foreign workers but there are no such possibilities in the Peloponnese.

Other Work
There are often jobs advertised in the classifieds of the English-language newspapers, or you can place an advertisement yourself. EU nationals can make use of the OAED (Organismos Apasholiseos Ergatikou Dynamikou), the Greek National Employment Service, in their search for a job. The OAED has offices throughout Greece.

Seasonal harvest work is handled by migrant workers from Albania and other Balkan nations, and is no longer a viable option for travellers.

ACCOMMODATION
There is a range of accommodation available in Greece to suit every taste and pocket. All places to stay are subject to strict price controls set by the tourist police. By law, a notice must be displayed in every room, stating the category of the room and the price charged in each season. The price includes a 4.5% community tax and 8% VAT.

Accommodation owners may add a 10% surcharge for a stay of fewer than three nights but this is not mandatory. A mandatory charge of 20% is levied if an extra bed is put into a room. During July and August, accommodation owners will charge the maximum price but, in spring and autumn, prices will drop by up to 20%, and perhaps by even more in winter. These are the times to bring your bargaining skills into action.

Rip-offs rarely occur, but if you suspect you have been exploited by an accommodation owner, report it to either the tourist police or regular police and they will act swiftly.

Mountain Refuges
There are eight mountain refuges dotted around the Peloponnese. They range from small huts with outdoor toilets and no cooking facilities to comfortable modern lodges, and are operated by local mountaineering and skiing clubs. Prices range from €4.70 to €5.90, depending on the facilities. The EOT publication *Greece: Mountain Refuges & Ski Centres* has details about each refuge.

Camping
Camping is a good option, especially in summer. There are almost 350 camping grounds in Greece (90 in the Peloponnese), a lot of them in great locations. Standard facilities include hot showers, kitchens, restaurants and minimarkets – and often a swimming pool.

Most camping grounds are open only between April and October. The **Panhellenic Camping Association** *(☎/fax 21-0362 1560; Solonos 102, Athens)* publishes an annual booklet (available from tourist offices) listing all the camp sites, their facilities and months of operation.

Camping fees are highest from 15 June to the end of August. Most camping grounds charge from €3.55 to €4.40 per adult and €2.35 to €2.95 for children aged four to 12.

There's no charge for children aged under four. Tent sites cost from €2.95 per night for small tents and from €3.55 per night for large tents. Caravan sites start at around €5.90.

Between May and mid-September it is warm enough to sleep out under the stars, although you will still need a lightweight sleeping bag to counter the pre-dawn chill. It's a good idea to have a foam pad to lie on and a waterproof cover for your sleeping bag.

Freelance (wild) camping is illegal, but the law is seldom enforced – to the irritation of camping-ground owners.

Hostels

There is only one youth hostel in Greece affiliated to the International Youth Hostel Federation (IYHF), the excellent **Athens International Youth Hostel** (☎ 21-0523 4170, fax 21-0523 4015; e info2002yh@yahoo com; Victor Hugo 16). You don't need a membership card to stay there; temporary membership costs €1.80 per day or daily stamp €2.05.

Other youth hostels are run by the **Greek Youth Hostel Organisation** (☎ 21-0751 9530, fax 21-0751 0616; e y-hostels@ otenet.gr; Damareos 75, Athens). There are affiliated hostels in Athens, Olympia and Patras.

Hostel rates vary from €4.70 to €5.90 and you don't have to be a member to stay in any of them. Few have curfews.

Domatia

Domatia are the Greek equivalent of the British B&B, minus the breakfast. Once upon a time domatia comprised little more than spare rooms in the family home that could be rented out to travellers in summer; nowadays, many are purpose-built appendages to the family house. Some come complete with fully equipped kitchens. Standards of cleanliness are generally high. The decor runs the gamut from cool grey marble floors, coordinated pine furniture, pretty lace curtains and tasteful pictures on the walls to so much kitsch you are almost afraid to move in case you break an ornament.

Domatia remain a popular option for budget travellers. They are classified A, B or C. Expect to pay from €17.60 to €29.35 for a single and €23.50 to €47 for a double,

depending on the class, whether bathrooms are shared or private, the season and how long you plan to stay. Domatia are found throughout the Peloponnese, except in large cities. Some are open only between April and October.

Traditional Settlements

Traditional settlements are old buildings of architectural merit that have been renovated and converted into tourist accommodation; you'll find them all over the country. There are some terrific places among them but they are expensive – most are equivalent in price to an A- or B-class hotel. Some of the best examples are in the old Byzantine town of Monemvasia in the Peloponnese.

Pensions

Pensions in Greece are virtually indistinguishable from hotels. They are classed A, B or C. An A-class pension is equivalent in amenities and price to a B-class hotel, a B-class pension is equivalent to a C-class hotel and a C-class pension is equivalent to a D- or E-class hotel.

Hotels

Hotels in Greece are divided into six categories: deluxe, A, B, C, D and E. Hotels are categorised according to the size of the room, whether or not they have a bar, and the ratio of bathrooms to beds, rather than standards of cleanliness, comfort of the beds and friendliness of staff – all elements that may be of greater relevance to guests.

As one would expect, deluxe, A- and B-class hotels have many amenities, private bathrooms and constant hot water. C-class hotels have a snack bar, rooms have private bathrooms, but hot water may only be available at certain times of the day. D-class hotels may or may not have snack bars, most rooms will share bathrooms, but there may be some with private bathrooms, and they may have solar-heated water, which means hot water is not guaranteed. E-class hotels do not have a snack bar, bathrooms are shared and you may have to pay extra for hot water – if it exists at all.

Prices are controlled by the tourist police and the maximum rate that can be charged for a room must be displayed on a board behind the door of each room. The classification is not often much of a guide to price.

Rates in D- and E-class hotels are generally comparable with domatia. You can pay from €35 to €60 for a single in high season in C class and €45 to €80 for a double. Prices in B class range from €50 to €80 for singles, and from €90 to €120 for doubles. A-class prices are not much higher.

Apartments

Some towns and villages also have self-contained family apartments that are available for either long- or short-term rental. Prices vary considerably according to the amenities offered. The tourist police may be able to help in other major towns; in rural areas, ask in a *kafeneio*.

FOOD

Greek food does not enjoy a reputation as one of the world's great cuisines. Maybe that's because many travellers have experienced Greek cooking only in tourist resorts. The old joke about the Greek woman who, on summer days, shouted to her husband 'Come and eat your lunch before it gets hot' is based on truth. Until recently, food was invariably served lukewarm – which is how Greeks prefer it. Most restaurants that cater to tourists have now cottoned on to the fact that foreigners expect cooked dishes to be served hot, and better methods of warming meals (including the dreaded microwave) have made this easier. If your meal is not hot, ask that it be served *zesto*, or order grills, which have to be cooked to order. Greeks are fussy about fresh ingredients, and frozen food is rare.

Greeks eat out regularly, regardless of socioeconomic status. Enjoying life is paramount to them and a large part of this enjoyment comes from eating and drinking with friends.

By law, every eating establishment must display a written menu including prices. Bread will automatically be put on your table and usually costs between €0.30 and €0.90, depending on the restaurant's category.

Where to Eat

Tavernas The taverna is usually a traditional place with a rough-and-ready ambience, although some are more upmarket, particularly in Athens, resorts and big towns. In simple tavernas, a menu is usually displayed in the window or on the door but you may be invited into the kitchen to peer into the pots and point to what you want. This is not merely a privilege for tourists. Greeks also do it because they want to see the taverna's version of the dishes on offer. Some tavernas don't open until 8pm and then stay open until the early hours. Some are closed on Sunday.

Greek men love their sport; they are football-(soccer) and basketball-mad. If you're eating in a taverna on a night when a big match is televised, expect indifferent service.

Psistaria These places specialise in spit roasts and charcoal-grilled food – usually lamb, pork or chicken.

Restaurants A restaurant *(estiatorio)* is normally more sophisticated than a taverna or *psistaria* – damask tablecloths, smartly attired waiters and printed menus at each table with an English translation. Ready-made food is usually displayed in a *bain-marie* and there may also be a charcoal grill.

Ouzeri An *ouzeri* serves ouzo. Greeks believe it is essential to eat when drinking alcohol so, in traditional establishments, your drink will come with a small plate of titbits or *mezedes* (appetisers) – perhaps olives, a slice of feta and some pickled octopus. *Ouzeri* are becoming trendy and many now offer menus with both appetisers and main courses.

Galaktopoleia A *galaktopoleio* (literally 'milk shop') sells dairy produce including milk, butter, yogurt, rice pudding, custard, eggs, honey and bread. It may also sell home-made ice cream in several flavours. Look for the sign '*pagoto politiko*' (city ice cream) displayed outside. Most *galaktopoleia* have seating and serve coffee and tea. They are inexpensive for breakfast and usually open from very early in the morning until evening.

Zaharoplasteia A *zaharoplasteio* (patisserie) sells cakes (both traditional and Western), chocolates, biscuits, sweets, coffee, soft drinks and, possibly, bottled alcoholic drinks. *Zaharoplasteia* usually have some seating.

Kafeneia *Kafeneia* are often regarded by foreigners as the last bastion of male chauvinism in Europe. With bare light bulbs, nicotine-stained walls, smoke-laden air, rickety wooden tables and raffia chairs, they are frequented by middle-aged and elderly Greek men in cloth caps who while away their time fiddling with worry beads, playing cards or backgammon, or engaged in heated political discussion.

It was once unheard of for women to enter a *kafeneio* but this situation is changing. In rural areas, Greek women are rarely seen inside *kafeneia*. When a female traveller enters one, she is inevitably treated courteously and with friendship if she manages a few Greek words of greeting. If you feel inhibited about going into a *kafeneio*, opt for outside seating. You'll feel less intrusive.

Kafeneia originally only served Greek coffee but now most also serve soft drinks, Nescafé and beer. Most *kafeneia* are open all day every day, but some close during siesta time (roughly from 3pm to 5pm).

Other Eateries You'll find plenty of pizzerias, creperies and *gelaterias* (which sell Italian-style ice cream in various flavours), but international restaurants are rare outside Athens – and expensive.

Meals

Breakfast There's some truth in the apocryphal story about the restaurant that serves a cup of coffee and two cigarettes as its Greek breakfast. Greeks are not big morning eaters; most have coffee and perhaps a cake or pastry for breakfast. Budget hotels and pensions offering breakfast provide it continental-style (rolls or bread with jam, and tea or coffee) while upmarket hotels serve breakfast buffets (Western and continental-style). Otherwise, restaurants and *galaktopoleia* serve bread with butter, jam or honey; eggs; and the budget travellers' favourite, yogurt *(yiaourti)* with honey. In tourist areas, many menus offer an 'English' breakfast – which means bacon and eggs.

Lunch This is eaten late – between 1pm and 3pm – and may be either a snack or a complete meal. The main meal can be lunch or dinner – or both. Once into their stride, Greeks enjoy eating and often have two large meals a day.

Dinner Greeks also eat dinner late. Many people don't start to think about food until about 9pm, which is why some restaurants don't bother to open their doors until after 8pm. In tourist areas dinner is often served earlier.

A full dinner in Greece begins with appetisers and/or soup, followed by a main course of either ready-made food, grilled meat, or fish. Only very posh restaurants or those pandering to tourists include Western-style desserts on the menu. Greeks usually eat cakes separately in a *galaktopoleio* or *zaharoplasteio*.

Greek Specialities

Snacks Favourite Greek snacks include pretzel rings sold by street vendors, *tyropitta* (cheese pie), *bougatsa* (custard-filled pastry) and *spanakopitta* (spinach pie). Street vendors sell various nuts and dried seeds such as pumpkin for €0.60 to €1.50 a bag. Chestnuts are roasted on the roadsides in winter.

Mezedes In a simple taverna, possibly only three or four *mezedes* (appetisers) will be offered – perhaps taramasalata (fish-roe dip), tzatziki (yogurt, cucumber and garlic dip), olives and feta (sheep or goat's milk) cheese. *Ouzeri* and restaurants usually offer wider selections.

Mezedes include *ohtapodi* (octopus), *garides* (shrimps), *kalamaria* (squid), dolmades (stuffed vine leaves), *melitzanosalata* (aubergine or eggplant dip) and *mavromatika* (black-eyed beans). Hot *mezedes* include *keftedes* (meatballs), *fasolia* (white haricot beans), *gigantes* (lima beans), *loukanika* (little sausages), *tyropitta*, *spanakopitta*, *bourekaki* (tiny meat pie), *kolokythakia* (deep-fried zucchini), *melitzana* (deep-fried aubergine) and *saganaki* (fried cheese).

It is quite acceptable to make a full meal of these instead of a main course. Three plates of *mezedes* are about equivalent in price and quantity to one main course. You can also order a *pikilia* (mixed plate).

Soups Soup is a satisfying starter or, indeed, an economical meal in itself with bread and a salad. *Psarosoupa* is a filling fish soup with vegetables, while *kakavia* (Greek bouillabaisse) is laden with seafood and more expensive. *Fasolada* (bean soup) is also a meal in itself. *Avgolemano soupa* (egg and lemon soup) is usually prepared from a chicken stock. If you're into offal, don't miss the traditional Easter soup *mayiritsa* at this festive time.

Salads The ubiquitous (and no longer inexpensive) Greek or village salad, *horiatiki salata*, is a side dish for Greeks, but many budget-conscious travellers make it a main dish. It consists of peppers, onions, olives, tomatoes and feta cheese, sprinkled with oregano and dressed with olive oil and lemon juice. A tomato salad often comes with onions, cucumber and olives, and, with bread, makes a satisfying lunch. In winter, try the cheaper *radhikia salata* (dandelion salad).

Main Dishes The most common main courses are *moussaka* (layers of eggplant or zucchini, minced meat and potatoes topped with cheese sauce and baked), *pastitsio* (baked cheese-topped macaroni and bechamel, with or without minced meat), dolmades and *yemista* (stuffed tomatoes or green peppers). Other main courses include *giouvetsi* (casserole of lamb or veal and pasta), *stifado* (meat stewed with onions), *soutzoukakia* (spicy meatballs in tomato sauce, also known as Smyrna sausages) and *salingaria* (snails in oil with herbs). *Melizanes papoutsakia* is baked eggplant stuffed with meat and tomatoes and topped with cheese, which looks, as its Greek name suggests, like a little shoe. Spicy *loukanika* (sausages) are a good budget choice and come with potatoes or rice. Lamb fricassee, cooked with lettuce, *arni fricassée me maroulia*, is usually filling enough for two.

Fish is usually sold by weight in restaurants but is not as cheap or as widely available as it used to be. *Kalamaria*, deep-fried in batter, remains a tasty option for the budget traveller at €3.55 to €4.70 for a generous serve. Other reasonably priced fish (about €3.55 a portion) are *marides* (whitebait), sometimes cloaked in onion, pepper and tomato sauce, and *gopes*, which are similar to sardines. More expensive are *ohtapodi*, *bakaliaros* (cod), *xifias* (swordfish) and *glossa* (sole). Ascending the price scale further are *synagrida* (snapper) and *barbounia* (red mullet). *Astakos* (lobster) and *karavida* (crayfish) are top of the range at about €44 per kilo.

Fish is mostly grilled or fried. More imaginative fish dishes include shrimp casserole and mussel or octopus *saganaki* (fried with tomato and cheese).

Desserts Greek cakes and puddings include baklava (layers of filo pastry filled with honey and nuts), *loukoumades* (puffs or fritters with honey or syrup), *kataïfi* (chopped nuts inside shredded wheat pastry or filo soaked in honey), *rizogalo* (rice pudding), *loukoumi* (Turkish delight), halva (made from semolina or sesame seeds) and *pagoto* (ice cream). Tavernas and restaurants usually only have a few of these on the menu. The best places to go for these delights are *galaktopoleia* or *zaharoplasteia*.

Vegetarian Food

Greece has few vegetarian restaurants. Unfortunately, many vegetable soups and stews are based on meat stocks. Fried vegetables are safe bets, as olive oil is always used – never lard. The Greeks do wonderful things with artichokes *(anginares)*, which thrive in Greece. Stuffed, served as a salad, as a *mezes*, and as the basis of a vegetarian stew, the artichoke warrants greater discovery by visitors. Vegetarians who eat eggs can rest assured that an economical omelette can be whipped up anywhere. Salads are cheap, fresh, substantial and nourishing. Other possibilities are yogurt, rice pudding, cheese-and-spinach pies, and nuts. Creperies also offer tasty vegetarian selections.

Lent, incidentally, is a good time for vegetarians because the meat is missing from many dishes.

Fast Food

Western-style fast food has arrived in Greece but, thankfully, patriotic Greeks seem to prefer the local chains, such as Goody's, which has a better salad bar than most of its rivals.

It's hard, though, to beat eat-on-the-street Greek offerings. Foremost among them are the *gyros* and the souvlaki. The *gyros* is a giant skewer laden with slabs of seasoned meat which grills slowly as it rotates while the meat is trimmed steadily from the outside; souvlakia are small individual kebab sticks. Both are served wrapped in pitta bread, with salad and lashings of tzatziki.

Another favourite is *tost*, which is a bread roll cut in half, stuffed with the filling(s) of your choice, buttered on the outside and then flattened in a heavy griddle iron. It's the speciality of the Everest fast-food chain, which has outlets nationwide.

Fruit

Greece grows many varieties of fruit. Most visitors will be familiar with *syka* (figs), *rodakina* (peaches), *stafylia* (grapes), *karpouzi* (watermelon), *milo* (apples), *portokalia* (oranges) and *kerasia* (cherries).

Many will not, however, have encountered the *frangosyko* (prickly pear). Also known as the Barbary fig, it is the fruit of the opuntia cactus, recognisable by the thick green spiny pads that form its trunk. The fruit are borne around the edge of the pads in late summer and autumn and vary in colour from pale orange to deep red. They are delicious but need to be approached with extreme caution because of the thousands of tiny prickles (invisible to the naked eye) that cover their skin. Never pick one up with your bare hands. They must be peeled before you can eat them. The simplest way to do this is to trim the ends off with a knife and then slit the skin from end to end.

Another fruit that will be new to many people is the *mousmoula* (loquat). These small orange fruit are among the first of summer, reaching the market in mid-May. The flesh is juicy and pleasantly acidic.

Self-Catering

Eating out in Greece is as much an entertainment as a gastronomic experience, so to self-cater is to sacrifice a lot. But if you are on a low budget you will need to make the sacrifice – for breakfast and lunch at any rate. All towns and villages of any size have supermarkets, fruit and vegetable stalls and bakeries.

Only in isolated villages and on remote islands is food choice limited. There may only be one all-purpose shop – a *pantopoleio*, which will stock meat, vegetables, fruit, bread and tinned foods.

Most larger towns have huge indoor food markets, known, perhaps not surprisingly, as *agora*, which feature fruit and vegetable stalls, butchers, dairies and delicatessens, all under one roof. They are lively places that are worth visiting for the atmosphere as much as for the shopping. The market at Kalamata is a good example.

Smaller towns have a weekly *laïki agora* (street market) filled with stalls selling local produce.

DRINKS
Nonalcoholic Drinks

Coffee & Tea Greek coffee is the national drink. It is a legacy of Ottoman rule and, until the Turkish invasion of Cyprus in 1974, the Greeks called it Turkish coffee. It is served with the grounds, without milk, in a small cup. Connoisseurs claim there are at least 30 variations of Greek coffee but most people know only three: *glyko* (sweet), *metrio* (medium) and *sketo* (without sugar).

The next most popular coffee is instant, called Nescafé (which it usually is). Ask for Nescafé *me ghala* (pronounced 'me **ga**-la') if you want it with milk. In summer, Greeks drink Nescafé chilled, with or without milk and sugar – this version is called *frappé*.

Espresso and filtered coffee, once sold only in trendy cafés, are now also widely available.

Tea is inevitably made with a tea bag.

Fruit Juice & Soft Drinks Packaged fruit juices are available everywhere. Fresh orange juice is also widely available but does not come cheap. The products of all the major soft-drink multinationals are available everywhere in cans and bottles, along with local brands.

Milk Fresh milk is available everywhere except the remotest villages. A litre costs about €1.20. UHT milk is available almost everywhere, as is condensed milk.

Water Tap water is safe to drink in Greece, although sometimes it doesn't taste too good because of the level of chlorine. Many tourists prefer to drink bottled spring water, sold widely in 500mL and 1.5L plastic bottles. Sparkling mineral water is rare.

Alcoholic Drinks

Beer Greek beers are making a strong comeback in a fast-growing market long dominated by the major northern European breweries. The most popular beers are still Amstel and Heineken, both brewed locally under licence and available everywhere, but many consumers are switching to local beers like Mythos, Alpha and Vergina. Mythos has claimed a healthy share of the market since it was launched in 1997 and is the most widely available. It has proved popular with drinkers who find the northern European beers a bit sweet.

Imported lagers, stouts and beers can be found in tourist spots; you might even spot Newcastle Brown, Carlsberg, Castlemaine XXXX and Guinness.

Supermarkets are the cheapest place to buy beer, and bottles are cheaper than cans.

Wine According to mythology, the Greeks invented or discovered wine (*krasi*) and it has been produced in Greece on a large scale for more than 3000 years. But the modern wine industry is still very much in its infancy. Until the 1950s most wines were sold in bulk and were seldom distributed any farther afield than the nearest town. It wasn't until industrialisation (and the resulting rapid urban growth) that there was much call for bottled wine. Quality control was unheard of until 1969, when appellation laws were introduced as a precursor to applying for membership of the European Community. Wines have improved significantly since then. Don't expect Greek wines to taste like French wines: the varieties grown in Greece are quite different.

Wine is produced throughout the Peloponnese. It seems that every smallholder has a piece of land set aside for grapes and every taverna sells local wine from the barrel. The best wines come from the north, particularly the low hills around Nemea, southwest of Corinth. The region has been known for its fine wines since Mycenaean times, when nearby Phlius supplied the Mycenaean court. Lovers of a good red should seek out Ktima Gaia and Ktima Papaionnou (*Ktima* means estate). Both are full-bodied dry reds, produced from the local *agioritiko* variety – which will grow nowhere else.

A second premium growing area is in the hills around Patras. The region is home of the Achaïa-Clauss winery, producers of Demestica, the country's most widely recognised label.

Aspro is white, *mavro* is red and *kokkinelli* is rosé.

Spirits Ouzo is the most popular aperitif in Greece. Distilled from grape stems and flavoured with anise, it is similar to the Middle Eastern *arak*, Turkish *raki* and French Pernod. Clear and colourless, it turns white when water is added. A 700mL bottle of a popular brand like Ouzo 12 Olympic or Sans Rival costs about €4.40 in supermarkets. In an *ouzeri*, a glass costs from €0.90 to €1.50. It will be served neat, with a separate glass of water to be used for dilution.

The second-most popular spirit is Greek brandy, which is dominated by the Metaxa label. Metaxa comes in a wide choice of grades, starting with three-star – a high-octane product without much finesse. You can pick up a bottle in a supermarket for about €4.40. The quality improves as you go through the grades: five-star, seven-star, VSOP, Golden Age and finally the top-shelf Grand Olympian Reserve (€18). Other reputable brands include Cambas and Votrys.

If you're travelling off the beaten track, you may come across *chipura*, a moonshine version of ouzo that packs a formidable punch. You will most likely encounter *chipura* in village *kafeneia* or private homes.

ENTERTAINMENT
Cinemas
Greeks are keen movie-goers and almost every town of consequence has a cinema. English-language films are shown in English with Greek subtitles. Admission ranges from €4.10 in small-town movie houses to €5.90 at plush big-city cinemas.

Clubs & Music Bars
Clubs can be found in big cities and resort areas, though not in the numbers of a decade ago.

Most young Greeks prefer to head for the music bars that have proliferated to fill the void. These bars normally specialise in a particular style of music – Greek, modern rock, 60s rock, techno and, very occasionally, jazz.

Ballet, Classical Music & Opera
Unless you're going to be spending a bit of time in Athens, you're best off forgetting about ballet, classical music and opera while you're enjoying your time in the Peloponnese.

Wine + Pine = Retsina

A holiday would not be the same without a jar or three of retsina, the famous – some might say notorious – pine-resinated wine that has become almost synonymous with Greece.

Your first taste of retsina may well leave you wondering whether the waiter has mixed up the wine and the paint stripper, but stick with it – it's a taste that's worth acquiring. Soon you will be savouring the delicate pine aroma, and the initial astringency mellows to become very moreish. Retsina is very refreshing consumed chilled at the end of a hot day, when it goes particularly well with tzatziki.

Greeks have been resinating wine, both white and rosé, for millennia. The ancient Greeks dedicated the pine tree to Dionysos, the god of wine, and believed that land that grew good pine would also grow good wine.

No-one seems quite sure how wine and pine first got together. The consensus is that it was an inevitable accident in a country with so much wine and so much pine. The theory that resin entered the wine-making process because the wine was stored in pine barrels does not hold water, since the ancients used clay amphora rather than barrels. It's more likely that it was through pine implements and vessels used elsewhere in the process. Producers discovered that wine treated with resin kept for longer and consumers discovered that they liked it.

Resination was once a fairly haphazard process, achieved by various methods such as adding crushed pine cones to the brew and coating the insides of storage vessels. The amount of resin also varied enormously. One 19th-century traveller wrote that he had tasted a wine 'so impregnated with resin that it almost took the skin from my lips'. His reaction was hardly surprising; he was probably drinking a wine with a resin content as high as 7.5%, common at the time. A more sophisticated product awaits the modern traveller, with a resin content no higher than 1% – as specified by good old EU regulations. That's still enough to give the wine its trademark astringency and pine aroma.

The bulk of the retsina found in the Peloponnese is produced from the white *savatiano* grape, which is grown around Nemea and in Arcadia. Not just any old resin will do; the main source is the Aleppo pine *(Pinus halepensis)*, which produces a resin known for its delicate fragrance.

Retsina is generally cheap and readily available. Supermarkets stock retsina in a variety of containers ranging from 500mL bottles to 5L casks and flagons. Kourtaki and Cambas are both very good, but the best (and worst) still flows from the barrel in traditional tavernas. Ask for *heema*, meaning unbottled (literally, 'loose').

Theatre

The highlight of the Greek dramatic year is the staging of ancient Greek dramas at the Theatre of Herodes Atticus in Athens during the Hellenic Festival from late June into September. Performances are also staged at the amazing Theatre of Epidavros. See Special Events in the Athens chapter, p86, and the Epidavros section of the Argolis chapter, pp120–1, for more information.

Rock

Western rock music continues to grow in popularity but live music remains a rarity outside Athens.

Traditional Music

Most of the live music you hear around the resorts is tame stuff laid on for the tourists. If you want to hear music played with a bit of passion, the *rembetika* clubs in Athens are highly recommended.

Folk Dancing

Greece's foremost folk dancers are the members of the Dora Stratou Dance Company, who perform nightly at their own theatre on Filopappos Hill in Athens between May and October (see Entertainment in the Athens chapter, p91). Folk dance is an integral part of all festival celebrations and there is often impromptu folk dancing in tavernas.

SPECTATOR SPORTS

Football (soccer) remains the most popular spectator sport, although basketball is catching up fast after the successes of Greek sides in European club competition in recent years. Greek soccer teams, in contrast, have seldom had much impact on European club competition and the national team is the source of constant hair-wrenching. The side's only appearance in the World Cup finals, in the USA in 1994, brought a string of heavy defeats.

The glamour clubs of Greek soccer are Olympiakos of Piraeus and Panathinaikos of Athens. Most soccer fans around the Peloponnese declare for one of these two in preference to local teams. At the time of writing, the only Peloponnese club in the Greek first division was Panahaiki from Patras. Athens supplies more than a third of the clubs.

The season lasts from September to mid-May; cup matches are played on Wednesday night and first-division games on Sunday afternoon. Games are often televised. Admission to a match costs around €5.90 for the cheapest terrace tickets, or €15 for a decent seat. Fixtures and results are given in the *Athens News*.

Olympiakos and Panathinaikos are also the glamour clubs of Greek basketball. Panathinaikos was European champion in 1996, and Olympiakos followed suit in 1997.

SHOPPING

Greece produces a vast array of handicrafts. The **National Welfare Organisation's Hellenic Folk Art Gallery** *(cnr Apollonos & Ipatias, Plaka, Athens)* has a good range.

Antiques

It is illegal to buy, sell, possess or export any antiquity in Greece (see Customs earlier in this chapter, p38). However, there are antiques and 'antiques'; a lot of items only a century or two old are regarded as junk, rather than part of the national heritage.

These items include handmade furniture and odds and ends from rural areas in Greece, ecclesiastical ornaments from churches and items brought back from far flung lands. Good hunting grounds for this 'junk' are Monastiraki and the flea market in Athens, and the Piraeus market held on Sunday morning.

Bags

Tagari bags are woven wool bags - often brightly coloured - which hang from the shoulder by a rope. Minus the rope, they make attractive cushion covers.

Ceramics

You will see ceramic objects of every shape and size – functional and ornamental – for sale throughout Greece. The best places for high-quality handmade ceramics are Athens and the islands of Sifnos and Skyros.

There are a lot of places selling plaster copies of statues, busts, grave stelae and the like.

Jewellery

Gold is good value in Greece and designs are of a high standard, but it is priced beyond the capacity of most travellers pockets. If you prefer something more reasonably priced, go for filigree silver jewellery.

Leather Work

There are leather goods for sale throughout Greece; most are made from leather imported from Spain. The best place for buying leather goods is Hania on Crete. Bear in mind that the goods are not as high quality or as good value as those available in Turkey.

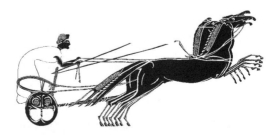

Getting There & Away

AIR

The only airport in the Peloponnese is at Kalamata, where services are restricted to two flights a week from Athens and the occasional charter flight from northern Europe.

Most visitors fly to Athens and then continue to the Peloponnese by land; see Land, p71, for details. Athens handles the vast majority of Greece's scheduled international flights, including all intercontinental traffic. Athens also receives a large number of charter flights.

Olympic Airways (W *www.olympic-airways.gr*) is still Greece's national airline, despite continuing attempts to sell off the ailing carrier. You'll find full details of Olympic's services on its website.

The baggage allowance on domestic flights is 15kg, or 20kg if the domestic flight is part of an international journey. Olympic offers a 25% student discount on domestic flights but only if the flight is part of an international journey.

Greece's only other international operator is **Aegean Airlines** (W *www.aegeanair.com*), which has daily flights from Athens to Rome, Düsseldorf and Stuttgart, and from Thessaloniki to Düsseldorf, Frankfurt, Munich and Stuttgart.

Buying Tickets

If you are flying to Greece from outside Europe, the plane ticket will probably be the most expensive item in your travel budget and buying it can be an intimidating business. There will be a multitude of airlines and travel agents hoping to separate you from your money, so take time to research the options. Start planning early – some of the cheapest tickets must be bought months in advance and popular flights tend to sell out early.

Discounted tickets fall into two categories: official and unofficial. Official discount schemes include advance-purchase tickets, budget fares, Apex, Super-Apex and a few other variations on the theme. These tickets can be bought from travel agents or direct from the airline. They often have restrictions – advance purchase being the usual one. There might also be restrictions on the period you must be away, such

as a minimum of 14 days and a maximum of one year.

Unofficial tickets are simply discounted tickets the airlines release through selected travel agents.

A return ticket can often be cheaper than a one-way ticket. Generally, you can find discounted tickets at prices as low as, or even lower than, Apex or budget tickets. Phone around travel agents for bargains.

If you are buying a ticket to fly out of Greece, Athens is one of the major centres in Europe for budget air fares.

In Greece, as everywhere else, always remember to reconfirm your onward or return bookings by the specified time – usually 72 hours before departure on international flights. If you don't, there's a risk you'll turn up at the airport only to find you've missed your flight because it was rescheduled or that the airline has given the seat to someone else.

Travel Agents Many of the larger travel agents use the travel pages of national newspapers and magazines to promote their special deals. Before you make a decision, there are a number of questions you need to ask about the ticket. Find out the airline, the route, the duration of the journey, the stopovers allowed, any restrictions on the ticket and – above all – the price. Ask whether the fare quoted includes all taxes and other possible inclusions.

You may discover when you start ringing around that those impossibly cheap flights, charter or otherwise, aren't available but the agent just happens to know of another one that 'costs a bit more'. Or the agent may claim to have the last two seats available for Greece for the whole of July, which it will hold for a maximum of two hours only. Don't panic – keep ringing around.

If you are flying to Greece from the USA, Southeast Asia or the UK, you may find the cheapest flights are being advertised by obscure agencies whose names haven't yet reached a phone directory – the proverbial 'bucket shops'. Many such firms are honest and solvent, but there are a few rogues who will take your money and disappear, only to reopen elsewhere a month or two later under a new name. If you feel suspicious, don't pay all the money at once – leave a small deposit and pay the balance when you get the ticket. If the agent insists on cash in advance, go somewhere else or be prepared to take a big risk. Once you have booked the flight with the agent, ring the airline to check that you have a confirmed booking.

It can be easier on the nerves to pay a bit more for the security of a better-known travel agent. Firms such as STA Travel, with offices worldwide, and Travel CUTS in Canada offer good prices to Europe (including Greece), and are unlikely to disappear overnight.

The fares quoted in this book are intended as a guide only. They are approximate and are based on the rates advertised by travel agents at the time of writing.

Charter Flights Charter-flight tickets are for seats left vacant on flights that have been block-booked by package companies. Charter-flight tickets are valid for up to four weeks and usually have a minimum-stay requirement of at least three days. Sometimes it's worth buying a charter ticket even if you think you want to stay for longer than four weeks. The tickets can be so cheap that you can afford to throw away the return portion.

The travel section of major newspapers is the place to look for cheap charter deals. More information on charter flights is given later in this chapter under specific point-of-origin headings.

Courier Flights Another budget option (sometimes even cheaper than a charter flight) is a courier flight. This deal entails accompanying freight or a parcel that will be collected at the destination. The drawbacks are that your time away may be limited to one or two weeks, your luggage is usually restricted to hand luggage (the parcel or freight you carry comes out of your luggage allowance), and you may have to be a resident of the country that operates the courier service and apply for an interview before you'll be taken on.

Travel Insurance The kind of cover you get depends on your insurance and type of ticket, so ask both your insurer and your ticket-issuing agency to explain where you stand. Ticket loss is usually covered.

Buy travel insurance as early as possible. If you buy it just before you fly, you may find you're not covered for such problems as delays caused by industrial action. Make sure you have a separate record of all your ticket details – preferably a photocopy.

Paying for your ticket with a credit card sometimes provides limited travel insurance, and you may be able to reclaim the payment if the operator doesn't deliver. In the UK, for instance, credit card providers are required by law to reimburse consumers if a company goes into liquidation and the amount in contention is more than UK£100.

Travellers with Special Needs

If you've broken a leg, require a special diet, are travelling in a wheelchair, are taking a baby, or whatever, let the airline staff know as soon as possible – preferably when booking your ticket. Check that your request has been registered when you reconfirm your booking (at least 72 hours before departure) and again when you check in at the airport.

Children under two years of age travel for 10% of the standard fare (or free on some airlines) as long as they don't occupy a seat. But they do not get a baggage allowance. 'Skycots' should be provided by the airline if requested in advance. These will take a child weighing up to about 10kg. Olympic Airways charges half fare for accompanied children aged between two and 12 years, while most other airlines charge two-thirds.

Departure Tax

The airport tax is €12 for passengers travelling to destinations within the European Union (EU) and €22 for other destinations. It applies to travellers aged over five years, and is paid when you buy your ticket, not at the airport.

Passengers aged over two departing from Athens are liable for a further €10.30 as a contribution to facilities at the new airport, and a security charge of €1.29. These charges are also paid when you buy your ticket.

Prices quoted in this book include these taxes and charges where applicable.

The UK

Discount air travel is big business in London. Advertisements for many travel agents appear in the travel pages of the weekend broadsheets, such as the *Independent* on Saturday and the *Sunday Times*. Look out for the free magazines, such as *TNT*, which are widely available in London – start by looking outside the main railway and underground stations.

For students or travellers under 26, popular travel agencies in the UK include **STA Travel** (☎ 020-7361 6161; W www.statravel.co.uk; 86 Old Brompton Rd, London, & other offices in London & Manchester).

Other recommended agents include **Trailfinders** (☎ 020-7937 1234; W www.trailfinders.com; 194 Kensington High St, London), **Bridge the World** (☎ 020-7734 7447; W www.b-t-w.co.uk; 4 Regent Place, London) and **Flightbookers** (☎ 020-7757 2000; W www.ebookers.com; 177 Tottenham Court Rd, London).

British Airways, Olympic Airways and Virgin Atlantic operate daily flights between London and Athens. Pricing is very competitive, with all three offering return tickets for around UK£220 in high season, plus tax. At other times, prices fall as low as UK£104, plus tax. British Airways has flights from Edinburgh, Glasgow and Manchester.

The cheapest scheduled flights are with **EasyJet** (☎ 0870-600 0000; W www.easyjet.com), the no-frills specialist, which has two Luton–Athens flights daily. One-way fares range from UK£89 to UK£139 in high season, and from a bargain UK£39 to UK£69 at other times.

There are numerous charter flights between the UK and Greece. Typical London–Athens charter fares are UK£99/149 one way/return in low season and UK£119/209 in high season. These prices are for advance bookings but even in high season it's possible to pick up last-minute deals for as little as UK£69/109. There are also charter flights from Birmingham, Cardiff, Glasgow, Luton, Manchester and Newcastle.

If you're flying from Athens to the UK, budget fares start at €75 to London or €90 to Manchester, plus airport tax.

Continental Europe

Athens is linked to every major city in Europe by either Olympic Airways or the flag carrier of each country.

London is the discount capital of Europe but Amsterdam, Frankfurt, Berlin and Paris are also major centres for cheap air fares.

Across Europe many travel agencies have ties with STA Travel, where cheap tickets can be purchased and STA-issued tickets can be altered (usually for a US$25 fee). Outlets in major cities include **Voyages Wasteels** (within France ☎ 08-03 88 70 04, fax 01-43 25 46 25; 11 rue Dupuytren, Paris), **STA Travel** (☎ 030-311 0950, fax 313 0948; Goethestrasse 73, Berlin) and **Passaggi** (☎ 06-474 0923, fax 482 7436; Stazione Termini FS, Gelleria Di Tesla, Rome).

France has a network of student-travel agencies which can supply discount tickets to travellers of all ages. **OTU Voyages** (☎ 01 44 41 38 50; W www.otu.fr; 39 Av Georges Bernanos (5e), Paris) has a central Paris office and another 42 offices around the country. **Acceuil des Jeunes en France** (☎ 01 42 77 87 80; 119 rue Saint Martin (4e), Paris), is another popular discount-travel agency.

General travel agencies in Paris include **Nouvelles Frontières** (☎ 08-03 33 33 33; W www.nouvelles-frontieres.com; 5 Av de l'Opéra (1er), Paris) and **Voyageurs du Monde** (☎ 01-42 86 16 00; 55 rue Sainte Anne (2e), Paris).

Belgium, Switzerland, the Netherlands and Greece are also good places for buying discount air tickets. In Belgium **Acotra Student Travel Agency** (☎ 02-512 86 07; rue de la Madeline, Brussels) and **WATS Reizen** (☎ 03-226 16 26; de Keyserlei 44, Antwerp) are both well-known agencies. In Switzerland **SSR Voyages** (☎ 01-297 11 11; W www.ssr.ch) specialises in student, youth and budget fares. In Zurich there is a branch at Leonhardstrasse 10 and there are branches in most major cities.

In the Netherlands, **Malibu Travel** (☎ 020-626 32 30; Prinsengracht 230, Amsterdam) is recommended.

If you're travelling from Athens to Europe, budget fares to a host of European cities are widely advertised by the travel agents around Syntagma.

Turkey

Olympic Airways and Turkish Airlines share the İstanbul–Athens route, with at least one flight a day each. The full fare is US$330 one way. Students qualify for a 50% discount on both airlines.

There are no direct flights from Ankara to Athens; all flights go via İstanbul.

Cyprus

Olympic Airways and Cyprus Airways share the Cyprus–Greece routes. Both airlines have three flights daily from Larnaca to Athens and there are five flights weekly to Thessaloniki. Cyprus Airways also flies from Paphos to Athens once a week in winter and twice a week in summer.

The USA

Discount-travel agents in the USA are known as consolidators (although you won't see a sign on the door saying Consolidator). San Francisco is the ticket consolidator capital of America, although some good deals can be found in Los Angeles, New York and other big cities. Consolidators can be found through the Yellow Pages or the major daily newspapers. The *New York Times*, the *Los Angeles Times*, the *Chicago Tribune* and the *San Francisco Examiner* all produce weekly travel sections in which you will find a number of travel-agency ads.

STA Travel (☎ 800-777 0112; w www.statravel.com) has offices in Boston, Chicago, Miami, New York, Philadelphia, San Francisco and other major cities. Call the toll-free 800 number for office locations.

New York has the widest range of options to Athens. The route to Europe is very competitive and there are new deals almost every day. At the time of research, Virgin Atlantic led the way, offering Athens for US$944 return in high season via London, falling to US$740 at other times. Olympic

Airways flies direct at least once a day and Delta Airlines flies direct three times week. Apex fares with Olympic range from US$730 to US$1015, depending on the season. These fares don't include taxes.

Boston is the only other east coast city with direct flights to Athens – on Saturday with Olympic Airways. Fares are the same as for flights from New York.

There are no direct flights to Athens from the west coast. There are, however, connecting flights to Athens from many US cities, either linking with Olympic Airways in New York or flying with one of the European national airlines to their home country, and then on to Athens. At the time of research, Virgin Atlantic was offering Los Angeles–Athens for US$982 return in high season, falling to US$879 at other times.

Courier flights to Athens are occasionally advertised in the newspapers or you could contact air-freight companies listed in the phone book. You may even have to go to the air-freight company to get an answer – the companies aren't always keen to give out information over the phone. **Travel Unlimited** (PO Box 1058, Allston, MA 02134, USA) is a monthly travel newsletter from the USA that publishes many courier flight deals from destinations worldwide. A 12-month subscription to the newsletter costs US$25 US$35 for residents outside the USA. Another possibility (at least for US residents) is to join the **International Association of Air Travel Couriers** (IAATC; ☎ 561-582-8320 w www.courier.org). The membership fee of $45 gets members a bimonthly update of air courier offerings, access to a fax-on-demand service with daily updates of last-minute specials and the bimonthly newsletter *Shoe string Traveler*. Be aware that joining this organisation does not guarantee that you'll get a courier flight.

If you're travelling from Athens to the USA, the travel agents around Syntagma offer the following one-way fares (prices do not include airport tax): Atlanta €340 Chicago €340, Los Angeles €380 and New York €265.

Canada

Canadian discount air-ticket sellers are also known as consolidators and their air fares tend to be about 10% higher than those sold in the USA. The *Globe & Mail*, the *Toronto*

Star, the *Montreal Gazette* and the *Vancouver Sun* carry travel agents' ads and are a good place to look for cheap fares.

Travel CUTS (☎ *1800-667 2887;* Ⓦ *www travelcuts.com)* is Canada's national student-travel agency and has offices in all major cities.

Olympic Airways has two flights weekly from Toronto to Athens via Montreal. There are no direct flights from Vancouver but there are connecting flights via Toronto, Amsterdam, Frankfurt and London on Canadian Airlines, KLM, Lufthansa and British Airways. You should be able to get to Athens from Toronto and Montreal for about C$1150/950 in high/low season or from Vancouver for C$1500/1300.

For courier flights originating in Canada, contact **FB On Board Courier Services** in Montreal (☎ *514-631 7929).* They can get you to London for C$760 return.

At the time of writing, budget-travel agencies in Athens were advertising flights to both Toronto and Montreal for €330, plus airport tax.

Australia

Two well-known agents for cheap fares are STA Travel and Flight Centre. **STA Travel** (☎ *03-9349 2411;* Ⓦ *www.statravel.com.au; central office, 224 Faraday St, Carlton, Victoria 3053)* has offices in all major cities and on many university campuses. Call ☎ 131 776 Australia-wide for the location of your nearest branch. **Flight Centre** (☎ *131 600 Australia-wide;* Ⓦ *www.flightcentre.com.au; central office, 82 Elizabeth St, Sydney, New South Wales 2000)* also has dozens of offices throughout Australia.

Thai International and Singapore Airlines also have convenient connections to Athens, plus a reputation for good service. If you're planning on doing a bit of flying around Europe, check around for special deals from the major European airlines. Alitalia, KLM and Lufthansa are three likely candidates with good European networks.

If you're travelling from Athens to Australia, a one-way ticket to Sydney or Melbourne costs about €550, plus airport tax.

New Zealand

Round-the-World (RTW) and Circle Pacific fares are usually the best value, often cheaper than a return ticket. Depending on which airline you choose, you may fly across Asia, with possible stopovers in India, Bangkok or Singapore, or across the USA, with possible stopovers in Honolulu, Australia or one of the Pacific Islands.

The *New Zealand Herald* has a travel section in which travel agents advertise fares. **Flight Centre** (☎ *09-309 6171; central office, National Bank Towers, cnr Queen & Darby Sts, Auckland)* has many branches throughout the country. **STA Travel** (☎ *09-309 0458;* Ⓦ *www.sta.travel.com.au; central office, 10 High St, Auckland)* has offices in Auckland as well as in Hamilton, Palmerston North, Wellington, Christchurch and Dunedin.

LAND
Athens

Athens has very good bus connections to all the major towns in the Peloponnese, as well as train services; see Getting There & Away in the Athens chapter, p92, for details.

Car & Motorcycle National Road 8 is the main road running west from Athens to the Peloponnese. The route is clearly signposted from central Athens (see the Athens chapter, p92, for details).

It can be painfully slow going for the first 21km from Athens to Elefsina. At Elefsina (one of the ugliest towns in Greece), drivers have the choice of following the old national road or paying €1.45 to use the new toll road. The toll road is strongly recommended, with at least two lanes in each direction all the way to Corinth, 84km west of Athens. The road divides at Corinth, with one route heading west along the coast to Patras, and the other heading southwest to Tripolis.

The new Athens ring road, under construction at the time of research, will link up with National Road 8 at Elefsina. In theory, this should make in possible to drive from the new Athens airport at Spata, 21km east of Athens, to Corinth in under 90 minutes.

The old national road from Elefsina to Corinth hugs the coast, but it's too busy – and the coast too developed – to be scenic.

See Car & Motorcycle in the Getting Around chapter, p77, for information about the road network in the Peloponnese.

Other Parts of Greece

There are buses to Patras from many parts of northern and central Greece, crossing the

Gulf of Patras on the ferries between Andirio and Rio, 6km northeast of Patras.

The Ionian islands of Kefallonia, Lefkada and Zakynthos can also be reached from Patras by bus – the fares include the price of the ferry ticket.

Albania

Bus There is a daily OSE (Organismos Sidirodromon Ellados, the Hellenic Railways Organisation) bus between Athens and Tirana (€35.20) via Ioannina and Gjirokastra. The bus departs Athens (Peloponnese train station) at 7pm arriving in Tirana the following day at 5pm. On the return trip, the bus departs Tirana at 7am.

Car & Motorcycle If you're travelling by car or motorcycle, there are two crossing points between Greece and Albania. The main one is at Kakavia, 60km northwest of Ioannina off the Ioannina–Konitsa road. The other border crossing is at Krystallopigi, 14km west of Kotas on the Florina–Kastoria road. Kapshtica is the closest town on the Albanian side. It is possible to take a private vehicle into Albania, although it's not a great idea because of security concerns and problems with obtaining spare parts. Always carry your passport in areas near the Albanian border.

Bulgaria

Bus The OSE operates two Athens–Sofia buses (€45.50, 15 hours) daily except Monday, leaving at 7am and 5pm.

Train There is an Athens–Sofia train daily (€30.65, 18 hours) via Thessaloniki (€15.60, nine hours). From Sofia, there are daily connections to Budapest (€48.10) and connections to Bucharest (€81) on Wednesday and Sunday.

Car & Motorcycle The Bulgarian border crossing is at Promahonas, 145km northeast of Thessaloniki and 50km from Serres.

Former Yugoslav Republic of Macedonia

Train Trains to the Former Yugoslav Republic of Macedonia (FYROM) leave from the northern city of Thessaloniki. There is a daily train to Skopje (€12.50, three hours) at 6.15am, crossing the border between Idomeni and Gevgelija. It continues from Skopje to the Serbian capital of Belgrade (€28.50, 12 hours).

There are no trains between Florina and FYROM, although there may be trains to Skopje from the FYROM side of the border.

Car & Motorcycle There are two border crossings between Greece and FYROM. One is at Evzoni, 68km north of Thessaloniki. This is the main highway to Skopje, which continues to Belgrade. The other border crossing is at Niki, 16km north of Florina. This road leads to Bitola, and continues to Ohrid, once a popular tourist resort on the shores of Lake Ohrid.

Turkey

Bus There are OSE buses between Athens and İstanbul (€67.50, 22 hours) daily except Wednesday, leaving the Peloponnese train station in Athens at 7pm.

Students qualify for a 20% discount and children under 12 travel for half fare.

Buses from İstanbul to Athens leave the Anadolu Terminal (Anatolia Terminal) at the Topkapı *otogar* (bus station) at 10am daily except Sunday.

Train There are daily trains between Athens and İstanbul (€58.70, 22 hours), although they are regarded as a poor alternative to the buses. The trains can get uncomfortably crowded, there are often delays at the border and the journey can take much longer than the supposed 22 hours. Inter Rail Passes are valid in Turkey but Eurail passes are not.

Car & Motorcycle If you're travelling between Greece and Turkey by private vehicle, the crossing points are at Kipi, 43km northeast of Alexandroupolis, and at Kastanies, 139km northeast of Alexandroupolis. Kipi is more convenient if you're heading for İstanbul.

Western Europe

Overland travel between Western Europe and Greece is almost a thing of the past. Air fares are so cheap that land transport cannot compete. Travelling from the UK to Greece through Europe means crossing various borders, so check whether any visas are required before setting out.

Bus There are no bus services to Greece from the UK or from anywhere else in northern Europe. Bus companies can no longer compete with cheap air fares.

Train Unless you have an Inter Rail or Eurail pass, or are aged under 26 and eligible for a discounted fare, travelling to Greece by train is prohibitively expensive. Indeed, the chances of anyone wanting to travel from London to Athens by train are considered so remote that it's no longer possible to buy a single ticket for this journey. The trip involves travelling from London to Paris on the Eurostar (UK£105 to UK£165 one way), followed by Paris–Brindisi (UK£102.50 one way), then a ferry from Brindisi to Patras – and finally a train from Patras to Athens.

Greece is part of the Inter Rail Pass system; tickets are available to those who have been resident in one of the participating European countries for more than six months. A one-month Global Pass (all zones) costs UK£355 for travellers over 26, and UK£249 for those under 26. See the **Inter Rail** website (W www.interrailnet.com) for details.

Greece is also part of the Eurail network. Eurail passes can only be bought by residents of non-European countries and are supposed to be purchased before arriving in Europe. They can, however, be bought in Europe as long as your passport proves that you've been there for less than six months. In London, head for **Rail Europe** (☎ 08705 848 848; 179 Piccadilly). Sample fares include US$420 for an adult Eurail Select-pass, which permits eight days 1st-class travel in two months, and US$294 for the equivalent youth pass for 2nd-class travel. Check the **Eurail** website (W www.eurail .com) for full details of passes and prices.

If you are starting your European travels in Greece, you can buy your Eurail pass from the **Hellenic Railways Organisation** (Karolou 1, Omonia, Athens • Sina 6, Syntagma, Athens) and at the station in Patras.

Car & Motorcycle Before the troubles in the former Yugoslavia began, most motorists driving from the UK to Greece opted for the direct route: Ostend, Brussels, Salzburg and then down the Yugoslav highway through Zagreb, Belgrade and Skopje and crossing the border to Evzoni.

These days most people drive to an Italian port and get a ferry to Greece. Coming from the UK, this means driving through France, where petrol costs and road tolls are exorbitant.

SEA
Ferries are a major feature of the Greek travel scene, and there's every chance that you'll be boarding a boat of some description in the course of your visit.

Ferries come in all shapes and sizes, from the giant 'superferries' that operate on the international routes between Patras and Italy to the small, ageing open ferries that chug around the backwaters.

Athens
Ferry There are regular and convenient ferry services from Piraeus to the port of Methana, 52km from Nafplio on the eastern coast of the Argolis.

Hydrofoil Minoan Lines operates its Flying Dolphin hydrofoil services from Piraeus to half a dozen ports along the east coast of the Peloponnese. The best served are Ermioni and Porto Heli, about 90km southeast of Nafplio, with at least four hydrofoils a day. There are also daily services that travel further south to Leonidio, Kyparissi, Gerakas and Monemvasia on the east coast of the Peloponnese.

These services are part of Minoan Lines' Argosaronic network, which calls at the islands of Poros, Hydra and Spetses (just off the Peloponnese coast). It's an interesting way of travelling to the Peloponnese.

Other Parts of Greece
There are regular ferries from the small western port of Kyllini to the Ionian islands of Kefallonia and Zakynthos. Neapoli is the main port for the island of Kythira, while Gythio has summer connections with both Kythira and Kastelli-Kissamos on Crete.

Italy
The northwestern Peloponnese city of Patras is Greece's principal port for ferries to Italy, with daily services to the Italian ports of Ancona, Bari, Brindisi, Trieste and Venice. Many of these services travel via the port of Igoumenitsa, in northwestern Greece, and Corfu.

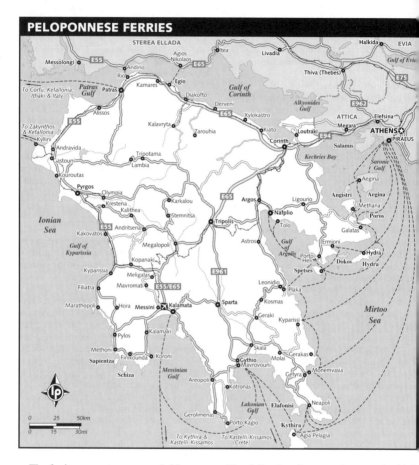

PELOPONNESE FERRIES

The ferries can get very crowded in summer. If you want to take a vehicle across it's a good idea to make a reservation. In the UK, reservations can be made on nearly all these ferries at **Viamare Travel Ltd** (☎ 020-7431 4560, fax 7431 5456; e ferries@viamare.com; 2 Sumatra Rd, London).

You'll find all the latest information about ferry routes, schedules and services on the Internet. For a good overview try W www.ferries.gr. Most of the ferry companies have their own websites, including:

ANEK Lines (W www.anek.gr)
Blue Star Ferries (W www.bluestarferries.com)
Hellenic Mediterranean Lines (W www.hml.it)
Minoan Lines (W www.minoan.gr)
Superfast (W www.superfast.com)

The following ferry services are for high season (July and August), and prices are for one-way deck class. Deck class on these services means exactly that. If you want a reclining, aircraft-type seat, you'll be up for another 10% to 15% on top of the listed fares. Most companies offer discounts for return travel. Prices are about 30% less in low season.

Ancona The route from Ancona has become increasingly popular in recent years. There can be up to three boats daily in summer and at least one a day year-round. All ferry operators in Ancona have booths at the *stazione marittima* (ferry terminal) off Piazza Candy, where you can pick up timetables and price lists and make bookings.

Ferries from Italy to Patras at a Glance

origin	company	time (hours)	price (€)	frequency
Ancona	ANEK	21	64	daily
Ancona	Blue Star	21	64	daily
Ancona	Minoan	20–25	72	6 weekly
Ancona	Superfast	19–21½	78	2 daily
Bari	Superfast	15½	52	daily
Bari	Ventouris	17½	45.50	3 weekly
Brindisi	Hellenic Mediterranean	15	46	4 weekly
Brindisi	Med Link	14	44	daily
Trieste	ANEK	29–31	64	daily
Venice	Blue Star	34	58	4 weekly
Venice	Minoan	26–35	75	daily

Superfast Ferries (☎ 071-207 0218) provides the fastest and most convenient service. It also accepts Eurail passes. Pass users must pay port taxes and a high-season loading of €8.80 in July and August. **ANEK Lines** (☎ 071-207 2275) and **Blue Star Ferries** (☎ 071-207 1068) are about 10% cheaper.

Bari Superfast Ferries (☎ 080-52 11 416) also accepts Eurail passes on its daily Bari–Patras route.

Brindisi The route from Brindisi to Patras is the cheapest and quickest of the Adriatic crossings. There can be up to five boats daily in high season. Most travel via Corfu and Igoumenitsa.

Hellenic Mediterranean Lines (☎ 0831-528 531; Corso Garibaldi 8) accepts Eurail passes, although, if using a pass, you will still have to pay the port tax of €6.45 and a high-season loading of €8.80 in July and August. Hellenic Mediterranean issues vouchers for travel with **Med Link Lines**

(☎ 0831-548 116/7; represented by Discovery Shipping, Costa Morena), on days when there is no Hellenic Mediterranean service.

Trieste ANEK Lines (☎ 040-322 0561; Stazione Marittima di Trieste) has daily boats via Igoumenitsa.

Venice Minoan Lines (☎ 041-240 7101), Stazione Marittima 123) travels to Patras via Corfu and Igoumenitsa. **Blue Star Ferries** (☎ 041-277 0559, Stazione Marittima 123) sails via Igoumenitsa.

ORGANISED TOURS

If a package holiday of sun, sand and sea doesn't appeal to you, but you would like to holiday with a group, there are several companies that organise special-interest holidays in Greece, including the Peloponnese.

There are several UK companies specialising in package holidays to the Peloponnese, including **Laskarina** (☎ 01629-824 881) and **Greek Options** (☎ 020-7233 5233).

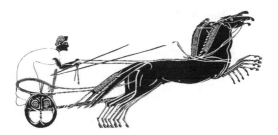

Getting Around

The Peloponnese is an easy place to travel around, thanks to a comprehensive public transport system.

AIR

There are no domestic flights within the Peloponnese. The only airport is at Kalamata; **Olympic Airways** (W *www.olympic -airways.gr*) operates flights between Athens and Kalamata for around €36/72 single/return (excluding airport tax).

BUS

Buses are the mainstay of public transport in the Peloponnese, with a network that reaches out to the smallest villages.

All long-distance buses are operated by regional collectives, which are known as KTEL (Koino Tamio Eispraxeon Leoforion). Each of the seven prefectures in the Peloponnese has its own KTEL, which operates services within the prefecture. They also operate services to the main towns of other prefectures and to Athens. You'll find details of the timetables for the prefectures of Argolis, Arcadia and Messinia on the Internet at W www.ktel.org. Fares are fixed by the government.

Most villages have a daily bus service of some sort, although in remote areas there may be only one or two buses a week. They operate for the benefit of people going to town to shop, rather than for tourists. The buses normally leave the villages very early in the morning and return early in the afternoon.

Larger towns usually have a central, covered bus station with seating, waiting rooms, toilets and a snack bar selling pies, cakes and coffee. Big cities like Athens and Patras have several bus stations, each serving different regions.

In small towns and villages the 'bus station' may be no more than a bus stop outside a *kafeneio* or taverna that doubles as a booking office. In remote areas, the timetable may be in Greek only, but most booking offices have timetables in both Greek and Roman script. The timetables give both the departure and return times – useful if you are making a day trip. Times are listed using the 24-hour clock system.

When you buy a ticket you will be allotted a seat number, noted on the ticket. The seat number is indicated on the back of each seat of the bus, not on the back of the seat in front; this causes confusion among Greeks and tourists alike. You can board a bus without a ticket and pay on board but, on a popular route or during the high season, this may mean that you have to stand. Keep your ticket for the duration of the journey; it will be checked several times en route.

It's best to turn up at least 20 minutes before departure to make sure you get a seat. Buses have been known to leave a few minutes before their scheduled departure time – another reason to give yourself plenty of time. Check the destination with the driver before you board the bus, and ensure your luggage has been placed in the hold.

Buses do not have toilets on board and they don't have refreshments available, so make sure you are prepared on both counts. Buses stop about every three hours on long journeys. Smoking is prohibited on all buses in Greece; only the drivers dare to ignore the 'no smoking' signs.

Bus fares are reasonably priced, with most journeys costing approximately €3.50 per 100km.

TRAIN

Most Greek people regard train travel as a poor alternative to road travel, although OSE (Organismos Sidirodromon Ellados, the Hellenic Railways Organisation) is gradually getting its act together and modernising its creaky rolling stock.

For starters, the rail system is not huge. The Peloponnese system uses a narrow-gauge track and exists quite independently of the main standard-gauge system connecting Athens with northern Greece.

There are also two very distinct levels of service: slow, stopping-all-stations services that crawl around the countryside and faster, modern, intercity trains.

The slow trains represent the country's cheapest form of public transport: 2nd-class fares are absurdly cheap and even 1st class is cheaper than bus travel. The downside is that the trains are painfully slow, uncomfortable and unreliable. There seems to be no effort o upgrade the dilapidated rolling stock on these services. Unless you are travelling on a very tight budget, they are best left alone – except on shorter runs. Sample journey times and fares on these trains include Athens–Patras (1st/2nd class €7.95/5.30, five hours) and Athens–Nafplio (2nd class only €4.70, 3½ hours).

The intercity trains which link the major cities are a much better way to travel. The services are not necessarily express – the Greek terrain is too mountainous for that – but the trains are modern and comfortable. There are 1st- and 2nd-class smoking/non-smoking seats and there is a café-bar on board. On some services, meals can be ordered and delivered to your seat.

Ticket prices for intercity services are subject to a distance loading on top of the normal fares. Seat reservations should be made as far in advance as possible, especially in summer. The Athens–Patras trip lasts for 3½ hours and costs €13.80/10.

Eurail and Inter Rail cards are valid in Greece, but it's not worth buying one if Greece is the only place you plan to use it. The passes can be used for 2nd-class travel on intercity services without paying the loading.

Another option if you're planning on using the trains a lot is to buy a tourist rail pass, which are available for individual passengers, as well as for families and groups of up to five people. They are valid for 10, 20 and 30 days (€43.15, €72.20 and €92.30, respectively) and entitle the holder to make an unlimited number of journeys on all the rail routes. Whatever pass you have, you must have a reservation. You cannot board a train without one.

Senior cards are available to passengers over 60 years of age on presentation of their IDs or passports. They cost €82.50 for 1st-class travel and €54.90 for 2nd class, and are valid for one year from the date of issue. Cardholders get a 50% reduction on train travel, plus five free journeys per year.

Tickets can be bought from OSE booking offices in a few major towns, otherwise from train stations. There is a 30% discount on return tickets and a 30% discount for groups of 10 or more.

You'll find information on fares and schedules on the Hellenic Railways Organisation website, w www.ose.gr.

CAR & MOTORCYCLE

No-one who has travelled on Greece's roads will be surprised to hear that the country's road-fatality rate is the highest in Europe. More than 2000 people die on the roads every year, with overtaking listed as the greatest cause of accidents. Ever-stricter traffic laws have had little impact on the toll; Greek roads remain a good place to practise your defensive-driving techniques.

Heart-stopping moments aside, your own car is a great way to explore off the beaten track. The road network has improved enormously in recent years; many roads marked as dirt tracks on older maps have now been asphalted – particularly in more remote mountain areas. It's important to get a good road map (see Maps under Planning in the Facts for the Visitor chapter, p35).

Greece is not the best place to initiate yourself into motorcycling; there are still a lot of gravel roads. Novices should be particularly careful; dozens of tourists have accidents every year.

There are two stretches of highway in the Peloponnese where tolls are levied: Corinth–Patras (€1.80) and Corinth–Tripolis (€2.65). The toll for the section of highway between Athens and Corinth is €1.50.

Petrol in Greece is expensive and the farther you get from a major city the more it costs. Prices vary from petrol station to petrol station. Super can be found as cheaply as €0.70 per litre at big city discount places but €0.75 to €0.85 is the normal range. You may pay closer to €0.90 per litre in remote areas. The price range for unleaded – available everywhere – is from €0.75 to €0.85 per litre. Diesel costs about €0.60 per litre.

See the Documents section in the Facts for the Visitor chapter, p37, for information

Road Distances (km)

	Athens	Corinth	Kalamata	Monemvasia	Nafplio	Patras	Sparta	Tripolis
Athens	---							
Corinth	84	---						
Kalamata	284	175	---					
Monemvasia	350	266	156	---				
Nafplio	165	63	163	215	---			
Patras	220	138	220	332	201	---		
Sparta	225	145	60	96	119	236	---	
Tripolis	194	110	90	157	81	176	61	---

Warning

If you are planning to use a motorcycle or moped, check that your travel insurance covers you for injury resulting from a motorbike accident. Many insurance companies don't offer this cover, so check the fine print!

on licence requirements and see the Useful Organisations section in the Facts for the Visitor chapter, p54, for information about the Greek automobile club (ELPA).

Road Rules

In Greece, as throughout Continental Europe, you drive on the right and overtake on the left. Outside built-up areas, traffic on a main road has right of way at intersections. In towns, vehicles coming from the right have right of way. Seat belts must be worn in front seats, and in back seats if the car is fitted with them. Children under 12 years of age are not allowed in the front seat. It is compulsory to carry a first-aid kit, fire extinguisher and warning triangle, and it is forbidden to carry cans of petrol. Helmets are compulsory for motorcyclists if the motorbike is 50cc or more.

Outside of residential areas the speed limit is 120km/h on highways, 90km/h on other roads and 50km/h in built-up areas. The speed limit for motorbikes up to 100cc is 70km/h and for larger motorbikes, 90km/h.

Drivers exceeding the speed limit by 20% are liable for a fine of €58.70; by 40%, €147. In practice, most tourists escape with a warning. Other offences and fines include

- going through a red light: €293.50
- illegal overtaking: €293.50
- driving without a seat belt: €147.75
- motorcyclist not wearing a helmet: €147.75
- driving the wrong way down a one-way street: €147.75
- illegal parking: €29.35

The police have also cracked down – at long last – on drink-driving laws. A blood-alcohol content of 0.05% is liable to incur a fine of €147.75 and over 0.08% is a criminal offence.

The police can issue traffic fines but payment cannot be made on the spot – you will be told where to pay.

If you are involved in an accident and no one is hurt, the police will not be required to write a report but it is advisable to go to a nearby police station and explain what happened. A police report may be required for insurance purposes. If an accident involves injury, a driver who does not stop and does not inform the police may face a prison sentence.

Rental

Car If the deadly driving has not put you off getting behind a wheel in Greece, then perhaps the price of hiring a car will. Rental cars are widely available but they are more expensive than in most other European countries. Most of the big multinational car-hire companies are represented in Athens.

The multinationals are, however, the most expensive places to hire a car. High season weekly rates with unlimited mileage start at about €380 for the smallest models such as a Fiat Seicento. The rate drops to about €300 per week in winter. To these prices must be added VAT of 18%. Then there are the optional extras, such as a collision damage waiver of €10 per day (more for larger models), without which you will be liable for the first €4400 of the repair bill (much more for larger models). Other costs include a theft waiver of at least €4.40 per day and personal accident insurance. It all adds up to an expensive exercise. The major companies offer much cheaper prebooked and prepaid rates.

You can find much better deals at some of the local companies. Their advertised rates can be up to 50% cheaper, and they are normally more open to negotiation, especially if business is slow.

If you want to take a hire car to another country or onto a ferry, you will need to have advance written authorisation from the hire company. Unless you pay with a credit card, most hire companies will require you to pay a minimum deposit of €120 per day. See the Getting Around sections of cities and islands in the appropriate chapters for details of places to rent cars.

The minimum driving age in Greece is 18 years, but most car-hire firms require you to be at least 21 – or 23 for larger vehicles.

Motorcycle Mopeds and motorcycles are available for hire wherever there are travellers to rent them. In many cases their maintenance has been minimal, so check the machine thoroughly before you hire it – especially the brakes: you'll need them!

Motorbikes are a cheap way to travel around. Rates range from €10 to €15 per day for a moped or 50cc motorbike to €25 per day for a 250cc motorbike. Out of season these prices drop considerably, so use your bargaining skills. By October it is sometimes possible to hire a moped for as little as €5 per day. Most motorcycle hirers include third-party insurance in the price but it's wise to check this. This insurance will not include medical expenses.

See Visas & Documents in the Facts for the Visitor chapter, p37, for information on moped and motorcycle licences.

BICYCLE

Cycling is a cheap, healthy, environmentally sound and, above all, fun way of travelling – and the Peloponnese is a region with a good reputation as a destination for cycling fans.

Cycling can be an excellent way to see the country, providing you pick the right time of year. It's too hot to cycle around in summer and it can get very cold in winter in the mountains but for the rest of the year conditions are ideal.

If you want a decent touring bike, you should bring your own. Bikes pose few problems for airlines. You can take it to pieces and put it in a bike bag or box but it's much easier simply to wheel it to the check-in desk, where it should be treated as a piece of baggage. You may have to remove the pedals and turn the handlebars sideways so that it takes up less space in the hold; check all this with the airline well in advance.

One note of caution: before you leave home, go over your bike with a fine-toothed comb and fill your repair kit with every imaginable spare. As with cars and motorbikes, you won't necessarily be able to buy spares for your machine if it breaks down in the middle of nowhere.

You can hire bicycles in some tourist places but they are not as widely available as cars and motorbikes. Prices range from €5.90 to €12 per day, depending on the type and age of the bike.

HITCHING

Hitching is never entirely safe in any country in the world and we don't recommend it. Travellers who decide to hitch should understand that they are taking a small but potentially serious risk. People who do choose to hitch will be safer if they travel in pairs and should let someone know where they are planning to go. Greece has a reputation for being a relatively safe place for women to hitch but it is still unwise to do it alone. It's better for a woman to hitch with a companion, preferably a male one.

Some parts of Greece are much better for hitching than others. Getting out of major cities tends to be hard work; Athens and Patras are both notoriously difficult. Hitching is much easier in remote areas. On country roads, it is not unknown for someone to stop and ask if you want a lift even if you haven't stuck a thumb out. You can't afford to be fussy about the mode of transport – it may be a tractor or a spluttering old truck.

WALKING

Unless you have come to Greece just to lie on a beach, the chances are you will do quite a bit of walking. You don't have to be a trekker to start clocking up the kilometres. The narrow, stepped streets of many towns and villages can only be explored on foot, and visiting the archaeological sites involves a fair amount of legwork. See the What to Bring, Health and Trekking sections in the Facts for the Visitor chapter, pp35, 47, 57, for more information about walking.

LOCAL TRANSPORT
Bus

Most towns are small enough for travellers to get around on foot. The only places where you may need to use local buses are Athens, Kalamata and Patras. The procedure for buying tickets for local buses is covered in the Getting Around section for each city.

Metro

Athens is the only city in Greece large enough to warrant an underground system. See the Athens chapter, p93, for details.

Taxi

Taxis are widely available in Greece except on very small or remote islands. They are reasonably priced by European standards, especially if three or four people share costs.

City cabs are metered. Flag fall is €0.74, followed by €0.24 per kilometre (€0.44 per kilometre outside town). These rates double between midnight and 5am. Costs additional to the per-kilometre rate are €1.18 from an airport, €0.59 from a bus, port or train station and €0.30 for each piece of luggage over 10kg. Grey rural taxis do not have meters, so you should always settle on a price before you get in.

The taxi drivers of Athens are legendary for their ability to part locals and tourists alike from their money. If you have a complaint about a taxi driver, take the cab number and report your complaint to the tourist police.

ORGANISED TOURS

Tours are worth considering only if your time is very limited, in which case there are countless companies vying for your money.

The major players are CHAT, GO Tours, Hop In Sightseeing and Key Tours, all based in Athens and offering almost identical tours. They include day trips to Delphi (€72) and Mycenae and Epidavros (€72). They also offer longer trips such as a four-day tour calling at Mycenae, Nafplio, Epidavros, Olympia and Delphi (€90 per day). These prices include twin-share accommodation and half board. See Organised Tours in the Athens chapter, p86, for more details.

Trekking

Trekking Hellas (☎ 21-0331 0323/26, fax 21-0323 4548; w www.trekking.gr; Filellinon 7, Athens) is a well-established company that specialises in treks and other adventure activities for small groups. It offers a wide range of treks in the Peloponnese lasting from one to nine days, including walking in the Lousios Gorge (€29, one day) and trekking the Taygetos foothills (€205, weekend).

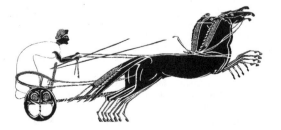

After admiring the views from the Acropolis...

...revive yourself in one of Plaka's tavernas

The splendour of the Parthenon: still breathtaking, even in ruins

Athens' street markets maintain the tradition of the *agora*

The 'face of Agamemnon', National Museum

Lose yourself in the local way of life

The Olympics get set to come full circle in 2004

Athens Αθήνα

postcode 102 00 (Omonia),
103 00 (Syntagma) • pop 3.7 million
Ancient Athens ranks alongside Rome and Jerusalem for its glorious past and its influence on Western civilisation, but the modern city is a place few people fall in love with.

However inspiring the Acropolis might be, most visitors have trouble coming to terms with the surrounding urban sprawl, the appalling traffic congestion and the pollution.

The city certainly is not without its redeeming features. The Acropolis remains one of the world's most inspiring sights, while the National Archaeological Museum stands tall among the great museums of the world.

Culturally, Athens is a fascinating blend of east and west. King Otto and the middle class that emerged after Independence may have been intent on making Athens a European city but the influence of Asia Minor is everywhere – the coffee, the kebabs, the raucous street vendors and the colourful markets.

HISTORY
The early history of Athens is so interwoven with mythology that it's hard to disentangle fact from fiction.

The Acropolis has been occupied since Neolithic times. It was an excellent vantage point and the steep slopes formed natural defences on three sides. By 1400 BC the Acropolis was a powerful Mycenaean city.

Its power peaked during the so-called golden age of Athens in the 5th century BC, after the defeat of the Persians at the Battle of Salamis. It fell into decline after its defeat by Sparta in the long-running Peloponnesian Wars, but rallied again in Roman times when it became a seat of learning. The Roman emperors, particularly Hadrian, graced Athens with many grand buildings.

After the Roman Empire split into east and west, power shifted to Byzantium and the city fell into obscurity. By the end of Ottoman rule, Athens was little more than a dilapidated village (the area now known as Plaka).

Then, in 1834, the newly crowned King Otto transferred his court from Nafplio and made Athens the capital of independent Greece. The city was rebuilt along neo-classical lines, featuring large squares and

Highlights

- Enjoying fine dining in the shadow of the Acropolis
- Exploring the world's finest collection of Greek antiquities at the National Archaeological Museum
- Listening to authentic *rembetika* in Athens' atmospheric clubs
- Catching a Greek tragedy at the annual Hellenic Festival

tree-lined boulevards with imposing public buildings. The city grew steadily and enjoyed a brief heyday as the 'Paris of the Mediterranean' in the late 19th and early 20th centuries.

This came to an abrupt end with the forced population exchange between Greece and Turkey that followed the Treaty of Lausanne in 1923. The huge influx of refugees from Asia Minor virtually doubled the population overnight, forcing the hasty erection of the first of the concrete apartment blocks that dominate the city today. The belated advent of Greece's industrial age in the 1950s brought another wave of migration, this time of rural folk looking for jobs.

The city's infrastructure, particularly road and transport, could not keep pace with such rapid and unplanned growth, and by the end of the 80s the city had developed a sorry reputation as one of the most traffic-clogged and polluted in Europe.

ATHENS

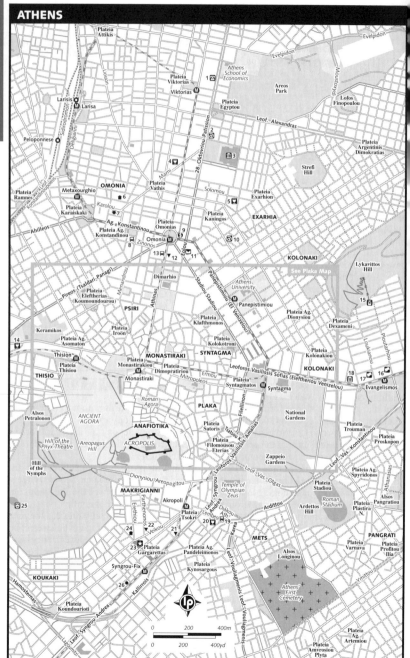

Plateia Attikis

Evelpidon

Evelpidon

Lofos Finopoulou

Athens School of Economics

1

Plateia Viktorias

Viktorias

Areos Park

Plateia Egyptou

Larisis

Larisa

Peloponnese

Leof.- Alexandras

Plateia Argentinis Dimokratias

2

3

Strefi Hill

4

OMONIA

Plateia Vathis

28 Oktovriou-Patission

Plateia Rammes

Metaxourghio

Plateia Karaiskaki

Karolou

6

7

Plateia Ag. Konstandinou

Plateia Omonias

Ahilleos

Ag. Konstantinou

8

Zinonos

Omonia

9

13

12

11

Solomou

Plateia Kaningos

5

Plateia Exarhion

EXARHIA

10

KOLONAKI

Lykavittos Hill

See Plaka Map

Dimarhio

Pireos (Tsaldari-Panagi)

Plateia Eleftherias (Koumoundourou)

PSIRI

Menandrou

Athinas

Panepistimiou (El Venizelou)

Stadiou

Athens University

Panepistimiou

Plateia Ag. Dionisiou

15

Plateia Dexameni

Keramikos

Plateia Ag. Asomaton

Plateia Iroön

Plateia Klafthmonos

14

Thision

Plateia Thisiou

THISIO

MONASTIRAKI

Plateia Monastirakiou

Monastiraki

SYNTAGMA

Plateia Kolokotroni

Leoforos Vasilissis Sofias (Eleftheriou Venizelou)

Plateia Kolonakiou

KOLONAKI

18

17

16

Evangelismos

Plateia Dimopratiriou

Mitropoleos

Ermou

Plateia Syntagmatos

Syntagma

Alsos Petralonon

Roman Agora

ANCIENT AGORA

PLAKA

Plateia Satoris

National Gardens

Hill of the Pnyx Theatre

Areopagus Hill

ACROPOLIS

ANAFIOTIKA

Plateia Filomousou Eterias

Plateia Trouman

Plateia Proskopon

Hill of the Nymphs

Dionysiou Areopagitou

Leoforos Vasilissis Amalias

Zappeio Gardens

Plateia Ag. Spyridonos

Alsos Pangratiou

25

MAKRIGIANNI

Akropoli

Parthenonos

Erehtiou

Temple of Olympian Zeus

Leof. Vas.- Olgas

Plateia Stadiou

Roman Stadium

Ardittou

Ardettos Hill

Plateia Plastira N.

PANGRATI

Plateia Varnava

Plateia Profitou Ilia

22

24

21

20

19

Plateia Tsokri

Lembesi

Veikou

METS

Athanasias

Ymittou

23

Plateia Gargarettas

Syngrou-Fix

Plateia Ag. Pandeleimonos

Plateia Kynosargous

Alsos Longinou

KOUKAKI

26

Kallirois

Athens' First Cemetery

Plateia Koundourioti

Leof. Syngrou Andrea

Plateia Ag. Artemiou

Plateia Amvrosiou Plyta

0   200   400m

0   200   400yd

ATHENS

PLACES TO STAY	OTHER		13	Bus No 049 to Piraeus
6 Athens International Youth Hostel	1	OTE main office	14	Plus Soda
	2	Museum Internet Cafe	15	Funicular
24 Art Gallery Hotel	3	National Archaeological Museum	16	British Embassy
			17	German Embassy
PLACES TO EAT	4	Rodon Club	18	Goulandris Museum of Cycladic & Ancient Greek Art
12 Marinopoulos Supermarket, Omonia	5	AN Club		
	7	OSE Office	19	Key Tours Office & Terminal
21 Taverna To 24 Hours	8	Bus No 051 to Bus Terminal A	20	Granazi Bar
	9	National Bank of Greece	23	Tourist Police
22 Veropoulos Supermarket	10	Bits & Bytes Internet Cafe	25	Dora Stratou Theatre
	11	Central Post Office	26	Olympic Airways

The 1990s appear to have been a turning point in the city's development. Jolted into action by the failed bid to stage the 1996 Olympics, authorities embarked on an ambitious programme to prepare the city for the 21st century. Two key elements in this programme have been an extension of the metro network and the construction of a new international airport.

These projects played an important role in the city's successful bid to stage the 2004 Olympics. (See the boxed text 'The Rocky Road to 2004', p91, for more about the Olympics.)

ORIENTATION

Although Athens is a huge, sprawling city, nearly everything of interest to short-term visitors is located within a small area bounded by Omonia Square (Plateia Omonias) to the north, Monastiraki Square (Plateia Monastirakiou) to the west, Syntagma Square (Plateia Syntagmatos) to the east and the Plaka district to the south. The city's two major landmarks, the Acropolis and Lykavittos Hill, can be seen from just about everywhere in this area.

Syntagma is the heart of modern Athens; it's flanked by luxury hotels, banks and expensive coffee shops and dominated by the old royal palace, home of the Greek parliament since 1935.

Omonia is destined to be transformed from a traffic hub into an expanse of formal gardens. This is guaranteed to increase traffic chaos, since all the major streets of central Athens meet here. Panepistimiou (El Venizelou) and Stadiou run parallel southeast to Syntagma, while Athinas leads south to the market district of Monastiraki.

Monastiraki is in turn linked to Syntagma by Ermou – home to some of the city's smartest shops – and Mitropoleos.

Mitropoleos skirts the northern edge of Plaka, the delightful old Turkish quarter that was virtually all that existed when Athens was declared the capital of independent Greece. Its labyrinthine streets are nestled on the northeastern slope of the Acropolis, and most of the city's ancient sites are close by. It may be touristy but it's the most attractive and interesting part of Athens and the majority of visitors make it their base.

Streets are clearly signposted in Greek and English. If you do get lost, it's very easy to find help. A glance at a map is often enough to draw an offer of assistance. Anyone you ask will be able to direct you to Syntagma (say **syn**-tag-ma).

INFORMATION
Tourist Offices

Athens' main office of the **Ellinikos Organismos Tourismou** (EOT; ☎ 21-0331 0561/ 0562, fax 21-0325 2895; e info@gnto.gr; Amerikis 2; open 9am-4pm Mon-Fri) is close to Syntagma. It has a useful timetable of the week's ferry departures from Piraeus and information about public transport prices and schedules from Athens. It also has a useful free map of Athens, which has most of the places of interest, and the main trolleybus routes, clearly marked. There is also an **EOT office at the airport** (☎ 21-0353 044; open 9am-9pm daily).

The **tourist police** (☎ 21-0920 0724; Veikou 43, Koukaki; trolleybus No 1, 5, 9 from Syntagma; open 24hrs) have a 24-hour information service, ☎ 171.

Money

Most of the major banks have branches around Syntagma and are open Monday to Thursday from 8am to 2pm and Friday from 8am to 1.30pm. The **National Bank of Greece** (cnr Karageorgi Servias & Stadiou, Syntagma; open for foreign-exchange dealings 3.30pm-6.30pm Mon-Thur, 3pm-6.30pm Fri, 9am-3pm Sat, 9am-1pm Sun) and **American Express** (☎ 21-0322 3380; Ermou 7, Syntagma; ·open 8.30am-4pm Mon-Fri, 8.30am-1.30pm Sat) are close by.

Eurochange (☎ 21-0322 0155; Karageorgi Servias 4, Syntagma; open 8am-8pm Mon-Fri, 10am-6pm Sat-Sun) changes Thomas Cook travellers cheques without commission.

The banks at the airport are open from 7am to 9pm.

Post & Communications

The **main post office** (Eolou 100, Omonia; open Mon-Fri 7.30am-8pm, Sat 7.30am-2pm, Sun 9am-1.30pm) is where mail addressed to poste restante will be sent unless specified otherwise. If you're staying in Plaka, it's best to get mail sent to the **Syntagma post office** (Plateia Syntagmatos 2), which is open the same hours. Parcels over 2kg going abroad must be posted from the **parcels office** (Stadiou 4, in the arcade). They should not be wrapped until they've been inspected.

The **Organismos Tilepikoinonion Ellados** (**OTE**) **telephone office** (28 Oktovriou-Patission 85; open 24hrs) is north of Omonia.

The following is a list of Internet cafés around the city centre. Most charge from €4 to €6 per hour of computer time, whether you're on the Net or not.

Bits & Bytes Internet Café Akadimias 78, Exarhia; open 24 hours
Museum Internet Café 28 Oktovriou-Patission 46, Omonia, next to National Archaeological Museum; open 9am-3am daily
Plaka Internet World Pandrosou 29, Monastiraki; open 11am-11pm daily
Skynet Internet Centre cnr Voulis & Apollonos, Plaka; open 9am-11pm Mon-Sat
Sofokleous.com Internet Café Stadiou 5, Syntagma, behind Flocafé; open 10am-10pm Mon-Sat, 1pm-9pm Sun

Travel Agencies

The bulk of the city's travel agencies are around Plateia Syntagmatos, particularly just south of it on Filellinon, Nikis and Voulis. Many of these agencies employ touts to roam the area looking for custom.

Reputable agencies include **STA Travel** (☎ 21-0321 1188, fax 21-0321 1194; e statravel@robissa.gr; Voulis 43, Syntagma) and **USIT-ETOS Travel** (☎ 21-0324 0483, fax 21-0322 8447; e usit@usitetos.gr; Filellinon 7, Syntagma). Both also issue International Student Identity Cards (ISIC).

Bookshops

Athens has four good English-language bookshops. The biggest is **Eleftheroudaki** (Panepistimiou 17, Syntagma & Nikis 20, Plaka). The others are **Pantelides Books** (Amerikis 11, Syntagma), **Compendium Books** (Nikis 28, Plaka) and **Booknest** (mezzanine level, arcade Panepistimiou 25-29, Syntagma). Compendium also has a second-hand books section. All of these shops stock Lonely Planet guides.

Cultural Centres

The **British Council** (☎ 21-0369 2314; Plateia Kolonakiou 17, Kolonaki) and the **Hellenic-American Union** (☎ 21-0362 9886; Massalias 22, Kolonaki) hold frequent concerts, film shows, exhibitions etc. Both also have libraries.

Laundry

Plaka has a convenient **laundrette** (Angelou Geronta 10, off Kydathineon), near the outdoor restaurants.

Medical Services

For emergency medical treatment, ring the tourist police (☎ 171) and they'll tell you where the nearest hospital is. Don't wait for an ambulance – get a taxi. Hospitals give free emergency treatment to tourists. For hospitals with outpatient departments on duty, ring ☎ 106. For first-aid advice, ring ☎ 166. For free emergency dental treatment go to the **Evangelismos Hospital** (Ipsilandou 45).

Dangers & Annoyances

Pickpockets A major problem in Athens is pickpockets. Their favourite hunting grounds are the metro system and the crowded streets around Omonia, particularly Athinas. The Sunday market on Ermou is another place where it pays to take extra good care of your valuables.

Bar Scams Lonely Planet receives a steady flow of letters warning about bar scams, particularly around Syntagma. The most popular version runs something like this: friendly Greek approaches solo male traveller and discovers that the traveller knows little about Athens; friendly Greek then reveals that he, too, is from out of town. Why don't they go to this great little bar that he's just discovered and have a beer? They order a drink and the equally friendly owner then offers another drink. Women appear, more drinks are provided and the visitor relaxes as he concludes that the women are not prostitutes, just friendly Greeks. The crunch comes at the end of the evening when the traveller is presented with an exorbitant bill and the smiles disappear. The con men who cruise the streets playing the role of the friendly Greek can be very convincing: some people have been taken in more than once.

THINGS TO SEE
Acropolis

Most of the buildings now gracing the Acropolis (☎ 21-0321 0291; adult/student €12/6 site & museum; site open 8am-6.30pm daily, museum open 8am-6.30pm Tues-Sun, noon-6.30pm Mon 1 Apr-31 Oct; site & museum open 8am-4.30pm daily Nov-Mar) were commissioned by Pericles during the golden age of Athens in the 5th century BC. The site had been cleared for him by the Persians, who destroyed an earlier temple complex on the eve of the Battle of Salamis.

The entrance to the Acropolis is through the **Beulé Gate**, a Roman arch that was added in the 3rd century AD. Beyond this is the **Propylaia**, the monumental gate that was the entrance in ancient times. It was damaged by Venetian bombing in the 17th century but it has since been restored. To the south of the Propylaia is the small, graceful **Temple of Athena Nike**, which is not accessible to visitors.

Standing supreme over the Acropolis is the monument that more than any other epitomises the glory of ancient Greece: the **Parthenon**. Completed in 438 BC, this building is unsurpassed in grace and harmony. To achieve perfect form, its lines were ingeniously curved to counteract optical illusions. The base curves upwards slightly towards the ends, and the columns become slightly narrower towards the top, with the overall effect of making them both look straight.

Above the columns are the remains of a Doric frieze, which was partly destroyed by Venetian shelling in 1687. The best surviving pieces are the controversial Elgin Marbles, carted off to Britain by Lord Elgin in 1801. The Parthenon, dedicated to Athena, contained an 11m-tall gold-and-ivory statue of the goddess completed in 432 BC by Phidias of Athens (only the statue's foundations exist today).

To the north is the **Erechtheion** with its much-photographed Caryatids, the six maidens who support its southern portico. These are plaster casts – the originals (except for the one taken by Lord Elgin) are in the site's museum.

The €12 admission charge buys a collective ticket that also gives entry to all the

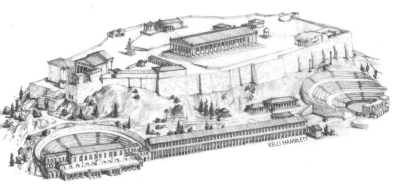

The Acropolis as it would have been at the height of its glory

other significant ancient sites: the Ancient Agora, the Roman Agora in Monastiraki, the Keramikos, the Temple of Olympian Zeus in Makrigianni and the Theatre of Dionysos. The ticket is valid for 48 hours, otherwise individual site fees apply.

Ancient Agora

The Agora (market; ☎ 21-0321 0185; western end of Adrianou; admission €4; open 8.30am-3pm Tues-Sun) was the marketplace of ancient Athens and the focal point of civic and social life. The main monuments are the well-preserved **Temple of Hephaestus**, the 11th-century **Church of the Holy Apostles** and the reconstructed **Stoa of Attalos**, which houses the site's museum (a good place to begin exploring the site).

Changing of the Guard

Every Sunday at 11am a platoon of traditionally costumed *evzones* (guards) marches down Vasilissis Sofias, accompanied by a band, to the Tomb of the Unknown Soldier in front of the **Parliament Building** on Syntagma.

National Archaeological Museum

The National Archaeological Museum (☎ 21-0821 7717; 28 Oktovriou-Patission 44; closed until April 2004) is one of the world's great museums, housing finds from all the major ancient sites around Greece. The main crowd-pullers are the magnificent, exquisitely detailed gold artefacts from Mycenae, including the famous Mask of Agamemnon, and the spectacular **Minoan frescoes** from Santorini (Thira). Sadly, it closed its doors for renovations in October 2002, and is scheduled to remain closed until April 2004.

Benaki Museum

The Benaki (☎ 21-0367 1000; cnr Vasilissis Sofias & Koumbari 1, Kolonaki; adult/student €5.90/2.95; open 9am-5pm Mon, Wed, Fri & Sat, 9am-midnight Thur, 9am-3pm Sun) houses the collection of Antoine Benaki, the son of an Alexandrian cotton magnate named Emmanual Benaki. It includes ancient sculpture, Persian, Byzantine and Coptic objects, Chinese ceramics, icons, two El Greco paintings and a superb collection of traditional costumes.

Goulandris Museum of Cycladic & Ancient Greek Art

This private museum (☎ 21-0801 5870; cnr Vasilissis Sofias & Neofytou Douka 4, Kolonaki; adult/student €2.95/1.50; open 10am 4pm Mon & Wed-Fri, 10am-3pm Sat) was custom-built to display a fabulous collection of Cycladic art, with an emphasis on the early Bronze Age. Particularly impressive are the beautiful marble figurines that inspired 20th-century artists such as Brancusi, Epstein, Modigliani and Picasso.

Lykavittos Hill

Pine-covered Lykavittos is the highest of the eight hills dotted around Athens. From the summit there are all-embracing views of the city, the Attic basin and the islands of Salamis and Aegina – pollution permitting.

The southern side of the hill is occupied by the posh residential suburb of Kolonaki. The main path to the summit starts at the top of Loukianou, or you can take the **funicular railway** (single/return €2/4, 9.15am 11.45pm daily) from the top of Ploutarhou.

ORGANISED TOURS

There are four main companies running organised tours around Athens: **Hop In Sightseeing** (☎ 21-0428 5500; Zanni 29, Piraeus) **CHAT** (☎ 21-0322 3137; Xenofontos 9), **GO Tours** (☎ 21-0921 9555; Diakou Athanassiou 20) and **Key Tours** (☎ 21-0923 3166/3266; Kaliroïs 4, Makrigianni).

Typical tours include a half-day sightseeing tour of Athens (€29.35), and Athens by Night (€40), which takes in the son et lumière (sound-and-light show) before a taverna dinner with folk dancing. You will find brochures for the tour companies everywhere; hotels often act as booking agents for at least one tour company and can offer substantial discounts on the official tour prices as a service to their customers – discounts that aren't available if you book directly. You will be informed of your pick-up point when you make your booking.

SPECIAL EVENTS

The annual **Hellenic Festival** is the city's most important cultural event, running from mid-June to late September. It features a line-up of international music, dance and theatre at the **Theatre of Herodes Atticus**. The setting is superb, backed by the floodlit Acropolis.

The festival also features performances at the famous Theatre of Epidavros in the Peloponnese, 2½ hours west of Athens. See the Epidavros section of the Argolis chapter, pp120–1, for more details.

Tickets for both venues can be bought at the **festival box office** (☎ 21-0322 1459, fax 21-0323 5172; **w** www.greekfestival.gr; Stadiou 4, Syntagma; open 8.30am-4pm Mon-Fri, 9am-2.30pm Sat). The box office opens three weeks before the start of the festival. There are student discounts for most performances on production of an ISIC.

The festival programme should be available on the festival website from the beginning of February.

PLACES TO STAY
Camping
Athens Camping (☎ 21-0581 4114, fax 21-0582 0353; Leoforos Athinon 198; adult/tent €4.70/3.55; open year-round) is 7km west of the city centre on the road to Corinth, making it the nearest camping ground to the city centre. It has reasonable facilities but nothing else going for it.

Hostels
Athens International Youth Hostel (☎ 21-0523 4170, fax 21-0523 4015; **e** info2002yh@yahoo.com; Victor Hugo 16, Omonia; members €8.40, joining fee €12.35, €2.05 for daily stamp) isn't situated in an overly salubrious location but otherwise this excellent HI-affiliated place is almost too good to be true. It occupies the former C-class Hotel Victor Ougo, which has been completely renovated: it even has double-glazed windows. The spotless rooms, with bathroom, sleep two to four people and include sheets and pillow cases. Facilities include a guest kitchen, Internet access, laundry and free safety-deposit boxes. There is no curfew.

Hotels
Plaka is the most popular place to stay, and it has a good choice of accommodation right across the price spectrum. Rooms fill up quickly in July and August, so it's wise to make a reservation.

Plaka The **Student & Travellers' Inn** (☎ 21-0324 4808, fax 21-0321 0065; **e** students-inn@ath.forthnet.gr; Kydathineon 16; dorms €18, singles/doubles €32/42, with bathroom

€36/52) occupies a converted nursing home and is a veritable maze of rooms large and small, some with fine old timber floors. The dorms here are good value, especially in the quieter months. All dorms share communal bathrooms. Rooms are heated in winter. Facilities include a courtyard with big-screen TV, Internet access and a travel service.

Acropolis House Pension (☎ 21-0322 2344, fax 21-0324 4143; Kodrou 6-8; singles/doubles with bathroom from €49.50/66) is a beautifully preserved 19th-century house retaining many original features. It boasts undoubtedly the most complex pricing structure in Athens, with discounts for stays of three days or more, supplements for air-con etc. All the rooms are heated in winter. Breakfast costs €4.95 per person.

Opposite the Acropolis House Pension, **Hotel Adonis** (☎ 21-0324 9737, fax 21-0323 1602; Kodrou 3; singles/doubles from €39/55.70) is a comfortable modern hotel that represents one of the best deals around. All the rooms come with air-con and TV. There are good views of the Acropolis from the 4th-floor rooms and from the rooftop bar. Prices include breakfast.

Monastiraki A friendly family-run place, **Hotel Tempi** (☎ 21-0321 3175, fax 21-0325 4179; **e** tempihotel@travelling.gr; Eolou 29; singles with shared bathroom €22, singles/doubles/triples with bathroom €27.90/37/44) was named one of the world's top 50 budget hotels by Britain's *Independent* newspaper. Yiannis and Katerina keep the place spotless, and the rooms at the front have balconies overlooking pretty Plateia Agia Irini with its flower market and church, not to mention views to the Acropolis. There is also a communal kitchen with a refrigerator and facilities for preparing hot drinks and snacks. Credit cards are accepted – unusual for a budget hotel.

If there were a prize for the best restoration job, it should go to the owners of the **Hotel Cecil** (☎ 21-0321 7909, fax 21-0321 8005; **e** cecil@netsmart.gr; Athinas 39; singles/doubles with bathroom €50/70.50). They have done a magnificent job of reviving this fine old hotel, with its beautiful, high, moulded ceilings and polished timber floors. The rooms are tastefully furnished and equipped with air-con and TV. Prices include breakfast.

ATHENS

PLAKA

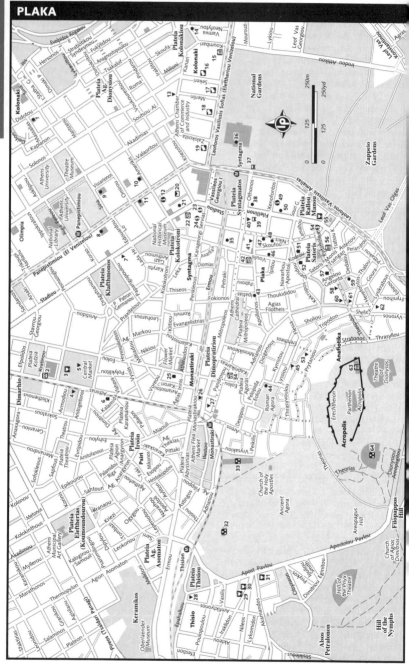

PLAKA

PLACES TO STAY		OTHER		32	Temple of Hephaestus
6	Hotel Cecil	1	Hellenic-American Union	33	Stoa of Attalos
25	Hotel Tempi	2	OTE	34	Plaka Internet World
51	Hotel Adonis	3	Rembetika Stoa Athinaton	35	American Express
52	Acropolis House Pension	8	Booknest	36	Parliament Building
57	Student & Travellers' Inn	9	OSE Syntagma Branch	37	Bus E95 to Airport
		10	Pantelides Books	38	USIT-Etos Travel
PLACES TO EAT		11	Eleftheroudakis Books	39	Bus No 040 to Piraeus
4	Fruit & Vegetable Market	12	EOT Main Tourist Office	42	Skynet Internet Centre
5	Meat Market	14	British Council	43	National Welfare
7	Vasilopoulou (Supermarket)	15	Benaki Museum		Organisation's Hellenic Folk
13	Marinopoulos Supermarket,	16	Italian Embassy		Art Gallery
	Kolonaki	17	Danish Embassy	44	Tower of the Winds
26	Savas	18	French Embassy	46	STA Travel
27	Thanasis	19	Egyptian Embassy	47	Eleftheroudakis Books
28	To Steki tou Elia	20	Parcel Post Office	48	Compendium
40	Neon Café	21	Athens Festival	49	CHAT Office
41	Furin Kazan Japanese		Box Office	50	Olympic Airways Branch
	Fast-Food Restaurant	22	Sofokleous.com	54	Eurochange
45	Eden Vegetarian Restaurant		Internet Café	55	Lava Bore
53	Taverna tou Psara	23	National Bank of Greece	56	Museum of Greek
58	Taverna Vizantino	24	Eurochange		Folk Art
60	Plaka Psistaria	29	Stavlos	59	Laundrette
61	Brettos	30	Berlin Club	63	Acropolis Museum
62	Daphne Restaurant	31	To Lizard	64	Theatre of Herodes Atticus

Koukaki A small, friendly place that's full of personal touches – like fresh flowers – the **Art Gallery Hotel** (☎ 21-0923 8376, fax 21 0923 3025; e ecotec@otenet.gr; Erehthiou 5; singles/doubles/triples with bathroom €58.60/70.40/84.50) is run by the brother-and-sister team of Ada and Yannis Assimakopoulos, who are full of information about the city. The rooms are heated in winter, when cheaper long-term rates are available.

PLACES TO EAT

Plaka For most people, Plaka is the place to be. It's hard to beat dining out beneath the floodlit Acropolis.

Taverna Vizantino (☎ 21-0322 7368; Kydathineon 18; mains €3.50-12) is the best of the outdoor restaurants around the square on Kydathineon. It prices its menu realistically and is popular with locals year-round. The daily specials are good value.

The **Eden Vegetarian Restaurant** (☎ 21-0324 8858; Lyssiou 12; mains €5.60-8.50; closed Tues) is unchallenged as the best vegetarian restaurant in Athens. It's been around for years, substituting soya products for meat in tasty vegetarian versions of moussaka (€4.70), and other Greek favourites. You'll also find vegie burgers (€5.30), mushroom

stifado (€8.50) and organically produced beer and wine.

Tucked away from the main hustle and bustle of the main tourist streets, **Taverna tou Psara** (☎ 21-0321 8734; Erehtheos 16; mains €12-17.35) is a cut above the Plaka crowd. The menu includes a fabulous choice of mezedes – the melizanakeftedes (aubergine croquettes; €5.30) are particularly good. You'll need to get in early to secure a table on the terrace, which has views out over the city.

Daphne Restaurant (☎ 21-0322 7971; Lysikratous 4; mains €11.75-17; open from 7pm nightly) is where former US First Lady Hillary Clinton and daughter Chelsea dined during their one-night stopover in 1996 on their way to light the Olympic flame at Olympia. It's an exquisitely restored 1830s neoclassical mansion decorated with frescoes from Greek mythology. The menu includes regional specialities like rabbit cooked in mavrodafni wine.

Syntagma Fast food is the order of the day around busy Syntagma, with an assortment of Greek and international offerings.

Neon Café (☎ 21-0324 6873; Mitropoleos 3, southwest cnr Plateia Syntagmatos; mains €3.40-5.75) is a stylish modern cafeteria with a good selection of meals, as well as coffee and cakes. You'll find spaghetti or fettucine napolitana for €3.40, or bolognese/carbonara for €4.40. Main dishes include *moussaka* (€4.25), roast beef with potatoes (€4.70) and pork kebab (€5.75).

It's reassuring to see that the **Furin Kazan Japanese Fast-Food Restaurant** (☎ 21-0322 9170; Apollonos 2; mains €5-16; open 11am-11pm Mon-Sat) is always full of Japanese visitors, obviously enjoying the food at the cheapest and best Japanese restaurant in town. There's a selection of rice and noodle dishes as well as old favourites like chicken yakitori, but it's the sashimi and sushi trays that steal the show.

Makrigianni Something of an institution among Athenian night owls, the **Taverna To 24 Hours** (☎ 21-0922 2749; Syngrou 44; mains €4-6.50; open 24hrs) never closes, except on Easter Sunday, and seems to be at its busiest in the wee small hours. The customers are as much of an attraction as the food: you'll be rubbing shoulders with an assortment of hungry cabbies, middle-aged couples dressed for the opera and leather-clad gays from the area's many bars, all tucking into steaming bowls of the house speciality: *patsas* (tripe soup). It also has a constantly changing choice of other popular taverna dishes.

Monastiraki There are some excellent cheap places around Monastiraki, particularly for *gyros* and *souvlaki* fans. **Thanasis** and **Savas**, opposite each other at the western end of Mitropoleos, are the places to go.

Thisio Cholesterol junkies in need of a hit should check out **To Steki tou Elia** (☎ 21-0345 8052; Epahalkou 5; mains €4.50-6), which specialises in lamb chops. Locals swear that they are the best in Athens and the place has achieved a sort of celebrity status. Eat here with Greek friends and they will constantly be pointing out famous personalities rolling up their sleeves to tuck into great piles of chops and a few jars of retsina. There are pork chops (€6) and steaks (€5.50) for those who don't eat lamb, as well as dips, chips and salads.

Self-Catering The following is a selection of supermarkets around central Athens:

Marinopoulos (Kanari 9, Kolonaki • Athinas 60, Omonia) **Vasilopoulou** (Stadiou 19, Syntagma) and **Veropoulos** (Parthenonos 6, Koukaki).

For the best range of fresh fruit and vegetables, head for the markets on Athinas They are opposite the meat and fish markets.

ENTERTAINMENT

The best source of entertainment information is the weekly listings magazine *Athenorama*, but you'll need to be able to read some Greek to make much sense of it. English-language listings appear daily in the *Kathimerini* supplement that accompanies the *International Herald Tribune*.

Bars

Most bars around Plaka and Syntagma are places to avoid, especially if there are guys outside touting for customers, but there are some gems out there.

Brettos (☎ 21-0323 2110; Kydathineon 41) is a delightful little place right in the heart of Plaka. Very little has changed here in years, except that being old-fashioned has suddenly become very fashionable. It's a family-run business that acts as a shop front for the family distillery and winery in Kalithea. Huge old barrels line one wall, and the shelves are stocked with a colourful collection of bottles that is backlit at night. Shots of Brettos-brand spirits (ouzo, brandy and many more) cost €1.80, as does a glass of wine.

Most bars in Athens have music as a main feature. Thisio is a good place to look, particularly on Iraklidon.

Stavlos (☎ 21-0345 2502; Iraklidon 10, Thisio) has a rock bar playing mainly alternative British music and more mellow sounds in the café/brasserie outside. Next door, the **Berlin Club** (☎ 21-0671 5455; Iraklidon 8, Thisio) is known for its special theme nights, which you'll see advertised around town.

Clubs

Clubs operate in central Athens between October and April only. In summer the action moves to the coastal suburbs of Glyfada and Ellinikon.

The **Lava Bore** (☎ 21-0324 5335; Filellinon 25; admission €6, includes free drink; open 10pm-5pm daily) is one city-centre

The Rocky Road to 2004

The eyes of the world will be upon Athens for 17 days in August 2004 when athletes from some 200 countries descend on the city for the 29th Olympiad.

It will be the end of a dramatic seven years of an emotional roller-coaster ride for the people of Athens. Back in 1997, when the city won the right to host the games, there was jubilation that the games were coming home to Greece after 108 years. Slowly but surely the magnitude of the task ahead began to sink in – and jubilation gave way to anxiety. Anxiety was replaced by alarm after Sydney raised the organisational standard to new heights in 2000.

Progress has been exasperatingly slow and some major public works projects have been scaled back before leaving the drawing board. The International Olympic Committee remains publicly optimistic that preparations are almost on track.

The Olympics seem sure to be a source of constant anxiety right up until the opening ceremony, but Greece is deeply committed – emotionally and financially – to making them work.

For the latest official progress reports, log on to Athens 2004 (W www.athens.olympic.org).

Rock & Jazz Concerts

The **Rodon Club** (Marni 24, north of Omonia) hosts touring international rock bands, while local bands play at the **AN Club** (Solomou 20, Exarhia).

Rembetika Clubs

The best-known of the clubs is the almost legendary **Rembetiki Stoa Athanaton** (π 21-0321 4362; Sofokleous 19, Dimhario; open 3pm-6pm & midnight-6am Mon-Sat, Oct-mid-May), which occupies a hall above the central meat market. Despite its strange location, it features some of the biggest names on the local *rembetika* scene. Access is by a lift in the arcade at Sofokleous 19.

Greek Folk Dances

The **Dora Stratou Dance Company** (π 21-0921 6650; Dora Stratou Theatre, Filopappos Hill; adult/child €12/6; performances 10.15pm daily, 8.15pm Wed & Sun, May-Oct) has earned an international reputation for authenticity and professionalism, performing a wide selection of dances from around the country. The theatre is signposted from the western end of Dionysiou Areopagitou. Tickets can be bought at the door.

Son et Lumière

The 'sound-and-light' spectacle (π 21-0322 1459; Hill of the Pnyx Theatre; adult/child €8.80/4.40; English shows 9pm nightly, French shows 10pm Wed, Thur, Sat-Mon, German shows 10pm Tues & Fri, Apr-end Oct) is not one of the world's best, but it is an enduring and integral part of the Athens tourist scene. The Hill of the Pnyx is west of the Acropolis off Dionysiou Areopagitou.

club that stays open year-round, although Filellinon 25 is its third address in five years. The formula remains much the same: a mixture of mainstream rock and techno and large beers for €3.

Gay & Lesbian Venues

The greatest concentration of gay bars is to be found around Makrigianni, south of the Temple of Olympian Zeus.

The **Granazi Bar** (π 21-0924 4185; Lembesi 20, Makrigianni; open 11pm-4am) has long been at the forefront of the gay scene. These days, the ambience is Pet Shop Boys – played at a volume that permits only body language. It's popular with the under-35 crowd, who come to party.

To Lizard (Apostolou Pavlou 3, Thisio; open from 11pm Fri-Sun) is a party bar that attracts a mostly lesbian crowd, with a few gays and the occasional straight; you can even see the Acropolis while dancing.

SPECTATOR SPORTS

Almost half of the 18 teams in the Greek soccer first division are based in Athens or Piraeus. The most popular are Olympiakos (Piraeus) and Panathinaikos (Athens). For details on seeing a match, see Spectator Sports in the Facts for the Visitor chapter, p65.

SHOPPING

The **National Welfare Organisation's Hellenic Folk Art Gallery** (cnr Apollonos & Ipatias, Plaka) is a good place to shop for handicrafts. It has top-quality goods and the money goes to a good cause – to preserve and promote traditional Greek handicrafts.

GETTING THERE & AWAY
Air
Athens is served by Eleftherios Venizelos International airport at Spata, 21km east of Athens.

For Olympic Airways flight information ring ☎ 21-0936 3363, and for all other airlines ring ☎ 21-0969 4466/7. The **head office of Olympic Airways** *(☎ 21-0926 7251; Leoforos Syngrou 96)* is in Koukaki, while the most central **Olympic Airways branch office** *(☎ 21-0926 7444, international ☎ 21-0926 7489; Filellinon 13, Syntagma)* is just off Plateia Syntagmatos.

Bus
Athens has two main intercity bus stations. Buses to the Peloponnese leave from **Terminal A**, which is northwest of Plateia Omonias at Kifissou 100. To get there, take bus No 051 from the junction of Zinonos and Menandrou, near Omonia. Buses run every 15 minutes from 5am to midnight. **Terminal B** *(5km north of Omonia off Liossion)* handles departures to central and northern Greece.

The EOT gives out schedules for both terminals with departure times and fares.

The following buses for the Peloponnese leave from Terminal A.

to	duration (hrs)	price (€)	frequency
Argos	2	7.70	hourly
Corinth	1½	5.70	half-hourly
Epidavros	2½	8.40	2 daily
Gythio	4¼	15.10	5 daily
Kalamata	3½	14.30	9 daily
Kalavryta	3½	10.90	daily
Monemvasia	5½	18.65	4 daily
Nafplio	2½	8.50	hourly
Olympia	5½	19.05	4 daily
Patras	3	12.25	half-hourly
Pylos	5½	17.45	2 daily
Pyrgos	5	17.70	10 daily
Sparta	3¼	12.65	11 daily
Tripolis	2¼	10.35	12 daily

Trains
Athens also has two train stations, located about 300m apart about 1km northwest of Plateia Omonias. Trains to the Peloponnese leave from the Peloponnese station on Sidiromon, while Larisis station, on Deligianni, handles trains to the north and all international services.

The easiest way to get to the stations i on metro line 2 to Larisa, outside Larisi station. The Peloponnese station is acros the footbridge at the southern end of Lari sis station. Tickets can be bought at the sta tions or at the OSE offices at Sina 6 an Karolou 1.

The following trains leave from Pelo ponnese station.

to	duration (hrs)	price (€)	frequency (daily)
Argos	3	3.85	5
Corinth	1¾	2.95	10
Corinth*	1½	5.30	5
Kalamata	6½	7.35	4
Nafplio	3½	4.70	2
Patras	4½	5.30	4
Patras*	3½	10.00	4
Pyrgos	6½	7.20	4
Pyrgos*	5	16.15	3
Tripolis	4	5.30	3

* Intercity service

Car & Motorcycle
National Road 8 is the road to the Peloponnese. Take Agiou Konstantinou from Plateia Omonias and keep following the signs.

The northern reaches of Leoforos Andrea Syngrou, just south of the Temple of Olympian Zeus, are packed solid with car-rental firms.

Hitching
Athens is the most difficult place in Greece to hitchhike from. For the Peloponnese take a bus from Panepistimiou station to Dafni, where National Road 8 begins.

Boat
You can't catch a boat to anywhere from Athens; they depart from Piraeus. See Getting to the Peloponnese in the Piraeus section, p95, for information on ferries and hydrofoils.

GETTING AROUND
To/From the Airport
There are two special express bus services operating between the airport and the city, as well as a service between the airport and Piraeus.

Service E94 operates between the airport and the eastern terminus of metro line 3 at

Ethniki Amyna. There are departures every 16 minutes, according to the official timetable, between 6am and midnight. The journey takes about 25 minutes.

Service E95 operates between the airport and Plateia Syntagmatos. This line operates 24 hours, with services approximately every 30 minutes. The bus stop is outside the National Gardens on Leoforos Vasilissis Amalias on the eastern side of Plateia Syntagmatos. The journey takes between an hour and 90 minutes, depending on traffic conditions.

Service E96 operates between the airport and Plateia Karaïskaki in Piraeus. This line also operates 24 hours, with services approximately every 40 minutes.

Tickets for all of these services cost €2.95. The tickets are valid for 24 hours and can be used on all forms of public transport in Athens: buses, trolleybuses and the metro. Tickets are sold at the kiosk next to the airport bus stop.

Taxi fares vary according to the time of day and level of traffic but you should expect to pay €15 to €20 from the airport to the city centre and €20 to €25 to Piraeus, depending on traffic conditions. Both trips should take no longer than an hour.

Bus & Trolleybus

Blue-and-white suburban buses operate from 5am to midnight. Route numbers and destinations, but not the actual routes, are listed on the free EOT map. The map does mark the routes of the yellow trolleybuses, making them easy to use. They also run from 5am to midnight.

There are special buses that operate 24 hours a day to Piraeus. Bus No 040 leaves from the corner of Syntagma and Filellinon, and No 049 leaves from the Omonia end of Athinas. They run every 20 minutes from 5am to midnight, and then hourly.

Tickets for all these services cost €0.45, and must be purchased before you board – either from a ticket booth or from a *periptero* (kiosk). The same tickets can be used on buses or trolleybuses and must be validated as soon as you board. The penalty for travelling without a validated ticket is €18.

Metro

The opening of the first phase of the long-awaited new metro system has transformed

travel around central Athens. Coverage is still largely confined to the city centre but that's good enough for most visitors. The following is a brief outline of the three lines that make up the network:

Line 1 This is the old Kifissia–Piraeus line. Until the opening of lines 2 and 3, this was the metro system. It is indicated in green on maps and signs. Useful stops include Piraeus (for the port), Monastiraki and Omonia (city centre), Viktorias (National Archaeological Museum) and Irini (Olympic Stadium). Omonia and Attiki are transfer stations with connections to line 2; Monastiraki will eventually become a transfer station with connections to line 3.

Line 2 This line runs from Sepolia in the northwest to Dafni in the southeast. It is indicated in red on maps and signs. Useful stops include Larisa (for the train stations), Omonia, Panepistimiou and Syntagma (city centre) and Akropoli (Makrigianni). Attiki and Omonia are transfer stations for line 1, while Syntagma is the transfer station for line 3.

Line 3 This line runs northeast from Syntagma to Ethniki Amyna. It is indicated in blue on maps and signs. Useful stops are Evangelismos (for the museums on Vasilissis Sofias) and Ethniki Amyna (buses to the airport). Syntagma is the transfer station for line 2.

Travel on lines 2 and 3 costs €0.75, while the fare for line 1 is split into three sections: Piraeus–Monastiraki, Monastiraki–Attiki and Attiki–Kifissia. Travel within one section costs €0.60, and a journey covering two or more sections costs €0.75. The same conditions apply everywhere: tickets must be validated at the machines at platform entrances before travelling. The penalty for travelling without a validated ticket is €23.50.

The trains operate between 5am and midnight. They run every three minutes during peak periods, dropping to every 10 minutes at other times.

Taxi

Athenian taxis are yellow. The flag fall is €0.75, with a €0.60 surcharge from ports and railway and bus stations, and a €0.90 surcharge from the airport. The day rate (tariff 1 on the meter) is €0.23 per kilometre. The rate doubles between midnight and 5am (tariff 2 on the meter). Baggage is charged at the rate of €0.30 per item over 10kg. The minimum fare is €1.50, which covers most journeys in central Athens.

Piraeus Πειραιάς

postcode 185 01 • pop 175,697

Piraeus (pir-ay-**ahs**), 10km southwest of central Athens, has been the port of Athens since classical times and is one of the major ports of the Mediterranean.

In ancient times, the two were linked by defensive walls; nowadays, Athens has expanded sufficiently to meld imperceptibly into Piraeus. The road linking the two passes through a grey, urban sprawl of factories, warehouses and concrete apartment blocks. The streets are every bit as traffic-clogged as those in Athens, and behind the veneer of banks and shipping offices most of Piraeus is pretty seedy. The only reason to come here is to catch a ferry or hydrofoil.

Orientation & Information

Most services of interest to travellers can be found around Great Harbour (Megas Limin). Located on the western side of the Piraeus Peninsula, it is the departure point for all ferry and hydrofoil services from Piraeus. The other two harbours, the Mikrolimano and Zea Marina, are on the eastern side of the peninsula and are reserved for yachts.

The metro line from Athens terminates at the northeastern corner of the Great Harbour on Akti Kalimassioti. Most ferry departure points are a short walk from here. A left turn out of the metro station leads after 250m to Plateia Karaïskaki, which is the terminus for buses to the airport.

Southeast of Plateia Karaïskaki, the waterfront becomes Akti Poseidonos, which leads into Vasileos Georgiou beyond Plateia Themistokleous. Vasileos Georgiou is one of the two main streets of Piraeus, running southeast across the peninsula; the other main street is Iroön Polytehniou, which runs southwest along the ridge of the peninsula, meeting Vasileos Georgiou by the main square, Plateia Korai.

Money There are lots of places to change money at the Great Harbour, including virtually all the ticket and travel agencies. The **Emporiki Bank** *(cnr Antistaseos & Makras Stoas)*, just north of Plateia Themistokleous, has a 24-hour automatic exchange machine. The **National Bank of Greece** *(cnr Antistaseos & Tsamadou)*, is 50m further north.

Post & Communications The main post office *(cnr Tsamadou & Filonos; open 7.30am-8pm Mon-Fri, 7.30am-2pm Sat)* is just north of Plateia Themistokleous. The **OTE** *(Karaoli 19; open 24hrs)* is just north of the main post office.

You can check email at the **Surf Internet Café** *(Platanos 3; open 8am-9pm Mon-Fri, 8am-3pm Sat)*, just off Iroön Polytehniou.

Places to Stay

There's no reason to stay at any of the shabby hotels around Great Harbour when Athens is so close. The cheap hotels are geared more towards accommodating sailors than travellers.

Places to Eat

There are dozens of fast-food places along the waterfront at Great Harbour.

You'll find fresh fruit and vegetables at the **markets** on Demosthenous. Opposite them is **Pairaikon supermarket** *(☎ 21-0411 7177; open 8am-8pm Mon-Fri, 8am-4pm Sat)*.

Getting There & Away

Bus There are two 24-hour bus services between central Athens and Piraeus. Bus No 049 runs from Omonia to the Great Harbour, and bus No 040 runs from Syntagma to the tip of the Piraeus Peninsula. The fare is €0.45 on each service. There are no intercity buses to or from Piraeus.

E96 buses to the airport leave from the southern side of Plateia Karaïskaki.

Train Railway services to the Peloponnese actually start and terminate at Piraeus, although most schedules don't mention it. See the Getting There & Away section for Athens, p92, for more information about trains.

Metro The metro is the fastest, easiest way of getting from the Great Harbour to central Athens (see the Getting Around section for Athens, p93). The station is at the northern end of Akti Kalimassioti.

Getting Around

Local bus Nos 904 and 905 run between the Great Harbour and Zea Marina. They leave from the bus stop beside the metro at Great Harbour, and drop you by the maritime museum at Zea Marina.

Getting to the Peloponnese

Ferry Few people use ferries to travel to the Peloponnese, although there are a couple of interesting – if roundabout – possibilities.

There are at least four ferries daily from Great Harbour to the port of Methana (€6, 2½ hours), on the east coast of Argolis. They continue to the Saronic Gulf island of Poros (€6.45, 2½ hours), opposite the town of Galatas – just south of Methana. Two ferries daily keep going to Hydra (€7.35, 3½ hours), and one goes all the way to Spetses (€10, 4½ hours). These ferries leave from the quay between Plateia Karaïskaki and Plateia Themistokleous.

There are also two ferries a week to the island of Kythira, which lies opposite the port of Neapoli at the southeastern tip of Lakonia.

Hydrofoil & Catamaran Hellas Flying Dolphins operates hydrofoils to a number of ports along the east coast of Peloponnese from early April to the end of October.

There are four services a day to Ermioni (€15.85, two hours), at least four to Porto Heli (€17, 2¼ hours) and daily services to Leonidio (€21.15, 2½ hours), Kyparissi (€22.30, three hours), Gerakas (€23.80, 3½ hours) and Monemvasia (€26.15, four hours). These services also call at the Saronic Gulf islands of Poros (€12.35, one hour), Hydra (€13.80, 1¼ hours) and Spetses (€19.10, two hours).

Tickets should be bought in advance from the **Hellas Flying Dolphins Booking Centre** (☎ 21-0419 9100; w www.dolphins .gr, cnr Akti Kondyli & Aitolikou Str).

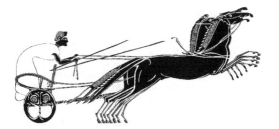

Corinthia Κορινθία

Corinthia occupies a strategic position adjoining the Isthmus of Corinth. The region was once dominated by the mighty, ancient city of Corinth, now one of its main attractions. Few travellers opt to linger long, although there are several minor sites in the pretty hinterland west of Corinth that are worth a detour if you have your own transport.

CORINTH Κόρινθος
postcode 201 00 • pop 29,787

Modern Corinth (in Greek, Korinthos; **ko**-rin-thoss), 6km west of the Corinth Canal, is the dull administrative capital of Corinthia prefecture. It was rebuilt here after the old town was destroyed by an earthquake in 1858. The new town was wrecked by another, equally violent, earthquake in 1928 and badly damaged again in 1981.

The modern town is dominated by concrete buildings built to withstand future earthquakes but it has a pleasant harbour, friendly people, tasty food and warrants an overnight stay because of its proximity to ancient Corinth and Nemea. Old Corinth is a mere village near the ancient site.

Orientation & Information
It is not difficult to negotiate Corinth, which is laid out on a grid of wide streets stretching back from the waterfront. Social activity centres around the large square by the harbour, Plateia El Venizelou, while transport and administrative activity is based around the small park 200m inland on Ethnikis Antistaseos.

There is no EOT (Ellinikos Organismos Tourismou, the Greek National Tourist Organization) office in Corinth. The **tourist police** (☎ 2741-023 282; Ermou 51; open 8am-2pm & 5pm-8pm daily May-Oct) and the regular **police** (☎ 2741-022 143) are in the same building, located across the road from the park. The National Bank of Greece is one of several banks on Ethnikis Antistaseos, the post office is on the edge of the park at Adimantou 33, and the OTE (Organismos Tilepikoinonion Ellados, the Greek telephone service operator) office is nearby on the corner of Kolokotroni and Adimantou.

Highlights
- Clambering through the columns of ancient Corinth
- Cruising down the Corinth Canal, which was 1800 years in the making!
- Exploring the Sanctuary of Zeus at Nemea

You can check email at the **Virtual Café** (☎ 2741-080 355; Ethnikis Antistaseos 3; open 10am-1am daily), and at **Stretto Internet Café** (☎ 2741-025 570; Pilarinou 70; open 8am-midnight Mon-Sat, 11am-midnight Sunday). Both charge €2.95 per hour (€1.50 minimum).

Folk Museum
The Folk Museum (☎ 2741-025 352; Ermou 1; admission €1.50; open 8.30am-1.30pm Tues-Sun), to the south of the wharf, focuses on bridal and festive costumes from the past three centuries. There are costumes from the islands and the mainland, metalwork, embroidery, gold and silver objects, and carvings, both secular and ecclesiastical.

Places to Stay
There are good camping grounds both east and west of Corinth, close to the sites of the ancient ports that served the ancient city.

Blue Dolphin Campground (☎ 2741-085 766/767, fax 2741-085 959; e skoupos@otenet.gr; adult/tent €4.55/2.80) is about

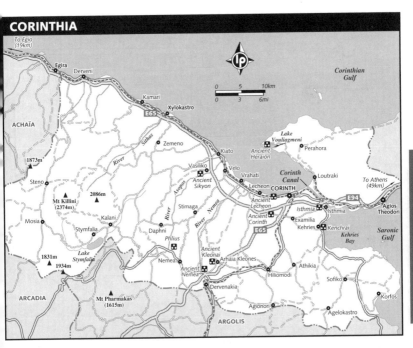

CORINTHIA

CORINTHIA

4km west of town just beyond the ruins of the ancient port of Lecheon. It's a well-organised site with its own stretch of Gulf of Corinth pebble beach. Buses from Corinth to Lecheon can drop you here.

Isthmia Beach Camping (☎ 2741-037 447/720, fax 2741-037 710; e isthmia@ otenet.gr; adult/tent €4.70/2.65, caravans for rent €5.90) is about 6km southeast of Corinth, close to the ruins of ancient Kenchrai. This is another excellent site, with lots of shade and green areas, plus a curve of secluded beach.

The rooms aren't the greatest, but the **Hotel Akti** (☎ 2741-023 337; Ethnikis Antistaseos 1; singles/doubles with bathroom €15/25) represents reasonable value at the price.

The **Hotel Apollon** (☎ 2741-022 587, fax 2741-083 875; Pirinis 18; singles/doubles with bathroom €41/55) is the best budget option in town. All the rooms are equipped with air-con and TV.

Architecturally, **Hotel Ephira** (☎ 2741-024 021, fax 2741-024 514; Ethnikis Antistaseos 52; singles/doubles/triples with bathroom €46/80/99) is probably the most boring building in town, but it houses the best rooms – they are comfortably furnished with air-con and TV. Breakfast is available for €5.

Hotel Corinthos (☎ 2741-026 701, fax 2741-023 693; Damaskinou 26; singles/ doubles with bathroom €42/50) has pleasant rooms with bathrooms and balconies.

The **Hotel Konstatatos** (☎ 2741-022 120, fax 2741-085 634; cnr Damaskinou & Dervenakion; singles/doubles with bathroom €47/52.85) seems to exist in some sort of 1950s time warp; it's a quaint, old-fashioned place with stuffed foxes in the foyer. The rooms are clean and comfortable, and the rates are negotiable.

Places to Eat
Just back from the waterfront near the Folk Museum, **Taverna O Theodorakis** (☎ 2741-022 578; Seferi 8; mains €2.95-8.80, fresh fish €20.55 per kg; open year-round) is a lively place specialising in fresh grilled fish. You can have a plate of sardines for €2.95, a large Greek salad for €2.95 and a litre of retsina for €2.35. It has outdoor seating in summer.

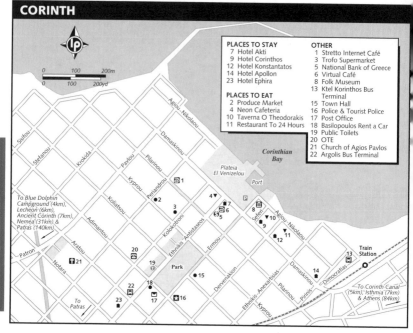

CORINTH

PLACES TO STAY
7 Hotel Akti
9 Hotel Corinthos
12 Hotel Konstantatos
14 Hotel Apollon
23 Hotel Ephira

PLACES TO EAT
2 Produce Market
4 Neon Cafeteria
10 Taverna O Theodorakis
11 Restaurant To 24 Hours

OTHER
1 Stretto Internet Café
3 Trofo Supermarket
5 National Bank of Greece
6 Virtual Café
8 Folk Museum
13 Ktel Korinthos Bus Terminal
15 Town Hall
16 Police & Tourist Police
17 Post Office
18 Basilopoulos Rent a Car
19 Public Toilets
20 OTE
21 Church of Agios Pavlos
22 Argolis Bus Terminal

As the name suggests, **Restaurant To 24 Hours** (☎ 2741-083 201; Agiou Nikolaou 19; mains €3.25-7.35) never closes, turning out an ever-changing selection of taverna favourites 24 hours a day.

Neon Cafeteria (☎ 2741-084 950; cnr Damaskinou & Ethnikis Antistaseos; mains €4.10-5.60) is a popular cafeteria with a good range of daily specials like macaroni with octopus (€4.25) or veal with rice (€4.85), as well as a salad bar (€3.25).

Trofo supermarket (☎ 2741-085 281; Kolokotroni 8; open 8am-9pm Mon-Fri, 8am-6pm Sat) is the biggest and best stocked of the supermarkets around the town centre. The main **produce market** is on the corner of Kyprou and Periandrou.

Getting There & Away

Bus Buses to Athens (€5.70, 1½ hours) leave every half-hour from the **Ktel Korinthos bus terminal** (☎ 2741-075 424; Dimocratias 4) located opposite the railway station. This is also the departure point for buses to ancient Corinth (€0.80, 20 minutes, hourly), Lecheon (€0.80, 15 minutes, hourly), Isthmia (€0.80, 20 minutes, six daily) and Nemea (€3.10, one hour, seven daily).

Buses to Argos (€3.10, one hour) and Nafplio (€3.95, 1¼ hours) leave from the **Argolis bus terminal** (cnr Aratou & Ethnikis Antistaseos). They also stop at Fihtio (€2.20, 45 minutes), on the main road 2km from Mycenae.

Catching a bus to other parts of the Peloponnese is a hassle. Buses to Patras don't come into town. They can be picked up from the bus stop on the Athens side of the Corinth Canal – meaning you have to get there on one of the frequent buses to Loutraki. You're better off catching the train (see the following section). The Corinth Canal stop is also the spot for buses south to Tripolis (€5, one hour), Sparta (€8.55, two hours) and Kalamata (€9.70, 2¾ hours).

Train There are 15 trains daily to Athens (€2.95, 1¾ hours). Four of them are intercity services but they are only 15 minutes faster than other trains. The Peloponnese rail network divides at Corinth, with eight trains daily heading along the north coast to Diakofto and Patras. It's worth checking the timetable before you set out; journey times to Patras range from under two hours on intercity trains to 3½ hours on the slowest slow train. Six trains continue down the west coast from Patras to Pyrgos, five go to Kyparissia and one takes 8½ hours to crawl all the way to Kalamata.

If Kalamata is your destination, you're better off taking the inland line. It has trains to Kalamata (€5.75, 4½ hours, four daily) via Argos (€2.05, one hour) and Tripolis (€2.65, 2¼ hours). There are also trains on the branch line to Nafplio (€2.95, 1¼ hours, three daily).

Car There are several car-rental outlets located around the city centre, including **Basilopoulos Rent a Car** (☎ 2741-025 573; Adimantou 39).

ANCIENT CORINTH & ACROCORINTH

The ruins of ancient Corinth lie 7km southwest of the modern city, surrounded by the attractive modern village of Ancient Corinth. Towering 575m above them is the Acrocorinth, a massive limestone outcrop that was the finest natural fortification in ancient Greece.

Most visitors come on whirlwind guided tours from Athens, but there's enough to see to warrant spending at least a full day. The village has a choice of restaurants and tavernas, and makes a great alternative to staying in modern Corinth. The tour groups disappear in the evening, and overnighters are left pretty much with the place to themselves.

History

During the 6th century BC, Corinth was one of ancient Greece's richest cities. It owed its wealth to its strategic position on the Isthmus of Corinth, which meant it was able to build twin ports: one on the Aegean Sea (Kenchrai) and the other on the Ionian Sea (Lecheon), and it traded throughout the Mediterranean. It survived the Peloponnesian Wars and flourished under Macedonian rule, but it was sacked by the Roman consul Mummius in 146 BC for rebelling against Roman rule. In 44 BC, Julius Caesar began rebuilding the city and it again became a prosperous port.

During Roman times, when Corinthians weren't clinching business deals, they were paying homage to the goddess of love, Aphrodite, in a temple dedicated to her (which meant they were having a rollicking time with the temple's sacred prostitutes, both male and female). St Paul, perturbed by the Corinthians' wicked ways, spent 18 fruitless months preaching here.

Ancient Corinth

The site of ancient Corinth (☎ 2741-031 207; site & museum €6; open 8am-7pm Apr-Oct, to 5pm Nov-Mar) lies right in the centre of the village.

Earthquakes and sackings by a series of invaders have left little standing in this ancient Greek city. The remains are mostly from Roman times. An exception is the 5th-century-BC Doric **Temple of Apollo**, the most prominent ruin on the site. To the south of this temple is a huge **agora**, or forum, bounded at its southern side by the foundations of a **stoa**. This was built to accommodate the bigwigs summoned here in 337 BC by Philip II to sign oaths of allegiance to Macedon. In the middle of the central row of shops is the **bema**, a marble podium from which Roman officials addressed the people.

At the eastern end of the forum are the remains of the **Julian Basilica**. To the north is the **Lower Peirene fountain** – the Upper Peirene fountain is on Acrocorinth. According to mythology, Peirene wept so much when her son Kenchrias was killed by Artemis that the gods, rather than let all the precious water go to waste, turned her into a fountain. It was the favourite watering hole of Pegasus, the winged horse, which explains why Pegasus features on old Corinthian coins. In reality, it's a natural spring which has been used since ancient times and still supplies old Corinth with water. The water tanks are concealed in a fountain house with a six-arched facade. Through the arches can be seen the remains of frescoes.

West of the fountain, steps lead to the **Lecheon road**, once the main thoroughfare to the port of Lecheon. On the east side of the road is the **Peribolos of Apollo**, a courtyard flanked by Ionic columns, some of which have been restored. Nearby is a **public latrine**; some seats remain. The site's **museum** houses statues, mosaics, figurines, reliefs and friezes.

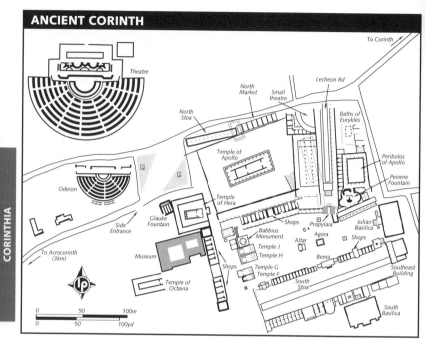

ANCIENT CORINTH

CORINTHIA

Acrocorinth

Earthquakes and invasions compelled the Corinthians to retreat to Acrocorinth (*admission free; open 8am-7pm Tues-Sun Apr-Oct, to 2.30pm Nov-Mar*), a sheer bulk of limestone which was one of the finest natural fortifications in Greece. The original fortress was built in ancient times but it has been modified many times over the years by a string of invaders. The ruins are a medley of imposing Roman, Byzantine, Frankish, Venetian and Turkish ramparts, harbouring remains of Byzantine chapels, Turkish houses and mosques.

On the higher of Acrocorinth's two summits is the **Temple of Aphrodite**, where the sacred courtesans, who so raised the ire of St Paul, catered to the desires of the insatiable Corinthians. Little remains of the temple but the views are tremendous.

Places to Stay & Eat

Several places in the village advertise rooms to rent:

Shadow Rooms to Rent (*☎/fax 2741-031 481; singles/doubles with bathroom €25/ 40*) is located on the northwestern edge of

the village on the road to Corinth and has wonderful views across the village to Acrocorinth. All rooms come with air-con. Greek-Australian owner Chris Marinis believes in a hearty breakfast (€4.40) before setting out to explore the sights.

Rooms to Rent Tasos (*☎ 2741-031 225/ 183; above Taverna O Tasos; singles/doubles with bathroom €20/28*) is closer to the centre of the village on the road into town from Corinth, next to the ruins of a so-called Turkish nunnery. Tasos describes them as deluxe, which they're not. But they are clean and bright, and convenient.

Taverna O Tasos (*see above; mains €3–6*) is a small family-run place with outdoor seating in the shade of a couple of large walnut trees. It's primarily a *psistaria* (grill restaurant) serving grilled meats and salads, but it also offers a small selection of taverna dishes.

Getting There & Away

There are hourly buses between Corinth and Ancient Corinth (€0.80, 20 minutes), which stop next to the site. There is no public transport to Acrocorinth.

CORINTH CANAL

The concept of cutting a canal through the Isthmus of Corinth to link the Ionian and Aegean seas was first proposed by the tyrant Periander, who ruled Corinth at the beginning of the 6th century BC. The magnitude of the task defeated him, so he opted instead to build a paved slipway across which sailors dragged small ships on rollers – a method used until the 13th century.

In the intervening years, many leaders, including Alexander the Great and Caligula, toyed with the canal idea, but it was Nero who actually began digging in AD 67. In true megalomaniac fashion, he struck the first blow himself using a golden pickaxe. He then left it to 6000 Jewish prisoners to do the hard work. The project was soon halted by invasions by the Gauls. Finally, in the 19th century (1883–93), a French engineering company completed the canal, a mere 1826 years after the first work had begun.

The Corinth Canal, cut through solid rock, is over 6km long and 23m wide. The vertical sides rise 90m above the water. The canal did much to elevate Piraeus' status as a major Mediterranean port. It's an impressive sight, particularly when a ship is passing through it.

The Old National Road to Athens crosses the canal at Isthmia by a submersible bridge, which is lowered to allow ships to pass over it.

Getting There & Away

The canal can be reached on a Loutraki bus from modern Corinth to the bridge. Any bus or train between Corinth and Athens will also pass over the canal. **Travel** (☎ 2741-080 028, fax 2741-074 820; e trv@yahoo.gr; Damaskinou 39) offers cruises through the canal every Sunday for €20.

ISTHMIA Ισθμία

Isthmia, 8km east of Corinth at the south-eastern end of the Corinth Canal, was once the site of the biennial Isthmian Games. These games were one of four events that made up the Panhellenic Games circuit along with the games at Delphi, Nemea and Olympia.

The first recorded games at Isthmia were staged in 582 BC, organised by the city of Corinth in honour of Poseidon, god of the sea, who had long been associated with the site. Corinth continued to host the games until its destruction by Rome in 146 BC, when they moved to Sikyon.

Ancient Isthmia

The site is spread across a hillside overlooking the modern town of Isthmia. It's on the road leading to the village of Kyras Vrisi, signposted to the right as you enter Isthmia from Corinth.

The entrance is via the **museum** (☎ 2741-037 244; museum & site €1.50; open 8.30am-3pm Tues-Sun). It's a good idea to take the hint and check out the museum first: it helps when it comes to making sense of the jumble of ruins awaiting beyond. A large section is devoted to explanation of an unusual style of glass mosaic called *opus sectile* discovered at nearby Kenchrai.

Immediately north of the museum lie the remains of the **Sanctuary of Poseidon**, a large temple erected in the 5th century BC on the ruins of an earlier temple. The temple was completely dismantled in Roman times and the stone reused elsewhere, leaving nothing but the foundations.

These foundations impinge on the original **stadium**, which began just east of the museum. The starting line can still be seen, marked by two square holes in the stone pavement that once held the supporting posts for an elaborate starting mechanism called a *hysplex*. The stadium was subsequently relocated to the valley southeast of the site, visible to the left of the road from Isthmia to the site.

The outline of an ancient theatre is clearly discernible dug into the hillside to the northeast of the Sanctuary of Poseidon. Further north, at the base of the hill, lie the ruins of a large Roman bath complex. Recent excavations uncovered some fine mosaics, but the complex was closed to visitors at the time of research.

The fortifications to the east of the site belong to a large Byzantine fortress that was built at the end of the 6th century using materials scavenged from the Sanctuary of Poseidon. It adjoins part of the Hexamilion Wall (see under Hexamilion, following, for more information).

The Hexamilion

The fortifications at Isthmia formed part of the Hexamilion, a defensive wall built

CORINTHIA

across the Isthmus of Corinth by the Byzantine Emperor Theodosius II in the first half of the 5th century to protect the Peloponnese against invasion by the Huns. It was called the Hexamilion because of its length – six Roman miles, or 7500m.

This earliest version was badly damaged by a major earthquake in the 6th century, and rebuilt by Justinian at the end of the 6th century BC. The wall was reconstructed by the Byzantine despot of Mystras, Manuel II, in 1415 in response to the growing threat posed by the Ottoman Empire. It proved little obstacle when the Ottoman general Turhan swept into the Peloponnese in 1423, and the wall was reinforced. The beefed-up version was equally ineffective when Turhan returned in 1453.

The remains of the wall can be seen beneath the Athens–Corinth toll road, 6km southeast of Corinth. Roadworks here uncovered about 150m of wall together with a small fort and several defensive towers. The site is signposted off the Corinth–Isthmia road. It's not enclosed, and there's no admission charge.

Getting There & Away
There are six buses a day between Isthmia and Corinth (€0.80, 20 minutes).

KENCHRAI
The ruins of the ancient port of Kenchrai lie 7km from Isthmia beside the main road south to Epidavros and Argolis.

Kenchrai served as Corinth's main port on the Saronic Gulf throughout antiquity and continued to be a major port in Roman and early Christian times. The sea level has risen appreciably since those days and most of the site now lies beneath the waters of Kehries Bay.

Despite this, the layout is easy enough to discern. Engineers improved what was already a fine natural anchorage by building moles out into the bay to create a perfect horseshoe harbour. The site's car park is right next to the southern mole, where the foundations of an early Christian basilica lie partly submerged on the shoreline. Beyond the basilica, now completely submerged, stood an ancient Temple of Isis. Exploration of the temple uncovered the exotic *opus sectile* glass mosaics now displayed in the museum at Isthmia.

LOUTRAKI Λουτράκι
postcode 203 00 • pop 11,383
Loutraki, 6km north of the Corinth Canal, lounges between a pebbled beach and the tall cliffs of the Gerania Mountains. Once a traditional spa town patronised by elderly and frail Greeks, it remains a major producer of bottled mineral water. The town was devastated by the 1981 earthquake, and subsequent reconstruction has resulted in its reincarnation as a tacky resort with dozens of modern, characterless hotels along the seafront. Loutraki hardly warrants an overnight stay.

Getting There & Away
Buses run from Corinth to Loutraki (€0.90, 20 minutes) every half-hour and there are nine buses daily from Athens (€4.70, 1½ hours). There are also two trains a day from Athens (€2.80, two hours).

LAKE VOULIAGMENI
Λίμνη Βουλιαγμενι
Tranquil Lake Vouliagmeni, 23km northwest of Loutraki, is a lovely little lagoon linked to the sea by a narrow channel. It's a popular spot at weekends and there are half-a-dozen small fish tavernas dotted around the shore.

The road continues beyond the lake to the ruins of **ancient Heraion**, surrounding a tiny natural harbour below Cape Melanhavi. The site was excavated by Humfry Payne from 1930 to 1933. Payne was accompanied by his wife, Dilys Powell, who describes her stay in the area in her book *An Affair of the Heart*. At the site are the ruins of an agora, a stoa and an 8th-century BC temple in a **Sanctuary to Hera**. The site is not enclosed and admission is free.

Getting There & Away
There is no public transport to Lake Vouliagmeni, so you will have to find your own way there. There are several places to rent motorcycles in Loutraki.

WEST OF CORINTH
The coastline stretching west from Corinth towards Patras is dotted with a series of fishing villages and small resorts. Places such as **Kiato**, **Xylokastro**, **Kamari** and **Derveni** (which has a sandy beach) are popular mainly with Greek holiday-makers and

groups from northern Europe. Beach buffs will be unimpressed. There are several interesting minor sites inland that are worth a detour if you have the time.

Ancient Sikyon Σικυον

Ancient Sikyon, known as the City of Pumpkins because of the plump terracotta pottery once produced here, is 6km south of Kiato. Founded in the 2nd millennium BC by the Ionians and later conquered by the Dorians, it became an important cultural centre focusing on wax painting, sculpture and pottery. It suffered at the hands of numerous invaders before it was finally destroyed by an earthquake in AD 23. The only obvious remains are those of a partially preserved **gymnasium** from Hellenistic and Roman times and the ruins of **Temple of Artemis**.

The site's **museum** (☎ 2742-028 900), housed in restored Roman baths, contains vases from various periods, terracotta statuettes from Archaic to Roman times, and a Praxiteles-styled marble head of Apollo. It was closed for renovations at the time of writing, so check the situation with Corinth's tourist police. The site is opposite the museum. It's not enclosed; admission is free.

Getting There & Away There's no public transport to the site, which is 1.5km west of the village of Vasiliko. If you're driving, you'll find signs to Vasiliko from Kiato; otherwise, a taxi from Kiato costs about €5. There are buses to Kiato from Corinth (€1.60, 40 minutes, six daily). All trains between Corinth and Patras stop at Kiato.

Stymfalia Στυμφαλία

If you've got your own transport, the 36km drive from Kiato to Stymfalia is worth the effort for the scenery as much as anything else. Little remains of the ancient site apart from the ruins of three temples. The site is next to a marshy lake of the same name, which was the home of the mythical man-eating Stymfalian birds that Heracles was ordered to shoo away as the sixth of his 12 labours. The birds were depicted in sculptures on the Temple of Artemis Stymfalia.

NEMEA Νεμέα

The tiny village of Nemea, 31km southwest of Corinth, lies at the heart of one of

Greece's premier wine-producing areas, famous for its full-bodied reds.

Nemea features prominently in the mythology of ancient Greece. It was here that Heracles carried out the first of his labours: slaying of the lion that Hera had sent to terrorise Nemea. Duly despatched by Heracles, the lion became the constellation Leo (each of the labours is related to a sign of the zodiac). See the boxed text 'Ancient Greek Mythology' in the Facts about the Peloponnese chapter, p30.

The modern village lies 4km southwest of the site of ancient Nemea. Like Olympia, Nemea was not a city but a sanctuary and venue for the biennial Nemean Games, held in honour of Zeus.

History

According to mythology, the Nemean Games began as a funeral festival to appease Zeus after the death of the son of Lycurgus (King of Sparta) and Eurydike, the infant Opheltes, who was killed by a snake while resting in a bed of wild celery at Nemea.

The first recorded games were held in 573 BC, when they became part of the Panhellenic circuit alongside Delphi, Isthmia and Olympia. Victors at Nemea were awarded a wreath of wild celery. These early games were organised by the city of Kleonai, in the hills 3km east of Nemea. The first Temple of Zeus was built about this time but was destroyed at the end of the 5th century during the Peloponnesian Wars. The site was left in ruins and the games were relocated to Argos.

The games didn't return to Nemea until 330 BC. Most of the remains that await the modern visitor were built between this date and 270 BC, when the games were again usurped by Argos.

The site fell into disrepair over the following centuries until it was reborn as an early Christian settlement in the 5th century AD. This settlement was abandoned after it was destroyed by the Avars during their invasion of the Peloponnese at the end of the 6th century.

Sanctuary of Zeus

The Sanctuary of Zeus (☎ 2746-022 739; site & museum €1.50; open 8.30am-3pm Tues-Sun) lies about 4km east of the modern village, tucked away behind a row of

CORINTHIA

cypress trees that provide precious shade for the car park.

It's a good idea to start your visit with a tour of the **museum**, which is on the right just inside the entrance. It has an excellent display on the history of the site, accompanied by old photographs and drawings. They include a sketch by Edward Lear, drawn during a flying visit to Nemea in 1849. There's a model of the site as it stood at the height of its prestige in 330 BC, and a second model of the site in the 5th century AD. Finds on display include a large collection of coins from all over ancient Greece, left behind by visitors to the games, and a delightful bronze jug engraved with the dedication *'Tou dios cimi tou Nemeai'* (I belong to Zeus at Nemea).

As you proceed north from the museum to the site, the first ruins encountered are those of an **early Christian basilica**, built in the 6th century. It stands on the foundations of the original **xenon**, a guesthouse for visiting VIPs and games officials.

Immediately to the west of here is the well-preserved **bath house**, protected by a modern roof, where athletes washed down after competing at the games. The foul, litter-filled watercourse next to the bath house was once the **Nemea River**.

The site's principal attraction is the **Temple of Zeus**, built in the 4th century BC on the foundations of an earlier temple. Three of the original columns survive. They have been joined by a further one-and-a-half columns, re-erected in 1984 as part of a scheme to rebuild the temple. East of the temple lies the long **Altar of Zeus**, where athletes would make their vows before heading off to compete.

Stadium

Nemea's ancient stadium (☎ 2746-022 739; admission €1.50; open 8.30am-3pm Tues-Sun) lies 400m southeast of the sanctuary. In ancient times, it was linked to the Sanctuary of Zeus by a sacred road. The road finished at the **apodytiria**, a small three-sided changing room where athletes would strip down and oil their bodies before entering the stadium. This changing room stands behind the kiosk at the entrance to the stadium area.

The entrance to the stadium itself is through a vaulted stone **tunnel** that disappears into the hillside behind the changing room. Built in 320 BC, it is in almost perfect condition. The walls are dotted with ancient graffiti scrawled by waiting athletes.

The tunnel emerges into an impressively large stadium that could hold an estimated 40,000 fans. It was created by carving out a small gully and using the spoil to build a terrace out into the surrounding Nemean Plain. The area of stone seating by the tunnel entrance was a VIP area; regular fans made do with sitting on ledges cut into the sides of the stadium.

The most interesting feature is the stone starting line at the southern end of the stadium. The square holes cut into the stone held the posts of the **hysplex**, an ingenious starting mechanism that was designed to ensure an even start. Its operation is explained by a video display in the museum.

Getting There & Away

There are buses to Nemea (€3.10, one hour, seven daily) from Corinth that travel past the site. There are also buses to Nemea from Argos (€2, two daily).

AROUND NEMEA
Ancient Kleonai

The meagre remains of ancient Kleonai, organiser of the Nemean Games, lie about 5km northeast of the Sanctuary of Zeus near the modern village of Arhaia Kleones. There's no public transport, but it makes a pleasant diversion if you have your own transport. The road to Arhaia Kleones is signposted 2km east of the Sanctuary of Zeus.

The only attraction is a small **Temple of Heracles** tucked away among the vineyards just north of the village. The ancient town lay in the low hills north of temple, and it's possible to discern the outline of the former acropolis.

Argolis Αργολίδα

The Argolis Peninsula, which separates the Saronic and Argolic Gulfs in the northeast of the Peloponnese, is a veritable treasure trove for archaeology buffs.

Argolis was the heartland of the mighty Mycenaean civilisation that dominated Greece from 1600 to 1200 BC and the ancient citadels of Mycenae and Tiryns are two of the region's major attractions, together with the magnificent Theatre of Epidavros.

The charming Venetian town of Nafplio was the first capital of independent Greece, while the town of Argos, from which the region takes its name, lays claim to being the longest continually inhabited town in the country.

ARGOS Αργος
postcode 212 00 • pop 24,239
Argos may be the oldest continuously inhabited town in Greece but most vestiges of its past glory lie buried beneath the uninspiring modern town. Although the town itself is of minor interest, it is a convenient base from which to explore the sites of Argolis, and it has a refreshing lack of tourist hype. It is also a major transport hub.

History
The site of modern Argos has been occupied since prehistoric times. According to legend, Mycenae was founded by Perseus, grandson of the Argive King Akritias, indicating that Argos has existed as a town since at least 2000 BC.

Argos slipped from the limelight during Mycenaean times but emerged from the Dark Ages as one of the main powers in the new Dorian-ruled Peloponnese. It reached the peak of its powers at the beginning of the 7th century BC under the tyrant Pheidon.

Argos continued to dominate the northern Peloponnese until the middle of the 6th century BC, when it was defeated by Sparta at the so-called Battle of the Champions at Thyrea. It remained an important player in Peloponnese affairs, but never regained its former glory. The Romans, who ruled from Corinth, also took a shine to Argos, investing it with some fine buildings.

It became part of the Duchy of Athens in 1212 after the Frankish carve-up of the

Highlights

- Entering ancient Mycenae through the Lion Gate

- Strolling the streets in the romantic Venetian town of Nafplio

- Marvelling at the remarkable Cyclopean walls of ancient Tiryns

- Testing the acoustics of the theatre at Epidavros

ARGOLIS

Byzantine Empire and remained under the duchy's control until it fell to the Turks in 1463.

Argos was captured by the Greeks early in the War of Independence and remained in Greek hands throughout the war.

Orientation & Information
Argos' showpiece and focal point is the central square, Plateia Agiou Petrou, with its Art-Nouveau streetlights, citrus and palm trees and the impressive Church of Agios Petros. Beyond, Argos deteriorates into an unremarkable working town.

There is no tourist office or tourist police; both are located in nearby Nafplio (see Orientation & Information under Nafplio later in this chapter, p112). The regular police can be contacted on ☎ 100. The post office and the OTE (Organismos Tilepikoinonion Ellados, the Greek telephone service operator) office are both close to Plateia

105

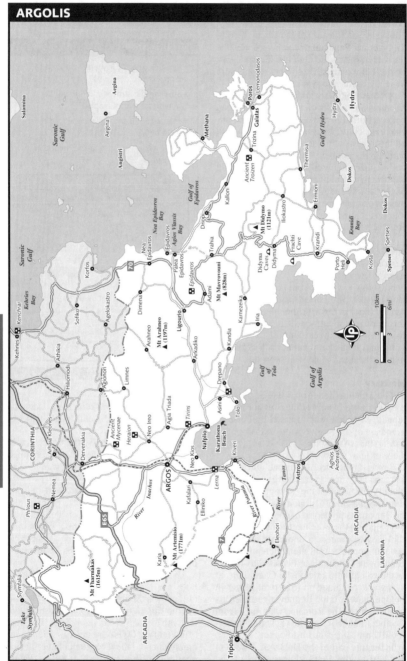

ARGOLIS

Agiou Petrou; the post office is clearly sign-posted on Kapodistriou and the OTE is on Nikitara, which leads off the square next to the National Bank of Greece. Check email at the **Café Net** (☎ 2751-029 677; 28th Oktavriou 4); it charges €3.55 per hour.

Archaeological Museum

Even if you're only passing through Argos, try to pause long enough to visit the archaeological museum (☎ 2751-068 819; admission €1.50; open 8.30am-3pm Tues-Sun), on the edge of the central square. The collection includes some outstanding Roman mosaics and sculptures; Neolithic, Mycenaean and Geometric pottery; and bronze objects from the Mycenaean tombs.

Roman Ruins

There are Roman ruins (admission free; open 8.30am-3pm daily) on both sides of Tripolis, which is the main Argos–Tripolis road. To get there from the central square, head south along Danaou for about 500m and then turn right onto Theatrou. Theatrou joins Tripolis opposite the star attraction, the enormous **theatre**, which could seat up to 20,000 people (more than at Epidavros). It dates from classical times but was greatly modified by the Romans. Nearby are the remains of a 1st-century-AD **odeion** (indoor theatre) and **Roman baths**.

The remains on the opposite side of Tripolis are those of the **Roman forum**, which is closed to the public.

Fortress of Larissa

This ancient fortress overlooks the city from the west from the summit of the Hill of Larissa. The site was first fortified in the 6th century BC, when it also housed temples to Zeus and to Apollo. The walls were rebuilt in Byzantine times and were subsequently modified by the Franks, the Venetians and the Turks. The outer wall, studded with squat towers, protects a large enclosure surrounding an inner citadel. Both sets of fortifications remain in reasonable condition.

You can walk up to the fortress by a path beginning above the Roman odeion. To get to the start of the path, take the first street on the right south of the ancient theatre. You can also get to the summit by road, which approaches from the west. The route is clearly signposted from Karantza.

Hill of Aspis

This small hill lies just northeast of the Hill of Larissa, connected by a low ridge. Its summit was the site of an early Bronze Age settlement, now occupied by the Church of Profitis Ilias. Excavations have uncovered the outline of an ancient wall, as well as chamber tombs and shaft graves belonging to a **Mycenaean necropolis**.

The ruins by the roadside on the southwestern slope of the hill belong to **Sanctuary of Apollo Deiradiotes & Athena Oxyderkis**, dating from the 5th century BC. It featured temples to both Apollo and Athena, built on terraces connected by a stone staircase carved out of the rock.

The hill and its various attractions are signposted from Karantza.

Places to Stay

All hotels in town are close to the central square.

Hotel Apollon (☎ 2751-068 065; Papaflessa 13; singles/doubles €15/20, with bathroom €17/24) is the best budget choice, tucked away on a quiet side street behind the National Bank of Greece, close to the main square. The rooms come with TV.

Hotel Mycenae (☎ 2751-068 754, fax 2751-068 332; Plateia Agiou Petrou 10; singles/doubles €30/40, apartment €65) is a C-class hotel on the central square with large, comfortable rooms and a four-bed 'apartment'. All rooms come with air-con and TV and are centrally heated in winter. Breakfast costs €6 per person.

Hotel Telesilla (☎ 2751-068 317, fax 2751-066 249; cnr Plateia Agiou Petrou & Danaou 2; singles/doubles with bathroom €30/50) has been transformed after a complete refit. It offers smart, modern rooms with air-con and TV.

Places to Eat

Restaurant Aigli (☎ 2751-067 266; Plateia Agiou Petrou 6; mains €2.65-5.30) is the place to check out. It offers pasta from €2.65, pizzas from €4.70 and burgers from €4.10, as well as traditional favourites like moussaka (€3.85). With outdoor seating in the main square, it's also perfect for people watching.

Taverna To Steki (☎ 2751-023 045; Agiou Konstantinou 10; mains €2.35-6.50) is a solid no-nonsense taverna with bargain

ARGOLIS

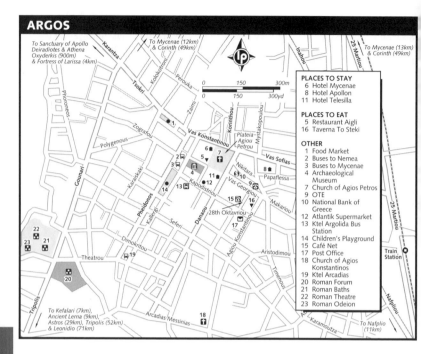

ARGOS

To Sanctuary of Apollo Deiradiotes & Athena Oxyderkis (900m) & Fortress of Larissa (4km)

To Mycenae (12km) & Corinth (49km)

To Mycenae (13km) & Corinth (49km)

To Kefalari (7km), Ancient Lerna (9km), Astros (29km), Tripolis (52km) & Leonidio (71km)

To Nafplio (11km)

Train Station

PLACES TO STAY
6 Hotel Mycenae
8 Hotel Apollon
11 Hotel Telesilla

PLACES TO EAT
5 Restaurant Aigli
16 Taverna To Steki

OTHER
1 Food Market
2 Buses to Nemea
3 Buses to Mycenae
4 Archaeological Museum
7 Church of Agios Petros
9 OTE
10 National Bank of Greece
12 Atlantik Supermarket
13 Ktel Argolida Bus Station
14 Children's Playground
15 Café Net
17 Post Office
18 Church of Agios Konstantinos
19 Ktel Arcadias
20 Roman Forum
21 Roman Baths
22 Roman Theatre
23 Roman Odeion

prices and fast, efficient service – plus an excellent line in local red wine.

Self-caterers can check out Argos' **food market** in the neoclassical agora on Tsokri. The Atlantik Supermarket on Kapodistriou is the most convenient of several **supermarkets** around town.

Getting There & Away

Bus Most services of interest to travellers are operated by **Ktel Argolida** (☎ 2751-067 324) from its office at Kapodistriou 8, just south of the main square. It has buses to Nafplio (€0.90, 20 minutes, every half-hour), Tripolis (€3.50, 1¼ hours, eight daily) and Athens (€7.70, two hours, hourly) via Corinth (€3.10). Buses to Mycenae (€1.25, 30 minutes, five daily) and Nemea (€2, one hour, two daily) leave from the stops on Kallergi.

Services south to Astros (€2.05, one hour) and Leonidio (€5.15, 2¼ hours) are operated by **Ktel Arcadias** (☎ 2751-023 162; Theatrou 40) from the Kafeneion Christos Klisaris. There are three services a day on this route, leaving at 10am, 1pm and 6pm.

Train There are five trains daily to Athens (€3.85, three hours), also stopping at Fihtio (near Mycenae; €1, 20 minutes) and Corinth (€2.05, one hour). There are three trains daily to Kalamata (€4.40, 3½ hours) via Tripolis (€2.35, one hour).

KEFALARI

Kefalari, 7km southwest of Argos, is a favourite beauty spot and a pleasant diversion for travellers with their own transport. The main attraction, the tiny **Church of Panagia Kefalariotissa** (Church of the Virgin & Life-Giving Spring), occupies the smaller of two caves in the cliff face north of the main square. Its name derives from a stream gushing from the rock above the caves. The bigger cave, its entrance framed by a spectacular red bougainvillea, is large enough to hold an army – as it did in the War of Independence.

Elliniko, 2km southwest of Kefalari, is home of the so-called **Pyramid of Elliniko**. It is believed to be the foundation of a small fort that guarded the ancient Argos–Arcadia road.

The road to Kefalari and Elliniko is signposted off the main road to Tripolis about 1.5km south of Argos.

MYCENAE Μυκήνες
postcode 212 00 • pop 422

The modern village of Mycenae (in Greek, Mikines; mih-**kee**-ness) is 12km north of Argos, just east of the main Argos–Corinth road. It is geared towards the hordes of package tourists visiting ancient Mycenae and has little to recommend it other than it being 2km south of the ancient site. There is accommodation along its single street. There's no bank, but there is a mobile post office with a currency-exchange service at the ancient site.

Ancient Mycenae

In the barren foothills of Mt Agios Ilias (750m) and Mt Zara (600m) stand the sombre and mighty ruins of ancient Mycenae (☎ 2751-076 585; citadel & Treasury of Atreus €6; open 8am-7pm daily Apr-Oct, to 5pm Nov-Mar), vestiges of a kingdom which, for 400 years (1600–1200 BC), was the most powerful in Greece, holding sway over the Argolid (the modern-day prefecture of Argolis) and influencing the other Mycenaean kingdoms.

After exploring, revive yourself with freshly squeezed Argolis orange juice, sold from a van opposite the mobile post office.

History & Mythology

Mycenae is synonymous with Homer. In the 9th century BC, Homer told in his epic poems, the *Iliad* and the *Odyssey*, of 'well-built Mycenae, rich in gold'. These poems were, until the 19th century, regarded as no more than gripping and beautiful legends. But in the 1870s, the amateur archaeologist Heinrich Schliemann (1822–90), despite derision from professional archaeologists, struck gold, first at Troy then at Mycenae.

In Mycenae, myth and history are inextricably linked. According to Homer, the city of Mycenae was founded by Perseus, the son of Danae and Zeus. Perseus' greatest heroic deed was the killing of the hideous snake-haired Medusa, whose looks literally petrified the beholder. Eventually, the dynasty of Perseus was overthrown by Pelops, a son of Tantalus. The Mycenaean Royal House of Atreus was probably descended from Pelops, although myth and history are so intertwined, and the genealogical line so complex, that no-one really knows. Whatever the bloodlines, in the

When Helen of Troy was abducted by Paris, the ensuing Trojan War precipitated the final act for the doomed House of Atreus

time of King Agamemnon – brother-in-law of Helen of Troy and a key player in the Trojan War caused by her abduction – the House of Atreus was the most powerful of the Achaeans (Homer's name for the Greeks). It eventually came to a sticky end, fulfilling the curse cast upon it because of Pelops' misdeeds – principally his killing instead of rewarding the man who helped him win his wife.

The historical facts are that in the 6th millennium BC Mycenae was first settled by Neolithic people. Between 2100 and 1900 BC, during the Old Bronze Age, Greece was invaded by people of Indo-European stock who had crossed Anatolia via Troy to Greece. They brought an advanced culture to the then-primitive Mycenae and other mainland settlements. This new civilisation is now referred to as the Mycenaean, named after Mycenae, its most powerful kingdom. The other kingdoms included Pylos, Tiryns, Corinth and Argos in the Peloponnese. Evidence of Mycenaean civilisation has also been found at Thiva (Thebes) and Athens.

The city of Mycenae consisted of a fortified citadel and surrounding settlement. Due to the sheer size of the walls of the citadel (13m high and 7m thick), the ancient Greeks believed they must have been built by a Cyclops, one of the giants described by Homer in the *Odyssey*.

Archaeological evidence indicates that the palaces of the Mycenaean kingdoms were destroyed around 1200 BC. It was long thought that the destruction was the work of the Dorians, but later evidence indicates that the decline of the Mycenaean

ARGOLIS

civilisation was symptomatic of the general turmoil around the Mediterranean at the time. The great Hittite Empire in Anatolia, which had reached its height between 1450 and 1200 BC, was now in decline, as was the Egyptian civilisation.

The Mycenaeans, Hittites and Egyptians had all prospered through their trade with each other, but this had ceased by the end of the 1200s. Many of the great palaces of the Mycenaean kingdoms were destroyed 150 years before the Dorians arrived.

Whether the destruction was the work of outsiders or due to internal division between the various Mycenaean kingdoms remains unresolved.

The Citadel The Citadel of Mycenae is entered through the celebrated **Lion Gate**, believed to be the oldest monumental structure in Europe. It is named because of the relief above the lintel of two lionesses supporting a pillar. This motif is believed to have been the insignia of the Royal House of Atreus.

Inside the citadel, you will find **Grave Circle A** on the right as you enter. This was the royal cemetery and contained six grave shafts. Five were excavated by Schliemann between 1874 and 1876 and the magnificent gold treasures he uncovered are in the National Archaeological Museum in Athens. In the last grave shaft, Schliemann found a well-preserved gold death mask with flesh still clinging to it. Fervently, he sent a telegram to the Greek king stating, 'I have gazed upon the face of Agamemnon'. The mask turned out to be that of an unknown king who had died some 300 years before Agamemnon.

To the south of Grave Circle A are the remains of a group of houses. In one was found the famous **Warrior Vase**, which Schliemann regarded as one of his greatest discoveries.

The main path leads up to **Agamemnon's palace**, centred on the **Great Court**. The rooms to the north were the private royal apartments. One of these rooms is believed to be the chamber in which Agamemnon was murdered by his wife Clytaemnestra, after her lover Aegisthus wimped out of the deed. Access to the **throne room**, west of the Great Court, would originally have been via a large staircase. On the southeastern side of the palace is the **megaron** (reception hall).

ARGOLIS

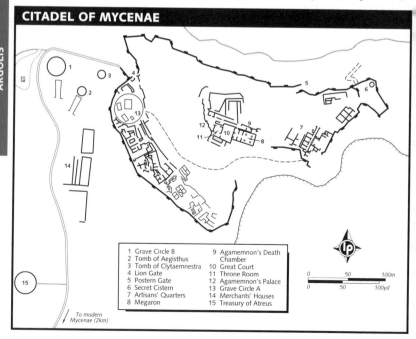

CITADEL OF MYCENAE

1 Grave Circle B	9 Agamemnon's Death
2 Tomb of Aegisthus	Chamber
3 Tomb of Clytaemnestra	10 Great Court
4 Lion Gate	11 Throne Room
5 Postern Gate	12 Agamemnon's Palace
6 Secret Cistern	13 Grave Circle A
7 Artisans' Quarters	14 Merchants' Houses
8 Megaron	15 Treasury of Atreus

0   50   100m
0   50   100yd

To modern
Mycenae (2km)

On the northern boundary of the citadel is the **Postern Gate** through which, it is said, Orestes escaped after murdering his mother and thus avenging the death of his father, Agamemnon. In the far northeastern corner of the citadel is the **secret cistern**. It can be explored by torchlight, but take care: the steps are slippery.

Until the late 15th century BC the Mycenaeans put their royal dead into shaft graves. They then devised a new form of burial: the tholos tomb, shaped like a beehive. The approach road to Mycenae passes to the right of the best preserved of these, the **Treasury of Atreus** or tomb of Agamemnon. A 40m-long passage leads to this immense beehive-shaped chamber. It is built with stone blocks that get steadily smaller as the structure tapers to its central point. Farther north along the road on the right is **Grave Circle B**, and nearby are the **tholos tombs of Aegisthus and Clytaemnestra**.

Places to Stay & Eat

Camping Mycenae (☎ 2751-076 121, fax 2751-076 850; e dars@arg.forthnet.gr; off Christou Tsounta; person/tent €4.10/3.25; open year-round) is a small camping ground conveniently located right in the middle of Mycenae village, opposite the Hotel Belle Helene.

There are several signs advertising rooms on the Fihtio side of the village, and half-a-dozen hotels.

The **Hotel Belle Helene** (☎ 2751-076 225, fax 2751-076 179; Christou Tsounta 15; singles/doubles €30/40) is a curious mixture of ancient and modern: a tiny old-fashioned hotel with a large modern restaurant tacked on the front. Heinrich Schliemann stayed here while excavating at ancient Mycenae. Dr Schliemann stayed in Room 3, now marked with a plaque.

Don't be put off by the cavernous restaurant that caters to tour buses at lunch time. The hotel part of **Hotel-Restaurant Klitemnistra** (☎ 2751-076 451, fax 2751-076 731; Christou Tsounta; doubles with bathroom €40) operates on a much smaller scale, with half-a-dozen clean, comfortable rooms. The friendly Greek-Australian owners can suggest walks in the area. Prices include breakfast.

The upmarket option is the B-class **La Petit Planete** (☎ 2751-076 240, fax 2751-076 610; Christou Tsounta; singles/doubles/triples with bathroom €45/60/75), which has great views from its hilltop location between the village and the ancient site. Facilities include a swimming pool, restaurant and bar.

Getting There & Away

There are buses to Mycenae from Nafplio (€2.10, one hour, three daily) and Argos (€1.40, 30 minutes, five daily). The buses stop in the village and at the ancient site.

Other bus services, such as Athens–Nafplio, advertise a stop at Mycenae but they actually go no closer than the village of Fihtio on the main road, leaving you 3km from the village and 5km from the site.

NAFPLIO Ναύπλιο
postcode 211 00 • pop 13,822
Nafplio, 63km southeast of Corinth on the Argolic Gulf, was the first capital of independent Greece and it's a town that still holds a special place in the hearts of many Greeks.

Nestled on the northern slopes of the ancient Akronafplia fortress, the old town is a maze of narrow streets lined with old Venetian and Ottoman buildings and gracious neoclassical mansions. Bursts of brilliant red bougainvillea blossom fill the streets in spring and early summer, making Nafplio one of the Peloponnese's most romantic destinations.

Not surprisingly, it's a favourite weekend destination for young Athenian couples. It's also a great base for exploring the ancient sites of Epidavros, Mycenae and Tiryns.

History

The site has been occupied since Neolithic times, and became the major port of the Argolis in Mycenaean times – when the Akronafplia was first fortified.

Nafplio survived the Dark Ages but was destroyed by Argos at the end of the 7th century BC in reprisal for forming an alliance with Sparta. It remained subservient to Argos until the end of the 12th century AD, when the Byzantines adopted the town as a naval base as part of their campaign against coastal pirates.

The town fell to the Franks in 1210, and became part of the Duchy of Athens until it was ceded to Venice in 1389. The Venetians held the town for the next 150 years,

ARGOLIS

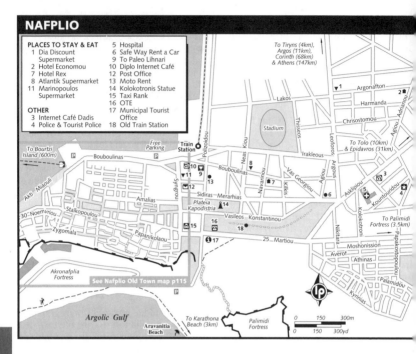

NAFPLIO

PLACES TO STAY & EAT
1 Dia Discount Supermarket
2 Hotel Economou
7 Hotel Rex
8 Atlantik Supermarket
11 Marinopoulos Supermarket

OTHER
3 Internet Café Dadis
4 Police & Tourist Police
5 Hospital
6 Safe Way Rent a Car
9 To Paleo Lihnari
10 Diplo Internet Café
12 Post Office
13 Moto Rent
14 Kolokotronis Statue
15 Taxi Rank
16 OTE
17 Municipal Tourist Office
18 Old Train Station

using it as a launching pad for their campaign to control the eastern Mediterranean. In the process, they transformed Nafplio into one of the strongest fortresses in the Peloponnese. It withstood various Turkish assaults before succumbing in 1540 after a three-year siege.

The Turks ruled the Peloponnese from Nafplio until 1686, when they were ousted by the Venetian general Francisco Morosini. The Venetians spent much of the next 29 years refortifying the town before they were ejected by the Turks for the last time in 1715.

It was captured by Independence forces led by Kolokotronis in November 1822, and remained in Greek hands throughout the war. It was declared capital of Greece in 1827, but slipped from the limelight when King Otto shifted the capital to Athens in 1834.

Orientation & Information

The old town occupies a narrow promontory with the Akronafplia fortress to the south and the promenades of Bouboulinas and Akti Miaouli to the north. The principal streets of the old town are Amalias, Vasileos

Konstantinou, Staïkopoulou and Kapodistriou. The old town's central square is Plateia Syntagmatos (Syntagma Square), at the western end of Vasileos Konstantinou.

The bus station is on Syngrou, the street separating the old town from the new. The main street of the new town, known to locals as Neapolis, is 25 Martiou – an easterly continuation of Staïkopoulou.

Tourist Offices Nafplio's municipal tourist office (☎ 2752-024 444; 25 Martiou, open 9am-1pm 4pm-8pm daily) is a short stroll east from the old town.

Money All the major banks have branches in town, including the National Bank of Greece on Plateia Syntagmatos, and the Ionian Bank at the western end of Amalias.

Post & Communications The post office is on Syngrou and the OTE is on 25 Martiou opposite the tourist office.

There are several Internet cafés around town; they include **Diplo Internet Café** (☎ 2752-021 280; Bouboulinas 43) and **Internet Café Dadis** (☎ 2752-029 688,

Ancient Nemea, where Heracles killed the lion

Corinth's famous wines start like this

Sightsee or sunbathe at ancient Heraion

The Corinth Canal, 1800 years in the making

Delightful Nafplio

'Wall-girt Tiryns', surely built by a Cyclops

Enjoy the romantic view over the island fortress of Bourtzi

Ancient Mycenae, where cursed King Agamemnon ruled

Lion Gate, ancient Mycenae

Asklipiou 15). Both are open daily from 9am to midnight.

Emergency The **tourist police** (☎ 2752-028 131; Kountouridou 16) can be found behind the hospital, sharing an office with the regular **police** (☎ 2752-022 100).

Bookshops In the old town, **Odyssey** (☎ 2752-023 430; Plateia Syntagmatos) stocks international newspapers as well as a small selection of novels in English, French and German. It also has maps.

Walking Tour

Nafplio's old town is a fascinating place to explore, full of surprises tucked away in the labyrinthine streets that weave over the undulating terrain. This walk takes in most of the main sites. It involves about 45 minutes' walking, but can take several hours if you linger and allow yourself to be lured into some of the many detours. (The route is marked on the Nafplio Old Town map.)

The tour begins on the southeastern edge of the old town outside the reconstructed **Land Gate**, once the principal land entrance to the town. The original was demolished in 1895, along with the surrounding eastern wall. The new gate, crowned by a splendid carved lion, stands on the old foundations, visible either side of the gate along with a small section of the moat.

The gate stands in the shadow of the **Grimani Bastion**, which was added to the Akronafplia complex at the beginning of the 18th century to protect the gate. The bastion's east wall sports a fine lion tableau.

From the gate, cross Syngrou and enter the old town along Plapouta. The first house on the right, on the corner of Syngrou and Plapouta, was the home of the regent Armansberg in 1833 during Nafplio's brief reign as capital of Greece. The elegant carved stone entrance speaks of grander times; today it stands sadly derelict.

Continue west along Plapouta for 50m to Plateia Agios Georgios. The large church at the eastern side of this small square is the **Church of Agios Georgios**, grandest of the city's many fine churches. Built in the 16th century towards the end of the first period of Venetian rule, it became a mosque in Ottoman times and now serves as the city's Greek Orthodox cathedral. The extravagant interior features a copy of Leonardo da Vinci's *Last Supper*. Famous names laid to rest here include the Venetian general Francisco Morosini and Bishop Germanos of Patras, who raised the flag of revolt that launched the War of Independence in 1821.

Head south across Plateia Agios Georgios, turn right into Papanikolaou and follow it west to Plateia Agios Spiridon. This small leafy square takes its name from the **Church of Agios Spiridon** on the western side of the square. It was at the entrance to this church, on Kapodistriou, that the first president of Greece, Ioannis Kapodistrias, was assassinated on 27 September 1831 by the Maniot chieftains Konstantinos and Georgos Mavromihalis.

Opposite the entrance are the remains of an old **hammam** (Turkish bath house).

The small fountain built into the wall at the southern side of Plateia Agios Spiridon is another reminder of Ottoman times. It looks at its best at night, when a spotlight highlights the ornate calligraphy of the Arabic script (inviting passers-by to drink).

The tour turns south from here onto Potamianou, which is the stepped street leading up towards the Akronafplia. The church on the right after the first flight of stairs is the **Frangoklisia** (Frankish church). Built originally as a Catholic convent by the Franks, it has also served as a Catholic church and an Ottoman mosque over the centuries.

Turn right above the Frangoklisia and follow Zygomala as it weaves its way west across the hillside. This is the oldest part of town. Many of the houses have stood since the earliest days of Venetian rule, although they have been repaired and modified so many times since that they are almost impossible to date. After 150m, turn right down the steps onto Labrinou, then left after the first flight of steps into Konstantinopoleos.

The restored Venetian building on the left served as the **konak** of the pasha (Ottoman governor) from 1715 to 1786. Further west, at the corner of Konstantinopoleos and Ethnikis Antistasis, the Greek Archaeological Service has taken up residence in a former **medersa** (Islamic college) built during this period.

Head down the steps of Ethnikis Antistasis and turn right onto Staïkopoulou – named after the first Greek to enter the Palamidi Fortress during the War of Independence.

The impressive domed building on the right was built as a mosque in 1730, and was linked to the *medersa*. After Independence, it was refitted to become the **Bouleutikon**, housing the Greek parliament from 1828 to 1834.

Head north from here into Plateia Syntagmatos (Constitution Square). This large paved square lay at the heart of the Venetian town, serving as the market place. It's dominated by the massive three-storey **arsenal** that forms the western side of the square and is the town's finest example of Venetian architecture. It was completed in 1713, just in time to be handed over to the Turks! It was used as a barrack house after Independence, and now houses the **archaeological museum** (see Museums later in this section, p116, for information).

Stroll east across the square and exit by Vasileos Konstantinou. The multi-domed building on the right as you leave the square was built as the town's principal mosque in the 16th century during the first period of Turkish rule. It's now used as a cinema.

Vasileos Konstantinou was the main street of Nafplio after Independence. Flanked by elegant neoclassical houses and overhung by bougainvillea blossoms, it's one of the prettiest streets in Greece. Head east along Vasileos Konstantinou until it opens up into Plateia Trion Navarchon, named in honour of the British, French and Russian admirals responsible for the destruction of the Turkish fleet at the Battle of Navarino in 1827.

The elegant cream-and-white neoclassical building on the southern side of the square, now the **town hall**, was once the first *gymnasio* (high school) in independent Greece, opened in 1834.

Educational activities have now been transferred to the opposite side of Plateia Trion Navarchon, to the site of the town's old northeastern bastion – demolished in the 1930s. The tour now heads back to the west along Amalias, which marks the course of the old northern wall, demolished in 1868. The neat grid of streets to the north of Amalias was developed at this time.

Amalias finishes in front of two of the town's finest examples of neoclassical architecture: the **Ionian Bank building** and the **public library**. Turn right into Koletti, and then left into Ypsilantou to emerge on Plateia Filellinon. The monument at the

centre of the square was erected in 1903 to honour French citizens who died fighting for Greek Independence.

The cafés around here are the perfect spot to finish the tour with a coffee.

Akronafplia Fortress

The Akronafplia fortress, which rises above the old part of town, is the oldest of Nafplio's three castles. Although sections of the walls date back to Mycenaean times, the fortress that stands today began to take shape in the 4th century BC with the construction of a wall to protect a settlement at the western end of the Akronafplia.

This wall was rebuilt by the Byzantines, and modified by the Franks – who split the castle into Greek and Frankish sections. The Venetians extended the fortress east with the addition of the **Castel di Toro Bastion** at the end of the 15th century. The squat, conical tower at the southeastern corner of this bastion is a superb example of the military architecture of this period. It's best viewed from the road leading up to the fortress from Plateia Arvanitia.

The defences were rendered useless by the development of cannon, which left the Akronafplia at the mercy of whoever controlled the **Hill of Palamidi** (see under Palamidi Fortress, following). Despite this, the Venetians bolstered the Akronafplia's defences further in the 17th century, reinforcing the Castel di Toro with the solid walls of the Grimani bastion.

The fortress was used as a political prison from 1936 to 1956, after which – to the horror of archaeologists – approval was granted for the government-run Xenia group to build hotels on the site.

There are several ways of approaching the Akronafplia. The old gateway to the fortress, crowned with a fine Venetian lion emblem, is at the top of Potamianou, the stepped street that heads uphill off Plateia Agios Spiridon. There's also a lift from Plateia Poliko Nosokomiou at the western edge of town – look for the flags at the entrance of the tunnel leading to the lift. It can also be approached by road from the east.

Palamidi Fortress

This vast citadel (☎ 2752-028 036; admission €4; open 8am-6.45pm daily Apr-Oct, to 5pm Nov-Mar) stands atop the Hill of

Palamidi, a 216m-high outcrop of rock that overlooks the old town from the east.

It was built by the Venetians between 1711 and 1714, and is regarded as a masterpiece of military architecture. Within its walls stands a series of independent bastions, strategically located across the hill. The most important – and best preserved – of these is the western **Agios Andreas Bastion**, which stands at the top of the steps from town. It was the home of the garrison commander and it is named after the tiny church in the interior courtyard. There are wonderful views over the Akronafplia and the old town from the bastion walls.

The **Miltiades Bastion**, to the northeast, is the largest of the bastions. It was used as a prison for condemned criminals from 1840 to 1920. War of Independence hero Theodore Kolokotronis was held here after being condemned for treason.

Southeast of here is the smaller **Epaminondas Bastion**, which guards the main northeastern gate to the fortress complex. It's overlooked from the south by the **Themistocles Bastion**, which occupies the highest point of the Palamidi. It was the site of a notorious massacre of Albanian mercenaries by Turkish forces in 1779. Hundreds were brought here and thrown to their deaths off the bastion's southern wall.

The fortress continues east to the **Achilles Bastion**. It was guarded by a ditch, designed to make the relatively low wall more impressive. It proved to be the Palamidi's weak point in 1715, when it was seized by

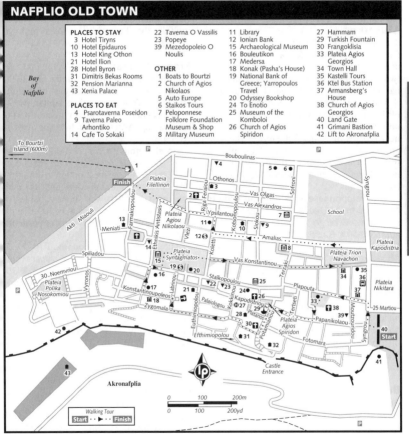

the Turks. The Turks added a further bastion beyond the moat.

There are two main approaches to the fortress. The energetic can tackle the seemingly endless 999 steps that begin southeast of the bus station. Climb early and take water. There's also a road to the fortress. A taxi costs about €3.50 one way.

Bourtzi

This small island fortress lies about 600m northwest of the old town and guards the entrance to the port. Although referred to by its Turkish name, it was built by the Venetians at the end of the 15th century. The square tower at the centre was added during the second period of Venetian rule. Boats to the island leave from the northeastern end of Akti Miaouli, provided there are at least four passengers. The trip costs €1.50 per person.

Museums

The **archaeological museum** (☎ 2752-027 502; Plateia Syntagmatos; admission €1.50; open 8.30am-3pm Tues-Sun) occupies the top two floors of the 18th-century Venetian arsenal at the western end of Plateia Syntagmatos.

The collection features pottery from Neolithic to classical times, including some unusual late-Mycenaean figurines from the nearby sites of Asini and Tiryns. The star attraction is a 15th-century-BC suit of bronze armour uncovered virtually intact near Mycenae, together with a helmet made from boar tusks.

The **Peloponnese Folklore Foundation Museum** (☎ 2752-028 947, fax 2752-027 960; W www.pli.gr; Vasileos Alexandros 1; adult/student €2.95/1.50; open 9am-3pm Wed-Mon, closed Feb) won the European Museum of the Year award in 1981 for its displays of traditional textile-producing techniques (with in-depth explanations in English) and folk costumes.

The **military museum** (Amalias 22; admission free; open 9am-2pm Tues-Sat, 9.30am-2pm Sun) traces Greece's military history from the War of Independence onwards through a collection of photographs, paintings, uniforms and assorted weaponry.

Beaches

Aravanitia Beach is a small pebble beach just a 10-minute walk south of town, tucked beneath the Palamidi Fortress.

If you're feeling energetic, you can follow a path east around the coast to sandy **Karathona Beach**, at the far side of the Palamidi Fortress. The walk takes about an hour.

Organised Tours

Staikos Tours (☎ 2752-027 950, fax 2752-028 000; e root@staikostravel.naf.forthnet.gr, Bouboulinas 50) and **Kastelli Tours** (☎ 2752-029 395, fax 2752-029 395; e kastelli@otenet.gr; Vasileos Konstantinou 33) both offer a range of tours around the Peloponnese, including Epidavros and Mycenae (€47) and cruises to Hydra and Spetses (€23.50).

Special Events

Nafplio hosts a **classical music festival** in late May and early June featuring both Greek and international performers. Venues include the Palamidi Fortress and the Bourtzi.

Places to Stay

The closest **camping grounds** are at the beach resorts around Tolo, east of Nafplio (see under Tolo later in this chapter, p119).

The cheaper rooms are in the new part of town along Argous, which is the road to Argos.

Hotel Argolis (☎/fax 2752-027 721; Argous 32; singles/doubles with bathroom €18/25) is the cheapest option, even at the official rates. It normally discounts its rooms to a bargain €8/16 for singles/doubles. If you're arriving by bus, ask to be let off at the Thanasenas stop, which is right opposite the hotel.

The nearby **Hotel Economou** (☎ 2752-023 955; Argonafton 22; beds in share room €10, doubles/triples with bathroom €30/35) is another popular choice. Owner George Economou was once the manager of the town's youth hostel (closed), and he keeps a couple of shared rooms aside for budget travellers. If you're arriving by bus, ask to be let off at the Thanasenas stop, opposite Hotel Argolis.

Most people prefer to stay in the old town, which is the most interesting place to be. Unfortunately, there is very little budget accommodation here.

Dimitris Bekas (☎ 2752-024 594; Efthimiopoulou 26; singles/doubles/triples with shared bathroom €15/21/24) is the only good budget option. His rooms are top value for a great location, above the Catholic church on the slopes of the Akronafplia. The rooftop terrace has great views over the old town.

Hotel Epidavros (☎/fax 2752-027 541; cnr Ypsilantou & Kokinou; doubles with bathroom €35.20) is a good fall-back, with a selection of rooms here and at the co-owned **Hotel Tiryns** (☎ 2752-021 020; Othonos 41) nearby.

For a room with a view, head to **Pension Marianna** (☎ 2752-024 256, fax 2752-021 783; W www.pensionmarianna.gr; Potaminou 9; singles/doubles/triples with bathroom €40/50/60), perched high above the town. It's a family business run by brothers Panos, Petros and Takis, with large rooms. Prices include a generous buffet breakfast, served on the terrace overlooking the town.

For many years it was the stylish **Hotel Byron** (☎ 2752-022 351, fax 2752-026 338; W www.byronhotel.gr; Platanos 2; singles/doubles/triples with bathroom €38.15/52.85-70.50/64.60-76.30) that set the standard for the city's hotel operators. It still remains a class act: a fine old building beautifully furnished in traditional style. It's worth paying more for a room with a view. The hotel is up the steps opposite the church of Agios Spiridon on Kapodistriou. Breakfast costs €5.90.

Hotel King Othon (☎/fax 2752-027 595; Farmakopoulou 4; singles/doubles €48/66, 4-bed family room €90) has come up looking a treat after a change of ownership and a complete refit. Prices include breakfast.

Hotel Rex (☎ 2752-026 907, fax 2752-028 106; Bouboulinas 21; singles/doubles €53/81) is another place that has been transformed after a change of ownership. It has large, comfortable rooms with air-con, TV and fridge. Prices include buffet breakfast.

The **Hotel Ilion** (☎ 2752-025 114, fax 2752-024 497; W www.ilionhotel.gr; Kapodistriou 6; doubles with bathroom €64.60-114.50) is the latest addition to Nafplio's range of luxury accommodation, aimed at well-heeled Athenian couples looking for a romantic weekend away. Housed in a renovated mansion, the 15 rooms carry names like the Room of Passion and the Suite of Dreams. The best room, the Suite of Love and Soul, has a Jacuzzi. Breakfast will set

you back €7.35. Hotel services include a hair stylist and an aesthetician – to ensure that guests look and feel their best!

Formerly one of the flagships of the government-run Xenia chain, the **Xenia Palace** (☎ 2752-028 981/5, fax 2752-028 783; W www.nafplionhotels.gr, Akronafplia; singles/doubles with bathroom €188/235, bungalows/suites €141/470) has lifted its game considerably under private ownership – but not enough to justify these prices.

The city's original **Xenia Hotel**, controversially built atop the Akronafplia's historic Castel di Toro Bastion, was closed at the time of research while new owners pondered the building's future. A demolition team would be the kindest choice for this pile of crumbling concrete and rusting iron rods. It's an eyesore of embarrassing proportions.

Places to Eat

The streets of the old town are filled with dozens of restaurants. Staïkopoulou, in particular, is one long chain of restaurants; it would take weeks to eat at all of them. Most of these places close down in winter and the choice shrinks to a few long-standing favourites.

Top of the list is the excellent **Taverna Paleo Arhontiko** (☎ 2752-022 449; cnr Ypsilantou & Siokou; mains €4.40-7.65). Owner Tassos runs the place like a party, and it's very popular with locals. There is live music every night from 10pm in summer, and on Friday and Saturday night in winter. Reservations are essential on weekends.

Mezedopoleio O Noulis (☎ 2752-025 541; Moutzouridou 21; meze €1.50-7.50) is another popular spot. It serves a fabulous range of mezedes (snacks) which can easily be combined to form a meal. Check out the saganaki flambé (€3.75), ignited with Metaxa (brandy) as it reaches your table.

Taverna O Vassilis (☎ 2752-025 334; Staïkopoulou 20-24; mains €4-7.65) is a popular family-run place at the heart of the restaurant strip on Staïkopoulou. It has a large choice of starters, and a good selection of main dishes – including a very tasty rabbit stifado (stew) for €4.85.

The restaurants along the promenade on Bouboulinas specialise in seafood.

Psarotaverna Poseidon (☎ 2752-027 515; Bouboulinas 77; kalamari €4.70, fish from

€23.50 per kg) is the territory of Kostas Bikakis, once acclaimed by a French travel magazine as 'the greatest kamaki (woman-iser) in the Argolid'. That was back in the 1950s. You can read about his exploits and study photos of a youthful Kostas with a bevy of glamorous girls while you munch on a plate of kalamaria or fresh fish.

Popeye (Staïkopoulou 32; breakfast €2.35-4.40) has a good selection of breakfast menus and reasonable prices. **Cafe To Sokaki** (☎ 2752-026 032; Ethnikis Antistasis 8) is an-other breakfast option.

Self-caterers will find a choice of **super-markets** in the new town, including **Marino-poulos** (cnr Syngrou & Flessa), **Atlantik** (Bouboulinas 24) and **Dia Discount Super-market** (cnr Leoforos Argous & Argonafton).

Entertainment
Nafplio seems to have almost as many nightclubs and bars as it has restaurants. Most of them are on Bouboulinas – just cruise along until you find a sound that you like at a volume you can handle.

You'll find live Greek music at **To Paleo Lihnari** (☎ 2752-022 041; Bouboulinas 39) on Friday and Saturday night.

Shopping
Despite the name, **Museum of the Komboloi** (☎/fax 2752-021 618; W www.komboloi.gr, Staïkopoulou 25; admission €1.50) is really more of a shop than a museum. It sells a wide range of komboloi (worry beads), evil-eye charms and amulets. The upstairs museum has a collection of ancient beads assembled by owner Aris Evangelinos.

To Enotio (☎ 2752-021 143; Staïkopoulou 40) produces and sells traditional and mod-ern Greek shadow puppets, priced from €6.

Getting There & Away
Bus The bus station (☎ 2752-027 323; W www.ktel.org; Syngrou 8) is a hive of activity. Local services include Argos (€0.85, 30 minutes, half-hourly), Epidav-ros (€2.15, 40 minutes, three daily), Gala-tas (€5.65, two hours, three daily), Myce-nae (€1.90, one hour, three daily), Porto Heli (€4.85, two hours, three daily) and Tolo (€0.85, 15 minutes, hourly).

There are also buses to Athens (€8.50, 2½ hours, hourly) via Corinth (€3.95, 1¼ hours), and to Tripolis (€4.25, 1½ hours).

Train Train services from Nafplio are of li[t]tle more than academic interest. There ar[e] trains to Athens (€4.70, three hours) leav[]ing at 6.10am and 6.30pm daily. The statio[n] is by the port on Bouboulinas. The **ticke[t] office** (☎ 2752-026 400) is in a converte[d] carriage behind an old steam train.

Hydrofoil Hydrofoil services from Nafpli[o] had been suspended at the time of writing[.] Check at **Yannopoulos Travel** (☎ 2752-02[]456, fax 2752-022 393; Plateia Syntagmatos[)].

Getting Around
There are several car-hire places in town, s[o] it pays to shop around. Two places wort[h] checking out are **Auto Europe** (☎ 2752-02[]160/1, fax 2752-024 164; Bouboulinas 5[?]) and **Safe Way Rent a Car** (☎ 2752-022 155[] fax 2752-025 738; Agiou 2). **Moto Ren[]** (☎ 2752-021 407, fax 2752-025 642; Poli[]zoidou 8) also has motorcycles.

AROUND NAFPLIO
Tiryns Τίρυνθα
The ruins of Homer's 'wall-girt Tiryns['] (☎ 2752-022 657; admission €1.50; ope[n] 8am-8pm daily Apr-Oct, to 2.30pm Nov[-] Mar) lie 4km northwest of Nafplio besid[e] the road to Argos.

They occupy a low hill that has been in[-] habited since Neolithic times. Its proximit[y] to the sea and the fertile soils of the sur[-] rounding plain made it an ideal location[.] This early settlement developed into one o[f] the major centres of the subsequent Myce[-] naean civilisation, with a palace complex t[o] rival those uncovered at Mycenae and a[t] Pylos, in Messinia. It was considered im[-] portant enough to justify the building of [a] fortifying wall in 1400 BC – well befor[e] Mycenae took similar action. Constructio[n] continued until 1200 BC, when the palac[e] was destroyed by fire and abandoned.

The walls which so impressed Homer re[-] main just an impressive today. They repre[-] sent the supreme example of the so-calle[d] Cyclopean style of construction found a[t] many Mycenaean sites. Stretching som[e] 725m, the walls are almost 20m thick i[n] parts, and the largest stones are estimated t[o] weigh 14 tons – so massive that subsequen[t] civilisations reasoned that they could only have been built by a Cyclops, a mythica[l] one-eyed monster with superhuman strength[.]

Within the walls lies a complex of vaulted galleries, secret stairways and storage chambers, topped by the remains of the palace at the high point of the hill. Fragments of frescoes uncovered at the site indicate that the palace was once richly decorated. These fragments now reside in the National Archaeological Museum in Athens. Other finds from the site, including a fine 12th-century-BC bronze helmet, can be seen at the Archaeological Museum in Nafplio.

Any Nafplio–Argos bus can drop you outside the site.

TOLO

postcode 210 56 • pop 1986

Tolo, 10km southeast of Nafplio, is the best known of a string of small resort towns on the south coast of the Argolis Peninsula. It lies at the western end of a large sheltered bay, protected by a headland to the east and the islands of Koronis and Romvi to the south.

Tolo has long been a favourite with the Brits, who come here in large numbers in July and August. In winter the place is almost deserted.

Orientation & Information

Tolo is virtually a one-street town. The street begins in the southeast as the road from Nafplio and curves around Tolo Bay one block back from the seafront before finishing at a large parking lot next to a picturesque little fishing port. The street doglegs in the middle of town, and its name changes from Bouboulinas to Seferi.

Most services of importance to travellers are in the centre of town on Seferi, including branches of the **Bank Emporiki** (Seferi 6) and the **Alpha Bank** (Seferi 28). The post office is opposite the giant Doukas Supermarket on Minoos, which runs inland off Sekeri in the middle of town. **In-Touch Internet Café** (☎ 2752-099 580; open 9am-11pm daily) is well set up.

Ancient Asini

Ancient Asini occupies a rocky promontory jutting out into Tolo Bay 1.5km southeast of Tolo. The site is not enclosed and can be visited at any time.

Asini was occupied from early Mycenaean times and destroyed by Argos, along with nearby Nafplio, in the 7th century BC

for allying itself with Sparta. Like Nafplio, it was reborn in the 4th century and some impressive sections of the defensive wall built at this time can be seen on the south side of the headland, next to Kastraki Camping.

Most of the site is very overgrown, although it's still possible to discern the ruins of a bath house added in Roman times and the foundations of various buildings. Excavations here in 1920s uncovered the celebrated **Lord of Asini**, an unusual male clay figurine sculpted in the 12th century BC. It now resides in the archaeological museum at Nafplio, along with other finds from the site.

Buses operating between Nafplio and Tolo stop at the site, which is an easy walk along the beach from Tolo.

Beaches

Tolo once boasted the best of the **beach** along this part of the coast but much of it has now disappeared – the victim of beach-front development. The beach gets better to the south of town and the best stretch is south of ancient Asini.

Places to Stay & Eat

Accommodation can be hard to find in July and August, when many hotels are block-booked by tour companies.

Kastraki Camping (☎ 2752-059 386/387, fax 2752-059 572; 1.5km east of Tolo; adult/tent €5.90/5.30; open Apr-Oct) is easily the best of the many camping grounds along this stretch of coast, with shady sites, good facilities and a great location on the beach right next to ancient Asini. It's signposted off the road to Tolo.

Mari Apartments (☎ 2752-059 006, fax 2752 059 918; 2-person apartments €50; open year-round) has a top spot overlooking the sea close to the centre of town on Bouboulinas. The apartments are equipped with kitchen, TV and air-con, and the balconies have views across Tolo Bay to the island of Koronis.

Having a prime position, overlooking Tolo Bay at the northern end of Bouboulinas, is doubtless the main reason that **Café-Restaurant Panorama** (☎ 2752-058 328; mains €4.50-12.50) is one of the few restaurants in town that does stay open year round.

ARGOLIS

There are plenty of **fast-food places** on Sekeri.

Getting There & Away

There are hourly buses from Nafplio to Tolo (€0.85, 30 minutes) via Asini. The buses stop at several points along the main street and terminate at the parking lot by the port, from where they leave for the return trip.

Getting Around

Moto Rent (*☎ 2752-058 303; Sekeri 74*) hires both cars and motorcycles.

ARKADIKO

The tiny village of Arkadiko, 14km west of Nafplio, is today little more than a blip on the map on the road to Ligourio and Epidavros. In Mycenaean times it was a settlement of some significance, strategically located above a fertile valley.

The foundations of a small **tholos tomb** by the roadside are overlooked by the ruins of **Kazarma Castle**. The crumbling walls have been modified many times over the centuries.

The main attraction around here, though, is the wonderful Mycenaean bridge about 500m west of town. It stands beside the Nafplio–Arkadiko road, on the northern side of a sharp bend.

LIGOURIO

postcode 210 52 • pop 2678

The town of Ligourio lies at the centre of the Argolis Peninsula 25km east of Nafplio. Its main attraction is the nearby Asklepion of Epidavros, home of the world-famous Theatre of Epidavros, and the town is sometimes referred to as Asklepiou.

All facilities of importance to travellers are spread out along the main street, Asklepiou, which doubles as the main road through town. There are a couple of banks and a post office, as well as hotels and restaurants.

Things to See

The small **Natural History Museum of Asklepion Epidavros** (*☎ 0753-022 587; admission €1.50; open 9am-8pm Mon-Sat*) is home to a large private collection of fossils and mineral crystals, as well as an interesting history of the evolution of the Greek landmass. It's at the eastern end of Asklepion, just beyond the small square with the tiny 11th century **Church of Agios Ioannou Eleimon** (St John the Merciful). It's typically Byzantine, and the walls are dotted with slabs and columns gleaned from earlier buildings.

Places to Stay & Eat

A small family-run hotel, the **Hotel Koronis** (*☎ 2753-022 267, fax 2753-022 450; Naf-plio-Epidavros road; singles/doubles with bathroom €25/30*) is the best bet for the independent traveller. It's conveniently situated in the middle of town on the main street.

Taverna Leonidas (*☎ 2753-022 115; Asklepiou 103; mains €3.50-7*) is a typical village taverna, with a small assortment of daily specials like *moussaka* (€4.50) and veal with potatoes (€5).

Getting There & Away

Ligourio is something of a transport hub, standing at the junction of the roads west to Nafplio, east to Palea Epidavros and south to the tip of Argolis. There are frequent buses to Nafplio (€2.15, 35 minutes), three a day to Palea Epidavros (€1.30, 20 minutes), three to Galatas (€4, 1½ hours) and three to Kranidi, Porto Heli and Kosta. The buses also run in the opposite direction.

Buses from Nafplio to the Asklepion of Epidavros stop in town; otherwise it's a comfortable 40-minute walk from town or €2.50 by taxi.

EPIDAVROS Επίδαυρος

Epidavros (*eh-**pee-dahv-ross**), 30km east of Nafplio, is one of the most renowned of Greece's ancient sites (*☎ 2753-022 006; admission €6*), as reflected by its listing as a World Heritage Site. Epidavros was a sanctuary of Asclepius, the god of medicine. The difference in the atmosphere here, compared with that of the war-oriented Mycenaean cities, is immediately obvious. Henry Miller wrote in *The Colossus of Maroussi* that Mycenae 'folds in on itself', but Epidavros is 'open, exposed…devoted to the spirit'. Epidavros seems to emanate joy, optimism and celebration.

History & Mythology

Legend has it that Asclepius was the son of Apollo and Coronis. While giving birth to

Asclepius, Coronis was struck by a thunderbolt and killed. Apollo took his son to Mt Pelion in Thessaly where the centaur physician Chiron instructed the boy in the healing arts.

Apollo was worshipped at Epidavros in Mycenaean and Archaic times but, by the 4th century BC, he had been superseded by his son. Epidavros became acknowledged as the birthplace of Asclepius. Although there were sanctuaries to Asclepius throughout Greece, the two most important were at Epidavros and on the island of Kos. The fame of the sanctuary soon spread beyond the Greek world. Livy and Ovid relate that Rome sent to Epidavros for help when the city was struck by plague in 293 BC.

It is believed that licks from snakes were one of the curative practices at the sanctuary. Asclepius is normally shown with a serpent, which – by renewing its skin – symbolises rejuvenation. Other treatments provided at the sanctuary involved diet instruction, herbal medicines and occasionally even surgery. The sanctuary also served as an entertainment venue. Every four years the Festival of Asclepieia took place at Epidavros. Dramas were staged and athletic competitions were held.

Theatre

Today the 3rd-century theatre, not the sanctuary, pulls the crowds to Epidavros. It is one of the best-preserved classical Greek buildings, renowned for its amazing acoustics. A coin dropped in the centre can be heard from the highest seat. Built of limestone, the theatre seats up to 14,000 people. Its entrance is flanked by restored Corinthian pilasters. The theatre is still used for live performances during the Hellenic Festival in July and August (see the Entertainment section).

Museum

The museum, between the sanctuary and the theatre, houses statues, stone inscriptions recording miraculous cures, surgical instruments, votive offerings and partial reconstructions of the sanctuary's once-elaborate **tholos**. After the theatre, the tholos is considered to have been the site's most impressive building and fragments of beautiful, intricately carved reliefs from its ceiling are also displayed.

Sanctuary

The vast ruins of the sanctuary are less crowded than the theatre. In the south is the huge **katagogeion**, a hostelry for pilgrims and patients. To the west is the large **banquet hall** in which the Romans built an **odeum**. It was here that the Festival of Asclepieia took place. Opposite is the **stadium**, venue for the festival's athletic competitions.

To the north are the foundations of the **Temple of Asclepius** and next to them is the **abaton**. The therapies practised here seemed to have depended on the influence of the mind upon the body. It is believed that patients were given a pep talk by a priest on the powers of Asclepius then put to sleep in the *abaton* to dream of a visitation by the god. The dream would hold the key to the healing process.

East is the **Sanctuary of Egyptian Gods**, which indicates that the cult of Asclepius was an adaptation of the cult of Imhotep, worshipped in Egypt for his healing powers. To the west of the Temple of Asclepius lie the foundations of the site's most unusual structure, known as the **tholos**. Built in the middle of the 4th century BC, it is so called because of its circular shape. Its function is unknown, but it may have been a ceremonial rotunda. It was being reconstructed at the time of research.

Set among the green foothills of Mt Arahneo, the air redolent with herbs and pine trees, it's easy to see how the sanctuary would have had a beneficial effect upon the ailing. Considering the state of Greece's current health system, perhaps the centre should be resurrected.

Entertainment

The Theatre of Epidavros is used to stage performances of ancient Greek dramas as part of the annual Hellenic Festival in July and August. Performances are held on Friday and Saturday night, starting at 9pm. Tickets can be bought in Epidavros at the **site office** (☎ 2753-022 006; open 9.30am-1pm & 6pm-9pm Thurs-Sat). Tickets can also be bought from the festival box office in Athens (see Special Events in the Athens chapter for more information, p86). Prices vary according to seating; student discounts are available. Special buses run from Athens and Nafplio during the festival.

ARGOLIS

Getting There & Away

There are buses from Nafplio to Epidavros (40 minutes, €2.15, four daily) via Ligourio (€2.15), and two buses daily to Athens (2½ hours, €8.40). The buses also operate return services.

PALEA EPIDAVROS
postcode 210 59 • pop 1733

Palea Epidavros is a pretty little seaside resort on the Saronic Gulf, 10km east of Ligourio. It is a favourite summer destination for Athenians, but is seldom visited by foreign tourists.

Activity is concentrated around the small central square by the sea, which is flanked with an assortment of cafés, hotels and restaurants. There's an **ATM** on the square but no bank.

The town is named Palea (old) because it is the site of ancient Epidavros – and to distinguish it from the nearby town of Nea Epidavros, 8km to the north. Nea Epidavros is best known for hosting the first meeting of the Greek national assembly in 1822.

Ancient Epidavros

The ancient city stood on the headland at the southern edge of town. It also has a theatre. This one is a pocket version compared with the mighty theatre at Asklepion Epidavros. It was built in the 4th century BC, nestled into the base of the headland. It's at the end of Archaia Theatrou, signposted off the southern road into town. Little else remains, except for a few sections of the ancient walls.

Beaches

The headland separates the small, sheltered town beach from tranquil Agios Vlassis Bay, with a pebble beach that curves away to the south. The water here is ideal for **swimming** and there is **snorkelling** around the headland.

Places to Stay & Eat

Small and well organised, **Camping Nicolas I** (☎ 2753-041 297; adult/tent €4.70/4.30) has a great position at the northern end of Agios Vlassis Beach and shady sites set among orange trees.

Hotel/Restaurant Mouria (☎ 2753-041 218, fax 2753-041 492; e gikasgroup@ forthnet.org.gr; doubles/triples with bathroom

€45/55) is run by the same family as Camping Nicolas I – an orange orchard separates the two. The location is even better, with comfortable rooms overlooking the bay. The shady beachside terrace restaurant is the perfect spot to feast on grilled fish and salad.

Getting There & Away

There are three buses a day to and from Nafplio (€2.60, one hour), and two a day to and from Athens (€7.60, 2¼ hours).

METHANA PENINSULA

The Methana Peninsula bulges out into the Saronic Gulf about 40km east of Ligourio, forming the eastern flank of the Gulf of Epidavros. It's virtually an island, connected to the mainland only by a narrow, swampy isthmus.

The air around the peninsula is dominated by the smell of sulphur that emanates from hot springs on the east coast. This betrays the area's volcanic origins; the old crater is at the northwestern tip of the peninsula.

The main town and port, also called Methana, is on the east coast. The sparse ruins of ancient Methana can be seen below the village of Megalohori. A road continues from here to Kameini Hora on the slopes of the volcano. A very rough path leads from here to the crater.

Methana lies on the bus route between Nafplio and Galatas, and there are three services a day in each direction. Methana also lies on the popular Saronic Gulf Islands ferry route from Piraeus. It has at least four ferries a day to Piraeus (2½ hours).

ANCIENT TROIZEN Τροιζα

The remains of ancient Troizen lie scattered across a hillside near the modern village of Trizina, 45km southeast of Ligourio.

Troizen's main claim to fame is that it was the birthplace of the mythical hero Theseus, who went on slay the Minotaur and become king of Athens. The myth suggests that Troizen was one of the few coastal cities in the Peloponnese where Ionian traditions continued after the arrival of Dorians, for Theseus was an Ionian hero (while the Dorians liked Heracles).

The myth also provides a basis for the close relationship between Troizen and Athens. The two shared many traditions and cults, and Troizen became a refuge for

Athenian women and children during the Persian invasion beginning in 480 BC.

The ruins themselves don't amount to much more than a good excuse to go for a walk. The principal feature is the foundation of the **Sanctuary of Hippolytos**, a large temple built in the 4th century BC – and destroyed by an eruption on Methana the following century. It stands on a wide terrace and overlooks the remains of the **asklepion**. A section of the 3rd-century-BC city wall remains intact, together with a square defensive tower. Small stones in the upper construction indicate Frankish rebuilding.

A footpath leads uphill from the site to the **Devil's Bridge**, a natural rock extension that bridges across the deep Gefyron Gorge.

Getting There & Away

The site is difficult to get to without your own transport. Buses from Galatas to Trizina can drop you at the turn-off to the site, leaving a walk of about 1km.

GALATAS

postcode 212 00 • pop 2592

The small seaside town of Galatas, 50km southeast of Ligourio, sits opposite the Saronic Gulf island of Poros, just 350m away across the narrow Poros Strait. Galatas is, in fact, best looked on as a mainland extension of Poros.

There are several hotels along the seafront, as well as cafés and restaurants, but the choice is much better on Poros (see the Islands chapter, p193, for details).

Visitors normally treat Galatas as a starting point for a walk along the coast to the celebrated citrus groves of **Lemonodassos** (lemon forest), which start 2km to the southeast, or for a visit to the ruins of ancient **Troizen**, legendary birthplace of Theseus, in the hills near the modern village of Trizina, 7.5km west of Galatas.

Getting There & Away

Bus The bus station (☎ 2298-022 480) is opposite the terminal for car ferries to Poros. There are three buses a day to and from Nafplio (€5.65, two hours), travelling via Methana. There are also buses to and from Trizina (€0.80, 15 minutes).

Ferry Small boats operate on the five-minute hop between Galatas and Poros (€0.30). They leave when they've got enough passengers, which seldom involves waiting long. There are also car ferries (€2.75, 15 minutes) every half-hour from 7am to 9.30pm. (See the Poros section of the Islands chapter, p193, for details of ferry and hydrofoil services from Poros to Piraeus, Methana and elsewhere.)

Getting Around

The district is ideal for exploring by bicycle, which can be hired on the seafront in Galatas.

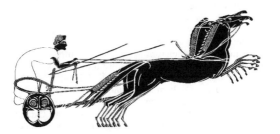

Arcadia Αρκαδία

The picturesque rural prefecture of Arcadia occupies much of the central Peloponnese. Its name evokes images of grassy meadows, forested mountains, gurgling streams and shady grottoes. It was a favourite haunt of Pan, who played his pipes, guarded herds and frolicked with nymphs in this sunny, bucolic idyll.

Almost encircled by high mountains, Arcadia was remote enough in ancient times to remain largely untouched by the battles and intrigues of the rest of Greece. It was the only region of the Peloponnese not conquered by the Dorians. It remains a backwater, dotted with crumbling medieval villages, remote monasteries and Frankish castles, visited only by determined tourists. It also has 100-odd kilometres of unspoilt coastline on the Argolic Gulf, running south from Kaveri to Leonidio.

Tripolis Τρίπολη

postcode 221 00 • pop 25,520

The violent recent history of Arcadia's capital, Tripolis (**tree**-po-lee), is in stark contrast with the surrounding rural idyll. In 1821, during the War of Independence, the town was captured by Kolokotronis and its 10,000 Turkish inhabitants were massacred. The Turks took the town again four years later, and burnt it to the ground before withdrawing in 1828.

Tripolis itself is not a place to linger long, but it's a major transport hub for the Peloponnese. It also has some impressive neoclassical buildings and Byzantine churches.

Orientation & Information

Tripolis can be a bit confusing at first. The streets radiate out from the central square, Plateia Vasileos Georgiou, like an erratic spider's web. The main streets are Washington, which runs south from the square to Kalamata; Ethnikis Antistaseos, which runs north from the square and becomes the road to Kalavryta; and Vasileos Georgiou, which runs east from the square to Plateia Kolokotroni. El Venizelou runs east from Plateia Kolokotroni, leading to the road to Corinth.

Highlights

- Visiting the superbly presented water power museum at Dimitsana
- Rafting on the magical Lousios River near Karitena
- Exploring unspoilt Leonidio, nestled below the sheer cliffs of the dramatic Badron Gorge

The main Arkadias bus station is conveniently central on Plateia Kolokotroni. The city's other bus station is opposite the train station, about a 10-minute walk away, at the southeastern end of Lagopati, the street that runs behind the Arkadias station.

There's a **tourist information office** (☎ 271-023 1844; Ethnikis Antistaseos 43; open 7am-2pm Mon-Fri) in the town hall, about 250m north of Plateia Vasileos Georgiou. The **tourist police** (☎ 271-022 2265) cohabit with the regular police at Plateia Petrinou, which is the square between Plateia Georgiou and the town hall. The police station is next to the ornate Malliaropoulio Theatre.

The **post office** (cnr Plapouta & Nikitara) is just off Plateia Vasileos Georgiou, behind Hotel Galaxy. The **Organismos Tilepikoinonion Ellados (OTE)** is nearby on 28 Oktovriou. Internet access is available at the **Pacman Net Café** (☎ 271-022 6407; Deligianni 3; open 10am-late daily), in the

ARCADIA

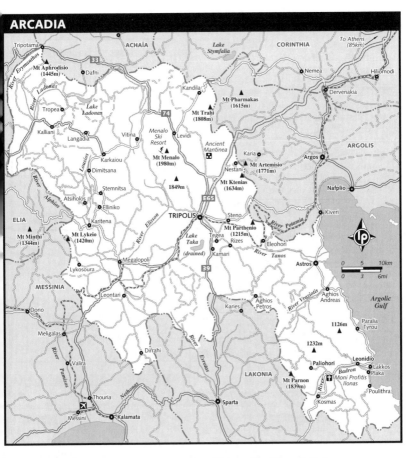

café-packed pedestrian precinct near Hotel Anactoricon.

Tripolis has branches of all the major banks. The **National Bank of Greece** (cnr 28 Oktovriou & Ethnikis Antistaseos • Plateia Kolokotroni) is centrally located. The bookshop on the northern side of Plateia Vasileos Georgiou sells English-language newspapers.

Archaeological Museum

The city's archaeological museum (☎ 271-024 2148; Evangistrias 2; admission €1.50; open 8.30am-3pm Tues-Sun) occupies a neoclassical mansion and is clearly signposted off Vasileos Georgiou next to Hotel Alex. The museum houses finds from the surrounding ancient sites of Megalopoli, Gortys, Lykosoura and Mantinea.

Places to Stay & Eat

Hotel Alex (☎ 271-022 3465, fax 271-022 3466; Vasileos Georgiou 26; singles/doubles/triples with bathroom €25/40/45) had just had a radical refit at the time of research. It's top value for spacious, air-con rooms, each with a TV.

Hotel Anactoricon (☎ 271-022 2545, fax 271-022 2021; Ethnikis Antistaseos 48; singles/doubles/triples with bathroom €45/60/70) is a friendly, family-run hotel beyond the town hall. It has comfortable rooms with air-con and TV, and discounts are normally negotiable.

Estiatorio Ioniko (☎ 271-022 2908; Plateia Vasileos Georgiou; mains €2.95-5.30) is a good no-nonsense taverna with a fine range of dishes, speedy service and bargain prices.

ARCADIA

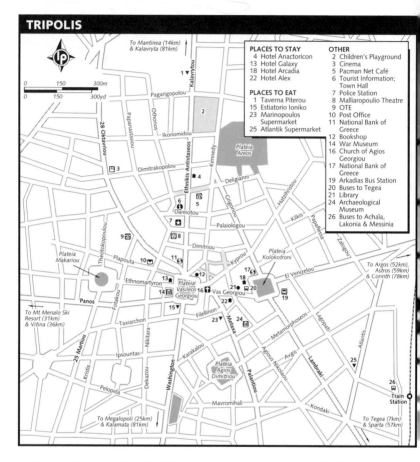

TRIPOLIS

To Mantinea (14km)
& Kalavryta (81km)

PLACES TO STAY	OTHER
4 Hotel Anactoricon	2 Children's Playground
13 Hotel Galaxy	3 Cinema
18 Hotel Arcadia	5 Pacman Net Café
22 Hotel Alex	6 Tourist Information;
	Town Hall
PLACES TO EAT	7 Police Station
1 Taverna Piterou	8 Malliaropoulio Theatre
15 Estiatorio Ioniko	9 OTE
23 Marinopoulos	10 Post Office
Supermarket	11 National Bank of
25 Atlantik Supermarket	Greece
	12 Bookshop
	14 War Museum
	16 Church of Agios
	Georgiou
	17 National Bank of
	Greece
	19 Arkadias Bus Station
	20 Buses to Tegea
	21 Library
	24 Archaeological
	Museum
	26 Buses to Achaïa,
	Lakonia & Messinia

To Argos (52km),
Astros (59km)
& Corinth (78km)

To Mt Menalo Ski
Resort (31km)
& Vitina (36km)

To Megalopoli (25km)
& Kalamata (81km)

To Tegea (7km)
& Sparta (57km)

Train Station

Taverna Piterou (☎ 271-022 2058; Kalavrytou 11A; mains €3.55-7.05) is a popular taverna for something a shade more upmarket. It's on the northern extension of Ethnikis Antistaseos, beyond the park with the old steam train.

There are numerous supermarkets around town, including a large **Atlantik** (☎ 271-022 3412; cnr Atlantis & Lagopati).

Getting There & Away

Bus The **Arkadias bus station** (☎ 271-022 2560) on Plateia Kolokotroni is the city's main terminal. There are 12 buses daily to Athens (€10.35, 2¼ hours) via Corinth (€5, one hour). There are also at least two buses daily west to Olympia (€8.10, 2½ hours) and Pyrgos (€9.40, three hours), and

three east to Argos (€3.50, one hour) and Nafplio (€4.25, 1½ hours).

Regional services include buses to:

to	fare (€)	duration (hrs)	frequency (daily)
Andritsena	5.15	1½	2
Dimitsana	4.60	1½	2
Karitena	3.40	1	5
Leonidio	6.10	2½	2
Megalopoli	2.20	35 min	8
Stemnitsa	4	1¼	3

Buses to Tegea (€0.80, 20 minutes) leave hourly from the stop outside Hotel Arkadia on Plateia Kolokotroni.

The **bus station** (☎ 271-024 2086) on Lagopati handles departures to Achaïa,

Lakonia and Messinia. It also includes departures to Sparta (€3.25, one hour, nine daily), Kalamata (€5, two hours, six daily), Kalavryta (€5.50, 2¼ hours, one daily) and Patras (€10.30, four hours).

Train Tripolis sits on the main Athens–Kalamata line. There are four trains daily to Athens (€5.30, four hours) via Argos (€2.35, 1¼ hours) and Corinth (€3.25, 2¼ hours). There are also trains to Kalamata (€3.10, 2½ hours, four daily).

Around Tripolis

Ancient Tegea, 8km southeast of Tripolis, was the most important city in Arcadia in classical and Roman times. Tegea was constantly bickering with its arch rival, Mantinea, and fought a long war with Sparta, to which it finally capitulated and became allied with in the Peloponnesian Wars. Tegea was laid waste in the 5th century AD but was rebuilt by the Byzantines, who called it Nikli. The ruins of the city lie scattered around the modern village of Tegea (also called Alea).

The bus from Tripolis stops outside Tegea's small **museum** (☎ 271-055 6540; admission €1.50; open 8.30am-3pm Tues-Sun), which houses thrones, statues and reliefs from the surrounding ruins. The collection includes a section of the pediment from the 4th-century-BC Doric **Temple of Athena Alea** showing Achilles dragging the body of Hector around the walls of Troy. The temple's pediment was regarded as one of the greatest artworks of its time. The ruins of the temple are 400m north of the museum and are clearly signposted. Another piece to look out for is the marble throne with the feet of a lion, found at the ancient theatre, 2km northwest of the museum near the **Church of Episkopi**.

Ancient Mantinea
Αρχαια Μαντινεα
Ancient Mantinea, 13km north of Tripolis, was the arch rival of Tegea in ancient times. The city covered a large area, spreading down onto the Plain of Mantinea from its acropolis on Gortsoli Hill, where sections of the ancient wall survive. The main section of the site is the area surrounding the agora, which is on the plain near the village of Milia – signposted off the Tripolis–Levidi road. Features include a small **theatre**, set on a low mound raised above the swampy plain.

Opposite the site stands the fabulous **Church of Agia Fotini**, an extraordinary building that appears to feature just about every architectural style in the history of Greece. It was built in 1973 and is surrounded by several other interesting pseudo-ancient monuments. It makes an interesting diversion for travellers with their own vehicle; there's no public transport.

MEGALOPOLI Μεγαλόπολη
postcode 222 00 • pop 5114
Despite its name, there's little left of Megalopoli (Great City) to reflect its former grandeur. The modern town is no more than a dull service centre that has grown up to feed and house workers at the enormous power station just north of town. It provides power for most of the Peloponnese, using coal strip-mined from the surrounding plains to fuel its steam turbines.

Few travellers pause for much longer than it takes to change buses or stock up on provisions.

History
Megalopoli was founded as the capital of Arcadia in 371 BC by the Theban general Epaminondas. His intention was to create a city strong enough to contain Sparta, recently defeated at the Battle of Leuctra. The new city was populated with reluctant citizens drawn from other Arcadian cities. It was sacked by Spartans 150 years later and never really recovered. It was finally abandoned in the 5th century AD.

Ancient Megalopoli
The ruins of the ancient city begin about 1km north of the modern town, on the road to Karitena. It must have been an idyllic spot in ancient times, nestled in a leafy valley on the banks of the Elisson River. These days, it stands almost in the shadow of the power station and giant smokestacks fill the sky with columns of thick, grey smoke.

The only feature worth stopping to check out more closely is the **ancient theatre**, which is signposted to the south of the Megalopoli–Karitena road. This suitably mega structure was excavated out of the slope of a low hill on the western bank of the River Elisson, and could seat an estimated 20,000 people. Traces of the stone seats remain, including the high-backed VIP bench that forms the front row. The foundations northwest of the theatre belong to the **bouleuterion** (council building).

The theatre and *bouleuterion* are fenced off, but there is no sign to indicate opening times. The gate was open at the time of research.

Places to Stay & Eat

There are six modest hotels to choose from, but most of them are booked out long-term by power-station workers.

Hotel Paris (☎ 2791-022 410; Agiou Nikolaou 9; singles/doubles with bathroom €20.55/32.30) is the best bet for tourists, with clean comfortable rooms close to the large central square, Plateia Polyvriou.

Psistaria O Meraklis (☎ 2791-022 789; Papanastasiou 8; mains €2.95-5.30) is a popular *psistaria* (grill restaurant), just north of Plateia Polyvriou on Papanastasiou, the road to Tripolis. It has a range of grilled food, including souvlaki sticks for €0.50, as well as salads and vegetable dishes. It's run by a Greek-Canadian family, and opens for dinner only.

Estiatorio Leontari (☎ 2791-025 580; Kolokotronis 15; mains €3.75-5.90) is one several restaurants around Plateia Polyvriou. It has a good selection of daily specials.

Getting There & Away

There are bus services to Athens (€11.85, three hours, eight daily) via Tripolis (€2.20, 35 minutes); Kalamata (€3.40, one hour, eight daily); and Andritsena (€3.20, one hour, two daily).

AROUND MEGALOPOLI
Ancient Lykosoura
Αρχαια Λυκοσουρα

Poetically described as the first city to see the sun, ancient Lykosoura lies nestled in the leafy hills 10km west of Megalopoli, near the small village of **Lykosoura**. It was the holy city of the Arcadians, and the only city that was not required to contribute citizens to populate Megalopoli.

Excavations here uncovered the remains of the **Sanctuary of Despina and Demeter**,

centred on a Doric temple. The site was closed at the time of research, but the ruins are visible from the fence. The small **museum** next to the site houses copies of colossal statues from the sanctuary. The originals are housed in the National Archaeological Museum in Athens. The museum is locked, but the key is available from the caretaker in Lykosoura.

Mt Lykeio Μτ Λυκειο

Mt Lykeio (1420m), 14km northwest of Lykosoura, was Arcadia's sacred mountain. It was here, according to local mythology, that Zeus was raised. It became the site of a mysterious cult involving human sacrifice and werewolves (*lykeio* means wolf).

It's possible to drive to the top of the mountain, although the road is not for the faint-hearted. The unsealed road begins above the village of Ano Karies, about 8km north of Lykosoura, where a signpost indicates the way. The first half of the journey is plain sailing, finishing at a large open terrace that was once the site of an ancient **stadium**. The second half of the journey is more difficult and should not be attempted in wet weather. Even in dry weather, it's a relief to find that there's enough space to turn around at the top! From here it's a short scramble to the summit, where a sign (blown horizontal by the winds) marks the **Altar of Zeus Lykeios**. Just below the summit to the northwest stand two column bases which once supported a pair of golden eagles.

Central Arcadia

The area to the west of Tripolis is a tangle of medieval villages, precipitous ravines and narrow winding roads, woven into valleys of dense vegetation beneath the slopes of the Menalon Mountains. This is the heart of the Arcadia prefecture, an area with some of the most breathtaking scenery in the Peloponnese. The region is high above sea level and nights are chilly, even in summer. Snow is common in winter.

You need your own transport to do the area justice, but the three most important villages – Karitena, Stemnitsa and Dimitsana – are within reach of Tripolis by public transport. Stemnitsa and Dimitsana are on the 37km stretch of road that cuts through the mountains from the Pyrgos–Tripolis road in the north to the Megalopoli–Andritsena road in the south. The road then follows the course of the River Lousios, its waters occasionally visible on the valley floor below.

KARITENA Καρίταινα
postcode 222 07 • pop 271

High above the Megalopoli–Andritsena road is the splendid medieval village of Karitena (kar-**eet**-eh-nah). A stepped path leads from the central square to the village's 13th-century **Frankish castle**, atop a massive rock. The castle was captured by Greek forces under Kolokotronis early in the War of Independence, and became a key stronghold as the war unfolded.

Before the advent of the euro, Karitena was best known as the home of the wonderful old, arched, stone bridge over the Alphios River that adorned the 5000-drachma note. The bridge remains, although it now sits beneath a large modern concrete bridge.

Karitena's 13th-century **Church of Agios Nikolaos** has well-preserved frescoes. The church is locked but if you ask around someone will direct you to the caretaker.

Activities
The Lousios River, which flows into the Alphios River northwest of Karitena, is a favourite spot with white-water sports enthusiasts. It's not one of the world's great rivers in terms of white water, with no rapids rated higher than three, but it makes up for that with some magnificent scenery. Fed by the countless springs that once powered the regions many mills, the Lousios is also one of the most reliable rivers in Greece.

Athens-based adventure specialist **Alpin Club** (☎ 21-0729 5486, fax 21-0721 2773; w www.alpinclub.gr) operates rafting trips every weekend between November and June, depending on the conditions. The trips cost €44 and involve about one to one-and-a-half hours of rafting. They start on the Lousios about 5km north of Karitena and ride the river to its confluence with the Alphios.

Alpin Club also offers kayaking (€44), hot-dogging in inflatable canoes (€44), canyoning (€23.50) and mountain biking (€23.50, including bike).

Alpin Club's Karitena base is on the main road, just north of the Alphios bridge.

Places to Stay & Eat
Christos Papadopoulos Rooms to Rent (☎ 2791-031 203; singles/doubles/triples with shared bathroom €17.60/23.50/29.35) is 200m north of town on the road to Gortys. The three rooms are clean but basic, with one shared bathroom.

Vrenthi Rooms (☎ 2791-031 650; doubles/triples with bathroom €35/45) is the best accommodation found in the village. The rooms at the front have fabulous views over the Alphios Valley. Café Vrenthi, 100m up the road, doubles as reception for the rooms.

Taverna To Konaki (☎ 2791-031 600; mains €2.65-4.40) is the only taverna in town. The food is not as inspiring as the views of the valley below.

Getting There & Away
Buses call at Karitena en route between Tripolis and Andritsena. A few will leave you on the main road, from where it's an arduous uphill walk to the village. The staff at the bus station from which you leave will be able to tell you where the bus will stop.

AROUND KARITENA
North of Karitena the road runs to the east of the Lousios Gorge. After 10km, south of the small village of Elliniko, a dirt track to the left leads to the site of **ancient Gortys**. It can be walked in 1½ hours or be reached by hardy vehicle. It's on the west side of the gorge, approached via a bridge. Gortys was an important city from the 4th century BC. Most ruins date from Hellenistic times, but to the north are the remains of a **Sanctuary to Asclepius**.

STEMNITSA Στεμνίτσα
postcode 220 24 • pop 412

Stemnitsa, 15km north of Karitena, is a spectacular village of stone houses and Byzantine churches. North of the village, signposts point the way to **Moni Agiou Ioannitou Prodromou**. The monastery is about 20-minutes' walk beyond the car park. A monk will show visitors the chapel's splendid 14th- and 15th-century frescoes. From here, paths lead to the deserted monasteries of **Paleou** and **Neou Philosophou**, and also south along the river bank to the site of ancient Gortys. The monks at Prodromou can direct you.

ARCADIA

Places to Stay & Eat

Hotel Triokolonion (☎ 2795-081 297, fax 2795-081 483; singles/doubles/triples with bathroom €24/35/42) is Stemnitsa's only hotel. The rooms are no better than average but the prices are nothing to complain about, and they include breakfast.

Taverna Klinitsas (☎ 2795-081 518/438; mains €3.75-6) is named after the highest peak in the surrounding hills, though the Klinitsas makes no great claims to culinary heights. It's so low-key that it doesn't have a menu, just a selection of daily specials. It's on the main street, on the Dimitsana side of the central square.

Getting There & Away

There are three buses daily between Stemnitsa and Tripolis (€4, 1¼ hours).

DIMITSANA Διμιτσάνα
postcode 220 07 • pop 611

Built amphitheatrically on two hills at the beginning of the Lousios Gorge, Dimitsana (dih-mit-**sah**-nah), 11km north of Stemnitsa, is a lovely medieval village.

Despite its remoteness, Dimitsana played a significant role in the country's struggle for self-determination. Its Greek school, founded in 1764, was an important spawning ground for the ideas leading to the uprisings against the Turks. Its students included Bishop Germanos of Patras and Patriarch Gregory V, who was hanged by the Turks in retaliation for the massacre in Tripolis. The village also had a number of gunpowder factories and a branch of the secret Filiki Eteria (Friendly Society), where Greeks met to discuss the revolution (see Russian Involvement under History in the Facts about the Peloponnese chapter, p15, for more on the Filiki Eteria).

From the heady days before Independence, Dimitsana has become a sleepy village where the most exciting event is the arrival of the daily bus from Tripolis.

Open Air Water Power Museum

This museum (☎ 2795-031 630; admission €1.20; open 10am-2pm & 5pm-7pm Wed-Mon 11 Apr-10 Oct, 10am-4pm Wed-Mon rest of year) offers a fascinating insight into the region's preindustrial past. It occupies the old Agios Yiannis mill complex, about 1.5km south of town, signposted off the road to Stemnitsa, where the waters of a spring-fed stream once supplied power for a succession of mills spread down the hillside. A flour mill, a gunpowder mill and a fulling tub (for treating wool) have been restored to working order.

A feature of this place is the high standard of the interpretive text (in Greek and English), and the use of videos (subtitled in English) to explain the processes of gunpowder and leather production.

Trekking

The best way to appreciate these magnificent surroundings is on foot. There are some wonderful walks in the Dimitsana area, particularly along the Lousios River. The principal walks are outlined in the *Walker's Map of the River Lousios Valley* (€2.95), available at the Open Air Water Power Museum.

Places to Stay

You'll see several signs for domatia (rooms) in the middle of town (Plateia Agia Kyriaki).

Tsiapas Rooms to Rent (☎ 2795-031 583; doubles with bathroom €35) has very comfortable rooms, signposted off Plateia Agia Kyriaki. All the rooms are equipped with a fridge and facilities for making tea and coffee. There's also a communal living room with a fireplace – perfect for a cold evening.

Hotel Dimitsana (☎ 2795-031 518; B&B doubles with bathroom €41.10) is Dimitsana's only hotel and it was closed for renovations at the time of research. It's 1km south of the village on the road to Stemnitsa and has great views of the Lousios Valley.

Getting There & Away

There are two buses daily from Tripolis to Dimitsana (€4.60, 1½ hours).

Kynouria

Kynouria is the name of the coastal region of Arcadia. It covers a narrow strip of territory that stretches from the tiny village of Kaveri, 41km east of Tripolis, to Kosmas, perched high in the Mt Parnon ranges close to the Lakonian border. Much of the land is incredibly rugged, with a narrow coastal plain and very little fertile ground.

In ancient times the region was contested by Argos and Sparta, with the Argives holding sway in the north and the Spartans controlling the south. Although modern Kynouria is part of Arcadia, the best access is from Argos.

KIVERI TO LEONIDIO
Κιβερι το Λεονιδιο
Kiveri is no more than a blip on the map, on the coast 41km east of Tripolis. It lies across the border in neighbouring Argolis, at the meeting point of the main roads east from Tripolis and south from Argos, just 12km to the north. The road re-enters Arcadia just south of Kiveri and hugs the coast for most of the 64km stretch south to Leonidio, curving above tiny pebble-beached villages.

The first town of consequence is Astros, perched in the hills 28km south of Argos and overlooking the resort of Paralio Astros. The town and resort, however, couldn't be more different. **Astros** is a pretty village, known for its dahlias and roses. The main attraction is the **villa of Herodes Atticus**, in the hills 2km west of Astros. It was built in the 2nd century AD for the wealthy Roman founder of the celebrated Theatre of Herodes Atticus in Athens. This was his modest country retreat, spread out over a small plateau and with views over the Argolic Gulf. Recent excavations have uncovered a stunning spread of more than 1000 sq metres of mosaics. They have been left in situ and will be put on display once a roof has been built to protect them from the elements.

Paralio Astros is an unattractive modern resort full of multistorey concrete apartment blocks that has sprung up next to a beach that is no better than average. Land for this development was created by bulldozing and filling the surrounding coastal wetlands – a prime example of environmental hooliganism. The saving grace of the place is the old fortress of **Paleo Astros**, which stands on a rocky outcrop to the north of the resort.

Apart from some magnificent coastal scenery, there's very little to see between Astros and the minor resort of **Paralia Tyrou**, 29km further south. Also known as **Tyrosapounakia**, it appears to be doing its best to emulate Paralio Astros. Development at this stage is limited to a smattering of hotels and tavernas.

LEONIDIO Λεονιδιο
postcode 223 00 • pop 3224
The small town of Leonidio, 76km south of Argos, has a dramatic setting at the mouth of the Badron Gorge. Its tiny Plateia 25 Martiou is an archetypal, unspoilt, whitewashed village square, surrounded by shady trees. The OTE is visible from the square, and the **police** (☎ 2757-022 222) are close at hand on Kiloso. Many of the older people around here still speak *Chakonika*, the language of ancient Sparta, in preference to Greek.

There are excellent, unspoilt beaches at the nearby seaside villages of **Plaka** and **Poulithra**. Plaka, which is no more than a cluster of buildings around a small square, is Leonidio's port. The fertile alluvial river flats between Leonidio and the coast are intensively farmed.

Places to Stay & Eat
There are apartments for rent in town, but most people head for the beach at Plaka, where there are several domatia.

Hotel Dionysos (☎ 2757-023 455; *doubles with bathroom* €40), opposite the port, is Plaka's only hotel. It's a good spot to unwind and do nothing for a few days.

Taverna Michel & Margaret (☎ 2757-022 379; *mains* €4.40-5.30) is a top spot for a long, lazy lunch: good food (fresh fish from €14.70 per kilo) friendly service and a great location overlooking Plaka's picturesque little port.

Getting There & Away
Bus There are three buses daily down the coast from Argos (€5.15, 2¼ hours) and two from Tripolis (€6.10, 2½ hours).

Hydrofoil Leonidio's port of Plaka is part of the Flying Dolphin circuit around the Saronic Gulf and the eastern Peloponnese. In summer there is a daily service to Piraeus (€21.15, 2½ hours), travelling via Spetses (45 minutes). There is also a daily service south to Monemvasia (80 minutes).

SOUTH OF LEONIDIO
The road south from Leonidio over the rugged Parnon Mountains to the town of Geraki in Lakonia, 48km away, is one of the most scenic in the Peloponnese. For the first 12km the road snakes west up the Badron Gorge, climbing slowly away from the river

ARCADIA

Take some time out for spiritual reflection or just to get away from it all in peaceful Arcadia

until at times it is no more than a speck of silver far below. The road then leaves the Badron and climbs rapidly through a series of dramatic hairpin bends towards Kosmas.

Just before the top of the climb there's a dirt road to the left leading to **Moni Profitis Ilias**, an amazing little monastery perched precariously on the mountainside. Visitors are welcome, providing they are suitably dressed. Few public phones in the world can match the location of the card phone outside, perched on the edge of the Badron Gorge, overlooking the monastery.

It's another 14km from the monastery to the peaceful, beautiful mountain village of **Kosmas**. There are no hotels, but there are several domatia (see Places to Stay & Eat following). Even if you don't stay overnight it's worth pausing for a cold drink beneath the huge plane trees in the square.

Beyond Kosmas the road descends, more gently this time, to the village of Geraki in Lakonia. From here you can head 40km west to ende, or continue south through Vlahiotis, Molai and Sikia to Monemvasia.

Places to Stay & Eat

Maleatis Apollo (☎ 2757-031 494; main square; singles/doubles/triples with bathroom €30/36/44) is named after an unusual brass statue of Apollo that was found nearby. The comfortable rooms here come complete with a TV and kitchen. The cosy co-owned taverna downstairs opens for lunch and dinner.

Kosmas Studios (☎ 2757-031 483; doubles with bathroom €30) has smaller rooms than Maleatis but they're equally well equipped. The owners of this place have been very busy on the sign-writing front; there are signs everywhere on the approaches to town, and one in the main square will point you in the right direction.

Lakonia Λακωνία

The modern region of Lakonia occupies almost identical territory to the powerful kingdom of Lacedaemon ruled by King Menelaus in Mycenaean times. The landscape is dominated by two great mountain ranges, the Taygetos Mountains in the west and the Parnon Mountains in the east. These mountains taper away to create the central and eastern fingers of the Peloponnese.

Between them lies the fertile valley of the Evrotas River, a region famous for its olives and oranges. The valley has been a focal point of human settlement since Neolithic times and was the home of the original Sparta of King Menelaus, although the location of this Mycenaean city has yet to be identified.

The city was re-established in its present location by the Dorians at the start of the 1st millennium BC. Unfortunately, the bulk of this ancient city lies beneath the modern town, leaving little to explore. The disappointment is more than compensated for by the glorious Byzantine churches and monasteries at Mystras, just to the west in the foothills of the Taygetos Mountains. Another place not to be missed is the evocative medieval town of Monemvasia, in the southeast.

English-speakers can thank the Lakonians for the word 'laconic', brief of speech, a description that still fits many modern Lakonians.

SPARTA Σπάρτη
postcode 231 00 • pop 14,817
Modern Sparta (in Greek, Sparti) is an easygoing town of wide, tree-lined streets that is very much in contrast with the ancient image of discipline and deprivation. The town lies at the heart of the Evrotas Valley, an important citrus- and olive-growing region. The Taygetos Mountains, snowcapped between November and May, provide a stunning backdrop to the city's west.

History
Sparta was a Doric city founded at the beginning of the 1st millennium BC. It was centred on a low hill rising from the Evrotas Valley just west of the river.

The Spartans ran their society in accordance with strict military guidelines that

Highlights

- Wandering among the haunting ruins of Byzantine Mystras
- Discovering the magic of medieval Monemvasia
- Enjoying a long, lazy lunch on the seafront in Gythio
- Exploring the isolated coastline north of Monemvasia

legend says were laid down by the famed 9th-century BC legislator Lycurgus. Sparta's steady march to become the leading power in the Peloponnese, and arch foe of Athens in classical times, is documented in the History section of the Facts about the Peloponnese chapter, pp9-12.

The myth of Spartan invincibility evaporated after its defeat at the Battle of Leuctra in 371 BC, and the city struggled in vain to reassert its authority. In 221 BC Spartans suffered the indignity of watching an occupying army march through the streets of their city for the first time.

The city enjoyed a revival under the Romans, who made it a free city, but went into steady decline in Byzantine times until it was abandoned in favour of nearby Mystras.

The town was refounded in 1834 on the orders of King Otto, who had just made the decision to move his court from Nafplio to Athens. Mindful of history, Otto and his court

133

LAKONIA

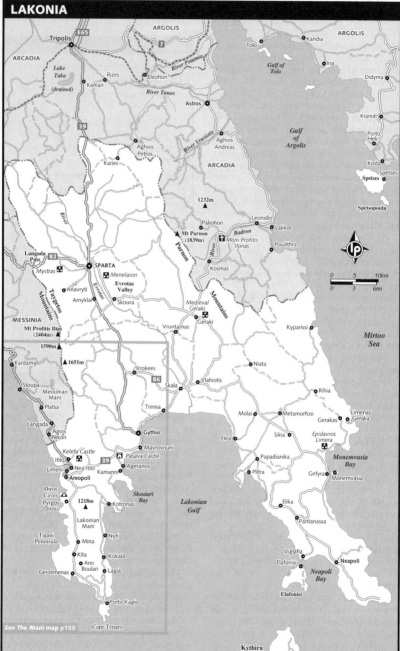

LAKONIA

See The Mani map p150

felt that since Athens was to be rebuilt to reflect its former glory, so too should Sparta.

Orientation & Information
It's hard to get lost in Sparta. The town is built on a grid system around two main thoroughfares: Palaeologou, which runs more or less north–south through the town, and Lykourgou, which runs east–west. They intersect in the middle of town. The central square, Plateia Kentriki, is one block west of the intersection. The bus station is at the eastern end of Lykourgou.

The **tourist information office** (☎ 2731-024 852; Plateia Kentriki; open 8am-2.30pm Mon-Fri) is on the 1st floor of the town hall, on the main square. The **tourist police** (☎ 2731-020 492; Hilonos 8) is one block east of the museum.

The post office is signposted off Lykourgou on Archidamou, and the Organismos Tilepikoinonion Ellados (OTE) is between Lykourgou and Kleomvrotou, one block east of Palaeologou. For Internet access, try the **Cosmos Club Internet Café** (☎ 2731-021 500; Palaeologou 34; open 8.30am-11pm daily), which charges €3.55 per hour, or **Aerodromio** (☎ 2731-029 268; Lykourgou 55; open 10am-midnight), which charges €4.70.

There are two central branches of the **National Bank of Greece** (Palaeologou 84 • Palaeologou 106); both have ATMs.

Foreign newspapers are available from **Libro** (☎ 2731-089 233; Palaeologou 52).

Ancient Sparta
If the city of the Lacedaemonians were destroyed, and only its temples and the foundations of its buildings left, remote posterity would greatly doubt whether their power were ever equal to their renown.

Thucydides, The Histories

A wander around ancient Sparta's meagre ruins bears testimony to the accuracy of Thucydides' prophecy. Head north along Palaeologou to the **statue** of a belligerent King Leonidas, standing in front of a soccer stadium. West of the stadium, signs point the way to the southern gate of the **acropolis**.

A dirt path leads off to the left (west) through olive groves to the 2nd- or 3rd-century-BC **ancient theatre**, the site's most discernible ruin. You'll find a reconstructed plan of the theatre on the wall at the Restaurant Elysse (see Places to Eat, p136).

The main cobbled path leads north to the acropolis, passing the ruins of the **Byzantine Church of Christ the Saviour** on the way to the hilltop **Sanctuary of Athena Halkioitou**. Some of the most important finds in the town's archaeological museum were unearthed here.

The history of the **Sanctuary of Artemis Orthia**, on the northeastern side of town, is more interesting than the site itself. Like most of the deities in Greek mythology, the goddess Artemis had many aspects, one of which was Artemis Orthia. In earliest times, this aspect of the goddess was honoured through human sacrifice. The Spartans gave this activity away for the slightly less gruesome business of flogging young boys in her honour. The museum houses a collection of clay masks used in ritual dances at the sanctuary. The sanctuary is signposted at the junction of Odos Ton 118 and Orthias Artemidos.

The **Tomb of Leonidas**, on shady Plateia Leonidou, is one of the few relics of ancient Sparta to be found among the streets of the modern town. Its original function is unknown, but legend has it that it was built to house the bones of King Leonidas.

Museums & Galleries
Sparta's **archaeological museum** (☎ 2731-028 575; cnr Lykourgou & Agios Nikolaos; admission €1.50; open 8.30am-3pm Tues-Sat, 8.30am-2.30pm Sun), just east of the town centre, includes votive sickles that Spartan boys dedicated to Artemis Orthia, heads and torsos of various deities, a statue of Leonidas, masks and a stele.

The **John Coumantarios Art Gallery** (☎ 2731-081 557; Palaeologou 123; admission free; open 9am-3pm Tues-Sat, 10am-2pm Sun) has a collection of 19th- and 20th-century French and Dutch paintings, and has changing exhibitions of works by contemporary Greek painters.

Places to Stay
The closest camping grounds are in nearby Mystras (see Places to Stay under Mystras, p139).

Hotel Cecil (☎ 2731-024 980, fax 2731-081 318; Palaeologou 125; singles/doubles with bathroom €30/40), to which most travellers head, is a small, family-run hotel. It offers good value for clean, comfortable rooms that come with a TV.

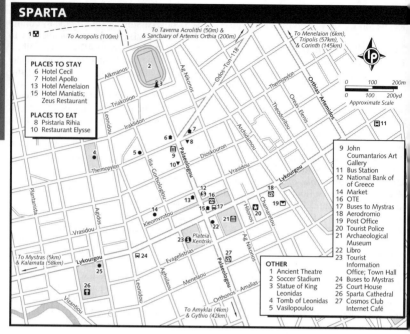

SPARTA

PLACES TO STAY
6 Hotel Cecil
7 Hotel Apollo
13 Hotel Menelaion
15 Hotel Maniatis;
   Zeus Restaurant

PLACES TO EAT
8 Psistaria Rihia
10 Restaurant Elysse

9 John
  Coumantarios Art
  Gallery
11 Bus Station
12 National Bank of
   of Greece
14 Market
16 OTE
17 Buses to Mystras
18 Aerodromio
19 Post Office
20 Tourist Police
21 Archaeological
   Museum
22 Libro
23 Tourist
   Information

OTHER
1 Ancient Theatre
2 Soccer Stadium
3 Statue of King
  Leonidas
4 Tomb of Leonidas
5 Vasilopoulou

Office; Town Hall
24 Buses to Mystras
25 Court House
26 Sparta Cathedral
27 Cosmos Club
   Internet Café

Hotel Apollo (☎ 2731-022 491/3, fax 2731-023 936; Thermopylon 84; singles/ doubles with bathroom €30/40) is a reasonable alternative to Cecil, with identical prices.

Hotel Maniatis (☎ 2731-022 665, fax 2731-029 994; Palaeologou 72-76; singles/ doubles/triples with bathroom €61.50/81/ 103.50) has spotless rooms and friendly and efficient service but the atmosphere is a little on the sterile side. Prices include breakfast.

Hotel Menelaion (☎ 2731-022 161/5, fax 2731-026 332; Palaeologou 91; singles/ doubles/triples with bathroom €61.50/81/ 103.50) has one of the finest neoclassical facades in town. When it comes to nominating the best hotel in town, the presence of a swimming pool gives the Menelaion the edge over the Maniatis. Prices include breakfast.

Places to Eat

There are lots of restaurants along Palaeologou in particular.

Restaurant Elysse (☎ 2731-029 896; Palaeologou 113; mains €4.50-8.80) is a popular place run by a helpful Greek-Canadian family. The menu features a couple of Lakonian specialities: chicken bardouniotiko (€4.80; chicken cooked with onions and feta cheese) and arni horiatiki (€5.50; lamb baked with bay leaves and cinnamon).

Psistaria Rihia (☎ 2731-027 350; Thermopylon 93; chicken €2.95, pork €3.55, lamb €3.85) is owned by Theodoros, another Spartan restaurateur who has spent time in Canada. His specialities are spit-roast meats and salads.

Zeus Restaurant (☎ 2731-022 665; Palaeologou 72-76; mains €3.50-12), next to Hotel Maniatis, has much more reasonable prices than the elegant decor would suggest. The air-conditioning is welcome on a hot day, too.

Taverna Acrolithi (☎ 2731-020 123; cnr Odos Ton 118 & Orthias Artemidos; mains €3-6.50), at the northeastern end of Odos Ton 118, has live Greek music from 10pm on Friday and Saturday night.

Vasilopoulou (☎ 2731-081 751; cnr Thermopylon & Gortsologlou), opposite the Sparta Inn, is bigger and better stocked than most supermarkets in Sparta. Nevertheless, self-caterers will find an abundance of choice.

Getting There & Away

Sparta's well-organised, modern **bus station** (☎ 2731-026 441) is at the eastern end of Lykourgou. Departures are displayed in English on a large information board outside above the entrance. They include 10 buses daily to Athens (€12.65, 3¼ hours) via Corinth (€8.55, two hours); five daily to Gythio (€2.60, one hour); four to Neapoli (€8.65, three hours) and Tripolis (€3.25, 1¼ hours); and three to Geraki (€2.60, 45 minutes) and Monemvasia (€6.35, two hours).

There is a twice-daily service to Kalamata (€3.40, 2½ hours), which involves changing buses at Artemisia (€2.05) on the Messinian side of the Langada Pass.

Departures to the Mani Peninsula include buses to Gerolimenas (€6.30, three hours, two daily) via Areopoli (€4.10, two hours) and a 9am service to the caves at Pyrgos Dirou (€4.70, 2¼ hours).

There are also 12 buses daily to Mystras (€0.80, 30 minutes). You can catch these on their way out to Mystras, at the bus stop on Leonidou.

Getting Around

Mavrakis Travels (☎ 2731-024 360, fax 2731-024 361; e trvunlim@otenet.gr) is the local agent for Hertz, which is the only car-hire company in town.

AROUND SPARTA
Amyklai Αμυκλαι
The village of Amyklai, 4km south of Sparta, was the site of one of the earliest-known settlements in the Evrotas Valley, occupied since Neolithic times.

It developed into an important Mycenaean settlement, and was later absorbed into Doric Sparta. The main point of interest for the modern visitor is the **Sanctuary of Apollo Amykles**, which occupies a low hill overlooking the Evrotas River about 1km east of the village. Built at the end of the 6th century BC, it was one of Sparta's most important temples. It was a large, square structure, with colonnades surrounding an open central courtyard. At the centre of the courtyard was a giant statue of

Apollo, which reportedly stood 13m high. The road to the temple is signposted on the northern edge of Amyklai, on the road from Sparta to Gythio.

The celebrated **tholos tomb of Vathio**, on the southeastern edge of the village, is further evidence of the region's importance in Mycenaean times. The tomb, which was covered by a low earth mound, was built in the Mycenaean 'beehive' style. All that remains is the bottom metre of the walls, but the stonework is of exceptional standard. Excavations here uncovered two fine gold cups decorated with scenes of hunting wild bulls. The cups are ranked among the prize exhibits at the National Archaeological Museum in Athens. The road to the tomb is signposted on the southern edge of Amyklai on the road from Sparta to Gythio. All buses heading south from Sparta travel via Amyklai.

Menelaion Μενελαιον
Some archaeologists believe that the Menelaion, southeast of Sparta, marks the site of the Mycenaean city ruled by King Menelaus (most famous for being married to Helen of Troy). No evidence has yet been uncovered to support this view, although finds indicate that the site has been occupied since Neolithic times.

The Menelaion is a small, crumbling, pyramid structure that stands at the tip of a steep spur that overlooks the Evrotas Valley from the east. Built in the classical period, it was part of a sanctuary to Menelaus and Helen, whose face launched a thousand ships.

Although the site is close to Sparta as the crow flies (2km), it's a fair way by road. Head north from Sparta and turn right immediately after the bridge across the River Evrotas, then take the road running south along the east bank of the river. The Menelaion is signposted to the left after about 4km. Bus services from Sparta are few and far between along this route.

MYSTRAS Μυστράς
The captivating ruins of the once-awesome town of Mystras (☎ 2731-083 377; admission €3.55; open 8am-6pm daily in summer, 8.30am-3pm daily in winter), crowned by an imposing fortress, spill from a spur of Mt Taygetos.

History

The fortress of Mystras (miss-**trahss**) was built by Guillaume de Villehardouin in 1249. When the Byzantines won back the Morea from the Franks, Emperor Michael VIII Palaeologus made Mystras its capital and seat of government. It soon became populated by people from the surrounding plains seeking refuge from the invading Slavs. From this time until the last despot, Dimitrios, surrendered to the Turks in 1460, a despot of Morea (usually a son or brother of the ruling Byzantine emperor) lived and reigned at Mystras.

While the empire plunged into decline elsewhere, Mystras enjoyed a renaissance under the despots. A school of humanistic philosophy was founded by Gemistos Plethon (1355–1452). His enlightened ideas attracted intellectuals from all corners of Byzantium. After Mystras was ceded to the Turks, Plethon's pupils moved to Rome and Florence where they made a significant contribution to the Italian Renaissance. Art and architecture also flourished, evidenced in the splendid buildings and vibrant frescoes of Mystras.

Mystras declined under Turkish rule. It was captured by the Venetians in 1687 and thrived again with a flourishing silk industry and a population of 40,000. It was recaptured by the Turks in 1715, and from then on it was downhill all the way. It was burned by the Russians in 1770, by the Albanians in 1780 and by Ibrahim Pasha in 1825. By the time of Independence in 1822

MYSTRAS

it was in a very sorry state, virtually abandoned and in ruins. Since the 1950s much restoration has taken place, and it is now listed as a World Heritage Site.

The Site

A day is needed to do Mystras justice. Wear sensible shoes, bring plenty of water and begin at the upper entrance to the site, so that you walk downhill rather than up. The site is divided into three sections: the *kastro* (the fortress on the summit), the *hora* (upper town) and the *kato hora* (lower town).

Kastro & Hora From opposite the upper-entrance ticket office, a path (signposted 'kastro') leads up to the fortress. The fortress was built by the Franks and extended by the Turks. The path descending from the ticket office leads to **Agia Sofia**, which served as the palace church and at which some frescoes survive. Steps descend from here to a T-junction. A left turn leads to the **Nafplio Gate**, which was the main entrance to the town. Near the gate is the huge **Palace of the Despots**, a complex of several buildings constructed at different times. The vaulted audience room, the largest of the palace's buildings, was added in the 14th century. Its facade is painted and its window frames are very ornate, but hundreds of years of neglect have robbed it of its former opulence.

From the palace, a winding, cobbled path leads down to the **Monemvasia Gate**, the entrance to the lower town.

Kato Hora Through the Monemvasia Gate, turn right to reach the well-preserved 14th-century **Convent of Pantanassa**. The nuns that live here are Mystras' only inhabitants. The building has beautiful carved stone ornamentation on its facade and the capitals of its columns. It's an elaborate, perfectly proportioned building – never overstated. Its exquisite, richly coloured 15th-century frescoes are among the finest examples of late Byzantine art. There is a wonderful view of the pancake-flat and densely cultivated plain of Lakonia from the columned terrace on the northern facade.

The path continues down to the **Monastery of Perivleptos**, built into a rock. Inside, the 14th-century frescoes equal those of Pantanassa and have been preserved

virtually intact. Each scene is an entity, enclosed in a simple symmetrical shape. The overall effect is of numerous icons placed next to one another to relate a visual narrative. The church has a very high dome. In the centre is the Pantokrator, surrounded by the 12 apostles and the Virgin.

As you continue down towards the Mitropolis you will pass **Agios Georgios**, one of Mystras' many private chapels. Further down, and above the path to the left, is the **Laskaris Mansion**, a typical Byzantine house where the ground floor was used as stables and the upper floor was the residence.

The **Mitropolis**, or Cathedral of Agios Dimitrios, consists of a complex of buildings enclosed by a high wall. The original church was built in the 13th century but was greatly altered in the 15th century. The church stands in an attractive courtyard surrounded by stoas and balconies. Its impressive ecclesiastical ornaments and furniture include a carved marble iconostasis, an intricately carved wooden throne and a marble slab in the floor, on which is carved a two-headed eagle (a symbol of Byzantium). The latter is located exactly on the site where Emperor Constantine XI was crowned. The church also has some fine frescoes. The adjoining **museum** houses fragments of sculpture and pottery from Mystras' churches.

Beyond the Mitropolis is the **Vrontokhion Monastery**. This was once the wealthiest monastery of Mystras, the focus of cultural activities and the burial place of the despots. Of its two churches, **Agios Theodoros** and **Aphentiko**, the latter is the most impressive, with striking frescoes.

Outside the lower entrance to Mystras is a *kantina* (mobile café) selling snacks and fresh orange juice.

Places to Stay

Camping Paleologio Mystras (☎ 2731-022 724, fax 2731-025 256; adult/tent €4.10/ 3.55; open year-round) is a friendly, well-organised site, 2km west of Sparta on the road to Mystras. Facilities include a swimming pool. Buses to Mystras can drop you off here.

Castle View Camping (☎ 2731-083 303, fax 2731-020 028; person/tent/campervan €4.70/2.65/55; open Apr-Oct), 3km from Sparta, is another good option.

LAKONIA

Hotel Byzantion (☎ 2731-083 309, fax 2731-020 019; e byzanhtl@otenet.gr; singles/doubles/triples with bathroom €40/60/70) is right in the centre of Mystras, on the road from Sparta. It is looking all the better for a recent facelift and offers rooms equipped with air-con and TV. Breakfast is included in the price.

There are also several domatia around the village.

Getting There & Away
Frequent buses go to Mystras from Sparta (see the Getting There & Away section under Sparta, p137). A taxi from Sparta to Mystras' lower entrance costs €6, and €7.50 to the upper entrance.

ANAVRYTI Ανάβρυτι
postcode 231 00 • pop 91
The pretty little mountain village of Anavryti, 12km southwest of Sparta, stands in magnificent isolation on a small plateau hidden away in the foothills of the Taygetos Mountains. At an altitude of more than 900m, the air is delightfully cool and fresh, and the high peaks of the surrounding mountains are so close that you can almost reach out and touch them.

It was once a substantial town of more than 3000 people, but it suffered badly at the hands of the Germans during WWII and during the subsequent years of the Greek civil war, prompting most residents to pack their bags for the USA or Canada.

Most visitors come to Anavryti for the trekking. The E4 trans-European trail passes through the village on the way from Mystras to the EOS (Ellinikos Orivatikos Syndesmos – Greek Alpine Club) Taygetos shelter on the slopes of Mt Profitis Ilias. (See under Mt Profitis Ilias, following, for more information about the mountain and the shelter.)

The climb from Anavryti to the shelter should only be attempted by properly equipped and experienced trekkers, but the Anavryti–Mystras section is relatively straightforward and clearly marked with the E4 trail's distinctive black-on-yellow signs. You'll need drinking water and a decent pair of hiking boots if you're going to walk it.

Accommodation and eating options are both covered at **Hotel Anavryti** (☎ 2731-021 788; singles/doubles with bathroom €15/24) which also has a restaurant. The owner of this hotel speaks English and can help with trekking directions.

The best approach is to catch a bus up to Anavryti from Sparta (€1.50, 40 minutes) and walk back down. There are buses from Sparta at 6.30am and 1.55pm on Monday, Thursday and Saturday. The walk back to Mystras takes about two hours.

MT PROFITIS ILIAS
Μτ Προφιτις Ηλιας
At 2404m, Mt Profitis Ilias is the highest peak of the imposing Taygetos Mountains, which separate Lakonia and Messinia. It lies southwest of Sparta, set among a cluster of five peaks known as 'the Pentadahilos'.

The tiny **Church of Profitis Ilias**, at the summit, is the target of an annual pilgrimage on 19 July, the prophet's name day. Hundreds of pilgrims head for the summit, timing their trek to arrive before sunrise.

It's possible to stay overnight at the EOS Taygetos shelter, set among pine trees at an altitude of 1650m on the eastern side of the mountain. Contact the **EOS** (☎ 2731-022 574) in Sparta for reservations, and to check that the shelter is open.

It's possible to drive most of the way to the shelter along a good sealed road. The turn-off is signposted on the Sparta–Gythio road 7.5km south of Sparta. The road winds up into the hills through the villages of Anoghia and Paleopanagia to the abandoned settlement of Boliana. Keep going for a further 2km beyond Boliana and you'll see the start of the walking track to the EOS shelter clearly marked on the left. The walk to the shelter takes about an hour.

The shelter doubles as base camp for the climb to the summit. The route to the top is clearly indicated and is relatively straightforward during the summer months, once the winter snow cover has gone. It takes about 2½ hours from the shelter.

You'll need good walking boots and warm clothing – it can get cold at any time of year. Water bottles can be filled at springs along the way.

LANGADA PASS Λανγαδα Πασσ
The 59km between Sparta and Kalamata is one of the most stunning routes in Greece, crossing the Taygetos Mountains by way of the Langada Pass.

The climb begins in earnest at the village of **Trypi**, 9km west of Sparta, where the road enters the dramatic **Langada Gorge**. To the north of this gorge is the site where the ancient Spartans abandoned babies too weak or deformed to become good soldiers.

From Trypi the road follows the course of the Langada River before climbing sharply through a series of hairpin bends to emerge in a sheltered valley. This is a good spot to stop for a stroll among the plane trees along the river bank. The road then climbs steeply once more to the high point of 1524m – crossing the boundary from Lakonia into Messinia on the way. You can stop overnight here (see Places to Stay & Eat, following).

The descent to Kalamata is equally dramatic, although the area will take a long time to recover from the devastating forest fires of 1998.

Travelling this route by bus involves changing buses at Artemisia, the closest Messinian settlement to the summit.

Places to Stay & Eat

Pandoheio Canadas (☎ 2721-099 281, 2721-022 436; singles/doubles/triples with bathroom €15/21/25), 22km from Sparta, is a small guesthouse perched on the upper slopes of the Taygetos Mountains, at an altitude of 1250m. As the name suggests, it's run by a Greek-Canadian couple. The restaurant is a major attraction, turning out delicious bean soup (€2.35). Specialities include home-cured smoked pork (€4) and home-made pork sausages (€2.50).

Hotel Taygetos (☎ 0721-099 236, fax 0721-098 198; singles/doubles with bathroom €25/30), 24km from Sparta, has a superb location at the very top of the Langada Pass. It also boasts a good restaurant with specialities such as rooster with red wine (€4.70), roast goat (€5.30) and rabbit *stifado* (stew; €5.60).

GERAKI Γεράκι
postcode 230 58 ● pop 1341
The village of Geraki (yeh-**rah**-kih) lies some 40km southeast of Sparta, in the foothills of the Parnon Mountains. It stands on the site of ancient Geronthrai, a settlement which dates back to Mycenaean times. Fragments of the ancient walls remain to the north and east of the village. The village also boasts several fine early Byzantine churches.

There are no hotels in Geraki, but locals in the village square can suggest domatia.

Medieval Geraki
This place is an unsung Mystras. While the latter is on almost everyone's list of 'must sees' in the Peloponnese, the medieval town of Geraki crumbles in obscurity on a remote hillside 4km east of the modern village.

The ruins are spread out below a Frankish fortress, built by Guy de Nivelet in 1245 as the seat of government of one of the 12 Frankish fiefdoms of the Peloponnese. It was ceded to the Byzantines, along with Mystras, in 1262 following the Frankish defeat at the Battle of Pelagonia.

Like Mystras, Geraki is noted for its churches, mostly dating from the final period of Byzantine rule. The finest is the Church of Agios Giorgios, which stands within the fortress. The iconostasis is adorned with the coat of arms of the De Nivelet family.

It would appear that the Ministry of Culture has big plans for the site, judging by the new sealed road leading to the entrance. At the time of research, it was locked and deserted. If that's still the case, it should be possible to get the key from one of the caretakers, Mr Giorgos Tsipouras (☎ 2731-071 096) or Mr Giorgos Kouris (☎ 2731-071 208), in modern Geraki. It's best to phone the night before.

Getting There & Away
The road to Geraki is signposted to the right, just north of Sparta along the Tripolis road. There are two buses daily from Sparta to the modern village (€2.60, 45 minutes).

MONEMVASIA & GEFYRA
Μονεμβασία & Γέφυρα
postcode 230 70 ● pop 1321
Monemvasia (mo-nem-vah-**see**-ah), 99km southeast of Sparta, is the Gibraltar of Greece – a massive rock rising dramatically from the sea just off the east coast.

Its name, meaning 'single entry' (*moni:* single, *emvasia:* entry), refers to the fact that the only access to the island is via a causeway from the mainland village of Gefyra (also called Nea Monemvasia).

From Gefyra, Monemvasia looks like a huge rock topped by a fortress, with a few modern buildings scattered at sea level. But cross the causeway and follow the road that curves around the side of the rock and you will come to a narrow tunnel in a fortifying wall. The tunnel zigzags, so you cannot see the other side until you emerge, blinking, into the magical old town of Monemvasia, concealed until that moment.

Unlike Mystras, Monemvasia's houses are inhabited, mostly by weekenders from Athens. In summer Gefyra and Monemvasia brim with tourists, but the extraordinary impact of the first encounter with the medieval town of Monemvasia – and the delights of exploring it – override the effects of mass tourism. The poet Yiannis Ritsos, who was born and lived for many years in Monemvasia, wrote of it: 'This scenery is as harsh as silence'.

History

Monemvasia has been a fortress since the earliest days of recorded history. It was originally known as Minoa, a name that has sparked speculation about a link to the Minoan civilisation that flourished on the island of Crete between 2900 and 1450 BC.

It was a defensive outpost built to protect Monemvasia Bay, a large half-moon bay that curves away to the north. This fine natural harbour was controlled by the now-destroyed city of Epidavros Limera (see under North of Monemvasia later in this chapter, p144, for details).

The first settlement was established at the end of the 6th century by mainlanders seeking refuge from barbarian incursions. By the 13th century it had become the principal commercial centre of Byzantine Morea, complementary to Mystras, the spiritual centre. It was famous throughout Europe for its highly praised Malvasia (also called Malmsey) wine.

It was the last town in the Peloponnese to succumb to the Franks, surrendering in 1248 after a three-year siege. It was ceded back to the Byzantines 14 years later, and remained in Byzantine hands until 1460. Hoping to save themselves from Turkish control, the citizens of Monemvasia then threw in their lot with Venice.

When the Turks eventually prevailed, local residents discovered their fears to be largely unfounded. Monemvasia continued to flourish, recording a population of more than 30,000 at the end of the 16th century.

The Venetians returned in 1690, making the city the capital of Lakonia. The subsequent 25 years of Venetian rule produced many of the town's finest buildings. A return to Turkish control in 1715 saw Monemvasia slip into decline.

Monemvasia's Turkish inhabitants were massacred in 1821 on their surrender following a three-month siege. The town remained in Greek hands throughout the War of Independence.

The island was once connected to the mainland by a natural causeway; this was destroyed by a devastating earthquake in AD 375. A narrow bridge now provides the only link to the mainland.

Orientation & Information

All of the practical facilities are located in Gefyra. The main street is 23 Iouliou, which runs south around the coast from the causeway, while Spartis runs north up the coast and becomes the road to Molai.

Malvasia Travel (☎ 2732-061 752), just up from the causeway on Spartis, acts as the bus stop. The post office and the National Bank of Greece are opposite. The OTE is at the top of 28 Oktovriou, which runs inland off 23 Iouliou. The **police station** (☎ 2732-061 210) is at Spartis 137.

Medieval Town

You can find everything you want in this city – except water.
An 18th-century Turkish traveller, recorded in the Monemvasia museum

The town is divided into two parts: the lower town occupies a large, walled compound on the island's southern slope; the ruins of the upper town overlook the southern slope.

Lower Town The road from Gefyra finishes outside the main **western gate**. This unusual zigzag gate was part of the fortifications built during the first period of Turkish rule; the finishing touches are Venetian.

The gate opens into the narrow, cobbled main street, lined with an assortment of cafés, souvenir shops and tavernas. It leads to the central square, Plateia Dsami, with its shady lilac trees and large brass canon. The square is named after the former Dsami Mosque, on the western side of the square, which now houses a small **archaeological** museum (☎ 2732-061 403; admission free; open 8.30am-3pm Tues-Sun). It contains finds unearthed during excavation and building works around the old town. The star turn is the *temblon* (chancel screen) from an 11th-century church near the sea gate. Other pieces of note include a marble door frame from the Church of Hagia Sofia.

Opposite the museum is the **Church of Christos Ekmonos** (Christ in Chains), sometimes referred to as Monemvasia's cathedral. The church has stood on this site since the 11th century, although it has been modified and repaired many times since. It retains several original features, including the fine carved lintel above the main entrance. The relief of two peacocks above the lintel was added during restoration work after Independence.

The steps to the south of the church lead down towards the **sea gate** in the centre of the southern wall. This part of town is a delightful maze of narrow, stepped streets flanked by old stone houses with walled gardens and courtyards.

The main street continues east from the main square, passing between the free-standing **bell tower** and the **Church of Mirtidiotissa**, reached by steps leading uphill from the northern edge of the square.

The main streets forks after about 50m, with the main passage heading downhill towards the **eastern gate**, passing the **Church of Agios Nikolaos** on the right. Look out for the relief of the Byzantine double eagle in the triangular tableau above the entrance.

From here it's possible to loop back to the main square by following the southern wall westwards, passing the whitewashed 16th-century **Church of Panagia Hrysaphitissa**.

Upper Town The upper town once stood within the walls of one of the Peloponnese's mightiest fortresses: a superb natural fortification rendered virtually impregnable by the efforts of Byzantine, Turkish and Venetian military architects.

Access to the upper town is by a **fortified path** that zigzags up a steep gully rising above the lower town. It ends at a massive gate that guards a long, vaulted entrance tunnel, which emerges onto the tree-lined old square.

The upper town itself is little more than a vast jumble of ruins, poking out here and there from the dense undergrowth. A well-trodden track leads north from the square to the most important surviving building, the **Church of Agia Sophia**, perched quite precariously on the sheer cliff edge on the northern side of the plateau. Although whitewashed when it was converted into a mosque while under Turkish rule, some fine 13th-century frescoes survive. Entrance to the church is via the triple-arched **loggia**, added by the Venetians in the 16th century.

The plateau's main track continues west from the church to the **citadel**, which stands at the high point of the plateau. The layout is still clearly discernible among the piles of stone, but the main attraction here is the views. From here, the path loops back to the main gate, following a depression that slopes down to the southern edge of the plateau. It passes two enormous **cisterns**, which were used to collect precious rainwater.

The path reaches the edge of the plateau next to the ruins of a substantial two-storey building, assumed to be the former headquarters of the Venetian military governor. Its position affords the best possible view of the lower town.

Places to Stay

Camping Paradise (☎ 2732-061 123, fax 2732-061 680; e paradise@otenet.gr; adult/ tent €4.30/2.80; open year-round) is a pleasant, well-shaded camping ground on the coast 3.5km south of Gefyra. It's right next to a beach and it has its own minimarket, bar and club, as well as big-screen cable TV.

There's no budget accommodation in Monemvasia, so if your budget is tight you'll have to stay in Gefyra. There are numerous domatia and plenty more hotels than the two we mention here, but the most interesting places are in Monemvasia.

Hotel Akrogiali (☎ 2732-061 360; Gefyra; singles/doubles with shower €18/27), a basic hotel, next to the National Bank of Greece on Spartis, has the cheapest rooms in town.

Hotel Monemvasia (☎ 2732-061 381, fax 2732-061 707; Gefyra; singles/doubles with bathroom €25/36) has rooms with balconies facing out to sea and towards Monemvasia. Prices include breakfast.

If you've got money to spend, Monemvasia is a good place to spend it. There's a range of impeccably restored traditional options to choose from. Bookings are recommended, especially at weekends.

Malvasia Hotel (☎ 2732-061 113/323, fax 2732-061 722; singles €35, doubles with bathroom €40-50, triples €55-110) has some beautifully furnished rooms spread around several locations in the old town. All prices include a generous breakfast.

Byzantino (☎ 2732-061 254, fax 2732-061 331; doubles with bathroom from €45, with view from €60) is similar to the Malvasia, with rooms spread around the old town. It has an inquiries office on the main street.

Kellia (☎ 2732-061 520, fax 2732-061 767; singles/doubles/triples €40/80/95) occupies a converted monastery down by the sea, next to the church of Panagia Hrysaphitissa. Formerly run by the EOT, this place is now under private ownership, and it looks all the better for the change. Breakfast is €6.

Places to Eat

Taverna O Botsalo (☎ 2732-061 486; 23 Iouliou 46, Gefyra; mains €3.85-6.45) has a good location overlooking Gefyra's small port, and offers tasty, reasonably priced dishes.

T' Agnantio Taverna (☎ 2732-061 754; Gefyra; mains €3.85-11.75) is a small place on the southern edge of town, with a strong local following.

To Kanoni (☎ 2732-061 387; main street, Monemvasia; mains €4.70-15.50) boasts an imaginative and extensive menu. Its specialities include stamna (stew with cheese, baked in a clay pot; €6.75) and hearty fish soup (€5.30).

Matoula (☎ 2732-061 660; Monemvasia; mains €4.50-7.50) has a great setting, with a terrace overlooking the sea.

Self-caterers will find most things at the **Lefkakis Supermarket** (☎ 2732-061 167), behind the post office in Gefyra. It also stocks international newspapers.

Getting There & Away

Bus Departures are from **Malvasia Travel** (☎ 2732-061 752), which also sells bus tickets. There are four buses daily to Athens (€18.65, 5½ hours) via Sparta (€6.35, two hours), Tripolis and Corinth. The 4.10am departure is an express service (€14.10, 4½ hours).

Hydrofoil In summer, there is at least one Flying Dolphin service daily to Piraeus (€27.60, four hours), travelling via Leonidio and Spetses. There are also four services a week south to Kythira (three hours). Buy tickets from **Angelakos Travel** (☎ 2732-061 219), by the petrol station on the Monemvasia side of the causeway.

Getting Around

A free shuttle bus operates between the causeway and old Monemvasia from 7.30am to 10pm June to September.

Cars can be hired from **Christos Rent Car & Moto** (☎ 2732-061 581, fax 2732-07 661; 23 Iouliou). Brother Mihalis (☎ 2732-061 173), opposite, rents motorcycles.

The medieval town of Monemvasia is inaccessible to cars and motorcycles. Cars are not allowed across the causeway between June and September; parking is available outside the old town at other times.

NORTH OF MONEMVASIA

If you have your own vehicle, there are some great opportunities to explore the isolated stretch of coastline north of Monemvasia.

The first point of interest is the acropolis of **Epidavros Limera**, 8km north of Monemvasia overlooking Monemvasia Bay. It was founded in the 8th century BC as a colony of the Argolid city of Epidavros, and was the master of Monemvasia in ancient times. Its ruined buildings later supplied much of the stone for the building of medieval Monemvasia. All that remains is a section of ancient wall on the hillside above the bay, visible from the road. The turn-off to Epidavros Limera is 6km north of Monemvasia.

This road continues northeast for a further 12km to the tiny fishing settlement of **Limenas Gerakas**, a ribbon of whitewashed houses hugging the northern flank of Gerakas Bay. This long, narrow bay snakes inland for almost 2km, flanked by steep hills, forming a perfect, calm anchorage. The headland east of the settlement was the site of ancient Zarax, destroyed by an earthquake in AD 376.

There are a couple of domatia signs along the seafront, but most visitors come just to eat at one of the seafood restaurants beside the quay.

Recent road improvements mean that it is now possible to continue north through the

Mellowing out – Kefalotiri cheese in Arcadia

Trek through the picture-perfect Dimitsana area

Little is left of Megalopoli, the 'great city'

Take in the magnificent coastal scenery around Paralia Tyrou

GEORGE TSAFOS

A street scene in the Mani

LEE FOSTER

Gythio, the port of ancient Sparta, is not spartan today

WAYNE WALTON

'As harsh as silence': mesmerising Monemvasia

GLENN BEANLAND

The tranquil fishing village of Gerolimenas makes a wonderful place to relax

hills from Limenas Gerakas to link up with the road from Molai to Kyparissi. This back route passes through the villages of **Gerakas**, built on the ruins of ancient Gerakas, and **Rihia**.

Kyparissi, 53km north of Monemvasia, existed in virtual isolation for much of its long history, cut off from the outside world by the southern peaks of the Parnon Mountains. It continues to exude a timeless charm, remote enough to deter all but the most determined.

The main settlement sits on a wide terrace overlooking a deep horseshoe bay, ringed on three sides by mountains. Below it are the satellite villages of **Paralia** and **Mitropolis**, on either side of a wide, sandy beach.

Strangely enough, given the absence of other transport, there are daily hydrofoil connections to Piraeus. Otherwise, the tourist infrastructure is limited to a couple of domatia and restaurants.

NEAPOLI Νεάπολη
postcode 230 70 • pop 2727
Neapoli (neh-**ah**-po-lih), 42km south of Monemvasia, lies close to the southern tip of the Peloponnese's eastern prong. It's a fairly uninspiring town, in spite of its location on a huge horseshoe bay. The western flank of the bay is formed by the small island of Elafonisi. Few travellers make it down this far, but the town is popular enough with local holiday-makers to have three seafront hotels and several domatia.

Orientation & Information
Most things of importance to travellers are found along the main street, Akti Voion, which curves around the seafront. They include branches of the National Bank of Greece and the Bank Agrotiki, both with ATMs. The post office is on the western side of town, behind the Hotel Aivali on Barbaressou.

Places to Stay & Eat
Hotel Aivali (☎ 2734-022 287/777; Akti Voion 164; singles/doubles with bathroom €21/30) is a small family hotel, ideally located right on the seafront. It has comfortable rooms, each equipped with a TV and fridge. Breakfast costs €5.

Psarotaverna O Vananas (☎ 2734-022 464; Akti Voion 158; mains €3-9, fish from €28 per kg) is busy place that has a small daily selection of taverna dishes, as well as a choice of fresh local fish.

Getting There & Away
Bus The bus station (☎ 2734-023 222; Dimocratias 3) is in the middle of town, just off Akti Voion. There are four buses daily to Sparta (€8.65, three hours) via Molai (€4.20, 1¼ hours), which is the place to change buses for Monemvasia.

Ferry There are daily ferries from Neapoli to Agia Pelagia (€4.70, one hour), on Kythira. Tickets are sold at **Alexandrakis Shipping** (☎ 2732-022 940, fax 2732-023 590; Akti Voion 160), opposite the ferry quay.

Hydrofoil In July and August there are hydrofoil services to Piraeus (€31.40, five hours, four weekly) via Monemvasia, and a Sunday service to Kythira (€9.40, 20 minutes).

ELAFONISI Ελαφονα
postcode 230 53 • pop 745
Like Neapoli, Elafonisi sees few foreign tourists but is popular with Greeks. They pop over from the mainland for fish lunches in summer, particularly on Sunday. Locals insist that the *barbounia* (red mullet) from the waters around here is the best you'll find. The island's main attractions, apart from the seafood, are its superb beaches, which the Greeks liken to those of the South Seas; they're not exaggerating.

As well as fish tavernas, there are two pensions and a few domatia. There is no official camping ground.

Getting There & Away
From July to September, there are frequent ferries to Elafonisi (€0.80, 10 minutes) from the village of Viglafia, about 14km west of Neapoli. They shuttle to and fro constantly from 9.30am to 10pm. There are also infrequent boats from both Neapoli and Viglafia.

GYTHIO Γύθειο
postcode 232 00 • pop 4489
Once the port of ancient Sparta, Gythio (**yee**-thih-o) is an attractive fishing town with a bustling waterfront of pastel-coloured

19th-century buildings, behind which old crumbling Turkish houses clamber up a steep, wooded hill.

It's become a popular destination in its own right, as well as being a good base for exploring the fascinating Mani Peninsula to the south.

Orientation & Information

Gythio is not too hard to figure out. Most things of importance to travellers are along the seafront on Akti Vasileos Pavlou. The bus station is at the northeastern end, next to the small triangular park known as the Perivolaki (Tree-filled).

Akti Vasileos Georgiou runs inland from here past the main square, Plateia Panagiotou Venetzanaki, and becomes the road to Sparta.

The square at the southwestern end of Akti Vasileos Pavlou is Plateia Mavromihali, the hub of the old quarter of Marathonisi. The ferry quay is opposite this square. Beyond it, the waterfront road becomes Kranais, which leads south to the road to Areopoli. A causeway leads out to Marathonisi Islet at the southern edge of town.

The **EOT tourist office** (*☎/fax 2733-024 484; Vasileos Georgiou 20; open 11am-3pm Mon-Fri*) is about 500m north of the waterfront. Apart from a couple of brochures, it's remarkably information-free, even by EOT's own lamentable standards. The **tourist police** (*☎ 2733-022 271*) and regular **police** (*☎ 2733-022 100*) share offices on the waterfront, between the bus station and Plateia Mavromihali.

The **post office** is on Ermou, three blocks north of the bus station, and the **OTE** (*cnr Irakleos & Kapsali*) is between the two. Travellers can access email at **Electron Computers** (*☎ 2733-022 120; Kapsali 5; open 8am-9pm Mon-Sat*), opposite the OTE. It charges €4.40 per hour, with a minimum of €0.90. Despite being opposite the OTE, poor lines are a major problem here – as they are everywhere in Gythio.

International newspapers are available from **Hassanakos Bookstore** (*☎ 2733-022 064; Akti Vasileos Pavlou 39*), below the Hotel Aktaion.

The Sea Turtle Protection Society runs an information tent next to the ferry quay from mid-June until the end of September. It has

films and displays about turtle-nesting sites on the beaches of the Lakonian Gulf east of Gythio.

Marathonisi Islet

According to mythology, tranquil pine-shaded Marathonisi is ancient Cranae, where Paris (prince of Troy) and Helen (wife of Menelaus) consummated the affair that sparked the Trojan War. The 18th-century Tzanetakis Grigorakis tower at the centre of the island houses a small **museum** (*☎ 2733-024 484; admission €1.50; open 9am-7pm*). It relates Maniot history through the eyes of European travellers, who visited the region between the 15th and 19th centuries. The top floor has a fascinating collection of plans of Maniot towers and castles.

Ancient Theatre

Gythio's small but well-preserved ancient theatre is next to an army camp on the northern edge of town. It's signposted off Plateia Panagiotou Venetzanaki, along Arheou Theatrou. You can scramble up the hill behind the theatre to the **acropolis**, now heavily overgrown. Most of ancient Gythio lies beneath the nearby Lakonian Gulf.

Beaches

There's safe swimming off the 6km of sandy beaches that extend from the village of **Mavrovouni**, 2km south of Gythio.

Places to Stay

Camping Meltemi (*☎ 2733-022 833, fax 2733-023 833; Mavrovouni; adult/tent €4.50/4; open year-round*), 3km southwest of Gythio, is a very well-organised place and the pick of the three camping grounds at Mavrovouni. It's right behind the beach and sites are set among 3000 olive trees. Buses to Areopoli stop outside the camping ground.

Camping Porto Ageranos (*☎ 2733-093 469, fax 2733-093 239; Vathy; adult/tent €4.40/3.25*), 8km southwest of Gythio, is hard to get to without your own transport. It offers good shady sites on an excellent beach, and is signposted off the road to Areopoli.

Xenia Karlaftis Rooms to Rent (*☎ 2733-022 719; Kranais; singles/doubles/triples with bathroom €20/30/35*), opposite Marathonisi Islet, is the best budget option in town. There's a communal kitchen area upstairs, with a fridge and a small stove for

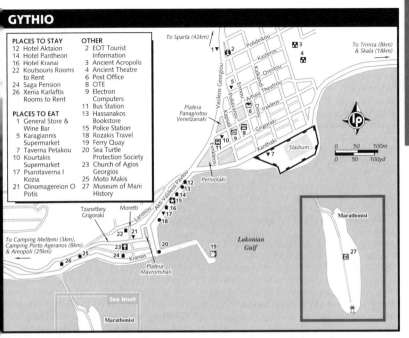

GYTHIO

PLACES TO STAY
12 Hotel Aktaion
14 Hotel Pantheon
16 Hotel Kranai
22 Koutsouris Rooms
   to Rent
24 Saga Pension
26 Xenia Karlaftis
   Rooms to Rent

PLACES TO EAT
1 General Store &
   Wine Bar
5 Karagiannis
   Supermarket
7 Taverna Petakou
10 Kourtakis
   Supermarket
17 Psarotaverna I
   Kozia
21 Oinomagereion O
   Potis

OTHER
2 EOT Tourist
   Information
3 Ancient Acropolis
4 Ancient Theatre
6 Post Office
8 OTE
9 Electron
   Computers
11 Bus Station
13 Hassanakos
   Bookstore
15 Police Station
18 Rozakis Travel
19 Ferry Quay
20 Sea Turtle
   Protection Society
23 Church of Agios
   Georgios
25 Moto Makis
27 Museum of Mani
   History

making tea and coffee. Manager Voula (daughter of Xenia) is a wonderful host, full of suitably laconic observations about life. Voula also has studios for rent at Mavrovouni, 3km southwest of town, beyond Mavrovouni.

Koutsouris Rooms to Rent (☎ 2733-022 321; Moretti; singles/doubles with bathroom €15/22, family room €25) is a quaint and old-fashioned place run by a retired merchant-navy captain and his wife. It's a long-standing favourite with independent travellers. To get here, walk up Tzanetbey Grigoraki from Plateia Mavromihali, turn right at the church with the clock tower and the rooms are on the left.

Saga Pension (☎ 2733-023 220, fax 2733-024 370; singles/doubles with bathroom €25/30), 150m from the port, is a French-run place and is good value for comfortable, tastefully furnished rooms with air-con and TV.

Hotel Kranai (☎/fax 2733-024 394; e kranai@forthnet.gr; Akti Vasileos Pavlou 17; singles/doubles with bathroom €42/56) is an attractive older-style place, with rooms overlooking the port.

Hotel Pantheon (☎ 2733-022 166, fax 2733-022 284; e pantelis@otenet.gr; Akti Vasileos Pavlou 33; singles/doubles with bathroom €55/60) has rooms with air-con, TVs and sea views. Breakfast is €5.30.

Hotel Aktaion (☎ 2733-023 500/1, fax 2733-022 294; Akti Vasileos Pavlou 39; doubles with bathroom €62, suites €77) is a beautifully restored neoclassical building, boasting the finest facade in town. It also has the best rooms in town. Breakfast is €5.

Places to Eat

Seafood is the obvious choice, and the waterfront is lined with numerous fish tavernas, especially on Kranais, where tourists have to walk the gauntlet of waiters touting for custom.

Psarotaverna I Kozia (☎ 2733-024 086; Akti Vasileos Pavlou 11; mains €4.40-5.90), between Rozakis Travel and the Hotel Kranai, has no touts, just lots of locals tucking into plates of grilled octopus (€4.40), calamari (€3.60) and other treats over a glass or two of ouzo.

Taverna Petakou (☎ 2733-022 889; mains €2.65-5.30), next to the stadium, is another favourite with locals. There are no frills here: the day's menu is written down in an exercise book in Greek. It may include a hearty fish soup (€5.30), which comes with a large chunk of fish on the side.

Oinomagereion O Potis (☎ 2733-024 253; Moretti 5; mains €2.95-8.80) is a cheerful and welcome addition to the restaurant scene. It has an interesting menu, with a good selection of salads. It's just up-hill from Plateia Mavromihali, on the cor-ner of Tzannibi Gregoraki and Moretti.

General Store & Wine Bar (☎ 2733-024 113; Vasileos Georgiou 67; mains €5.30-10.30) is a tiny restaurant run by the Greek-Canadian Thomakos family and it offers something completely different. You'll find an unusually varied and imaginative menu, featuring dishes such as orange and pump-kin soup (€2.95) and fillet of pork with black pepper and ouzo (€10.30).

Kourtakis (☎ 2733-023 408; Irakleos) and **Karagiannis** (cnr Vasileos Georgiou & Orestou) are two supermarkets at which self-caterers can stock up on supplies. The latter is located around the corner from the bus station.

A street market is held along Ermou on Tuesday and Friday mornings.

Getting There & Away

Bus The bus station (☎ 2733-022 228) is at the corner of Evrikleos and Irakleos. There are buses south to Areopoli (€1.70, 30 minutes, four daily); Athens (€15.10, 4¼ hours, five daily) via Sparta (€2.50, one hour); Gerolimenas (€3.70, two hours, two daily); the Diros Caves (€2.30, one hour, one daily); and Vatheia (€4.20, 1¼ hours, one daily). Getting to Kalamata is hard work, and involves changing buses at Itilo (€2.60, 45 minutes), to which there are only two buses daily (6am and 1pm).

Ferry ANEN Lines operates services from Gythio to Kastelli-Kissamos on Crete (€15.60, seven hours) via Kythira (€7.10, 2½ hours) three times weekly between June and September. The schedule is subject to constant change, so check with **Rozakis Travel** (☎ 2733-022 207, fax 2733-022 229; e rosakigy@otenet.gr), on the waterfront near Plateia Mavromihali, before coming here to catch a boat.

Getting Around

Rozakis Travel (see Ferry, above) hires out cars. Mopeds and scooters are available from **Moto Makis** (☎ 2733-022 950; Kranais).

The Mani Η Μάνη

The region referred to as the Mani covers the central peninsula in the south of the Peloponnese. For centuries the Maniots were a law unto themselves, renowned for their fierce independence and resentment of any attempt to govern them.

Today the Maniots are regarded by other Greeks as independent, royalist and right wing. But don't be deterred from visiting the region by descriptions of the Maniots as hostile, wild and hard people. Contact with the outside world and lack of feuding have mellowed them. The Maniots are as friendly and hospitable as Greeks elsewhere, despite the fierce appearance of some older people, who dress like the Cretans and offer fiery raki as a gesture of hospitality.

The Mani is generally divided into the Lakonian Mani (also called the inner Mani) and the Messinian (or outer) Mani. The Messinian Mani starts southeast of Kalamata and runs south between the coast and the Taygetos Mountains, while the Lakonian Mani covers the rest of the peninsula south of Itilo. Such was the formidable reputation of the inhabitants of the remote inner Mani that foreign occupiers thought they were best left alone.

The Mani has no major ancient sites, but it compensates well with medieval and later remains, bizarre tower settlements (particularly in the inner Mani) built as refuges from clan wars from the 17th century onwards, and magnificent churches, all enhanced by the distant presence of the towering peaks of the Taygetos Mountains. The Diros Caves in the south are also a major attraction.

History

The people of the Mani regard themselves as direct descendants of the Spartans. After the decline of Sparta, citizens loyal to the principles of Lycurgus, founder of Sparta's constitution, chose to withdraw to the mountains rather than serve under foreign masters. Later, refugees from occupying powers joined these people, who became known as Maniots – derived from the Greek word *mania*.

The Maniots claim they are the only Greeks not to have succumbed to foreign

THE MANI

invasions. This may be somewhat exaggerated but the Maniots have always enjoyed a certain autonomy and a distinctive lifestyle. Until Independence, the Maniots lived in clans led by chieftains. Fertile land was so scarce that it was fiercely fought over. Blood feuds were a way of life and families constructed towers as refuges.

The Turks failed to subdue the Maniots, who eagerly participated in the War of Independence. Although reluctant to relinquish their independence, in 1834 they became part of the new kingdom.

For background reading on the region and its people, try *Mani: Travels in the Southern Peloponnese* by Patrick Leigh Fermor, *Deep into Mani* by Greenhalgh & Eliopoulis and *The Architecture of Mani* by Ioannis Saïtis.

The Mani, by longtime Stoupa resident Bob Barrow, is worth seeking out in local shops if you're planning on doing any exploring. The author manages Thomeas

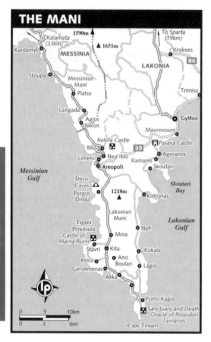

THE MANI

To explore the Lakonian Mani, head from Gythio to Areopoli and then south to Gerolimenas, loop around and return to Areopoli via Kotronas. You can then continue north from Areopoli to Itilo and continue to the Messinian Mani.

AREOPOLI Αρεόπολη
postcode 230 62 • pop 774

Areopoli (ah-reh-**o**-po-lih), capital of the Mani, is aptly named after Ares, the god of war. Its citizens adopted the name on 17 March 1821, when local leader Petrobey Mavromihalis marched north from the town at the head of a Maniot army to launch the War of Independence. Prior to that date it had been known as Tzimova.

The main square is dominated by a statue of Petrobey Mavromihalis, looking suitably warlike, and the town retains many other reminders of its rambunctious past. It is also a good base from which to explore the region.

Orientation & Information

The town is split into two parts: the new upper town around Plateia Athanaton, and the old lower town, around Plateia 17 Martiou 1821. The two squares are linked by Kapetan Mapetan, one of the few streets in town with a street sign – albeit badly faded and barely legible. All the features of interest are to be found in the narrow alleyways surrounding Plateia 17 Martiou 1821.

The bus stop is in front of the Europa Grill on Plateia Athanaton. There is no tourist office or tourist police. The post office is at the northern edge of town on Petrobey Mavromihalis, while the Organismos Tilepikoinonion Ellados (OTE) is on Plateia Athanaton. The **National Bank of Greece** (*Petrobey Mavromihalis*) is the only bank in town. It's open during normal banking hours in July and August, and 9am to noon on Tuesday and Thursday for the rest of the year. There's an ATM outside.

Foreign newspapers and a small selection of books are available from **Konstantinakos** (☎ 2733-051 253; *Plateia Athanaton*).

Churches

They start with the 18th-century **Church of Taxiarhes**, on the southern side of square. Its four-storey bell tower marks it as the most important of the town's many churches. Look out for the extremely well-preserved

Travel in Stoupa, and spends all his spare time exploring the Mani. His self-published guide is full of little gems of information about the region's villages, towers and churches.

You'll find more information on the Internet at **w** http://users.macunlimited.net /maniguide.

Lakonian Mani

Grey rock, mottled with defiant clumps of green scrub, and the occasional stunted olive or cypress tree characterise the bleak mountains of the inner Mani. The lower slopes are terraced wherever this unyielding soil has been cultivated. A curious anomaly is the profusion of wildflowers which mantle the valleys in spring, exhibiting nature's resilience by sprouting from the rocks.

The indented coast's sheer cliffs plunge into the sea, and rocky outcrops shelter pebbled beaches. This wild and barren landscape is broken only by austere and imposing stone towers, mostly abandoned, standing sentinel over the region.

relief carving above the main door. It depicts the archangels Michael and Gabriel, flanked by two saints, Agios Georgios and Agios Theodoros, on horseback. Above them is the hand of God and a dove.

The much older **Church of Agios Ioannis**, which stands in a small square on the southern edge of the old town, contains a series of frescoes relating the life of Jesus. It was built by the Mavromihalis family.

The twin **Churches of Panagia and Agios Haralambos**, at the junction of Kapetan Mapetan and Petrobey Mavromihalis, also have interesting frescoes.

Tower Houses

There are numerous examples of tower houses, although some are in very poor condition. The towers in the best condition are those that have been converted into accommodation (see Tsimova Rooms, Pyrgos Kapetanakas and Londas Pension under Places to Stay, following, for details).

There are several towers south of Plateia 17 Martiou 1821 along Tzani Tzanaki, including the **Mavromihalis Tower**. It was once the mightiest tower in town but now stands sadly derelict. The **Pikoulakis Tower**, further south, had recently undergone a complete facelift at the time of research.

West of these lie the **Barelakos Tower**, which sports some fine *akroceramica* (roof

tiles), and the ruins of another tower once occupied by the Mavromihalis family.

Places to Stay

Tsimova Rooms (☎ 2733-051 301; *Plateia 17 Martiou 1821; singles/doubles with bathroom €22/38, apartment €45*) is in a beautiful old, renovated tower behind the Church of Taxiarhes. Owner George Versakos has cosy rooms, filled with ornaments, family photos and icons, and a two-room apartment with a kitchen. George loves to show off his private collection of daggers and pistols! You'll see a sign at the Church of Taxiarhes pointing the way.

Pierros Bozagregos Traditional Guest House (☎ 2733-051 354; *doubles with bathroom €40-45, triples €50*) has large, comfortable rooms, each with fridge. Breakfast is available for €6. Pierros is opposite Tsimova Rooms, behind the Church of Taxiarhes.

Pyrgos Kapetanakas (☎ 2733-051 233, fax 2733-051 401; *singles/doubles/triples with bathroom €40/45/50*), signposted to the right at the bottom of Kapetan Mapetan, is an excellent place. It occupies the tower house built by the powerful Kapetanakas family at the end of the 18th century. The architecture is austerely authentic, in keeping with the spirit of the Mani, but rooms are comfortably furnished and equipped with air-con. Breakfast is €3.55.

THE MANI

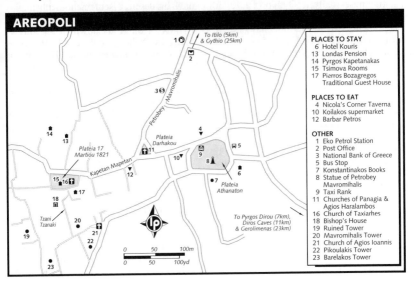

AREOPOLI

To Itilo (5km) & Gythio (25km)

Plateia Darhakou

Plateia 17 Martiou 1821

Kapetan Mapetan

Plateia Athanaton

Petrobey (Mavromihalis)

Tzani Tzanaki

To Pyrgos Dirou (7km), Diros Caves (11km) & Gerolimenas (23km)

0   50   100m
0   50   100yd

PLACES TO STAY
6 Hotel Kouris
13 Londas Pension
14 Pyrgos Kapetanakas
15 Tsimova Rooms
17 Pierros Bozagregos Traditional Guest House

PLACES TO EAT
4 Nicola's Corner Taverna
10 Koilakos supermarket
12 Barbar Petros

OTHER
1 Eko Petrol Station
2 Post Office
3 National Bank of Greece
5 Bus Stop
7 Konstantinakos Books
8 Statue of Petrobey Mavromihalis
9 Taxi Rank
11 Churches of Panagia & Agios Haralambos
16 Church of Taxiarhes
18 Bishop's House
19 Ruined Tower
20 Mavromihalis Tower
21 Church of Agios Ioannis
22 Pikoulakis Tower
23 Barelakos Tower

Hotel Kouris (☎ 2733-051 340, fax 2733-051 331; Plateia Athanaton; singles/doubles with bathroom €38/47) is a fairly characterless modern hotel but it's a useful fallback option.

Londas Pension (☎ 2733-051 360, fax 2733-051 012; e londas@otenet.gr; doubles/triples with bathroom €70/90) has the most stylish rooms in town. This 200-year-old tower is signposted to the right off Kapetan Mapetan at the Church of Taxiarhes. The tower's rooms have whitewashed stone walls and beamed ceilings, and prices include breakfast.

Places to Eat

Nicola's Corner Taverna (☎ 2733-051 366; Plateia Athanaton; mains €3.50-7) is open all day and is the most popular place to eat. It has a good choice of tasty taverna staples.

Barbar Petros (☎ 2733-051 205; dishes €2.95-5.30) is primarily a psistaria (grill restaurant) serving steak and chops, but it also has daily specials such as eggplant-and-potato pie (€3.75 for an enormous serving).

There is a small **Koilakos supermarket** (☎ 2733-051 221; Kapetan Mapetan) near the square.

Getting There & Away

The **bus office** (☎ 2733-051 229; Plateia Athanaton) is inside the Europa Grill. There are five buses daily to Gythio (€1.70, 30 minutes); three to Itilo (€0.80, 20 minutes) via Limeni; two to Gerolimenas (€2.15, 45 minutes) and the Diros Caves (€0.80, 15 minutes); one daily to Lagia (€2.35, 40 minutes) via Kotronas; and three weekly (Monday, Wednesday and Friday) to Vathia (€2.60, one hour).

DIROS CAVES Σπηλαίο Διρού

These extraordinary caves (☎ 2733-052 222; admission €10.90 including tour; open 8am-5.30pm June-Sept, 8am-3pm Oct-May) are 11km south of Areopoli, near the village of Pyrgos Dirou – notable for its towers, which are signposted to the left off the road to the caves.

The natural entrance to the caves is on the beach. Locals like to believe the legend that the caves extend as far north as Sparta; speleologists have so far traced them inland for 5km. The caves were inhabited in Neolithic times, but were abandoned after an

earthquake and weren't rediscovered until 1895. Systematic exploration began in 1949. The caves are famous for their stalactites and stalagmites, which have fittingly poetic names such as the Palm Forest, Crystal Lily and the Three Wise Men.

Unfortunately, the guided tour through the caves covers only the lake section, and bypasses the dry section that features the most spectacular formations.

Finds from the caves are housed in the nearby **Neolithic Museum** (☎ 2733-052 223; admission €1.50; open 8.30am-3pm Tues-Sun).

Places to Stay

Most people visit the caves on a day trip from Areopoli or Gythio, but there is accommodation closer to the caves.

To Panorama (☎ 2733-052 280; singles/doubles with bathroom €22/28) is a small family-run hotel and is the closest accommodation to the caves. It's 1km south of the caves on the road to Pyrgos Dirou. The comfortable rooms have air-con and TV.

PYRGOS DIROU TO GEROLIMENAS
Πύργος Διρού το Γερολιμένας
Journeying south down the Mani's west coast from Pyrgos Dirou to Gerolimenas, the barren mountain landscape is broken only by deserted settlements with mighty towers. A turning to the right 9km south of Pyrgos Dirou leads down to the Bay of Mezapos, sheltered to the east by the frying pan–shaped Tigani Peninsula. The ruins on the peninsula are those of the **Castle of Maina**, built by the Frankish leader Guillaume de Villehardouin in 1248, and subsequently adapted by the Byzantines.

Kita, 13km south of Pyrgos Dirou, positively bristles with the ruins of war towers and fortified houses. It was the setting for the last great interfamily feud recorded in the Mani, which erupted in 1870 and required the intervention of the army, complete with artillery, to force a truce.

Places to Stay

Tsitsiris Castle Guest House (☎ 2733-056 297, fax 2733-056 296; Stavri; singles/doubles with bathroom €41.10/54.90) is the only place to stay along the 17km stretch between Pyrgos Dirou and Gerolimenas. The 'castle' is a restored tower house on the edge of the village of Stavi. Rooms have air-con and a bathroom, and rates include a generous breakfast. The castle has its own restaurant, with home-cooked meals at standard taverna prices. The guesthouse is signposted off the main road 4km north of Gerolimenas.

GEROLIMENAS & AROUND
postcode 230 71 • pop 55

Gerolimenas (yeh-ro-lih-**meh**-nahss) is a tranquil fishing village built around a small, sheltered bay at the southwestern tip of the peninsula. It's a wonderful place to relax for a few days, and is an ideal base for exploring the surrounding villages and sites.

Keria Κερια

The tiny village of Keria, about 4km northwest of Gerolimenas, is home to the magnificent **Church of Agios Ioannis**. Built in the 13th century, it is a fine example of the art of recycling. The walls are studded with numerous ancient gravestones and with masonry gleaned from earlier buildings. Sadly, the best of the gravestones, which occupied pride of place to the right of the entrance, was prised from the wall and stolen in 2000.

The walk from Gerolimenas to Keria takes about 1½ hours, along the track that leads north into the hills from the western side of the village. It is possible to drive to Keria via the village of Kounos, signposted to the east 3km north of Gerolimenas.

Ano Boulari & Kato Boulari
Ανο Βουλαρι & Κατω Βουλαρι

The twin villages of Ano Boulari and Kato Boulari lie in the hills about 2.5km northeast of Gerolimenas. Both have some fine towers, although the best are found in Ano (Upper) Boulari. The **Mantouvali Tower**, on the main street, was the stronghold of the ruling Mantouvali clan. The **Anemodoura Tower**, in Kato (Lower) Boulari, was built around 1600 and is thought to be one of the earliest Maniot towers.

The 11th-century **Church of Agios Stratigos**, which overlooks Ano Boulari, has a wonderful slate roof that blends almost perfectly with the grey hillside. It has some well-preserved frescoes, most dating from the 12th century, but the doors are locked.

The Boulari villages lie on a loop road that begins just north of Gerolimenas, running

northeast to Ano Boulari and returning to the main road via Kato Boulari about 3km north of Gerolimenas. It takes about three hours to walk the circuit.

Places to Stay & Eat

Hotel Akrotenaritis (☎ 2733-054 205; singles/doubles with bathroom €14.70/29.35) is a good budget option. All rooms are equipped with air-con, and some have views over the harbour. Akrotenaritis also has a restaurant.

Hotel Akrogiali (☎ 2733-054 204, fax 2733-054 272; singles/doubles with bathroom €23.50/35.20, apartments €47) has a great setting overlooking the small pebble beach on the way into town. It has a choice of rooms, all with air-con, ranging from standard doubles in the original hotel building to 'superior' rooms in a new wing, which is beautifully crafted from local stone. Breakfast costs €3.55. The owners also rent out four-person apartments nearby.

There is a small supermarket facing the harbour on the road into town.

Getting There & Away

There are buses to/from Gerolimenas to Sparta (€6.30, 2¼ hours), Gythio (€3.70, 1¼ hours) and Areopoli (€2.15, 45 minutes). The Hotel Akrotenaritis acts as the bus station.

GEROLIMENAS TO PORTO KAGIO
Γερολιμένας το Πόρτο Κάγιο

South of Gerolimenas, the road continues 4km to the small village of Alika, where it divides. One road leads east to Lagia and the other goes south to Vathia and Porto Kagio. The southern road follows the coast, passing pebbly beaches. It then climbs steeply inland to **Vathia**, the most dramatic of the traditional Mani villages, comprising a cluster of closely packed tower houses perched on a rocky spur.

A fork to the right 9km south of Alika leads to two sandy beaches at Marmari. Just before Marmari, a turn-off to the left leads south towards Cape Tenaro, the southernmost point of the Greek mainland. This road finishes at a parking area overlooking a deep bay. The meagre ruins in front of the parking area are those of the **Sanctuary and Death Oracle of Poseidon Tainarios**, a name which reflects the ancient belief that a deep cave at Cape Tenaro was the entrance to Hades.

A fork to the left 9km south of Alika cuts across the peninsula to the tiny east-coast fishing village of **Porto Kagio**, set on a perfect horseshoe bay.

Places to Stay & Eat

Akroteri Domatia (*☎/fax 2733-052 013; Porto Kagio; singles/doubles with bathroom €30/40*) is a great place to hang out for a few days. The rooms are large and have balconies overlooking the bay. The only decision to make is whether to eat at the Akroteri's own restaurant, or at one of its two rivals on the beachfront. Not surprisingly, all specialise in fish.

Vathia Towers is magnificent and was once part of a government-run traditional hotel, which closed several years ago for renovation. The place remains closed, with no indication of renovation work in progress and no clues as to when it might reopen.

LAGIA TO KOTRONAS
Λάγια το Κοτρώνας

Lagia was once the chief town of the southeastern Mani. Perched 400m above sea level, it's a formidable-looking place, especially when approached from Halikia.

Heading north along the coast from Lagia, the road winds downwards and provides spectacular views of the little fishing harbour of **Agios Kyprianos**, a short detour from the main road. The next village is **Kokala**, busy, friendly and with two pebbled beaches. The bus stop is in front of Synantisi Taverna.

Once through Kokala, the road climbs again. After 4km there are more beaches at the sprawling village of **Nyfi**. A turn-off to the right leads to the sheltered beach of **Halikia**. Continuing north, a turn-off beyond Flomohori descends to Kotronas.

Places to Stay & Eat

The accommodation on the east coast is disappointing. There is nothing that can be recommended with enthusiasm. Lagia has nothing, but there are possibilities in Kokala.

Pension Kokala (*☎ 2733-021 107; singles/doubles with bathroom €18/25; open May-Oct*) is a small, modern pension, conveniently located on the main street in the middle of the village.

To Kastro Pension (*☎ 2733-021 090; doubles from €30*) is perched high above the village and is reached by a steep, concrete road leading up the hill next to Hotel Soleteri. You'll see signs promoting this pension, formerly Papa's Rooms, all the way down the east coast.

Marathos Taverna (*mains €2.95-7.35, fresh fish from €26.40; open May-Oct*) is on the beach north of Kokala and is the best eatery in town, with good food and a great setting. The road down to the taverna is signposted on the northern edge of the village.

KOTRONAS Κοτρώνας
postcode 230 66 • pop 288

Around Kotronas the barrenness of the Mani gradually gives way to relatively lush hillsides, with olive groves and cypress trees. Kotronas bustles compared with the Mani's half-deserted tower villages. Its main thoroughfare leads to the waterfront, where the bus turns around. To the left is a bay with a small, sandy beach. The post office is on the right of the main thoroughfare as you face the sea. The islet off the coast is linked by a causeway. Walk inland along the main thoroughfare and turn left at the fork. Take the first left and walk to a narrow road, which soon degenerates into a path, leading to the causeway. On the islet are ruins surrounding a small, well-kept church.

Places to Stay & Eat

Adelfia Pension (*☎ 2733-021 209; singles/doubles €15/18*) is on the right of the main road as you head towards the sea.

Kotronas Bay Bungalows (*☎ 2733-021 340, fax 2733-021 402; bungalows €95*) is 500m east of the village, on the road that skirts the bay. The bungalows can accommodate up to four people and come with fully equipped kitchens.

There are two minimarkets and a bakery on the main street.

KOTRONAS TO SKOUTARI
Κοτρώνας το Σκουταρι

The upgrading of the coast road from Kotronas to Skoutari, 14km to the northeast, means that it's now possible to complete a circuit of the Mani without doubling back to Areopoli.

Skoutari is a quiet little village overlooking pretty Skoutari Bay, which terminates at a long, sandy beach where there is a small, summer *psarotaverna* (seafood taverna). There are domatia (rooms) in the village. There's a good sealed road from Skoutari to the Gythio–Areopoli road, about 5km to the north.

LIMENI Λιμένι

The tiny village of Limeni is 3km north of Areopoli, on the southern flank of beautiful Limeni Bay.

Limeni Village Bungalows (☎ 2733-051 111, fax 2733-051 182; singles/doubles with bathroom €55/70), on the south side of Limeni Bay, offers spectacular views over the bay to Itilo. This replica of Maniot towers is located on the cliff top overlooking the village and its facilities include a pool, bar and restaurant.

The village proper has domatia as well as a taverna.

ITILO & NEA ITILO

Οίτυλο & Νέο Οίτυλο
postcode 230 62 • pop 331

Itilo (**eet**-ih-lo), 11km north of Areopoli, was the medieval capital of the Mani.

The village is now a crumbling and tranquil backwater, perched on the northern edge of a deep ravine traditionally regarded as the border between outer and inner Mani. On the southern side of the ravine stand the ruins of **Kelefa Castle**, built by the Turks in the 17th century in an attempt to contain the Maniots. Access to the castle is from the Areopoli–Gythio road.

Nea Itilo, 4km south of Itilo, lies at the back of secluded Limeni Bay.

Places to Stay

Apart from a few domatia situated down by Limeni Bay in Nea Itilo, there is no budget accommodation.

Hotel Itilo (☎ 2733-059 222, fax 2733-059 234; Nea Itilo; singles/doubles with bathroom €35.20/47) is a comfortable C-class hotel, right by the beach at the middle point of the bay. Breakfast is included in the price.

Getting There & Away

Itilo is the changeover point for bus services between the Lakonian and Messinian Mani. There are three buses daily going to Areopoli (€0.80, 20 minutes) via Nea Itilo

and Limeni, and two a day north to Kalamata (€4.30, 2¼ hours) via Stoupa and Kardamyli.

Messinian Mani

The Messinian Mani, or outer Mani, lies to the north of its Lakonian counterpart, sandwiched between the Taygetos Mountains and the west coast of the Mani Peninsula. Kalamata lies at the northern end of the peninsula, just beyond the Messinian Mani border. The rugged coast is scattered with numerous small coves and beaches backed by mountains that remain snowcapped until late May. There are glorious views along the way, particularly on the descent from Stavropigi to Kardamyli and further south around the small village of Agios Nikon.

STOUPA Στούπα

postcode 240 24 • pop 625

Stoupa, 10km south of Kardamyli, has undergone a rapid transformation from fishing village to upmarket resort. Tourist development remains fairly low-key; it's billed as a resort for discriminating package tourists intent on discovering the unspoilt Greece. Although not as picturesque as Kardamyli, it does have two lovely beaches.

Celebrated author Nikos Kazantzakis lived here for a while and based the protagonist of his novel *Zorba the Greek* on Alexis Zorbas, a coal-mine supervisor in Pastrova, near Stoupa.

Orientation & Information

Stoupa is 1km west of the main Areopoli–Kalamata road, connected by link roads both north and south of town. Both roads lead to the larger of Stoupa's two main beaches, a glorious crescent of golden sand.

Stoupa's development has been so rapid that its amenities have yet to catch up. Katerina's supermarket, on the coast road behind the main beach, doubles as both the post office and the OTE. It sells stamps, accepts mail for delivery, changes money and sells phonecards.

There is no tourist office, but most tourists treat **Thomeas Travel** (☎ 2721-077 689, fax 2721-077 571; e antthom@otenet.gr) as if it were one. The manager, Bob Barrow, is a keen student of Mani history and a mine of information about local attractions. He can also change money, organise hire cars and advise on accommodation.

Places to Stay
Camping Ta Delfinia (☎ 2721-077 237, fax 2721-077 318; adult/tent €4/3; open Mar-Oct) is a good site to try if you're keen to escape the crowds. It's located near Kaminia Beach, 2km away on the Kardamyli side of Stoupa.

Stoupa's growing band of pensions and custom-built domatia seem to be block-booked by package-tour operators. Thomeas Travel may know of vacancies.

Stoupa Hotel (☎ 2721-054 308, fax 2721-077 568; singles/doubles with bathroom €40/45) is on the southern approach road to Stoupa. This modern C-class hotel has comfortable rooms with air-con, but nothing else to recommend it.

Hotel Lefktron (☎ 2721-077 322, fax 2721-077 700; e info@lefktron-hotel.gr; singles/doubles with bathroom €40/45), which takes the town's name from ancient times, is signposted off the southern approach road to Stoupa. Rooms here have a fridge and air-con.

Places to Eat
Stoupa has lots of restaurants and tavernas, none particularly cheap.

Taverna Akrogiali (☎ 2721-077 335; mains €5-12.50) has a top location at the southern end of the beach, and good food.

Taverna Dionysos (☎ 2721-077 442; mains €3.85-6.15) is a popular spot with a reputation for hearty meals at reasonable prices. It's signposted off the road behind the main beach.

Katerina's Supermarket (☎ 2721-077 777; waterfront) carries a remarkable range of stock for a small-town supermarket. Ouzo fans will be pleased to find their favourite tipple promoted as a health food.

Getting There & Away
Stoupa is on the main Itilo–Kalamata bus route, with four buses daily in each direction, three on Saturday and Sunday. You can stop at Kardamyli (€0.80) or go through to Kalamata (€2.60, 1¼ hours). There are bus stops at the junctions of both the southern and northern approach roads, but the buses don't go into town.

KARDAMYLI Καρδαμύλη
postcode 240 22 • pop 329
The tiny village of Kardamyli (kah-dah-mee-lih) has one of the prettiest settings in the Peloponnese, nestled between the calm waters of the Messinian Gulf and the peaks of the Taygetos Mountains. The deep Vyros Gorge, which emerges just north of town, runs straight up to the foot of **Mt Profitis Ilias** (2407m), the highest peak of the Taygetos (see the Lakonia chapter). The gorge and surrounding areas are very popular with trekkers.

Kardamyli was one of the seven cities offered to Achilles by Agamemnon.

Orientation & Information
Kardamyli is on the main Areopoli–Kalamata road. The bus stops at the central square, Plateia 25 Martiou 1821, at the northern end of the main thoroughfare. The post office is back towards Stoupa on the main street. **Koursaros Internet Café** (☎ 2721-073 963; open 10am-2am daily) is on the street opposite the post office. It charges €5.30 per hour, with a minimum of €2.95 for 30 minutes.

Kardamyli's main pebble-and-stone beach is off the road to Kalamata; turn left just north of the main square.

Old Kardamyli
Old (or upper) Kardamyli is the name given to the Trikoupis family compound, which stands on a low spur overlooking the Vyros Gorge about 800m northeast of town.

The imposing walled compound was built in the 17th century and it encloses the stunning late-Byzantine **Church of Agios Spiridon**. Check out the fine detail of the carving on the marble frame surrounding the arched window to the right of the door.

Opposite stands the **Mourtzinos Tower**, once occupied by the head of the Trikoupis clan, Kapetanios Mourtzinos Trikoupis. It was being restored at the time of research, unlike the surrounding towers belonging to lesser members of the clan.

The road up to Old Kardamyli is signposted on the right before the bridge over the Vyros River at the northern edge of town.

Trekking
Trekking has become Kardamyli's biggest draw card. The hills behind the village are crisscrossed with an amazing network of

olour-coded trails. All the accommodation places in the village can supply you with a map that explains the routes. Most are strenuous. Strong footwear is essential to support your ankles on the rough ground, particularly if you venture into the boulder-strewn Vyros Gorge. You will also need to carry plenty of drinking water. Kardamyli is not set up for long treks, and there is no agent or local guide offering guided treks.

Many treks pass through the mountain village of **Exohorio**, perched on the edge of the Vyros Gorge at an altitude of 450m. The village is also accessible by road, and it's a good place for nontrekkers to do a spot of more gentle exploration. The turn-off to Exohorio is 3km south of Kardamyli.

Places to Stay

Melitsina Camping (☎ 2721-073 461, fax 2721-073 334; adult/tent €4/3.25; open May-Sept) has good shady sites at the northern end of Kardamyli's main beach. The beachfront road terminates at the gate.

There are plenty of domatia signs along the main road. The street leading down to the sea from opposite the post office is the place to look:

Olympia Koumounakou rooms (☎ 2721-073 623, 2721-021 026; singles/doubles with bathroom €20/25), 150m along on the left, has double rooms with a communal kitchen.

Stratis Bravacos (☎ 2721-073 326; double/triple studios €28/35) has spotless studio apartments with kitchen facilities. The rooms are located opposite Olympia Koumounakou.

Lela's Taverna & Rooms (☎ 2721-073 541; doubles with bathroom €35) has decent rooms but the real attraction is the restaurant, with terrace seating overlooking the sea. If you keep going down the street past Statis Bravacos and turn right, you'll come to this place.

Anniska Apartments (☎ 2721-073 600, fax 2721-073 000; studios/apartments from €61.50/91.50) has a range of spacious, well-appointed studios and apartments, all with kitchen facilities. The studios sleep two people, while the larger apartments accommodate up to four. Anniska is by the sea, 200m north of Lela's.

Vardia (☎ 2721-073 513, fax 2721-073 156; studios/apartments from €58.70/79.25, low season €47/58.70) offers a range of fully equipped studios and apartments. The views are a major attraction at Vardia, which has a wonderful setting on the hillside overlooking Old Kardamyli. Breakfast costs €5.90. Contact Dimitreas Supermarket (see Places to Eat, following) for information and directions.

Places to Eat

There are nine tavernas in the village, so there's no shortage of eating options.

Lela's Taverna & Rooms (☎ 2721-073 541; mains €2.95-5.90) has a fabulous setting, with a terrace overlooking the sea, and taverna favourites such as *gemista* (stuffed tomatoes and peppers; €3.25). See Places to Stay for details on getting here.

Taverna Perivolis (☎ 2721-073 713; mains €3.55-7.35) is a popular taverna run by a friendly Greek-Australian family. It's on the left as you head towards Anniska Apartments (see Places to Stay, earlier) from the main road.

Taverna Dioskouroi (☎ 2721-073 236; mains €2.95-4.70) is another local favourite. It overlooks the sea from the hillside just south of town.

Pizza Pavlos (☎ 2721-073 688; mains from €3.55) turns out daily specials such as *moussaka* (€4.70) as well as pizzas (€7.05).

Dimitreas Supermarket (☎ 2721-073 513; open 7am-9.30pm daily) is one of two supermarkets side by side at the northern edge of the village.

Getting There & Away

Kardamyli is on the main bus route from Itilo to Kalamata and there are four buses daily in each direction (three on Saturday and Sunday). The trip to Kalamata takes an hour and costs €2.45; to Stoupa costs €0.80. Early birds can catch the sole daily bus to Exohorio at 6.15am; most people prefer to take a taxi (€5).

THE MANI

Messinia Μεσσηνία

Messinia occupies the fertile southwestern corner of the Peloponnese. Its boundaries have changed little since Mycenaean times, when the fabled King Nestor ruled from his palace near Pylos.

The region was conquered by Sparta at the end of the 8th century. Despite several uprisings, ruthlessly suppressed, it remained in Spartan hands for more than 300 years. Messinia's boundaries were restored in 371 BC, following Sparta's defeat by the Thebans at the Battle of Leuctra. Its capital was ancient Messini, about 25km northwest of Kalamata on the slopes of Mt Ithomi.

Today, Pylos and ancient Messini rate among the region's main attractions. Finikounda, in the southwest, boasts one of the best beaches in the country, while the old Venetian strongholds of Koroni and Methoni are delightful little hideaways that have yet to feel the weight of package tourism.

KALAMATA Καλαμάτα
postcode 241 00 • pop 49,154

Kalamata is Messinia's capital and is the second-largest city in the Peloponnese, after Patras.

Built on the site of ancient Pharai, the city takes its modern name from a miracle-working icon of the Virgin Mary, known as *kalo mata* (good eye). It was discovered in the stables of the Ottoman *aga* (governor), who converted to Christianity as a result of the miracles it performed.

Kalamata featured prominently in the War of Independence. On 23 March 1821 it became the first Greek city to be liberated. Independent Greece's first newspaper, *To Salpinx (The Clarion)*, was published here.

The city was subsequently recaptured by Ali Pasha's troops and almost totally destroyed. It was rebuilt unimaginatively by French engineers in the 1830s.

Kalamata was devastated again on 14 September 1986, this time by an earthquake measuring 6.2 on the Richter scale. Twenty people died, hundreds were injured and more than 10,000 homes were destroyed.

Orientation & Information

The old town around the *kastro* (walled compound) is picturesque and the waterfront

along Navarinou is lively – but it's a long hot walk between the two. The main streets linking the old town with the waterfront are Faron and Aristomenous. The city centre is around Plateia Georgiou on Aristomenous.

The **main bus station** *(Artemidos)* is on the northwestern edge of town, although local buses leave from Plateia 25 Martiou. The **train station** *(Frantzi)* is near Plateia Georgiou.

Tourist Offices The town is dotted with arrowed 'tourist information' signs, most directing people to the unusually helpful **tourist police** (☎ 2721-095 555; *Miaouli, open 8am-9.30pm Mon-Fri*), close to the port and opposite the Lambos supermarket. Other signs point to the old Ellinikos Organismos Tourismou (EOT) tourist office (now closed) by the yachting marina. None of them point to the new **EOT office** (☎ 2721-022 059; e detak@compulink.gr, *1st floor, Polyvriou 5; open 8am-2pm Mon-Fri*), just north of Plateia Georgiou.

158

MESSINIA

Post & Communications The main post office *(Iatropoulou 4; open 7.30am-2pm Mon-Fri)* is near the train station; another is opposite the port on Bouboulinas. The Organismos Tilepikoinonion Ellados (OTE) is on the northwestern side of Plateia Georgiou.

Diktyo Internet Café *(☎ 2721-097 282; Nedontos 75; open 10am-midnight daily)* charges €2.95 per hour, €1.50 minimum.

Money All the major Greek banks are represented in Kalamata. Like the **National Bank of Greece** *(Aristomenous • cnr Ariti & Navarinou)*, most have two branches: one in the city centre and one by the waterfront.

Laundry There is a **laundrette** *(☎ 2721-095 978; Methonis 3; open 9am-2pm &* 6pm-9pm Mon-Fri, 9am-3pm Sat) near the waterfront. It charges €5.30 to wash and dry 6kg of laundry.

Kastro

The crumbling remains of the city's 13th-century *kastro (off Vileardouinou; admission free; open 10am-1.30pm Mon-Fri)* stand on a low hill on the northern edge of the city.

It was built by the Frankish ruler Geoffrey de Villehardouin in 1208, on the foundations of the acropolis of the Mycenaean city Pharai. It was rebuilt by the Venetians at the beginning of the 18th century, and its most impressive surviving feature is the **arched entrance gate** – topped by a fine Venetian lion emblem. Remarkably, it survived the 1986 earthquake. Some sections of the walls

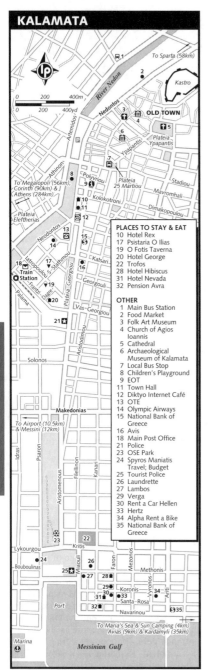

KALAMATA

To Sparta (58km)

River Nedon

Nedontos

Kastro

OLD TOWN

Plateia
Ypapantis

Ypapantis

Artemidos

Athinon

0   200   400m
0   200   400yd

To Megalopoli (56km),
Corinth (90km) &
Athens (284km)

Plateia
Eleftherias

Polyvriou

Plateia
25 Martiou

Stadiou

Mavromihali

Kolokotroni

Dimakopoulou

Neodontos

Katsari

Georgouli

Plateia Georgiou

Iatropoulou   S Stathmou

Train
Station   Dagre

Frantz.

Palama

Vas. Georgiou

Aristodimou

Makedonias

Solonos

To Airport (10.5km)
& Messini (12km)

Idras

Psaron

Filellinon

Kanari

Aristomenous

Lykourgou

Bouboulinas

Kritis

Miaouli

Faron

Mezonos

Methonis

Koronis

Vyronos

Anit.

Santa-Rosa

Navarinou

Port

Marina

To Maria's Sea & Sun Camping (4km)
Avias (9km) & Kardamyli (35km)

Messinian Gulf

PLACES TO STAY & EAT
10 Hotel Rex
17 Psistaria O Ilias
19 O Fotis Taverna
20 Hotel George
22 Trofos
28 Hotel Hibiscus
31 Hotel Nevada
32 Pension Avra

OTHER
1 Main Bus Station
2 Food Market
3 Folk Art Museum
4 Church of Agios
   Ioannis
5 Cathedral
6 Archaeological
   Museum of Kalamata
7 Local Bus Stop
8 Children's Playground
9 EOT
11 Town Hall
12 Diktyo Internet Café
13 OTE
14 Olympic Airways
15 National Bank of
   Greece
16 Avis
18 Main Post Office
21 Police
23 OSE Park
24 Spyros Maniatis
   Travel; Budget
25 Tourist Police
26 Laundrette
27 Lambos
29 Verga
30 Rent a Car Hellen
33 Hertz
34 Alpha Rent a Bike
35 National Bank of
   Greece

MESSINIA

were badly damaged, however, and much of
the *kastro* is off limits to visitors. Wide steps
lead to the summit, where you'll find the
tiny **Church of Agios Konstantinos** tucked
away among shady pine trees. It's a pleasant spot to bring a picnic lunch, with good
views over the city to the sea.

The modern theatre on the southwestern
slope of the hill is the setting for an annual
summer festival, which includes cultural
events such as contemporary musical performances and plays.

Archaeological Museum of Kalamata

This archaeological museum (☎ 2721-026
209; e protocol@zepka.culture.gr; Papazog-
lou 6; admission €1.50; open 8am-2.30pm
Tues-Sat, 8.30am-3pm Sun) is just north of
Plateia 25 Martiou, signposted off Ypapantis. It's one of the best local museums
around. The 1st-floor prehistoric displays
are particularly good, with comprehensive
explanations in English.

Folk Art Museum

This new museum (☎ 2721-028 499; Plateia
Agiou Ioannou) had yet to open its doors at
the time of research. It occupies a beautifully restored neoclassical building. If the
display is half as good as the restoration
job, it's worth a visit. The museum is on the
northern edge of the square, opposite the
massive Church of Agios Ioannis.

OSE (Railway) Park

The leafy park at the southern end of Aristomenous is home to a collection of old
steam locomotives and carriages, parked
next to the city's quaint old train station.

Places to Stay

Maria's Sea & Sun Camping (☎ 2721-041
314, fax 2721-041 251; Verga; adult/tent
€4.40/3) is the pick of the city's many
camping grounds, located right on the beach
4km east of town. It has a minimarket, bar,
restaurant and two-person bungalows. Buses
to Avias from the main bus station can drop
you close by.

Hotel Nevada (☎ 2721-082 429; Santa
Rosa 9; singles/doubles/triples with shared
bathroom €13.50/19.40/26.75) is a small
old-fashioned hotel offering the best value
in town, especially outside July and August.

when prices drop 25% on the listed rates. It's tucked away on Santa Rosa, one block back from the waterfront.

Pension Avra (☎ 2721-082 759; Santa Rosa 10; singles/doubles with shared bathroom €23/27) is almost opposite the Nevada. A key feature is the communal kitchen upstairs.

Hotel George (☎ 2721-027 225; cnr Frantzi & Dagre; singles/doubles with bathroom €25/30) has the best budget rooms in the city centre. All rooms come with a TV. Ask for a room away from the street.

The waterfront east of Faron is lined with characterless C-class hotels that are best avoided. Following are some better midrange and top-end options.

Hotel Hibiscus (☎2721-062 511, fax 2721-082 323; Faron 196; singles/doubles with bathroom €58.70/88.05) is a welcome addition to the accommodation scene, occupying a beautifully restored, neoclassical building at the seafront end of Faron. Lovely polished-timber floors and elegant furnishings make this place a real treat. Breakfast costs €5.90.

Xenones Pola (☎ 2721-058 400, fax 2721-058 040; Avia; singles €35.20-52.85, doubles €52.85-76.30) is in the village of Avias, about 9km southeast of Kalamata, and operated by the owners of the Hibiscus. Occupying an old stone house in spacious grounds above the village, it is classified as a traditional settlement. Breakfast costs €5.90.

Hotel Rex (☎ 2721-094 440, fax 2721-023 293; e rex@galaxynet.gr; Aristomenous 26; singles/doubles with bathroom from €80.70/113) has reclaimed its title as the best hotel in town, following a major renovation that has restored, to its former glory, one of the city's finest neoclassical buildings. Prices include buffet breakfast.

Places to Eat

O Fotis Taverna (☎ 2721-028 925; Sidirodromikou Stathmou 15; mains €2.95-5.30) is a cheery place, with a good choice of dishes and a loyal local following.

Psistaria O Ilias (Sidirodromikou Stathmou 22; mains €2.65-4.70) is a busy place specialising in grilled food, but it also has a small selection of taverna dishes such as boiled goat with vegetables (€3.85) and tripe (€3.55).

Down by the seafront, Navarinou is lined with countless cafés, fast-food restaurants and seafood tavernas.

Self-caterers should visit Kalamata's large food market, across the bridge from the bus station. Kalamata is noted for its olives, olive oil, figs, raki and *mastica* (a surprisingly smooth mastic-based liqueur). There are dozens of supermarkets around

MESSINIA

Kalamata Olives

Kalamata is best known as the home of the famous Kalamata olive. While not all olives grown around here are the Kalamata variety, it is this plump, purple-black variety that is found in delicatessens around the world. They are also grown extensively in neighbouring Lakonia and on the islands of Crete and Lesvos.

Locals insist, though, that the finest olives are grown on Messinian soil, particularly in the Pamisos Valley, north of Messini. The region's reliable winter rains and hot summers make for perfect olive-growing conditions.

The Kalamata tree can be distinguished from the common olive, grown for oil, by the size of its leaves. Like its fruit, the leaves of the Kalamata are twice the size of other varieties – and greener. Another important difference is that the Kalamata is alternate bearing – which means a heavy crop one year followed by a light crop.

Unlike other varieties, Kalamata olives cannot be picked green. They ripen in late November and must be hand-picked to avoid bruising. The olives are then graded according to size and brine-cured.

You can check out a selection of these famous olives at the markets in Kalamata.

NICK KELLY

town, including **Trofos** (☎ 2721-092 811; Kritis 13), the biggest and the best.

Getting There & Away

Air There are two flights weekly to Athens (€47.55). **Olympic Airways** (☎ 2721-022 724, fax 2721-027 868; ⓦ www.olympic -airways.gr; Giatrakou 3) is in the centre of town.

Bus Heading north, there are buses to Athens (€14.30, 4¼ hours, nine daily) via Tripolis (€5, 1¼ hours) and Corinth (€9.70, 2¾ hours); Kyparissia (€4.40, 1¼ hours, five daily); and Patras (€13.35, four hours, two daily) via Pyrgos (€7.65, two hours). Heading west, there are buses to Koroni (€3.30, 1½ hours, nine daily) and Pylos (€3.20, 1¼ hours, nine daily). Five of the buses to Pylos continue to Methoni (€3.80, 1¾ hours) and three keep going to Finikounda (€5.10, 2 hours). Heading east, there are buses to Sparta (€3.40, 1½ hours, two daily) via Artemisia (€1.60), and to Itilo (€4.30, 2¼ hours, three daily) via Kardamyli and Stoupa. (Details of services also apply for the reverse direction.)

Train Kalamata is the end of the line for both branches of the Peloponnese railway. There are four trains daily to Athens (€7.35, 6½ hours) on the inland line via Tripolis (€3.10, 2½ hours), Argos (€4.40, 3½ hours) and Corinth (€4.85, 4½ hours). There are two trains daily to Patras (€5.30, six hours) on the west-coast line via Kyparissia (€2.35, 1¾ hours) and Pyrgos (€3.25, 3¼ hours). (Details of services also apply for the reverse direction.)

Ferry AMEN Lines operates a weekly ferry service to Kastelli-Kissamos (Crete) via Kythira and Antikythira. The service is subject to constant change; contact **Spyros Maniatis Travel** (☎ 2721-020 704; Psaron), by the port, for the latest information.

Getting Around

To/From the Airport Kalamata's airport is 10.5km west of the city, near Messini. There is no airport shuttle bus. A taxi costs about €7.50.

Bus Local buses leave from Plateia 25 Martiou. The most useful service is bus No 1,

which goes south along Aristomenous to the seafront, then east along Navarinou. The flat fare is €0.60. Buy tickets from the kiosk on Ypapantis, just north of Plateia 25 Martiou.

Car & Motorcycle Kalamata is a good place to hire a car thanks to the hot competition between the many agencies. Most, but not all, are clustered together at the waterfront end of Faron. Agencies include:

Avis (☎ 2721-020 352) Kessari 2
Budget (☎ 2721-027 694, fax 2721-028 136) Maniatis Travel, Iatropoulou 1
Hertz (☎ 2721-088 268) Faron 235
Rent a Car Hellen (☎ 2721-094 644) Faron 210
Verga (☎ 2721-095 190, fax 2721-041 753) Faron 202

Alpha Rent a Bike (☎ 2721-093 423, fax 2721-025 370; Vyronos 156) hires a range of bikes from 50cc to 500cc.

MAVROMATI & ANCIENT MESSINI

postcode 240 04 • pop 388

The ruins of ancient Messini lie scattered across a small valley below the picturesque village of Mavromati, 25km northwest of Kalamata. The village, nestled on the slopes of Mt Ithomi, takes its name from a spring that rises near the main square; the water gushes from a hole in the rock that looks like a black eye – *mavro mati* in Greek.

Most visitors come here on day trips, but there's enough to see to warrant an overnight stay. The attractions are spread over a large area, so it's easy to spend a whole day exploring – especially if you are energetic enough to climb to the top of Mt Ithomi.

History

Ancient Messini was founded in 371 BC, after the Theban general Epaminondas defeated Sparta at the Battle of Leuctra, freeing Messinians from almost 350 years of Spartan rule.

Built on the site of an earlier settlement, the new Messinian capital was one of a string of defensive positions designed to keep watch over Sparta. As well as its defensive potential, the site was favoured by the gods. According to local myth, Zeus was born here – not on Crete – and raised by the nymphs Neda and Ithomi, who bathed him in the same spring that gives the modern village its name.

The city flourished under Roman rule, but slipped into steady decline following the break-up of the empire. It was abandoned for several centuries following the Avar invasions at the end of the 6th century, then reoccupied between the 10th and 13th centuries before being abandoned for good.

Museum

The small museum (☎ 2724-051 201; admission €1.50; open 8.30am-3pm Tues-Sun) is on the main road, about 200m northwest of the village. It houses an assortment of finds from the site. Unfortunately the finds do not include the splendid statue of Hermes unearthed from the gymnasium.

Fortifications

The massive fortifications, designed by Epaminondas himself, are an impressive reminder of the capabilities of ancient engineers. They were based on a mighty wall, studded with squat towers, stretching 9km around the surrounding ridges, completely enclosing the town.

Numerous sections of the wall survive, and its entire course is clearly visible; the finest section is in the northwest, 800m beyond the museum, surrounding the celebrated **Arcadian Gate**. This unusual circular gate guarded the ancient route to Megalopoli, now the modern road north to Meligala and Zerbisia. The road still runs through the gate, dodging an enormous fallen stone slab. The wall climbs steeply away to the east, towards the summit of Mt Ithomi. The ruins beyond the gate are those of a hotpotch of grave monuments and tombs.

The city's second major gate was the eastern **Lakonian Gate**, destroyed at the end of the 19th century during the building of the road from Mavromati to the Voulkarno Monastery (see Mt Ithomi, later in this section, p164, for details).

Major Monuments

Ancient Messini remained unexplored until very recent times, and is only slowly being revealed. Much of the land is still covered with olive trees and small patches of vineyard, fenced off using sections of the ancient columns that lie scattered everywhere.

The best views of the site are from Mavromati's main square, where it's worth spending a few minutes examining the layout before heading down for a closer look. Access is by a couple of roads that lead steeply downhill from either side of the museum. They link up and lead to a car park, passing the small Byzantine **Church of Agios Nikolaos** along the way. The church walls are dotted with slabs of stone gleaned from the ancient site, creatively recycled into lintels and door frames.

The car park is next to the ruins of the **theatre**, which is carved into the hillside below. A path leads to the east of the theatre, connecting with a small section of old paved street. The foundations to the left of this path belong to the **Arsinoe Fountain**, once fed by waters from the Mavromati spring – known as Klepsydra in ancient times. Today the waters are carried across the site by a concrete drainage channel. The fountain stood between the theatre and the wide **northern stoa** (colonnaded building) of the agora (commercial area).

The flat expanse of the unexcavated **agora** is easy enough to discern east of the main path running south from the theatre. The path leads to the main attraction, the **asklepion**, a large complex of shrines and meeting rooms that formed the heart of the ancient city. The *asklepion* was centred on a **Doric temple**, which once housed a huge, golden statue of Ithomi.

The entrance from the north is down a grand stone staircase at the centre of an area divided into two large function rooms used to host visiting VIPs. The columns to the north belong to a **Roman stoa** standing at the southern edge of the agora.

The principal entry was from the east through the **propylon** (elaborate entrance way), built in alignment with the temple. The surviving column bases give a good idea of its imposing proportions. North of the propylon is the well-preserved **ekklesiasterion** (assembly hall), which was used for public meetings and served as a theatre. It was being restored at the time of research. The **bouleuterion** (council house), south of the propylon, was reserved for meetings of the Messinian council, attended by representatives from all towns in the territory. The apparently haphazard assortment of ruins immediately east of the propylon are those of

MESSINIA

an early Christian settlement, superimposed on a much older grave enclosure.

The western side of the complex is lined with a row of small rooms that functioned as shrines. Pride of place goes to the so-called **artemision**, where fragments of an enormous statue of Artemis Orthia were found. It is protected by a modern awning.

The *asklepion* is flanked to the north by the **valaneion** (bath house), identifiable by the circular furnaces that heated water. Many of the bronze coins on display in the museum were unearthed here. East of here, a shady oak tree has sprouted from the base of funerary monument.

A track leads downhill from the *asklepion* to the **stadium**, used to stage athletics contests in honour of Zeus. It remains largely intact, although suffering badly from the effects of centuries of waterlogging, which has caused much of the stone seating to subside. The stone bench in the front row on the eastern side was where the judges sat; next to it is the 'throne', occupied by the priest who presided over games.

The stadium is surrounded by the ruins of an enormous **gymnasium**, entered by the recently reassembled propylon of the gymnasium.

Mt Ithomi

The main route to the top of Mt Ithomi begins about 1.5km east of Mavromati, along the road to Moni Voulkanou. A signpost points to the start of a rough track that zigzags up the hillside. It's supposedly passable by 4WD but was in very poor condition at the time of research. The walk to the top takes about 45 minutes, passing the ruins of a couple of temples on the way. The summit is occupied by the 13th-century Voulkanou Monastery, now abandoned in favour of the newer (16th-century) monastery on the eastern side of the mountain, beyond the old Lakonian Gate.

The turn-off to Moni Voulkanou (the monastery) is in the centre of Mavromati, opposite the main square. It looks like somebody's driveway at first, but don't be put off.

Places to Stay & Eat

Rooms to Rent Zeus (☎ 2724-051 025/005; *doubles with shared bathroom €47*) has just two cosy double rooms with a communal kitchen. The rooms overlook the site from the family jewellery shop on the main square.

Rooms to Rent Lykourgos (☎ 2724-051 297; *singles/doubles with bathroom €30/ 38*) offers larger rooms than available at Zeus. The rooms are signposted next to the Taverna/Psistaria Ithomi.

Taverna/Psistaria Ithomi (☎ 2724-051 298; *mains €4.10-5.90*), opposite the spring in the middle of the village, is a typical village *psistaria*, which specialises in grilled food and salads. The small selection of taverna dishes has normally gone by the evening.

Getting There & Away

There are two buses daily to Mavromati (€2.20, one hour) from Kalamata, leaving at 5.40am and 2.05pm. They also operate in the opposite direction.

KORONI Κορώνη
postcode 240 04 • pop 1668

Koroni (ko-**ro**-nih) is a delightful old Venetian town on the coast, 43km southwest of Kalamata. Its narrow streets lead up to an old castle, most of which is occupied by the **Timios Prodromos Convent**. The small promontory beyond the castle is a tranquil place for a stroll, with lovely views over the Messinian Gulf to the Taygetos Mountains. Koroni's main attraction is **Zaga Beach**, a long sweep of golden sand just south of the town.

Orientation & Information

Buses drop passengers in the main square outside the Church of Agios Dimitrios, one block back from the harbour. There is no tourist office, but you'll find all the information you need on the large map of town on the church wall. It shows the location of the post office, OTE and both banks, all of which are nearby. There is no tourist police in Koroni. The main street runs east from the square, one block back from the sea. Most locals appear unaware that it has a name, Perikli Ralli.

It takes about 20 minutes to walk to Zaga Beach; take the road that leads up to the castle from above the square, turn right at the top of the hill and follow the road that curves up around the castle. You'll see a sign to the beach on the left after 500m.

Places to Stay & Eat

Camping Koroni (☎ *2725-022 119, fax 2725-022 884; adult/tent €4.70/3.55*) is a small camping ground, 500m north of town on the road from Kalamata. It's a friendly place, although the grounds look badly in need of attention. Buses stop outside.

Koroni does not have a lot of accommodation. Most of the options are spread around a cluster of domatia (rooms) by the sea at the eastern end of the main street. Expect to pay around €20.50/26.50 for singles/doubles with a private bathroom. There are more domatia overlooking Zaga Beach, but they are often block-booked in summer.

Hotel Diana (☎/*fax 2725-022 312;* e *dhotel@hol.gr; singles/doubles with bathroom €25/40*) represents top value for good rooms with a TV, fridge and air-con. It's just off the main square, on the road leading to the seafront. Some rooms also have sea views. Breakfast is available for €3.55.

Symposium Restaurant (☎ *2725-022 385; mains around €3.55*), on the main street, is about as traveller-friendly as you could ever want a restaurant to be. Years of New York living have taught George, the amiable Greek-American owner, all about keeping the customer satisfied. He has seafood and grills, as well as a daily selection of taverna staples. Vegetarians will find a range of dishes to choose from.

Psarotavera Ifigenia (☎ *2725-022 097; mains €2.95-8.80*) is one of a couple of seafood restaurants on the seafront; it also does pizzas.

Self-caterers will find everything they need at the shops around the main square, including **Sifas Supermarket** (☎ *2725-022 198; Plateia Kentriki*).

Getting There & Away

There are nine buses daily from Koroni to Kalamata (€3.30, 1½ hours); they also operate in the reverse direction.

FINIKOUNDA Φοινικούντα
postcode 240 06 • pop 560

The pretty little fishing village of Finikounda, midway between Koroni and Methoni, no longer qualifies as an undiscovered gem, though it remains sufficiently off the beaten track to avoid being overrun. It occupies a prime location, nestled below a small headland at the western end of Finikounda Beach.

Orientation & Information

Finikounda has spread steadily along the beach over the years, having started as a cluster of houses around the port.

Most shops and facilities are around the port, including a post office and a bank. Internet access is available at **To Akrogialia Bar & Café** (☎ *2723-071 325; open 6pm-late*). The bus stop is outside Hotel Finikountas, 100m from the port on the way to Methoni.

Beaches

Finikounda Beach is the pick of three fine beaches along this stretch of coastline, with 500m of golden sand stretched between two headlands. Anemomilos Beach, to the east, and Loutros Beach, to the west, offer the same golden sands but are more exposed.

The reliability of the summer *maistros*, a light to moderate northwesterly wind that rises in the afternoon, has made Finikounda a prime destination for **windsurfing**. Dipha Surf Station, 3km west of Finikounda at Anemomilos Beach, hires out boards.

Places to Stay

Camping Anemomilos (☎ *2723-071 360, fax 2723-071 121; adults/tents/camper vans €4.40/2.65/5*), 3km west of Finikounda off the road to Methoni, serves as a base for most young campers. It has good shady sites by the beach on the western side of Finikounda headland.

Akti Studios (☎ *2723-071 316; doubles/triples with bathroom €35.20/41.10*) is set back from the beach road, about 250m east of the port. This small, family-run place has comfortable studios with kitchen facilities.

Hotel Korakakis Beach (☎ *2723-071 221, fax 2723-071 232;* e *korakaki@otenet.gr; singles/doubles with bathroom €49/540*) is a comfortable, modern hotel at the eastern end of the town's main beach. It serves breakfast (€4.40) and also has studios nearby.

Golden Sun Hotel (☎ *2723-071 141, fax 2723-071 145; singles/doubles with bathroom €44/73.40*) has a great location on the headland at the western end of Finikounda Beach. British tour operator Neilson Holidays brings small groups here for windsurfing holidays, but the hotel retains some rooms for independent travellers. Prices include breakfast.

Places to Eat

Estiatorio To Steki (☎ 2723-071 304; mains €3.50-5) is a popular spot that turns out a range of grilled food, as well as daily specials such as *moussaka* (€4); the servings are designed for the hungry. It's tucked away on a small side street, signposted off the main drag.

Taverna Elena (☎ 2723-071 235; mains €4-12.50) has a prime position on the headland overlooking the port at the western end of town. It's the perfect spot to relax and take in the views.

Getting There & Away

Three buses daily go to (and come back from) Kalamata (€5.10, 2 hours) via Methoni (€1.30, 15 minutes) and Pylos.

METHONI Μεθώνη

postcode 240 06 ● pop 1169

Methoni (meh-**tho**-nih), 12km south of Pylos, was one of the seven cities offered to Achilles by Agamemnon. Homer described it as 'rich in vines'. Today Methoni is a pretty seaside town, with a sandy beach that's crowded in summer and with a magnificent 15th-century Venetian fortress.

Orientation & Information

The road from Pylos forks on the edge of town to create Methoni's two main streets, which run parallel through town to the fortress. The fork to the right is the main shopping street and has a supermarket and National Bank of Greece. The fork to the left leads directly to the fortress car park, passing the post office on the way. Turn left at the fortress end of either street onto Miaouli, which leads to Methoni Beach. The small square by the beach is surrounded by fairly characterless C-class hotels and several seafood restaurants.

Methoni has no tourist office or tourist police. The office of the regular **police** (☎ 2723-031 203) is signposted near the post office.

Methoni Castle

This splendid fortress (admission free; open 8.30am-5pm Tues-Sat, 9am-5pm Sun) is a supreme example of medieval military architecture. It stands on a promontory south of the modern town, surrounded on three sides by the sea and separated from the mainland by a moat. The medieval town, enclosed within the fortress walls, was the Venetians' first and longest-held possession in the Peloponnese. It was also a stopover point for pilgrims en route to the Holy Land.

Places to Stay

Camping Methoni (☎ 2723-031 228; adult/tent €3.25/2.05) has a good location right behind the beach, but it could use a few shade trees.

Rooms to Rent Giorgos (☎ 2723-031 640/588; doubles/triples with bathroom €20/25) is above Cafeteria George at the fortress end of the main shopping street. This is one of many domatia for which you'll see signs in the streets near the fortress.

Hotel Castello (☎ 2723-031 300/280, fax 2723-031 300; e psiharis@methoni.gr; Miaouli; singles/doubles/triples with bathroom €37/44/52) is a small, family-run hotel facing the fortress. The rooms are tastefully furnished and there's a tranquil garden at the back. Breakfast costs €4.40.

Hotel Albatros (☎ 2723-031 160, fax 2723-031 114; singles/doubles with bathroom €40/50) is next to the post office, in the centre of town. It has comfortable air-con rooms, each with TV and refrigerator.

Hotel Achilles (☎/fax 2723-031 819; e achilefs@conxion.gr; singles/doubles with bathroom €40/56) is the smartest of a range of small, family hotels in town. It offers comfortable, modern, air-con rooms.

Places to Eat

Taverna Nikos (☎ 2723-031 282; Miaouli; mains €2.75-5; open year-round) is a no-frills taverna, halfway along Miaouli near the fortress. It's always full of locals.

Restaurant Kali Karthia (☎ 2723-031 260; mains €3.60-7.50) is a small, family-run place halfway along the shopping street. It serves good food and good wine.

Café La Mare (☎ 2723-031 311; pasta from €3, pizzas from €4.70) is a popular local hang-out on the small square near Methoni Beach. It has a range of pastas and pizzas, as well as ice creams and snacks.

Getting There & Away

Buses leave from where the two main streets meet at the Pylos end of town. You'll find a timetable pinned to the door of the adjacent

Assimakis Food Market. There are seven buses daily to Kalamata (€3.80, 1¼ hours) and Pylos (€0.80, 15 minutes), and three to Finikounda (€1.30, 15 minutes). The same services run in the reverse direction.

PYLOS Πύλος
postcode 240 01 • pop 2104
Pylos (**pee**-loss), 51km southwest of Kalamata, presides over the southern end of an immense bay. It was here, on 20 October 1827, that the British, French and Russian fleets, under the command of Admiral Codrington, fired at point-blank range on Ibrahim Pasha's combined Turkish, Egyptian and Tunisian fleet, sinking 53 ships and killing 6000 men, with negligible losses on the Allies' side.

It was known as the Battle of Navarino (the town's former name), and was decisive in the War of Independence, but it was not meant to have been a battle at all. The Allied fleet wanted to achieve no more than to persuade Ibrahim Pasha and his fleet to leave, but things got out of hand. On hearing the news, George IV described it as a 'deplorable misunderstanding'.

Pylos is one of the most picturesque towns in the Peloponnese, with its huge natural harbour almost enclosed by the Sfaktiria islet, a delightful tree-shaded central square, two castles and surrounding pine-covered hills.

Orientation & Information
Everything of importance is within a few minutes' walk of the central square, Plateia Trion Navarhon, down by the seafront. The bus station is on the inland side of the square. There is no tourist office. The post office is on Nileos, which runs uphill from the bus station towards Arviniti Hotel. The **police station** (☎ 2723-022 316; *Plateia Trion Navarhon*) and National Bank of Greece are on the square, while the main Kalamata–Methoni road runs around it.

Neo Kastro
There are castles on each side of Navarino Bay, but the more accessible is **Neo Kastro** (☎ 2723-022 010; *admission €2.35; open 8.30am-3pm Tues-Sun*), on the hilltop at the southern edge of town, off the road to Methoni. It was built by the Turks in 1573 and was later used as a launching pad for

the invasion of Crete. It remains in good condition, especially the formidable surrounding walls. Within its walls are a citadel, a mosque converted into a church and a courtyard surrounded by dungeons (it was used as a prison until the 1900s). The road to Methoni from the central square goes past the castle.

The ancient Paleokastro, 6km north of Pylos, is covered under Around Gialova, later in this chapter.

Boat Tours
You can ask around the waterfront for fishing boats to take you around Navarino Bay and the island of Sfaktiria. The price will depend on the number of passengers; you can reckon on about €10 per person for a group of four or more. On the trip around the island, stops can be made at memorials to admirals of the Allied ships. Boats may also pause so you can see wrecks of sunken Turkish ships, discernible through the clear waters.

Places to Stay
Rooms to Rent Stavroula Milona (☎ 2723-022 724; *Paralia Pylos; doubles €17.60 with shared bathroom*) is a charming little place right on the seafront, to the south of the harbour above the Café-Bar En Plo. The rooms are small but clean and comfortable. It has a communal kitchen and a TV room.

12 Gods (Dodeka Theoi; ☎ 2723-022 179/ 324/878, fax 2723-022 878, e a12gods@ otenet.gr; doubles with bathroom €30) is perched high above the harbour, about 1km south of the main square on Kalamatas, which becomes the main road to Kalamata. Rooms are named after the gods of the ancient Greek pantheon. Appropriately enough, Poseidon has superb views over Navarino Bay.

Arviniti Hotel (☎ 2723-023 050, fax 2723-022 934; Nileos; singles/doubles with bathroom €32.30/41.10), near the post office, has large, air-con rooms, each with TV; breakfast costs €3.55.

Hotel Miramare (☎ 2723-022 751, fax 2723-022 226; singles/doubles/triples with bathroom €41.10/58.70/64.60) is on the seafront, 150m north of the harbour. This comfortable mid-range hotel is the town's finest and has views over Navarino Bay. Prices include breakfast.

MESSINIA

Places to Eat

Psarotaverna 4 Epohes (☎ *2723-022 739; mains €2.65-7.35, fresh fish from €29.35 per kg*), on the seafront beyond Hotel Miramare, is a popular family-run place. It has taverna favourites such as stuffed tomatoes (€2.95) and *moussaka* (€3.20), as well as a good selection of fresh seafood.

Restaurant 1930 (☎ *2723-022 032; mains €3.55-11.75, seafood €35.20 per kg*) has a mix of traditional fare, such as *spetsofai* (sausages in spicy sauce; €4.10), and modern Mediterranean dishes, such as pork fillet in Roquefort (€11.75). The decor is an amusing recreation of scenes from the 1930s.

There is an **Atlantik supermarket** on the main square.

Getting There & Away

There are buses to Kalamata (€3.20, 1¼ hours, nine daily); Kyparissia (€3.80, 1¼ hours, five daily) via Nestor's Palace (€1.50, 30 minutes) and Hora (€1.50, 35 minutes); Methoni (€0.80, 20 minutes, five daily); Finikounda (€1.80, 30 minutes, three daily). On weekends there are two buses each day to Athens (€17.45, five hours). The same services also operate into Pylos.

GIALOVA
postcode 240 01 • pop 258

The village of Gialova lies 8km north of Pylos on the northeastern side of Navarino Bay. It boasts a fine sandy beach and safe swimming in the sheltered waters of the bay. The Gialova Lagoon is a prime bird-watching site in winter, as well as home to some unlikely critters (see the boxed text 'Chameleon Colonists').

Bird-Watching

The Gialova Lagoon is one of the best – and most accessible – bird-watching sites in the Peloponnese. Between November and March the lagoon is home to up to 20,000 assorted water birds, while many others pause here on their spring migration between Africa and Eastern Europe.

The Hellenic Ornithological Society has recorded here 262 of the 423 species found in Greece, including 10 species of duck and eight of heron. Waders descend in their thousands, along with flamingos and glossy ibis. Birds of prey include the imperial eagle, osprey, peregrine falcon and species of harrier.

The lagoon and associated wetlands cover an area of some 500 hectares at the northern end of Navarino Bay, separated from the bay only by a narrow spit of land leading out to Koryphasion Hill. The wetlands are fed by two freshwater streams, which flow into the reed beds on the northern and eastern flanks of the lagoon and empty into Navarino Bay below Koryphasion Hill.

The entire ecosystem was seriously compromised by an ill-considered attempt to drain the wetlands in the 1950s. The work left the area scarred by a network of drains and embankments, which have had a serious impact on water flows and salinity levels.

The birds don't seem to mind. The waters of the lagoon are a prime breeding habitat for at least 20 species of fish, including sea bream and mullet.

The wetlands and surrounding coastal habitats were declared a protected area in 1996. Since then environmental groups have been campaigning to resurrect the area. The old pump house, the former nerve centre of the drainage scheme, has been converted into an **information centre**. The pump house is also the starting point for a **walking trail** that guides visitors through a range of habitats, with information boards explaining the fauna and flora.

Places to Stay & Eat

Camping Erodios (☎ *2723-028 240, fax 2723-028 241;* e *erodioss@otenet.gr; adult/tent €4/3.50, 2-bed/4-bed cabins €45/55*), Erodios being the Greek for heron, is a

---

Chameleon Colonists

The sandy coastal scrub around the lagoon is home to Europe's only known population of African chameleons, which are thought to have hitched over from Egypt with the Romans. The colony went unnoticed until 1998, when it was first identified as being a species of Africa rather than Europe. After the colony had been quietly ignored for 2000 years, the discovery brought almost instant disaster in the shape of reptile collectors, who walked off with half the population in 2001.

new site northwest of the village, on the road leading out to the lagoon and Paleokastro. It has a good stretch of beach on Navarino Bay and great facilities, although the shade trees here still have some growing to do.

Navarino Beach Camping (☎ 2723-022 761, fax 2723-023 512; adult/tent/camper van €4.10/2.95/5) is just south of the village, on the road to Pylos. It has good shady sites right by the beach.

Hotel Zoe (☎ 2723-022 025, fax 2723-022 026; e hotelzoe@otenet.gr; singles/doubles with bathroom €40/50) is a small hotel near the pier in Gialova. The owners have lots of information about bird-watching and walks around the wetlands.

Taverna To Spitiko (☎ 2723-022 137; mains €4.50-7) has a strong Cypriot presence in its kitchen and turns out a very tasty *saganaki* (fried cheese) made with Cypriot cheese, and delicious *seftaljes* (Cypriot-style pork meatballs flavoured with fresh herbs).

Getting There & Away
There are five buses a day going south to Pylos (€1.50, 15 minutes) and five going north to Kyparissia via Nestor's Palace and Hora. The services also run in the opposite direction.

AROUND GIALOVA
Paleokastro
The ruins of this ancient castle lie 5km west of Gialova on rugged Koryphasio Hill, a formidable natural defensive position overlooking the northern entrance to Navarino Bay.

The road to the castle is signposted on the northern edge of the village. It crosses the narrow spit of land that separates Navarino Bay from the Gialova Lagoon, and finishes at a car park at the southern end of the hill. Signs point to a rough track that snakes up the steep hillside to the castle entrance.

The castle was built by the Franks at the end of the 13th century and occupies the site of the acropolis of ancient Pylos. It was occupied in 1381 by Spanish mercenaries from Navarra, after whom the bay is named.

The car park is also the starting point for another track that skirts around the base of Koryphasio Hill to **Voidokilias Beach**, a beautiful, sandy horseshoe bay. This is presumed to be Homer's 'sandy Pylos', where

Telemachus was warmly welcomed when he came to ask wise old King Nestor the whereabouts of his long-lost father, Odysseus, King of Ithaca. There's another path up to the castle from the southern side of the beach and this path passes **Nestor's Cave**. According to myth, this is the cave where Hermes hid the cattle he stole from Apollo. It boasts some impressive stalactites.

Voidokilias Beach can also be approached by road from the village of Petrohori, about 4km north of Gialova off the road to Hora.

NESTOR'S PALACE
The palace (☎ 2763-031 437; admission €2; open 8.30am-3pm Tues-Sun Apr-Oct, 8am-2.30pm Nov-Mar), originally a two-storey building, is the best preserved of all Mycenaean palaces. Its walls stand 1m high, giving a good idea of the layout of a Mycenaean palace complex. The main palace is in the middle and was a vast building of many rooms. The largest, the **throne room**, was where the king dealt with state business. In the centre was a large, circular hearth surrounded by four ornate columns which supported a 1st-floor balcony. Some of the fine frescoes discovered here are in the museum in the nearby village of Hora. Rooms surrounding the throne room include the sentry box, pantry, waiting room, a vestibule and, most fascinating, a bathroom with a terracotta tub still in place.

The most important find was about 1200 Linear B script tablets, the first discovered on the mainland. Some are in Hora's museum. The site was excavated later than the other Mycenaean sites, between 1952 and 1965. An excellent guidebook by Carl Blegen, who led the excavations, is sold at the site.

Hora's fascinating little **archaeological museum** (☎ 2763-031 358; admission €1.50; open 8.30am-3pm Tues-Sun), 3km northeast of Nestor's Palace, houses finds from the site and other Mycenaean artefacts from Messinia. The prize pieces are the frescoes from the throne room at Nestor's Palace.

Getting There & Away
Nestor's Palace is 9km north of Gialova on the main road between Pylos and Kyparissia. There are five buses a day in each direction, which stop at both Nestor's Palace and Hora.

MESSINIA

KYPARISSIA

postcode 245 00 • pop 4894
Kyparissia (Ki-par-is-**sía**), on the coast 61km northwest of Kalamata, is the main town of the Tryfilia region of northwestern Messinia.

Orientation & Information
Kyparissia is an easy place to negotiate. Most facilities are in the new part of town, which is laid out on a neat grid system stretching back from the seafront. The post office is on the main square, which is also flanked by branches of the National Bank of Greece and the Bank Agrotiki.

Travellers can check email at **Heaven's Net Internet Café** (☎ 2761-062 136; *El Venizelou 76; open 10am-3am daily)*; it's 250m southwest of the main square and charges €4.40 per hour. Newspapers can be purchased from 25th Martiou 44.

There is no tourist office. The **police station** (☎ 2761-022 500; *El Venizelou)* is just northeast of Plateia Kalanzakou.

Kyparissia Castle
Kyparissia's pride and joy is its fine Frankish castle (no phone, free, always open), which overlooks the town from a rocky spur extending from the mountains to the east. It stands on the site of a Mycenaean citadel, later extended by the Byzantines before assuming its present form under the Franks. Its remains in good condition, especially the formidable surrounding walls. There are wonderful views over the town from the Café To Kastro, atop the walls on the western side of the castle. It opens 9am to 2am daily, with seating beneath shady pines.

Places to Stay & Eat
Camping Kyparissia (☎ 2761-023 491, fax 2761-024 519; *adult/tent €4.25/3)* is an excellent site, right opposite the best section of beach on the northern side of town.

Hotel Trifylia (☎ 2761-022 066; *25th Martiou 40; singles/doubles with shared bathroom €20.55/26.40)* is a convenient budget option, located close to the bus station and the main square.

Kyparissia Beach Hotel (☎ 2761-024 492/4, fax 2761-024 495; *singles/doubles with bathroom €58.70/80)* is the best hotel in town and is just a stone's throw from the beach. It also has a swimming pool.

Psarotaverna Karavisos (☎ 2761-025 007; *mains €3.50-9)* gets the locals' vote over a number of similar seafood restaurants along the seafront.

Getting There & Away
Bus The bus station *(Nosokomiou)* is 50m north of the main square. It has services to Kalamata (€4.40, 1¼ hours, five daily); Athens (€14.90, 4¼ hours, four daily); Pylos (€3.80, 1¼ hours, six daily) via Hora (€2.35, 40 minutes); and Patras (€9.40, 2½ hours, two daily) via Pyrgos (€3.55, one hour). The same services also operate into Kyparissia.

Train The train station *(cnr Nosokomiou & Kalanzakou)* is 100m north of the bus station. Seven trains a day go to (and from) Pyrgos and Patras; six continue to Athens. It's a hell of a long journey on the slow trains (€8.50, seven to nine hours). Two of the trains are intercity services but even these take six hours. There are also two trains a day to and from Kalamata (€2.35, 1¾ hours).

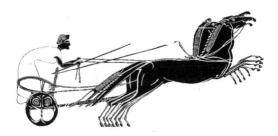

Elia Ηλεία

The western prefecture of Elia is home to some of the best farming country in Greece. The main agricultural areas are along the broad valley of the Alphios River, the 'Sacred Alph' of Samuel Taylor Coleridge's *Kubla Khan*, and in the northwest around Gastouni and Andravida. The rich alluvial flats in the northwest are watered by the Pinios River, which has been dammed upstream to create Lake Pinios, the largest water-storage facility in the Peloponnese.

Ancient Elia took its name from the mythical King Helios. Its capital was the city of Elis, now a forgotten ruin on the road from Gastouni to Lake Pinios. When the Franks arrived, they made Andravida the capital of their principate of Morea. Pyrgos is the dull modern capital. Most people come to Elia for one reason: to visit Ancient Olympia.

Southern Elia

Heading north into Elia from Messinia, the mountains to the east give way to interrupted plains fringed by golden sand beaches. Interspersed by pebbled shores and rocky outcrops, these beaches stretch right around Elia's coastline. The best beaches in the south are at **Tholos**, and there's a camping ground, and at **Kakovatos**. There's seaside accommodation in each village, but most of it is in uninspiring concrete buildings.

PYRGOS Πύργος
postcode 271 00 • pop 23,274
Pyrgos, 98km southwest of Patras and 24km from Olympia, is an agricultural service town that has little of interest for the traveller, except its municipal theatre and market. It is, however, the capital of Elia prefecture and all forms of public transport pass through here, including buses and trains to Olympia. The bus and train stations are about 400m apart, the former in the town centre on Manolopoulou and the latter at the northern edge of town on Ypsilantou.

Places to Stay
There are several hotels on the streets leading into town off Ypsilantou.

Highlights

- Exploring Ancient Olympia, birthplace of the Olympic Games
- Visiting the remote Temple of Vasses, currently cocooned in an enormous white tent
- Seeing Hlemoutsi Castle, the best-preserved Frankish castle in the Peloponnese

Hotel Pantheon (☎ 2621-029 746, fax 2621-036 791; Themistokleous 7; singles/ doubles with bathroom €38.15/57.85) is nothing special but it's clean and centrally located. The official rates apply only at peak times; it's normally possible to get a double for €30. Breakfast is available for €4.10.

Getting There & Away
Bus There are 16 buses daily running from Pyrgos to Olympia (€1.50, 30 minutes) on weekdays, 14 on Saturday and nine on Sunday. There are 10 buses daily running from Pyrgos to Athens (€17.70, five hours) and Patras (€6.20, two hours); and three daily to each of Kyllini (€3.60, 50 minutes), Kyparissia (€4.70, 1¼ hours), Tripolis (€9.40, 3½ hours), Kalamata (€7.65, two hours) and Andritsena (€5.70, 1½ hours). The same services also operate into Pyrgos.

ELIA

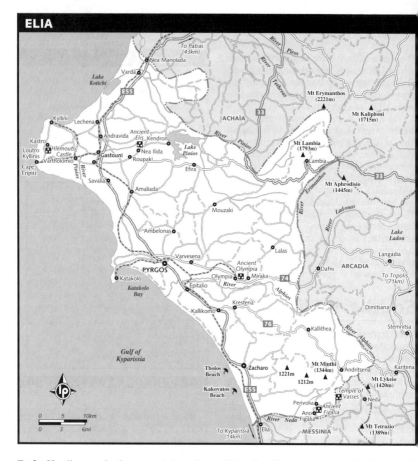

ELIA

Train Heading north, there are eight trains daily to Patras (€2.95, two hours), seven of which continue to Athens (€7.20, 6½ hours). Three of these trains are intercity and take five hours to reach Athens. Heading south, there are five trains daily to Kyparissia (€2.20, 1¼ hours), two of which continue to Kalamata (€3.25, 3¼ hours). Train services to Olympia and Pyrgos had been suspended at the time of research.

OLYMPIA Ολυμπία
postcode 270 65 • pop 1286
The modern village of Olympia (o-lim-**bee**-ah) panders unashamedly to the hundreds of thousands of tourists who pour through here each year on their way to Ancient Olympia, 500m south on the road to

Tripolis. The main street is lined with countless overpriced souvenir shops, cafés and restaurants.

Orientation & Information
The modern village lies along the main Pyrgos–Tripolis road, known as Praxitelous Kondyli, which runs through town. The bus stops for Pyrgos and Tripolis are opposite one another by the tourist office, towards the southern end of Praxitelous Kondyli. The train station is close to the centre on Douka.

Olympia's helpful municipal **tourist office** (☎ 2624-023 100/173; Praxitelous Kondyli; open 9am-9pm daily June-Sept, 8am-2.45pm Mon-Sat Oct-May) comes as a pleasant surprise after dealing with government-run

Ellinikos Organismos Tourismou (EOT) offices elsewhere. The friendly staff have a good map of the village, comprehensive information on bus, train and ferry schedules (from Kyllini and Patras) and can change currency. The **tourist police** (☎ 2624-022 550; *Spiliopoulou 5)* is on the block behind the tourist office.

The **post office** *(Pierre Coubertin)* is up the first street to the right from the tourist office as you walk along Praxitelous Kondyli towards Ancient Olympia. The Organismos Tilepikoinonion Ellados (OTE) is on Praxitelous Kondyli, beyond the turn-off for the post office. The National Bank of Greece is on the corner of Praxitelous Kondyli and Stefanopoulou. Travellers can check email at the **Café-Bar Aiolos** (☎ 2624-023 481; *cnr Spiliopoulou & Stefanopoulou; open 10.30am-3am daily)*, which charges €4.50 per hour.

Historical Museum of the Olympic Games

This museum (☎ 2624-022 544; *admission €1.50; open 8.30am-3.30pm Mon-Sat, 9am-4pm Sun)* is located two blocks west of Praxitelous Kondyli on Kosmopoulou. Most of the labelling is in French, though the collection of victors' medals, commemorative stamps and literature needs little explanation.

Ancient Olympia

Ancient Olympia (☎ 2624-022 517; *admission €6, €9 site & museum; open 8am-7pm daily Apr-Oct, 8am-5pm Mon-Fri, 8.30am-3pm Sat-Sun Nov-Mar)* was formerly a complex of temples, priests' dwellings and public buildings. It was also the venue of the Olympic Games, which took place every four years. During the games the city-states were bound by *ekeheiria* (a sacred truce) to stop beating the hell out of one another, and compete in races and sports instead.

The site is now World Heritage listed.

History The origins of Olympia date back to Mycenaean times. The Great Goddess, identified with Rea, was worshiped here in the 1st millennium BC. By the classical era Rea had been superseded by her son Zeus. A small regional festival, which probably included athletic events, was begun in the 11th century BC.

The first official quadrennial Olympic Games were declared in 776 BC by King Iphitos of Elis. By 676 BC they were open to all male Greeks, reaching their height of prestige in 576 BC. The games were held in honour of Zeus, popularly acclaimed as the games' founder. They took place at the time of the first full moon in August.

The athletic festival lasted five days and included wrestling, chariot and horse racing,

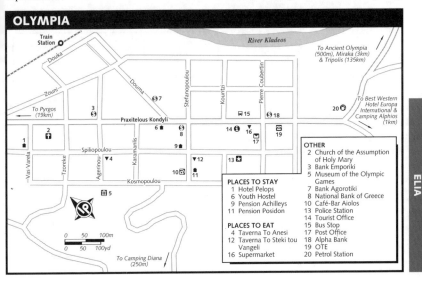

the pentathlon (wrestling, discus and javelin throwing, long jump and running), and the pancratium (a vicious form of fisticuffs).

Originally only Greek-born males were allowed to participate, but later Romans were permitted. Slaves and women were not allowed to enter the sanctuary as participants or spectators. Women trying to sneak in were thrown from a nearby rock.

The event served purposes besides athletic competition: writers, poets and historians read their works to a large audience, and the citizens of various city-states got together. Traders clinched business deals and city-state leaders talked in an atmosphere of festivity that was conducive to resolving differences through discussion rather than battle.

The games continued during the first years of Roman rule. By this time, however, their importance had declined and, thanks to Nero, they had become less edifying. In AD 67 Nero entered the chariot race with 10 horses, while other competitors could have no more than four. Despite this advantage, he fell and abandoned the race. Nevertheless, he was declared the winner by the judges.

The games were held for the last time in 394, before being banned by Emperor Theodosius I as part of a purge of pagan festivals. In 426 Theodosius II decreed that the temples of Olympia be destroyed.

The modern Olympic Games were instituted in 1896 and, other than during WWI and WWII, have been held every four years in different cities around the world ever since. The Olympic flame is lit at the ancient site and carried by runners to the games' host city.

The Site Ancient Olympia is signposted from the modern village. The entrance is beyond the bridge over the Kladeos River (a tributary of the Alphios). Thanks to Theodosius II and various earthquakes, little remains of the magnificent buildings of Ancient Olympia, but there is enough to sustain an absorbing visit in an idyllic, leafy setting. The first ruin encountered is the **gymnasium**, which dates from the 2nd century BC. South of here is the partly restored **palaestra**, or wrestling school, where contestants trained and practised their sport. Next to this was the **theokoleon** (priests' house), and behind the *theokoleon* was the **workshop** where Phidias sculpted the gargantuan, ivory-and-gold *Statue of Zeus*, one of the Seven Wonders of the Ancient World. The workshop was identified by archaeologists after the discovery of tools and moulds. Beyond the *theokoleon* is the **leonidaion**, an elaborate structure that accommodated dignitaries.

The **altis**, or Sacred Precinct of Zeus, lies to the left of the path. Its most important

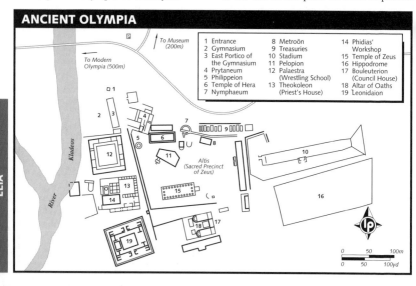

ANCIENT OLYMPIA

1 Entrance	8 Metroön	14 Phidias'
2 Gymnasium	9 Treasuries	Workshop
3 East Portico of	10 Stadium	15 Temple of Zeus
the Gymnasium	11 Pelopion	16 Hippodrome
4 Prytaneum	12 Palaestra	17 Bouleuterion
5 Philippeion	(Wrestling School)	(Council House)
6 Temple of Hera	13 Theokoleon	18 Altar of Oaths
7 Nymphaeum	(Priest's House)	19 Leonidaion

MARTIN HARRIS

The pentathlon, which included a foot race, featured in the ancient Olympics

building was the immense 5th-century **Doric Temple of Zeus** in which stood Phidias' statue. The 12m-high statue was later removed to Constantinople by Theodosius II, where it was destroyed by a fire in 475 BC. The temple consisted of 13 lateral columns and six at either end; none is still standing.

The **stadium** lies to the east of the *altis* and is entered through an archway. The judges' seats and the start and finish lines of the 120m sprint track still survive. There are normally plenty of athletic types weaving through the tourists as they time themselves over the distance. The stadium could seat at least 30,000 spectators. Slaves and women spectators had to be content to watch from the Hill of Cronos. South of the stadium was the **hippodrome**, where the chariot contests thrilled the crowds.

To the north of the Temple of Zeus was the **pelopion**, a small, wooded hillock with an altar to Pelops. It was once surrounded by a wall and the remains of its Doric portico can be seen. Many artefacts, now displayed in the museum, were found buried on the hillock.

Further north is the 6th-century Doric **Temple of Hera**, the site's most intact structure. Hera was worshipped along with Rea until the two were superseded by Zeus.

Situated to the east of this temple is the **nymphaeum**, erected by the wealthy Roman banker Herodes Atticus between AD 156 and 160. Typical of buildings financed by Roman benefactors, it was grandiose, consisting of a semicircular building with Doric columns flanked at each side by a circular temple. The building contained statues of Herodes Atticus and his family. Despite its elaborate appearance, the *nymphaeum* had a practical purpose: it was a fountain house supplying Olympia with fresh spring water.

From the *nymphaeum*, a row of 12 **treasuries** stretched east to the stadium. These looked like miniature temples. Each was erected by a city-state for use as a storehouse. These buildings marked the northern boundaries of the *altis*. The remains are reached by ascending a flight of stone steps.

At the bottom of these steps are the scant remains of the 5th-century-BC **metroön**, a temple dedicated to Rea, the mother of the gods. Apparently the ancients worshipped Rea in this temple with orgies.

To the west of the Temple of Hera are the foundations of the **philippeion**, a circular construction with Ionic columns, built by Philip of Macedon to commemorate the Battle of Khaironeia (338 BC), where he defeated a combined army of Athenians and Thebans. The building contained statues of Philip and his family.

North of the *philippeion* was the **prytaneum**, the magistrate's residence. Here, winning athletes feasted and were entertained.

South of the Temple of Zeus is the **bouleuterion** (council house), where competitors swore to obey the rules decreed by the Olympic Senate.

Museum The museum (☎/fax 2624-022 529; admission €6, museum & site €9; open 8am-7pm Tues-Sun, noon-7pm Mon Apr-Oct, 8.30am-3pm Tues-Sun, 10.30am-5pm Mon Nov-Mar) is 200m north of the site, on the opposite side of the road. The star piece is the 4th-century Parian marble statue of **Hermes of Praxiteles**, a masterpiece of classical sculpture from the Temple of Hera. Hermes was charged with taking the infant Dionysos to Mt Nysa.

Other important exhibits are a sculptured **Head of Hera** and the pediments and metopes from the Temple of Zeus. The eastern pediment depicts the chariot race between Pelops and Oinomaos. The western pediment shows the fight between the Centaurs and Lapiths, and the metopes depict the 12 Labours of Heracles.

Places to Stay
Camping Diana (☎ 2624-022 314, fax 2624-022 425; adult/tent €5/3.35; open year-round) is a friendly, well-run place, nestled on a leafy hillside just 250m west of the village. It's clearly signposted from the village.

ELIA

Camping Alphios (☎/fax 2624-022 950; adult/tent €4.50/2.50; open Apr-Oct) shares a million-dollar view with the neighbouring Hotel Europa, in the hills 1km southwest of town.

The **Youth Hostel** (☎ 2624-022 580; Praxitelous Kondyli 18; dorm beds €7) isn't able to offer deluxe conditions but is much better than the Greek average. Rates include hot showers and there's no curfew. Breakfast is available for €2.05.

Pension Achilleys (☎ 2624-022 562; Stefanopoulou 4; singles/doubles/triples €20/ 30/35) is a small, family-run pension, just uphill from the National Bank of Greece. Breakfast costs €4.40.

Pension Posidon (☎ 2624-022 567; Stefanopoulou 9; singles/doubles with bathroom €20/28/36) is further up the hill from the Achilleys and has spotless rooms. Breakfast is available for €2.95.

Hotel Pelops (☎/fax 2624-022 543; e hotel_pelops@hotmail.com; cnr Spiliopoulou & Vas Varela; singles/doubles/triples with bathroom €39.60/57.25/72.20) is a comfortable, family-run place on the western side of town. The Greek-Australian owners are full of ideas for exploring the area. Prices include a generous buffet breakfast.

Best Western Hotel Europa International (☎ 2624-022 650, fax 2624-023 166; e hotel europa@hellasnet.gr; singles/doubles/triples €78/110/126.75) is an excellent A-class hotel that offers a bit of style. It has sensational views from its hilltop location southwest of the village. Facilities include a bar, restaurant, swimming pool and tennis court, and prices include a buffet breakfast.

Places to Eat

With so many one-off customers passing through, Olympia's restaurants have little incentive to strive for excellence – and they don't.

Taverna To Anesi (☎ 2624-022 644; cnr Agerinou & Spiliopoulou; mains €3.85-5.30) is a busy psistaria (grill restaurant). It's a favourite with locals, who come here to feast on portions of succulent roast chicken (€3.55) or pork (€4.70), washed down with a local red wine.

Taverna To Steki tou Vangeli (☎ 2624-022 530; Stefanopoulou 13; mains €3.85-6.15) is another place that stands out from the crowd, with hearty servings of tasty food.

Self-caterers will find **supermarkets** along Praxitelous Kondyli.

Getting There & Away

There are four buses running daily to Athens (€19.05, 5½ hours) via Pyrgos and the coast, as well as numerous services to Pyrgos (€1.50, 30 minutes). Three buses daily head east to Tripolis (€8.10, 3½ hours).

Train services between Olympia and Pyrgos had been suspended at the time of research. The line was being upgraded, which is likely to be a lengthy process given the rate of progress.

MIRAKA Μιρακα
pop 330

The tiny village of Miraka, in the hills about 3km east of Ancient Olympia, occupies the site of ancient Pisa. This was the city responsible for organising the earliest games staged at Olympia, before the job was assumed by Elis. Nothing, however, remains of ancient Pisa and the main reason people come here is to eat:

Taverna Bacchus (☎ 2624-022 498; mains €5-7.50) serves up specialities such as lamb with oregano (€7.50). While bus groups make do with the tourist restaurants in Olympia, you'll find the drivers and guides feasting up here.

There's no public transport to Miraka, so you'll need to catch a taxi from Olympia or else drive. The turn-off is 1.5km east of Olympia on the road to Tripolis.

ANDRITSENA Ανδρίτσαινα
postcode 270 61 • pop 575

The village of Andritsena, 81km west of Tripolis, is perched on a hillside overlooking the valley of the Alphios River. Crumbling stone houses with rickety wooden balconies flank its narrow cobbled streets and a stream gushes through its central square, Plateia Agnostopoulou. Look out for the fountain emerging from the trunk of a huge plane tree.

The post office, OTE and bank are near the central square. Travellers can check email at the **Café Club Mylos** (☎ 2626-022 301; open 2pm-2am daily), which charges €3.55 per hour. Most people come to Andritsena to visit the World Heritage–listed Temple of Vasses, 14km away.

Traditions live on in Messinia

Fry it before you try it!

If you can't get an Athens 2004 ticket, try Ancient Olympia

An unforgettable ride through the spectacular Vouraïkos Gorge

The Temple of Vasses in Elia

Kick back in pretty Kapsali on Kythira, the island where Aphrodite was born

Hanging out in Poros

Stylish Hydra's harbour

A whitewashed church on Kythira

Temple of Vasses

The Temple of Vasses (☎ 2626-022 254; admission €2; open 8am-5pm daily) must qualify as the most isolated temple in Greece, perched at an altitude of 1130m on the slopes of Mt Kolition, 14km south of Andritsena.

It was built in 420 BC by the people of nearby Figalia, who dedicated it to Apollo Epicurus (the Helper) for delivering them from pestilence. Designed by Ictinus, the architect of the Parthenon, it combines Doric and Ionic columns and a single Corinthian column – the earliest example of this order. Ancient traveller and writer Pausanias, writing in the 2nd century AD, marvelled at the beauty of the stone and symmetry of its proportions.

It was in a sorry state by the time it was rediscovered by European travellers at the beginning of the 19th century. The cella (inner temple room) was reconstructed by the Greek Archaeological Society between 1902 and 1908, with the exception of its Ionic frieze, depicting scenes from the Battle of the Amazons and the Battle of the Centaurs, which was pilfered and sold to the British Museum in 1814.

The temple now stands enclosed in an enormous, custom-built white tent, erected in 1987 to protect the structure from the ravages of the weather while further essential preservation work is carried out. The tent is due to remain in position until the work is finished, which could well be forever given the rate of progress. The terraced fields below the temple are filled with a jigsaw of stones from the site.

There is no public transport to the temple. In summer, it's sometimes possible to find fellow travellers in Andritsena willing to share the cost of taxi – about €20 return. If you have your own transport, you can head southeast from Vasses to visit ancient Figalia (see later in this chapter). This road keeps going all the way to the coast and makes an interesting, if slow, alternative for people not wishing to return to Andritsena. Most maps don't show that this road has recently been upgraded and sealed.

Places to Stay

Hotel Theoxenia (☎/fax 2626-022 219; singles/doubles/triples with bathroom €29.35/ 41.10/47) is one of the last of the true Xenia hotels, the chain of government-run hotels in which nothing quite works. If Greece were to produce a hotel sitcom, it would be set in a Xenia hotel. It would feature a receptionist who was always watching sitcoms in the bar, guests bumping around a labyrinth of corridors trying to locate their rooms in the dark, door handles falling off in your hand and showers exploding when the water is turned on. Most Xenia hotels have now been transferred to private ownership, making Andritsena's Theoxenia one of the last of a dying breed. It's on the main road on the eastern side of town.

Epikourios Apollon (☎ 2626-022 840; Plateia Agnostopoulou; doubles with bathroom €35.20), opposite of the Theoxenia, is a smart new place that comes complete with an enthusiastic owner who's keen to please. Strangely, most of the rooms overlook the main square rather than the magnificent Alphios Valley. The price includes breakfast.

Places to Eat

There are lots of places to eat around the main square.

Psistaria Paparis (☎ 2626-022 375; mains €3.55-5.30) is one of the few places open at lunch time, serving grilled meats and salads. It's opposite the post office, on the main street.

Psistaria Baskozos (☎ 2626-022 455; mains €4-8.50; open from 8pm), on the main road just 150m east of the square, is a favourite with locals. It serves similar fare to Paparis.

Getting There & Away

There are two buses daily to Andritsena from Athens Bus Terminal A (€13.95, four hours). There are also services to Pyrgos (€5.70, 1½ hours), and to Tripolis (€5.15, two hours) via Karitena and Megalopoli (€3.20, one hour). The services also operate in the reverse direction.

ANCIENT FIGALIA
Αρχαία Φιγαλια

The citizens of ancient Figalia, 14km southeast of the Temple of Vasses, must have been early believers in the great real-estate mantra – 'location, location, location'.

The location of their city is little short of spectacular, set among lush hills high above the dramatic Neda Gorge. Today the gorge marks the boundary of Elia and Messinia but in ancient times it was part of Arcadia – and it's not hard to imagine Pan propped up against a shady oak, playing his pipes and keeping watch over the shepherds.

The ruins are spread around the tiny stone village of Ano Figalia, itself now abandoned by all except a few hardy older residents. The main features are signposted at the entrance to the village. They include a small **Temple of Athens**, perched on a spur above the Neda Gorge. A path continues beyond the temple to a **lookout point** with great views of the gorge, the waters of Neda a mere flash of silver far below. At the time of research, authorities appeared to be in the process of fencing off the temple and its surrounds.

Some impressive sections of the **ancient wall** survive, notably in the west, but the ruins are little more than an excuse to enjoy a walk in magnificent surroundings. The area is becoming increasingly popular as a walking destination, and there are a number of marked trails that go down to the gorge. These trails start from opposite the ruins of the **fountain house**, still gushing water, on the southeastern side of the village. A large map board details the walking possibilities.

The village churchyard is home to the tiny 11th-century **Church of Hryssa Panagia**, which features ancient columns salvaged from the site. Faded frescoes cover the walls and ceilings.

Getting There & Away
The turn-off to Ano Figalia is 11km southeast of Vasses at the village of Perivolia. The signpost is beside the church with the amazing arched windows, the Church of Agiou Dimitriou. There is no public transport to Ano Figalia.

Northern Elia

ANCIENT ELIS Αρχαια Ελις
The ruins of ancient Elis lie scattered amid rich farming country about 45km north of Pyrgos, near the tiny village of Nea Ilida.

The city is best known for the role it once had in organising of the Olympic Games. It is also known as the setting for the fifth of the Labours of Heracles, the cleansing of the stables of King Augeas, ruler of Elis. The feat was achieved by redirecting the waters of the nearby Pinios River. The tactic would have to be rethought if the feat were to be repeated today: the modern Pinios has been reduced to a sorry trickle by the demands of irrigation.

History
Elis began as an early Bronze Age settlement, but remained something of a rural backwater until the arrival of the Dorians. They transformed Elis into the dominant city-state in the northwest of the Peloponnese, controlling an area roughly corresponding to the region of modern Elia. Their territory included the Sanctuary of Olympia, at Olympia, where the Eleans upgraded a local athletics festival into the first official Olympic Games.

First staged in 776 BC, the hosts required participating city-states to observe a sacred truce to ensure the success of the event. The growing popularity of the Olympics, and the prestige reflected on the hosts, didn't go down well with everyone. In 668 BC the Eleans were defeated by Argos, so handed the running of the Olympiad back to the previous owners, the city of Pisa.

Elis resumed control in 580 BC and thereafter devoted itself almost entirely to the staging of games. Athletes were required to spend the month preceding the games training at Elis, resulting in a proliferation of gymnasia, palaestra and other facilities.

Less publicised than its role as organiser of the Olympics, Elis was also the organiser of the Heraean Games for women, staged every four years in honour of the goddess Hera. Elis was one of the few city-states to grant its women a significant role in public life, establishing a special council of arbitration, made up of women chosen from each of the 16 principal towns in its territory. The council was charged with resolving disputes.

The city continued to prosper under Roman rule, but went into terminal decline when the Emperor Theodosius I outlawed the Olympics in AD 394. The site was identified in the early years of the 19th century, and was excavated between 1911 and 1914.

Elis Archaeological Museum
The museum (☎ 2622-041 415; admission €2; open 8.30am-3pm Tues-Sat) houses finds from the site dating back to the early Bronze Age. A highlight is the central

medallion from a Roman mosaic depicting the 12 Labours of Heracles. It was recovered from a 3rd-century villa nearby, together with another mosaic with representations of the Nine Muses.

The Site

There's really very little to be seen, despite an encouraging-looking reconstruction of the agora on the museum brochure.

The city was spread over a wide area stretching from the Pinios River to Ayannis Hill, the low hill to the south of the museum that was the site of the city's acropolis. Fragments of ancient walls poking from the fields provide some indication of the city's former extent, while sections of excavations along the roadside presumably provided the basis for the plan of the agora.

The main attraction is the ancient theatre, which is signposted down a gravel road next to the museum. It was built in the 4th century BC, with the seating excavated into a low hill looking north over the Pinios Valley. The *cavea* (stage area) was built on the river flats, requiring a sophisticated network of drains to prevent flooding; the remains of this system can be seen running north through dense rushes. Dozens of the bronze theatre 'tickets' on display in the museum were uncovered here during excavations.

Getting There & Away

The turn-off to Elis is about 30km northwest of Pyrgos, near the town of Gastouni. The route is signposted via the villages of Roupaki and Sosti.

KYLLINI Κυλλήνη
postcode 270 68 • pop 1079

The tiny port of Kyllini (kih-**lee**-nih), 54km northwest of Pyrgos, was the port of Elis during ancient times, and later the chief port of the Frankish principate of the Morea. It was destroyed in 1430, and little remains of the old town except the shell of an old castle that is slowly crumbling into the sea. Nearby, and worth a visit, is the wonderful Hlemoutsi Castle.

The only reason to pass this way is to catch a ferry to Kefallonia or Zakynthos. Most people pass through Kyllini by bus

from Patras on their way to board the ferry. If you get stuck in Kyllini, the **tourist/port police** (☎ 2623-092 211) at the quay can suggest accommodation.

Hlemoutsi Castle

Hlemoutsi Castle (☎ 2623-095 033; admission free; open 8am-5pm Tues-Sat, 8am-3pm Sun), 6km south of Kyllini, is the largest and best preserved of the Frankish castles in the Peloponnese, and well worth a detour if you have your own transport.

It's a hard place to miss if you're anywhere in the vicinity. It's perched above the appropriately named village of Kastro, on top of the only hill for miles, and dominates the surrounding agricultural plain.

Originally known as Clermont, it was built between 1220 and 1223 by the Frankish ruler of the principate of Achaïa, Geoffrey de Villehardouin, to guard the port of Glarenza (Kyllini) and his capital of Andreville (Andravida). It comprises a massive hexagonal inner citadel on the high point of the hill and an outer enclosure protected by a marginally less formidable wall.

The castle's outer wall and main gate were rebuilt in the 15th century by the Turks, who also added a mosque, but the inner citadel represents an almost perfect example of Frankish military architecture. The massive vaulted galleries that surround the inner citadel are the most impressive feature, and some of the original arched windows remain intact.

Restaurant Apollon (☎ 2623-095 100), below the castle on Kastro's main square, is a good spot to stop for lunch after visiting the castle.

Getting There & Away

Bus There are between three and seven buses daily to Kyllini (€4.40, 1¼ hours) from the Zakynthos bus station in Patras, as well as at least three buses daily from Pyrgos (€3.60, 50 minutes). The services also run in the opposite direction.

Ferry There are boats to Zakynthos (€4.40, 1½ hours, up to five daily), and to Poros (€6.15, 1¼ hours, three daily) and Argostoli (€8.65, 2¼ hours, two daily) on Kefallonia.

ELIA

Achaïa Αχαία

Achaïa owes its name to the Achaeans, an Indo-European branch of migrants who settled on mainland Greece and established what is more commonly known as the Mycenaean civilisation. When the Dorians arrived, the Achaeans were pushed into this northwestern corner of the Peloponnese, displacing the original Ionians. Legend has it that the Achaeans founded 12 cities, which later developed into the powerful Achaean Federation that survived until Roman times. Principal among these cities were the port settlements of Patras and Egio.

The coast of modern Achaïa consists of a string of resorts more popular with Greeks than with tourists. Inland are the high peaks of Mt Panahaïko (1924m), Mt Erymanthos (2221m), where Heracles captured the Erymanthian boar, and Mt Helmos (2338m).

The village of Diakofto, 55km east of Patras, is the starting point for the fantastic rack-and-pinion railway to Zahlorou and Kalavryta. Overnight stops at both places are highly recommended.

PATRAS Πάτρα
postcode 260 01 • pop 160,400
Achaïa's capital, Patras (in Greek, Patra), is Greece's third-largest city and is the principal port for boats to and from Italy and the Ionian Islands. It is named after King Patreas, who ruled Achaïa in about 1100 BC. Despite a history stretching back 3000 years, Patras is not wildly exciting. Few travellers stay around any longer than it takes to catch the next boat, bus or train.

The city was destroyed by the Turks during the War of Independence and rebuilt on a modern grid plan of wide and arcaded streets. It features large squares and ornate neoclassical buildings, many of which were being restored at the time of research in preparation for the city's role as Europe's City of Culture for 2006.

The higher you climb up the steep hill behind the teeming, somewhat seedy waterfront, the better Patras gets.

Orientation & Information
Patras' grid system of streets means easy walking. The waterfront is known as Iroön

Highlights

- Experiencing the colourful Patras carnival
- Riding the mountain railway up the spectacular Vouraïkos Gorge
- Exploring the wonderful rock formations of the Cave of the Lakes, near Kalavryta

Polytehniou at its northeastern end, Othonos Amalias at its middle and Akti Dimeon to the south. Customs is at the Iroön Polytehniou end, and the main bus and train stations are on Othonos Amalias. Most of the agencies selling ferry tickets are on Iroön Polytehniou and Othonos Amalias. The main thoroughfares of Agiou Dionysiou, Riga Fereou, Mezonos, Korinthou and Kanakari run parallel to the waterfront. The main square is Plateia Vasileos Georgiou, up from the waterfront along Gerokostopoulou.

Tourist Offices The **EOT** (*Ellinikos Organismos Tourismou;* ☎ 261-062 0353; *Iroön Polytehniou*) is outside the international arrivals terminal at the port. In theory, it's open 8am to 10pm Monday to Friday; in practice, it's invariably closed. The most useful piece of information is an arrow pointing to the helpful **tourist police** (☎ 261-045 1833; *Iroön Polytehniou; open 7.30am-11pm daily*), upstairs in the embarkation hall.

ACHAÏA

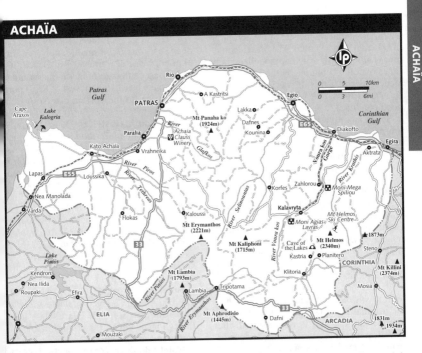

Money The **National Bank of Greece** (*Plateia Trion Symahon*) is opposite the train station. Weekday opening times are 8am to 2pm (8am to 1.30pm on Friday) and 6pm to 8.30pm. On weekends, in summer only, it opens 11am to 1pm and 6pm to 8.30pm.

Post & Communications The **main post office** (*cnr Zaïmi & Mezonos*) is centrally located. It's open 7.30am to 8pm Monday to Friday, 7.30am to 2pm Saturday, and 9am to 1.30pm Sunday. The main **OTE** (*Organismos Tilepikoinonion Ellados; cnr Dimitriou Gounari & Kanakari*) is in the western part of the city. There's another office opposite the tourist office at the port.

There are lots of Internet cafés around the city. The closest to the port is **Internet Café Paradise** (☎ 261-062 5867; *Zaïmi 7; open 5am-1am daily*) charges €4 per hour.

There are several cheaper places around the upper reaches of Gerokostopoulou, including **Netp@rk** (☎ 261-027 9699; *Gerokostopoulou 37; open 10am-2am daily*) and the co-managed **Netrino Internet Café** (☎ 261-062 3344; *Karaiskaki 133; open 10am-2am daily*); both charge €2.50 per hour.

Bookshops For travel-oriented material, **Road Editions** (☎ 261-027 9938; *Agiou Andreou 50*) stocks a large range of Lonely Planet guides as well as maps and travel literature.

News Stand (☎ 261-027 3092; *Agios Andreou 77*) has a small selection of novels, as well as international newspapers and magazines. You'll also find international newspapers at the *periptera* (kiosks) on Plateia Trion Symahon.

Laundry Take those travel-soiled clothes to the laundrette on Zaïmi, just uphill from Korinthou. It charges €6.75 to wash and dry a load and is open 9am to 3pm and 5.30pm to 9pm Monday to Friday, 9am to 3pm on Saturday; it's closed on Sunday.

Emergency Patras has a **first-aid centre** (☎ 261-027 7386; *cnr Karolou & Agiou Dionysiou*) and **port police** (☎ 261-034 1002) in the customs building by the port.

Fortress

The city's wonderful old fortress (*admission free; open 8am-7pm Tues-Sun Apr-Oct;*

8.30am-5pm Tues-Fri, 8.30am-3pm Sat-Sun Nov-Mar) stands on the site of the acropolis of ancient Patrai (Patras). The present structure is of Frankish origin, remodelled many times over the centuries by the Byzantines, Venetians and Turks. It was in use as a defensive position until WWII, and remains in good condition.

Set in an attractive park of pencil pines, it is reached by climbing the steps at the end of Agiou Nikolaou. Great views over the city to the Ionian islands of Zakynthos and Kefallonia are the reward.

Ancient Odeion

The elegant Ancient Odeion (☎ 261 0276 207; admission free; open 8.30am-3pm), 200m south of the fortress, is the sole reminder of the city's importance in Roman times. It was built in the middle of the 2nd century, and could hold an audience of some 2300 in its 11 tiered rows of seats. It lay hidden beneath a small hill for centuries until it was rediscovered in 1889. Much of the original Roman brickwork survived in good condition, and it was restored after WWII. It is still used in summer for performances of music and drama.

Archaeological Museum

The small museum (☎ 261-027 5070; Mezonos 42; admission free; open 8.30am-2.30pm Tues-Sun) houses a collection of finds from the Mycenaean, Hellenic and Roman periods. It's well laid out and exhibits are labelled in English.

Patras Carnival

Patras is noted for the exuberance with which its citizens celebrate the city's annual carnival.

The carnival programme begins in mid-January, and features a host of minor events leading up to a wild weekend of costume parades, colourful floats and celebrations at the end of February or early March. The event draws big crowds, so hotel reservations are essential if you want to stay overnight. Contact the Greek National Tourist Organisation for dates and details.

Places to Stay

There's a shortage of decent budget accommodation in Patras, one of the reasons few travellers stick around.

Camping Rion (☎ 261-099 1585, fax 261-099 3388; Rio; adult/tent €4.10/3.60; open year-round) is a small, family-run site, 5km northeast of Patras at Rio Beach. It's the closest camping ground to Patras and is right on the beach, 500m west of Rio's port. You can get to the port on bus No 6 from Plateia Agios Georgios.

YHA Youth Hostel (☎ 261-042 7278; Iroön Polytehniou 62; dorm beds €6), which belongs to the Greek-run Youth Hostels Association, not to Hostelling International, is a grubby dump that is very hard to recommend. It's also a long haul from the city centre, 1.5km north of the customs building.

Pension Nicos (☎ 261-062 3757; cnr Patreos & Agiou Andreou; singles/doubles/triples with bathroom €18/30/40, doubles/triples with shared bathroom €25/35) is easily the best budget choice in town. The sheets are clean, the water is hot and it's close to the waterfront.

Hotel Rannia (☎ 261-022 0114, fax 261-022 0537; Riga Fereou 53; singles/doubles with bathroom €30/45) is a C-class hotel facing Plateia Olgas. It has comfortable aircon rooms, each with a TV.

Hotel Adonis (☎ 261-022 4213, fax 261-022 6971; Zaïmi 9; singles/doubles with bathroom €59/75) has good views out over the port, though its rooms aren't really good enough to justify the price (which does include breakfast).

Places to Eat

Europa Centre (☎ 261-043 7006; Othonos Amalias 10; mains €4.50-7) is a convenient cafeteria-style place close to the international ferry dock. It serves up taverna dishes, spaghetti and a choice of vegetarian meals.

Restaurant Tzorou Erimioni (☎ 261-027 1487; Riga Fereou 3; mains €2.95-4.70) is a favourite with locals. It specialises in traditional dishes, such as *patsas* (tripe), though travellers will probably be happier with a large bowl of fish soup (€4.10) or roast chicken with potatoes (€3.55). Don't look for this place by name; the sign outside says only 'restaurant'.

Nitro English Bar (☎/fax 261-027 9357; e nitrobar@hotmail.com; Pantanasis 9; mains €7.50-10.50; open 1pm-late) is the perfect spot for Brits pining for a taste of the 'Old Dart'. You'll find daily specials, such as steak-and-kidney pie, shepherd's pie and Sunday roast, and a choice of English beers. It's also well set up for travellers, with a shower room and Internet access.

Dia Discount Supermarket *(Agiou Andreou 29)* is not the largest supermarket in town, but it's ideally located for travellers who plan to buy a few provisions and keep moving.

Getting There & Away

Bus Buses to Athens (€12.25, three hours) depart from the **main bus station** *(Othonos Amalias)* every 30 minutes, and travel via Corinth (€7.65, 1½ hours). There are also 10 services daily to Pyrgos (€6.20, two hours), two of which continue to Kalamata (€13.35, four hours); four services go to

Kalavryta (€5.10, two hours) and two to Tripolis (€10.30, four hours).

Buses to the Ionian islands of Lefkada (€9.70, two daily) and Kefallonia leave from the **bus station** (☎ 261-027 7854) at the corner of Othonos Amalias and Gerokostopoulou. Services to Kefallonia use the ferries from the port of Kyllini to Poros (€8.45) and continue by road to Argostoli (€10.90). Buses to Zakynthos (€9.80, 3½ hours) leave from the **Ktel Zakynthos bus station** (☎ 261-022 0219; Othonos Amalias 58). They also travel via Kyllini.

Train There's a left-luggage office at the train station. It charges €3.25 per item per day, or €1.65 with a train ticket – so buy your ticket before you drop off your bags.

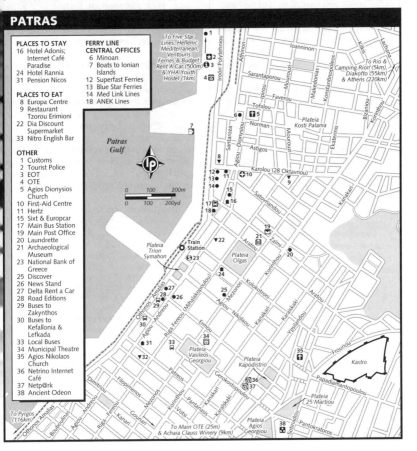

PATRAS

PLACES TO STAY
16 Hotel Adonis; Internet Café Paradise
24 Hotel Rannia
31 Pension Nicos

PLACES TO EAT
8 Europa Centre
9 Restaurant Tzorou Erimioni
22 Dia Discount Supermarket
33 Nitro English Bar

OTHER
1 Customs
2 Tourist Police
3 EOT
4 OTE
5 Agios Dionysios Church
10 First-Aid Centre
11 Hertz
15 Sixt & Europcar
17 Main Bus Station
19 Main Post Office
20 Laundrette
21 Archaeological Museum
23 National Bank of Greece
25 Discover
26 News Stand
27 Delta Rent a Car
28 Road Editions
29 Buses to Zakynthos
30 Buses to Kefallonia & Lefkada
33 Local Buses
34 Municipal Theatre
35 Agios Nikolaos Church
36 Netrino Internet Café
37 Netp@rk
38 Ancient Odeon

FERRY LINE CENTRAL OFFICES
6 Minoan
7 Boats to Ionian Islands
12 Superfast Ferries
13 Blue Star Ferries
14 Med Link Lines
18 ANEK Lines

ACHAÏA

A Drop of Mavrodafni?

The historic **Achaïa Clauss winery** (☎ 261-032 5051, fax 261-033 8269, **e** aclauss@mail.otenet.gr) stands in the hills 9km south of Patras near the village of Saravali.

It was founded in 1854 by Baron Gustav Clauss, a Bavarian visitor who had been impressed by the potential of the surrounding wine-growing region to produce high-quality estate-bottled wines – a new concept in Greece. From the outset he left no doubt about the seriousness of his intentions. His estate, approached by an elegant, tree-lined avenue, was centred on a grand stone mansion. It was surrounded by enough outbuildings to resemble a small village.

The winery's signature product, first released in 1873, is its celebrated Mavrodafni of Patras, Greece's favourite fortified wine. The winery likes to promote a romantic tale that the wine was named after the baron's unrequited love, who died of tuberculosis. In reality, the name has much more to do with the local *mavrodafni* grapes, a prized but low-yielding variety that makes up at least 50% of the blend.

The standard Achaïa Clauss Mavrodafni, fortified with brandy to 16% proof, is matured in oak barrels for eight years before it is bottled and released. It's widely available from good supermarkets for about €5.50. Greeks like to serve it as an aperitif, but most tourists feel happier enjoying a glass at the end of meal – much like a port. The Old Reserve is aged 20 years in the barrel.

Unless you're a visiting VIP, you won't get to sample the winery's top drop. It's based on two barrels laid down in 1882 and continually reblended with younger wines ever since. The annual output of a dozen or so bottles is reserved for state banquets.

The winery is open 10am to 6pm daily for tours, tastings and sales.

You can get there by bus No 7 from Plateia Agios Georgiou. It will drop you at the bottom of the driveway, leaving a walk of some 600m. If you're driving, take Dimitriou Gounari southeast out of Patras and keep following the main drag for about 4km to the huge, concrete soccer stadium on the edge of the city. The road turns south after the stadium; there are reassuring signposts pointing up the hillside to the winery and Saravali.

There are at least eight trains daily to Athens. Half of them are slow trains, which take five hours and cost €5.30. They travel via Diakofto (€2.05, one hour) and Corinth (€3.55, 2½ hours). The intercity trains to Athens take 3½ hours and cost €10. The last intercity train leaves Patras for Athens at 6.30pm. Holders of Eurail passes can travel free but need to make a reservation.

There are also trains to Pyrgos (€2.95, two hours, seven daily) and Kalamata (€5.30, six hours, two daily).

Ferry Domestic There are daily ferries from Patras to the Ionian islands of Kefallonia (€10, 2½ hours), Ithaki (€10.90, 3¾ hours) and Corfu (€17.90, seven hours).

Ferries to central Greece operate from Rio, 5km northeast of Patras, to Andirio every 15 minutes between 7am and 11pm and every 30 minutes through the night (€0.40/5.60 foot passenger/car, 15 minutes).

International Patras is Greece's main port for ferry services to Italy. The most popular crossing is between Patras and Brindisi, and in summer there are up to five boats daily on this route. Crossing times and fares vary a lot between companies. With the exception of express services to Ancona, most ferries stop at Igoumenitsa and Corfu. Some allow a free stopover on Corfu – ask when you buy your ticket. See the Getting There & Away chapter, pp73-5, for further details of services.

The services and ferries out of Patras are

ANEK Lines (☎ 261-022 6053; **W** www.anek.gr) Othonos Amalias 25
Services: Ancona & Trieste via Corfu & Igoumenitsa

Blue Star Ferries (☎ 261-063 4000; **W** www.bluestarferries.com) Othonos Amalias 12-14
Services: Brindisi direct; Ancona & Venice via Igoumenitsa & Corfu

Hellenic Mediterranean (☎ 261-045 2521; **W** www.hml.it) cnr Iroön Polytehniou & Pente Pigadion
Services: Brindisi via Kefallonia and Corfu

Med Link Lines (☎ 261-062 3011) Giannatos Travel, Othonos Amalias 15
Services: Brindisi direct or via Kefallonia & Igoumenitsa

Minoan (☎ 261-042 1500; **W** www.minoan.gr) cnr Norman 1 & Athinon
Services: Ancona via Igoumenitsa; Venice via Igoumenitsa & Corfu

Superfast Ferries (☎ 261-062 2500; **W** www
.superfast.com) Othonos Amalias 12
Services: Ancona direct or via Igoumenitsa;
Bari via Igoumenitsa
Ventouris Ferries (☎ 261-045 4873/4; **W** www
.ventouris.gr) Iroön Polytehniou 44-46
Services: Bari direct

Getting Around

Local buses leave from the northwestern
corner of Plateia Vasileos Georgiou. Car-
rental agencies include:

Budget (☎ 261-045 5190) Iroön Polytehniou 36
Delta Rent a Car (☎ 261-027 2764, fax 261-
022 0532) Othonos Amalias 44
Europcar (☎ 261-062 1360) Agiou Andreou 6
Hertz (☎ 261-022 0990) Karolou 2
Sixt (☎ 261-027 5677) Agiou Andreou 10B

DIAKOFTO Διακοφτό
postcode 251 00 • pop 2290

Diakofto (dih-ah-kof-**to**), 55km east of Patras
and 80km northwest of Corinth, is a serene
village, tucked between steep mountains and
the sea, amid lemon and olive groves.

Orientation & Information

Diakofto's layout is easy to figure out. The
train station is in the middle of the village.
To reach the waterfront, cross the railway
track and walk down the road ahead. After
1km you will come to pebbly Egali Beach.

There is no EOT or tourist police. The
post office, OTE and the National Bank of
Greece are all on the main street that leads
inland from the station.

Things to Do

The main reason people come to Diakofto
is to ride the **rack-and-pinion railway** up the
Vouraïkos Gorge to Kalavryta (see the
boxed text 'Diakofto–Kalavryta Railway').

If you want to relax by the sea, the best
section of **Egali Beach** is on the western side
of town; turn right when you reach the
seafront on the road from the station.

Places to Stay & Eat

Hotel Lemonies (☎ *2691-041 229/820;
singles/doubles with bathroom* €24/36) is a
quiet, old-fashioned hotel, 500m north of the
train station on the road leading to the beach.

Chris Paul Hotel (☎ *2691-041 715/855, fax
2691-042 128;* **e** *chris-pa@otenet.gr; singles/
doubles/triples with bathroom* €30.80/

55.75/66.95) is a modern C-class hotel and
home to Diakofto's best rooms, each with
air-con and TV. It also has a swimming pool,
bar and restaurant (breakfast costs €4.40).
It's conveniently situated near the train station and is well signposted.

Costas (☎ *2691-043 228; mains* €2.95-
7.50), opposite the National Bank of Greece
on the main street, is a popular taverna-
psistaria and the pick of the town's restaurants. Run by a friendly Greek-Australian
family, it has a good choice of taverna-style
dishes, along with the usual grilled meats.

People heading up to Kalavryta on the
train can stock up for the trip at the shops
opposite the station, which include **Elvar
Supermarket** (☎ *2691-043 361*).

Getting There & Away

There's not much point in catching a bus
to/from Diakofto – the trains are much more
convenient. Patras–Athens buses bypass the
village on the E65.

Diakofto is on the main Athens–Patras
train line and there are frequent trains in
both directions. There are trains on the rack-
and-pinion line to Kalavryta (2nd/1st class
€3.70/4.50, one hour, four daily) via
Zahlorou (€3.30/4.10) departing at 8am,
10.30am, 1.15pm and 3.45pm Monday to
Friday; and at 9am, 11am, 2.10pm and
4.48pm on the weekend. (See the boxed
text, p186, for further information.)

ZAHLOROU Ζαχλωρού
postcode 250 01 • pop 101

The picturesque and unspoilt settlement of
Zahlorou, at the halfway stop on the
Diakofto–Kalavryta train line, straddles
both sides of the river and railway line.
Many people take the train to this point and
walk back to Diakofto.

Moni Mega Spileou
Μονή Μεγάλου Σπήλαιου

A steep path (signposted) leads up from
Zahlorou to the Moni Mega Spileou
(Monastery of the Great Cavern). The original monastery was destroyed in 1934, when
gunpowder stored during the War of Independence exploded. The new monastery
houses illuminated gospels, relics, silver
crosses, jewellery and the miraculous icon
of the Virgin Mary, which, like numerous
icons in Greece, is said to have been painted

ACHAÏA

Diakofto–Kalavryta Railway

The railway from Diakofto to Kalavryta takes travellers on an unforgettable ride through the dramatic Vouraïkos Gorge. The train climbs over 700m in 22.5km, using a rack-and-pinion (cog) system for traction on the steep sections. Built by an Italian company between 1885 and 1895, the railway was a remarkable feat of engineering for its time.

The opening section of the journey is fairly sedate, climbing gently through the lush citrus orchards that flank the lower reaches of the river. The ascent begins in earnest about 5km south of Diakofto and the section from here to Zahlorou is spectacular as the line switches back and forth across the gorge in search of a foothold. As the gorge narrows, the train disappears into a long curving tunnel and emerges clinging to a narrow ledge that seems to overhang the river. This stretch is quite awesome in spring, when the waters are swollen by snowmelt from the surrounding mountains.

South of the charming village of Zahlorou, the line follows the river beneath a leafy canopy of plane trees, before meandering through open country for the final run to Kalavryta.

The journey takes just over an hour, stopping en route at Zahlorou. Second-class fares are €3.30 to Zahlorou and €3.70 to Kalavryta, but spending €4.10/4.50 for a 1st-class compartment at the front or rear of the train is well worth the extra – they have the best views.

The line was commissioned by Greece's great railway-building prime minister, Harilaos Trikoupis, who had the romantic notion of using the new train technology of the time to provide access to the birthplace of the modern Greek nation – Moni Agias Lavras, near Kalavryta. It was at this monastery that Bishop Germanos of Patras raised the flag of revolt that launched the War of Independence on 25 March 1821.

The steam engines that first plied the route were replaced in the early 1960s by diesel cars, but the old steam engines can still be seen outside Diakofto and Kalavryta stations.

See the Diakofto and Kalavryta Getting There & Away sections, pp185, 188, for information on departure times.

by St Luke. It was supposedly discovered in the nearby cavern by St Theodore and St Simeon in AD 362. A monk will show visitors around. Modest dress is required of both sexes – that means no bare arms or legs. The 3km walk up to the monastery takes about an hour.

Places to Stay & Eat

Hotel Romantzo (☎/fax 2692-022 758; singles/doubles/triples with bathroom €25/35/45) is a quaint D-class place and one of Greece's more eccentric small hotels. It stands right next to the railway line at the end of the platform. You can almost reach out and touch the trains from the windows of its seven rooms. It's a wonderful place, with timber floors and old-fashioned furnishings – and not a square edge in sight. It's advisable to book at weekends. During the week, the manager uses one triple room as a dorm where hikers can roll out their sleeping bags (€5.90). The hotel has a good restaurant, with outdoor seating on the opposite side of the railway. It also serves breakfast.

Messinia Rooms to Rents (☎/fax 2692-024 103; doubles with bathroom €35) is right next to the Romantzo and offers a reasonable alternative to it. The prices and facilities are very similar, but not the style.

Getting There & Away

All Diakofto–Kalavryta trains stop at Zahlorou. You can drive to Zahlorou on a dirt road leading off the Diakofto–Kalavryta road. The turn-off is 7.5km north of Kalavryta.

KALAVRYTA Καλάβρυτα
postcode 250 01 • pop 1747

At an elevation of 756m, Kalavryta (kah-**lah**-vrih-tah) is a cool mountain resort with copious springs and shady plane trees. Two relatively recent historical events have assured the town a special place in the hearts of all Greeks. The revolt against the Turks began here on 25 March 1821 when Bishop Germanos of Patras raised the banner of revolt at the Moni Agias Lavras, 6km from Kalavryta. Also, on 13 December 1943, in one of the worst atrocities of WWII, the Nazis set fire to the town and massacred all male inhabitants over 15 years old as punishment for Resistance activity. The total number killed in the region was 1436. The

hands of the old cathedral clock stand eternally at 2.34, the time the massacre began.

Orientation & Information

Most people arrive at the train station, on the northern edge of town. Opposite is a large building that will eventually become the Municipal Museum of the Kalavryta Holocaust. Kalavryta is the founding member of the Union of Martyred Towns. To the right of the museum-to-be is Syngrou, a pedestrian precinct, which turns into 25 Martiou. To the left of the museum is Konstantinou.

The central square, Plateia Kalavrytou, is between these two streets, two blocks up from the train station.

The bus station is on Kapota. From the train station, walk up Syngrou and turn right at Hotel Maria onto Kapota; cross Ethnikis Antistassis and you'll see the buses parked at the bottom of the hill on the left. Kalavryta has neither EOT nor tourist police. The post office is on the main square and the OTE is on Konstantinou. Internet access is available at Cybernet (☎ 2692-023 555; Agiou Alexiou 17), on the corner of the road leading to the Martyrs' Monument.

The National Bank of Greece is on 25 Martiou, just before the central square. It has an ATM.

Martyrs' Monument

A huge white cross on a cypress-covered hillside just east of the town marks the site of the 1943 massacre. Beneath this imposing monument is a poignant little shrine to the victims. The site is signposted off Konstantinou.

Places to Stay

Kalavryta does not have a lot of accommodation. Peak season here is the ski season, from late November to April. Reservations are essential at this time and at weekends throughout the year, when Athenians come to enjoy the cool mountain air. The prices listed below are slashed by as much as 50% at other times.

There are no budget hotels, but there are several domatia (rooms) on the streets behind the train station.

Megas Alexandros (☎ 2692-022 221; Kapota 1; singles/doubles with bathroom €35.20/41.10) is the cheapest hotel in town.

Hotel Maria (☎ 2692-022 296, fax 2692-022 686; Syngrou 10; singles/doubles with bathroom €41.10/52.85) is conveniently located opposite the museum. It's a small, family-run hotel that has cosy rooms, each with a TV. Breakfast served in the café downstairs for €4.40.

Hotel Anesis (☎ 2692-023 070; e anesis@ otenet.gr; Plateia Kalavrytou; singles/doubles/ triples with bathroom €44/55.80/66) is a smart, modern hotel run by Greek-Australian brothers Nikos and Dimitris Mihalopoulos, who've quickly established the Anesis as the best hotel in town. The rooms are stylishly furnished and well appointed; the best room has its own fireplace. In summer prices drop to just €23.50/29.35/38.15, making it also the best deal in town. Breakfast costs €5.90 and is served in the restaurant downstairs.

Hotel Filoxenia (☎ 2692-022 422, fax 2692-023 009; e filoxenia@otenet.gr; Ethnikis Antistaseos 10; singles/doubles/triples with bathroom €62.25/79.25/98.65) is another good choice. It's an old-fashioned place where not much has changed in years, except that the rooms now have a minibar, safe and TV. The price includes breakfast.

Places to Eat

You'll find most places to eat in Kalavryta are on 25 Martiou.

Taverna O Australos (☎ 2692-023 070; Plateia Kalavrytou; mains €3.85-6.45) is located below the Hotel Anesis. This taverna has built up a strong local following, with specialities such as rabbit stifado (stew; €5.30) and goat in lemon sauce (€5.90).

To Tzaki Taverna (☎ 2692-022 609; cnr 25 Martiou & Plateia Kalavrytou; mains €4.10-8.25) is another popular spot, offering a good choice of daily specials.

Taverna Pezodromos (☎ 2692-024 455; Syngrou 8; mains €4-8.50), opposite the National Bank of Greece, has an excellent selection of staples. You can wash down house specialities such as roast goat in white sauce (€6.45) or roast lamb in vine leaves (€7.35) with a litre of house wine (€3.55).

Entertainment

Air Music Club, about 1km north of town on the road to Diakofto, is housed in one of the original Boeing 720-68 planes bought by Aristotle Onassis for the launch of Olympic Airways in the 1960s. It was transported here in pieces and reassembled in situ.

Getting There & Away

There are bus services to Patras (€5.10, four daily) via Diakofto (€2.50), Athens (€10.90, two daily) and Tripolis (€5.50, one daily).

There are trains to Diakofto (via Zahlorou) that depart at 9.15am, 11.45am, 2.30pm and 5pm Monday to Friday, and 10.12am, 12.45pm, 3.20pm and 6pm on weekends.

Kalavryta's **taxi rank** (☎ 2692-022 127) is on the central square.

AROUND KALAVRYTA
Moni Agias Lavras

Moni Agias Lavras (admission free; open 10am-1.30pm daily), 6km southwest of Kalavryta, is regarded as the birthplace of the modern Greek nation. It was here, according to popular account, that Bishop Germanos of Patras raised the flag of revolt that launched the War of Independence on 25 March, 1821.

While the historical accuracy of this claim is debatable, there's no doubting the importance of the place in the minds of most Greeks. Indeed, the main reason for building the Diakofto–Kalavryta railway was to provide access to the monastery for pilgrims.

The monastery dates back to the 10th century, but virtually all trace of the original was destroyed by Ibrahim Pasha in 1826. It was rebuilt in 1839, and again in the 1950s after it was torched by the Nazis during WWII.

The new monastery has a small museum where the banner standard is displayed along with other monastic memorabilia.

The road to the monastery is clearly signposted from Kalavryta. There's no public transport. A taxi from Kalavryta costs about €5.

Cave of the Lakes

The remarkable Cave of the Lakes (☎ 2692-031 633; w www.kastriacave.gr; adult/child €6/3; open 9.30am-4.30pm Mon-Fri, 9am-6pm Sat-Sun) lies 16.5km south of Kalavryta near the village of Kastria. The cave features in Greek mythology and is mentioned in the writings of the ancient traveller Pausanias. In modern times its whereabouts remained unknown until 1964, when locals noticed water pouring from the roof of a smaller, lower cave after heavy rain and decided to investigate. They found themselves in a large bat-filled cavern at the start of a winding 2km-long cave carved out by a subterranean river.

The cavern is now reached by an artificial entrance, from where a 350m raised walkway snakes up the riverbed. It passes some wonderfully ornate stalactites, but they are mere sideshows alongside the lakes themselves. The lakes are actually a series of 13 stone basins formed by mineral deposits left over the millennia. In summer the waters dry up to reveal a curious lacework of walls, some up to 3m high.

Getting to the cave is difficult without your own transport. The daily bus from Kalavryta to Kastria isn't much help. A taxi from Kalavryta will cost about €20 return.

Planitero Πλανίτερο

Nestled in a leafy valley about 22km south of Kalavryta, the tiny settlement of Planitero is one of the best-kept secrets in the northern Peloponnese. The valley is watered by a wonderful, bubbling mountain stream that descends from nearby Mt Helmos (2338m). The conditions are perfect for trout farming, which is the main activity here.

Places to Stay & Eat Taverna Planiteros (☎ 2692-032-055; doubles €44; mains €4.70-5.30) has rooms to rent nearby the tavern. Trout is the only item on the menu at this small, family-run taverna, which comes with its own trout farm attached. You can have your trout made into soup (€3.55), grilled, fried or baked (€4.70) or stuffed (€5.30).

Taverna Laleousa (☎ 2692-031 035; mains €4.50-9), nearby, also features grilled trout (€5) as its house speciality. The menu also includes salmon (€9), as well as specials such as rooster with homemade pasta (€8.50).

Getting There & Away There's no public transport to Planitero, so getting there is hard work without your own wheels. The turn-off to Planitero is 1km south of Kastria, from where it's another 2.5km to the village.

Ski Centre

The ski centre (elevation 1650m to 2100m), with nine pistes and one chairlift, is 14km east of Kalavryta on Mt Helmos. It has a cafeteria and first-aid centre but no overnight accommodation. The ski centre has a Kalavryta office (☎ 2692-022 661, fax 2692-022 415; 25 Martiou 18; open 7am-3pm Mon-Fri) and there are several outlets on Konstantinou which rent skis. **Ski Time Center** (☎ 2692-022 030; Agiou Alexiou 11) charges €8.80 per day for skis, poles and bindings, €17.60 per day for snowboards and €5.90 for toboggans. There is no transport to the centre from Kalavryta, so you will need to organise your own. A taxi costs about €20 return. The season lasts from November to February, snow permitting.

Mt Helmos Refuge

The EOS-owned B Leondopoulos Mountain Refuge is situated at 2100m on Mt Helmos. A marked footpath leads to the refuge from the ski centre (one hour's walk). Another path leads from the village of Ano Loussi (1½ hours), on the way to Kastria. To stay in the refuge, or for details on walks or climbs on Mt Helmos, talk to the ski-centre staff in the Kalavryta office.

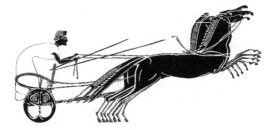

The Islands

Although not strictly 'the Peloponnese', the islands lying off its coast are just a short hop away and can offer a welcome diversion from the sights of the mainland.

KYTHIRA Κύθηρα
postcode 80 100 • pop 3334

The island of Kythira (**kee**-thih-rah), 12km south of Neapoli, is a perfect destination for people who want to unwind for a few days.

Some 30km long and 18km wide, Kythira dangles off the tip of the Peloponnese's eastern Lakonian Peninsula, between the often-turbulent Ionian and Aegean Seas. More than 40 villages are scattered evenly across the island, and ghosts are said to roam the inland settlements. It is looked on as one of Greece's remotest places; many Greeks regard it as the Holy Grail of island-hopping, a reputation that was enhanced by Dimitris Mitropanos' 1973 song, 'Road to Kythira'.

Despite its proximity to the Peloponnese, Kythira was grouped with the far-off Ionian Islands by the British Ionian Protectorate in the 19th century. Today it is administered from Piraeus, along with the Saronic Gulf Islands.

Mythology suggests that Aphrodite was born in Kythira. She is supposed to have risen from the foam where Zeus had thrown Cronos' sex organ after mutilating him. The goddess of love then re-emerged near Paphos in Cyprus, so both islands haggle over her birthplace.

You'll find more information on the Internet at W www.kythira.com.

Hora Χώρα
pop 267

Perched on a long, slender ridge 2km uphill from the village of Kapsali, Hora (also known as Kythira; Κύθηρα) is the island's pretty capital, with white, blue-shuttered houses. The central square, planted with hibiscus, bougainvillea and palms, is Plateia Dimitriou Staï. The main street runs south of it.

The post office is on the square, as are the National Bank of Greece and Agricultural Bank, both with ATMs. Just south of the square is Anonymo (also called Cafe No-Name), a café-bar offering Internet

Highlights

- Visiting the tranquil villages of Kythira and swimming at its unspoilt beaches
- Staying at one of Hydra's gracious old stone mansions
- Wandering around the old harbour at Spetses Town

access for €6 per hour. The **police station** (☎ 2736-031 206) is near the *kastro* (walled compound).

Things to See Hora's Venetian **kastro**, built in the 13th century, is at the southern end of town. If you walk to its southern extremity, passing the Church of Panagia, you will come to a sheer cliff, from here there's a stunning view of Kapsali, extending all the way to Antikythira on a good day.

The **archaeological museum** (☎ 2736-031 789; admission free; open 8.45am-3pm Tues-Sat, 9.30am-2.30pm Sun) is north of the central square, near the turn-off to Kapsali. It features gravestones of British soldiers and their infants who died on the island in the 19th century. A large marble lion from around 550 BC is also exhibited.

Places to Stay & Eat Castello Rooms (☎ 2736-031 069, fax 2736-031 869; e jfat seas@otenet.gr; double rooms/3-person studios €36/45) has both spacious rooms and

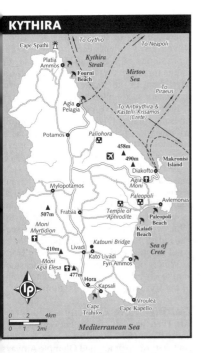

KYTHIRA

Cape Spathi
To Gythio
To Neapoli
Platia Ammos
Kythira Strait
Fourni Beach
Mirtoo Sea
To Piraeus
Agia Pelagia
To Antikythira & Kastelli-Kissamos (Crete)
Potamos
Paliohora
458m
490m
Makronisi Island
Diakofto
Mylopotamos
Agia Moni
Paleopoli
Avlemonas
507m Fratsia
Temple of Aphrodite
Paleopoli Beach
Moni Myrtidion
Kaladi Beach
410m
Katouni Bridge
Sea of Crete
Livadi
Kato Livadi
Fyri Ammos
Moni Agia Elesa
477m
Hora
Kapsali
Vroulea
Cape Trahilos
Cape Kapello
Mediterranean Sea
0 2 4km
0 1 2mi

studios. It's signposted at the southern end of the main street.

Hotel Margarita (☎ 2736-031 711, fax 2736-031 325; e fatseasp@otenet.gr; singles/doubles €70/85), off the main street between the central square and *kastro*, is in a renovated 19th-century mansion. This charming hotel offers very pleasant rooms, each with a TV and telephone, and serves breakfast on a lovely whitewashed terrace.

Eating options in Hora are limited to the cafés clustered around the central square and along the main street.

Fournos (☎ 2736-034 289; snacks €2.50-12) has a selection of snacks a cut above the usual fare, including tasty antipasto plates, home-made quiche and pies and a very decent burger. It has tables and chairs on the square, although the café itself is tucked away on a side street.

Kapsali Καψάλι
pop 71

Kapsali is a picturesque village located down a winding road from Hora. It looks particularly captivating from Hora's *kastro*, with its twin sandy bays and curving waterfront.

Restaurants and cafés line the waterfront, and Kapsali's trademark is its safe, sheltered swimming. It can get very crowded in July and August.

As well as cars and mopeds, bicycles, canoes and pedal boats can be hired from Panayotis, at **Moto Rent** (☎ 2736-031 600), on the waterfront. It also offers water-skiing.

Places to Stay & Eat Accommodation bookings are essential in July and August.

Vassilis Studios (☎ 2736-031 125, fax 2736-031 553; double studios €75), on the road between Hora and Kapsali and not far from the beach, is an attractive green-and-white complex. Olga, the friendly owner, offers spacious studios with lovely wooden floors and good bay views.

Raikos Hotel (☎ 2736-031 629, fax 2736-031 801; e raikoshotel@techlink.gr; doubles/triples €85/105) is a very smart, friendly hotel. It has spacious, pleasantly decorated rooms, with terraces overlooking Kapsali and Hora's *kastro*, and a lovely pool and bar area, too. It's signposted off the Hora–Kapsali road.

Hydragogio (☎ 2736-031 065; mains to €12.50) is a lively eatery at the far end of town, by the rocks. It specialises in *mezedes* and fresh fish, with lobster and fish priced by the kilo. It's a good place to splurge on lobster, if your budget will stretch that far. The wine list is comprehensive and excellent.

Mylopotamos Μυλοποταμό
pop 49

Mylopotamos is an alluring, verdant village. Its central square is flanked by a much-photographed church and a *kafeneio* (traditional male-only coffee house), which serves excellent fare in a gorgeous setting. It's worth a stroll to the **Neraïda** (Water Nymph) waterfall, with luxuriant greenery and mature, shady trees. As you reach the church, take the right fork and follow the signs to an unpaved road leading down to the falls.

Potamos Ποταμός
pop 396

Potamos, 10km from Agia Pelagia, is the island's commercial hub. On Sunday morning almost every islander is attracted to its market. The National Bank of Greece (with ATM) is on the central square. The post office is just north of the central square.

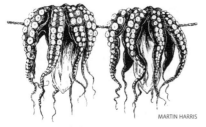

MARTIN HARRIS

Octopus could be one of the fine seafood dishes you try in the Islands

Hotel Porfyra (☎ 2736-033 329, 2736-033 924; double studios €50) is Potamos' only hotel. It has spotless, self-contained units surrounding a pleasant courtyard. The sign, almost opposite the post office north of the main square, is in Greek only.

Taverna Panaretos (☎ 2736-034 290; mains to €9) is a bustling taverna on the central square. It serves well-prepared international and Greek dishes, including tempting seafood risotto and pasta.

Agia Pelagia Αγία Πελαγία
pop 281

Kythira's northern port of Agia Pelagia is a simple, friendly waterfront village ideal for relaxing and swimming. Mixed sand and pebble beaches flank the quay.

Places to Stay & Eat Reservations are essential if you want to stay in Agia Pelagia in July and August.

Georgos Kambouris Domatia (☎ 2736-033 480; doubles €50) is one of the friendliest and most pleasant places to stay. Georgos' wife, Maria, maintains spotless, airy rooms. The building is just in front of Hotel Romantica.

Hotel Kytheria (☎ 2736-033 321, fax 2736-033 825; doubles €65) is a welcoming hotel, owned by the helpful Angelo, from Australia. It has very comfortable, tidy rooms right on the beachfront.

Faros Taverna (☎ 2736-033 343; mains to €7.50) is a blue-and-white taverna close to the quay that serves good, economical Greek staples.

Moustakias (☎ 2736-033 519; mains to €8.80), next to the minimarket, is an *ouzeri* that offers not only ouzo but *mezedes*, grilled meats, seafood and all the traditional Greek favourites.

Around the Island

There are lots of opportunities to explore if you have independent transport. The monasteries of **Agia** and **Agia Elesa** are mountain refuges with superb views. **Moni Myrtidion**, in the southeast, is a beautiful monastery surrounded by trees.

From Hora, drive northeast to the picturesque village of **Avlemonas** via **Paleopoli**, with its wide, pebbled beach. Around here, archaeologists spent years searching for evidence of a temple at Aphrodite's birthplace.

Just north of the village of Kato Livadi, make a detour to see the remarkable, and seemingly out-of-place, British-built **Katouni Bridge**, a legacy of Kythira's time as part of the British Protectorate in the 19th century. Beachcombers should seek out **Kaladi Beach**, near Paleopoli. Another good beach is **Fyri Ammos**, closer to Hora.

While you're in the island's northeast, be sure to visit the spectacularly situated ruins of the Byzantine capital of **Paliohora**.

Getting There & Away

Air There are daily flights between Kythira and Athens (€52.80). The airport is 10km southeast of Potamos, and **Olympic Airways** (☎ 2736-033 362) is on the central square in Potamos. You can also make bookings at **Kythira Travel** (☎ 2736-031 390) in Hora.

Ferry The *Nisos Kythira* shuttles between Agia Pelagia and Neapoli two or three times daily (€4.40, one hour). Tickets are sold at the quay just before departure and from **Sirenes Travel Club** (☎ 2736-034 371) in Potamos. In bad weather the boat arrives and departs from Diakofti, not Agia Pelagia.

ANEN Lines operates the *Myrtidiotissa* on a circuit that takes in Piraeus, Kythira, Kastelli-Kissamos (Crete) and Gythio (Peloponnese). From mid-June to mid-September there are two boats weekly to Piraeus (€16.50, 6½ hours), three to Gythio (€7.10, 2½ hours) and four to Kastelli-Kissamos (€12.90, four hours). Information and tickets are available from **Porfyra Travel** (☎/fax 2736-031 888; e porfyra@ otenet.gr) in Livadi.

Hydrofoil From June to mid-September there are daily hydrofoils from Diakofti to Zea Marina in Piraeus (€30.80): the journey takes 3½ hours direct (three times a week), or five hours via Neapoli, Monemvasia, Kyparissi and Leonidio, all in the eastern Peloponnese (four times a week). Tickets are available from **Kythira Travel** (☎ 2736-031 490) on the main square in Hora.

Getting Around
There is no regular public transport on the island, but there are many taxis. The best way to see the island and explore the small villages and difficult-to-access beaches is with your own transport. **Moto Rent** (☎ 2736-031 600, fax 2736-031 789), on Kapsali's waterfront, rents out cars and mopeds.

POROS Πόρος
postcode 180 20 • pop 4348
The island of Poros is little more than a stone's throw from the small Peloponnese town of Galatas on the east coast of the Argolis Peninsula.

Poros was once two islands, Kalavria and Sferia. These days they are connected by a narrow isthmus, cut by a canal for small boats and rejoined by a road bridge. The vast majority of the population lives on the small volcanic island of Sferia, which is more than half-covered by the town of Poros. Sferia hangs like an appendix from the southern coast of Kalavria, a large, well-forested island that has a smattering of package hotels.

Poros Town
postcode 180 20 • pop 4102
Poros is also the name of the island's main settlement. It's a pretty place of white houses with terracotta-tiled roofs and it offers wonderful views over to the mountains of Argolis. It is a popular weekend destination for Athenians, as well as for package tourists and cruise-ship passengers.

Orientation & Information The main ferry dock is at the western tip of town, overlooked by the striking blue-domed clock tower. A left turn from the dock puts you on the waterfront road leading to Kalavria. The Organismos Tilepikoinonion Ellados (OTE) building is on the right after 100m. A right turn at the ferry dock leads along the waterfront facing Galatas. The first square (a triangle actually) is Plateia Iroön, where the hydrofoils dock. The bus leaves from next to the kiosk at the eastern end of the square.

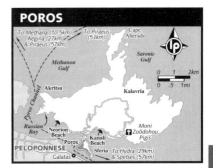

The next square along is Plateia Karamis, which is where you'll find the post office. **Coconuts Internet Café** (☎ 2298-025 407; waterfront; open 10am-2pm & 5pm-11pm daily) charges €5.90 per hour, with a €1.50 minimum.

The National Bank of Greece is 500m further along the waterfront. The Alpha Bank and the Bank Emporiki have branches on Plateia Iroön.

Poros does not have a tourist office. The **tourist police office** (☎ 2298-022 462/256; Dimosthenous 10) is behind the Poros high school. Dimosthenous runs inland from the road to Kalavria, starting just beyond the small supermarket.

Suzi's Laundrette Service, next to the OTE, charges €9 to wash and dry a 5kg load.

Places to Stay Poros has very little cheap accommodation.

If things are not too hectic, a domatia (rooms) owner may offer you accommodation when you get off the ferry. Otherwise, head left along the waterfront and turn right after about 400m, beyond the small supermarket. There are lots of domatia on the streets around here.

Seven Brothers Hotel (☎ 2298-023 412, fax 2298-023 413; e 7brothrs@hol.gr; Plateia Iroön; singles/doubles with bathroom €40/48) is a smart C-class hotel, with large, comfortable rooms equipped with aircon and TV.

Hotel Dionysos (☎ 2298-023 953; Papadopoulou 78; singles/doubles with bathroom €36/60) occupies a beautifully restored mansion opposite the car-ferry dock from Galatas. The rooms are comfortably furnished, each with air-con and TV. Breakfast is €4.40.

Places to Eat Poros has some excellent restaurants.

Taverna Karavolos (☎ 2298-026 158; mains €3.25-6; open from 7pm daily) is signposted behind the Cinema Diana, on the road to Kalavria. Karavolos means 'big snail' in Greek and this is the nickname of cheerful owner Theodoros. Sure enough, snails are a speciality of the house – they're served in a delicious thick tomato sauce. You'll find a range of imaginative *mezedes*, such as *taramokeftedes* (fish-roe balls), and a daily selection of main courses, such as pork stuffed with garlic (€5). Theodoros has a strong local following and only a dozen tables, so bookings are advisable.

Taverna Platanos (☎ 2298-024 249; Plateia Agios Georgiou; mains €4-7.50) is another popular spot, with seating beneath a large, old plane tree in the small square at the top of Dimosthenous. Owner Tassos is a butcher by day, so, unsurprisingly, the restaurant specialises in spit-roast meats. You'll find specialities such as *kokoretsi* (offal) and *gouronopoulo* (suckling pig).

The Flying Dutchman (☎ 2298-025 407; off Plateia Karamanos; mains €8.50-17.50) has brought a touch of the exotic to Poros' restaurant scene, with a menu that includes Indonesian and Chinese dishes.

Getting There & Away
Small boats shuttle constantly between Poros and the mainland (Galatas, €0.30), leaving Poros Town from the quay opposite Plateia Iroön. Car ferries to Galatas leave from the dock on the road to Kalavria.

There are also regular ferries daily to Piraeus (€6.45, three hours) via Methana and Aegina (€3.85, 1½ hours), two daily ferries to Hydra (€3.25, one hour) and one to Spetses (€5, two hours). Ticket agencies are opposite the ferry dock.

Minoan Flying Dolphin operates six services daily from Piraeus (€12.95, one hour), one from Great Harbour and five from Zea Marina. There are also six hydrofoils south to Hydra (€6.15, 30 minutes), two of which continue to Spetses (€10.60, one hour).

Flying Dolphin (Plateia Iroön) has a timetable of departures outside its agency.

Getting Around
The Poros bus operates almost constantly along a route that starts near the hydrofoil dock on Plateia Iroön. It crosses to Kalavria and goes east along the south coast as far as Moni Zoödohou Pigis (€0.60), then turns around and heads west as far as Neorion Beach.

There are several places on the road to Kalavria offering bikes for hire, both motorised and pedal-powered.

HYDRA Υδρα
postcode 180 40 • pop 2719

Hydra (**ee-drah**) is the Saronic Gulf island with the most style. The gracious stone, white and pastel mansions of Hydra township are stacked up the rocky hillsides that surround the fine natural harbour. Filmmakers were the first foreigners to be seduced by the beauty of Hydra. They began arriving in the 1950s, when the island was used as a location for *Boy on a Dolphin*, among other films.

If you've been in Greece for some time you may fall in love with Hydra for one reason alone – the absence of kamikaze motorcyclists. There is no motorised transport in Hydra, except for sanitation and construction vehicles. Donkeys (hundreds of them) are the only means of transport.

History
Like many islands, Hydra was ignored by the Turks, so many Greeks from the Peloponnese settled here to escape Ottoman suppression and taxes. The population was further boosted by an influx of Albanians. Agriculture was impossible, so these new settlers began building boats. By the 19th century the island had become a great maritime power. The canny Hydriots made a fortune by running the British blockade of French ports during the Napoleonic Wars. The wealthy shipping merchants built most of the town's grand, old *arhontika* (mansions) from the considerable profits they made. Hydra became a fashionable resort for Greek socialites and lavish balls were a regular feature.

Hydra made a major contribution to the War of Independence. Without the 130 ships supplied by the island, the Greeks wouldn't have had much of a fleet with which to blockade the Turks. It also supplied leadership in the form of Georgios Koundouriotis, who was president of the emerging Greek nation's national assembly from 1822 to 1827, and Admiral Andreas Miaoulis, who commanded

HYDRA

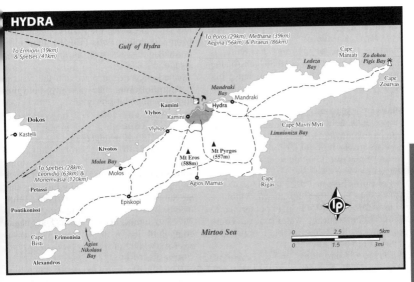

To Poros (29km), Methana (39km),
Aegina (56km) & Piraeus (86km)

Gulf of Hydra

To Ermioni (19km)
& Spetses (41km)

Cape
Maniati

Zo dohou
Pigis Bay

Ledeza
Bay

Cape
Zourvas

Mandraki
Bay

Mandraki

Kamini

Hydra

Vlyhos

Kamini

Dokos

Vlyhos

Cape Mavri Myti

Kastelli

Limnioniza Bay

Kivotos

Mt Eros
(588m)

Mt Pyrgos
(557m)

Molos Bay

To Spetses (28km),
Leonidio (63km) &
Monemvasia (120km)

Molos

Petassi

Agios Mamas

Cape
Rigas

Episkopi

Pontikonissi

Mirtoo Sea

0   2.5   5km
0   1.5   3mi

Cape
Bisti

Erimonisia

Agios
Nikolaos
Bay

Alexandros

the Greek fleet. Streets and squares all over Greece are named after these two.

You can find further information about the island on the Internet at w www.compulink.gr/hydranet.

Hydra Town
postcode 180 40 • pop 2526

Most of the action in Hydra town is concentrated around the waterfront cafés and shops; the upper reaches of the narrow, stepped streets are virtually deserted and are a joy to explore.

Orientation & Information Ferries and hydrofoils dock on the eastern side of the harbour. The town's three main streets all head inland from the harbour. Walking around from the ferry dock, the first street you come to is Tombazi, at the eastern corner. The next main street, on the left before the clock tower, is Miaouli, which is the town's main thoroughfare. The third street is Lignou, at the western extreme, which links up with Kriezi and runs west over the hills to Kamini. Lignou is best reached by heading up Votsi, on the left after the clock tower, and taking the first turn right.

Most things of importance are close to the waterfront. The post office is on a small side street between the Commercial (Emporiki) Bank and the National Bank of Greece. From mid-May until the end of September the **tourist police office** (☎ 2298-052 205) is located at the police station, opposite the OTE on Votsi.

You can check email at the **Flamingo Internet Café** (☎ 2298-053 485; Tombazi; open noon-11pm daily), which charges €7.50 per hour, with a €1.50 minimum.

There's a laundry service in the small market square near the post office. It's open 10am to 1.30pm and 5pm to 8.30pm daily and charges €10 to wash and dry a load.

Things to See & Do The **Historical Archives Museum of Hydra** (☎ 2298-052 355; admission €1.50; open 10am-4.30pm Tues-Sun) is close to the ferry dock, on the eastern side of the harbour. It houses a collection of portraits and naval oddments and has an emphasis on the island's role in the War of Independence.

The **Byzantine Museum** (☎ 2298-054 071; admission €1.50; open 10am-5pm Tues-Sun), upstairs at the Monastery of the Assumption of Virgin Mary, houses a collection of icons and assorted religious paraphernalia. The entrance is through the archway beneath the clock tower on the waterfront.

Lisa Bartsiokas (☎ 2298-053 836, fax 2298-053 842; e hydragr@otenet.gr) offers a range of guided walks around the island in spring and autumn. The walks take between five and eight hours, including breaks, and cost €14.70 per person with a minimum of four.

Hydra Divers *(☎ 2298-053 900;* w *www .divingteam.gr)* is a new business offering dives at a range of locations around the nearby Peloponnese coast.

Places to Stay Accommodation in Hydra is generally of a very high standard, and you pay accordingly for it. The prices listed here are for the high season, which in Hydra means every weekend as well as July and August.

Pension Theresia *(☎ 2298-053 984, fax 2298-053 983; Tombazi; singles/doubles with bathroom €30/45)* is a popular place, about 300m from the waterfront on Tombazi. It has clean, comfortable rooms and a small communal kitchen.

Pension Alkionides *(☎/fax 2298-054 055; singles/doubles with bathroom €35/45)* is another good budget choice, tucked away off Oikonomou about 250m from the port. All rooms have a fridge.

Hotel Orloff *(☎ 2298-052 564, fax 2298-053 532;* e *orloff@internet.gr; singles/doubles with bathroom from €85/95)* is a beautiful old mansion, with a cool, vine-covered courtyard at the back. The furnishings are elegant without being overstated, and each of the 10 rooms has a character of its own. Prices include buffet breakfast, served in the courtyard in summer.

Hotel Bratsera *(☎ 2298-053 971, fax 2298-053 626;* e *tallos@hol.gr; Tombazi; doubles with bathroom €105-165, 4-bed suites from €175)* has loads of character. It occupies a converted sponge factory, about 300m from the port on Tombazi. It also has the town's only swimming pool. It's for guests only but you'll qualify to use if you eat at Bratsera's restaurant. Room prices include breakfast.

Places to Eat Hydra has dozens of tavernas and restaurants. Unlike the hotels, there are plenty of cheap places around, especially if you're prepared to head away from the waterfront.

Taverna Gitoniko *(☎ 2298-053 615; Spilios Haramis; mains €2.95-8.80)* is better known by the names of its owners, Manolis and Christina. The menu is nothing special, but it's built up an enthusiastic local following through the simple formula of turning

out consistently good traditional taverna food. Try the beetroot salad – a bowl of baby beets and boiled greens served with garlic mashed potato. The flavours complement each other perfectly. Get in early or you'll have a long wait.

To Kryfo Limani *(The Secret Port; ☎ 2298-052 585; mains €3.55-8.50)* is tucked away on a small alleyway. This charming spot has seating beneath a large lemon tree and serves delicious specials, such as hearty fish soup (€4.70).

Entertainment Hydra boasts a busy nightlife. The action is centred on the bars on the southwestern side of the harbour, where places such as **Pirate** *(☎ 2298-052 711)* and **Saronikos** *(☎ 2298-052 589)* keep going until close to dawn. Pirate plays western rock while Saronikos plays Greek.

Amalour *(☎ 69-7746 1357; Tombazi)* is a more sophisticated café-bar that sells a wide range of fresh juices, as well as alcohol.

Getting There & Away

Ferry There are two ferries daily to Piraeus (€7.35, 3½ hours), sailing via Poros (€3.25) and Methana (€4.40). There's also a daily boat to Spetses (€3.55, one hour). Departure times are listed on a board at the ferry dock.

You can buy tickets from **Idreoniki Travel** *(☎2298-054 007)*, next to the Flying Dolphin office overlooking the port.

Hydrofoil Hydra is well served by the Flying Dolphin fleet, with up to nine services daily to Piraeus (€13.50) – two to the Great Harbour, the rest to Zea Marina. Direct services take 1¼ hours but most go via Poros (€5.90, 30 minutes) and take 1½ hours. There are also frequent services to Spetses (€6.75, 30 minutes), some of which call at Ermioni, adding 20 minutes to the trip. Many of the services to Spetses continue to Porto Heli (€7.35, 50 minutes). There is also a daily service to Leonidio, Kyparissi, Gerakas and Monemvasia.

The **Flying Dolphin office** *(☎ 2298-053 814)* is on the waterfront opposite the ferry dock.

Getting Around

Water taxis *(☎ 2298-053 690)* will take you anywhere you like around the island. Sample fares include €4.70 to Kamini and €7.35 to Mandraki and Vlyhos.

The donkey owners clustered around the port charge about €8 to transport your bags to the hotel of your choice.

SPETSES Σπέτσες
postcode 180 50 • pop 3976
Pine-covered Spetses, the most distant of the Saronic group from Piraeus, has long been a favourite with British holiday-makers.

Spetses' history is similar to Hydra's: it became wealthy through shipbuilding, ran the British blockade during the Napoleonic Wars and refitted its ships to join the Greek fleet during the War of Independence. Spetsiot fighters achieved a certain notoriety through their pet tactic of attaching small boats laden with explosives to the enemy's ships, setting them alight and beating a hasty retreat.

Spetses Town
postcode 180 50 • pop 3846
Spetses township sprawls along almost half the northeast coast of the island, reflecting the way in which the focal point of settlement has changed over the years.

There's evidence of an early Helladic settlement near the old harbour, about 1.5km east of the modern commercial centre and port of Dapia. Roman and Byzantine remains have been unearthed in the area behind Moni Agios Nikolaos, about halfway between the two.

The island is thought to have been uninhabited for almost 600 years before the arrival of refugees fleeing the fighting between the Turks and Venetians in the 16th century. They settled on the hillside just inland from Dapia, the area now known as Kastelli.

The Dapia district has a few impressive *arhontika*, but the prettiest part of town is around the old harbour.

Orientation & Information The quay at Dapia Harbour serves both ferries and hydrofoils. A left turn at the end of the quay leads east along the waterfront on Sotirios Anargyris, skirting a small square where the horse-drawn carriages wait. The road is flanked by a string of uninspiring, concrete C-class hotels and emerges after 200m on Plateia Agias Mamas, right next to the town beach. The bus stop for Agioi Anargyri is

Lascarina Bouboulina

Spetses contributed one of the most colourful figures of the War of Independence, the dashing heroine Lascarina Bouboulina. Her exploits on and off the battlefield were the stuff of legend. She was widowed twice by the time the war began; both of her ship-owning husbands had been killed by pirates, leaving her a very wealthy woman. She used her money to commission her own fighting ship, the *Agamemnon*, which she led into battle during the blockade of Nafplio.

Bouboulina was known for her fiery temperament and countless love affairs, and her death was in keeping with her flamboyant lifestyle – she was shot during a family dispute in her Spetses home. Bouboulina featured on the old 50-drachma note, depicted directing cannon fire from the deck of her ship.

The Bouboulina mansion, behind the OTE building, has now been converted into a **museum** (☎ 2298-072 416; adult/child €3/1; open 9am-5pm Tues-Sun). Billboards around town advertise the starting times for tours in English.

next to the beach. The post office is on the street running behind the hotels; if you're coming from the quay, turn right at Hotel Soleil and then left.

The waterfront to the right of the quay is also called Sotirios Anargyris. It skirts Dapia Harbour, passes the grand Hotel Possidonion and continues west around the bay to the Hotel Spetses, to become the road to Ligoneri.

N Spetson is the main road inland from Dapia, running southwest off the small square where the horse-drawn carriages wait. It soon becomes Botassi, which continues inland. These two streets are among the very few on Spetses with street signs.

There is no tourist office on Spetses. The **tourist police office** (☎ 2298-073 100) is in the police station, on the well-signposted road to the museum, and operates from mid-May to September.

The OTE is behind Dapia Harbour, opposite the National Bank of Greece. Internet access is available at **Delfinia Net Café** (☎ 2298-075 051; Plateia Agias Mamas; open 9am-2am daily).

THE ISLANDS

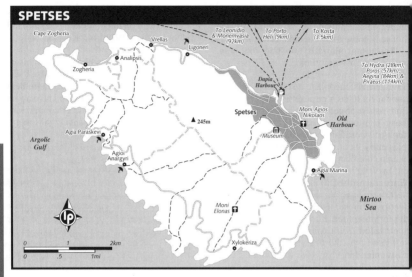

Things to See & Do The **old harbour** is a delightful place to explore. It is ringed by old buildings and filled with boats of every shape and size – from colourful little fishing boats to sleek luxury cruising yachts. The shipbuilders of Spetses still do things the traditional way and the shore is dotted with the hulls of half-built caïques. The walk from Dapia Harbour takes about 20 minutes.

The **museum** (☎ 2298-072 994; admission €1.50; open 8.30am-2.30pm Tues-Sun) is housed in the *arhontiko* of Hadzigiannis Mexis, a ship owner who became the island's first governor. While most of the collection is devoted to folklore items and portraits of the island's founding fathers, there is also a fine collection of ships' figureheads. The museum is hidden away in the back streets of Evangelistras but is clearly signposted from Plateia Orologiou.

Places to Stay The prices listed here are for the high season in July and August. Travellers should be able to negotiate substantial discounts at other times – particularly for longer stays.

Orloff Apartments (☎ 2298-072 246, fax 2298-074 470; singles/doubles with bathroom €25/35) is a good quiet spot to unwind for a few days. Manager Christos has a dozen or so well-equipped studio rooms in the gardens of the family home, on the road leading

out to Agioi Anargyri, above the old harbour about 1.5km from the port. All have fridge and facilities for making tea and coffee.

Villa Marina (☎ 2298-072 646; singles/doubles with bathroom €32/50) is a small, friendly place just off Plateia Agias Mamas, beyond the row of restaurants. It has good rooms that look out onto a delightful little flower garden. All rooms have a refrigerator and there is a well-equipped communal kitchen downstairs.

Hotel Possidonion (☎ 2298-072 308, fax 2298-072 208; singles/doubles/triples B&B with bathroom €49.90/64.60/73.40) is a wonderful old Edwardian-style hotel, overlooking the seafront just south of the Dapia Harbour. It has seen better days but remains an imposing building, with wide wrought-iron balconies looking out to sea.

Nisia (☎ 2298-075 000, fax 2298-075 012; e nisia@otenet.gr; doubles around €135), about 200m west of the Hotel Possidonion, represents the luxury end of the market, with apartment-style rooms clustered around a large swimming pool.

Places to Eat **Taverna O Lazaros** (☎ 2298-072 600; mains 4-6.50) is in the district of Kastelli, about 600m inland at the top end of Spetson. Treat yourself to a plate of taramasalata (€2.50); its home-made version of this popular fish-roe dip is unrecognisable from the mass-produced muck served at many restaurants. The speciality of the house is baby goat in lemon sauce (€5).

Restaurant Patralis (☎ 2298-072 134; mains €4.50-7.80, fish from €34 per kg), about 1.5km west of Dapia on the road to Ligoneri, is the place to which fish fans should go. It has a great setting, a good menu and fish supplied by the restaurant's own boat. The fish à la Spetses (€7.50), a large tuna or swordfish steak baked with vegetables and lots of garlic, goes down perfectly with a cold beer.

Entertainment Bar Spetsa (☎ 2298-074 131) is good for a quiet beer and a great selection of music from the 1960s and 1970s. It's 50m beyond Plateia Agias Mamas on the road to Agioi Anargyri.

I **Vouli** (☎ 2298-074 179) is a classic old-fashioned wine bar. Call in at 10am in the morning and you'll realise why nothing very much ever happens on Spetses; it's always busy with locals gossiping over a morning tumbler of wine (€0.90), poured from one of the giant barrels that line the walls. Come along equipped with a few snacks to share around.

Getting There & Away
There is one ferry daily to Piraeus (€10, 4½ hours) via Hydra (€3.55), Poros (€5) and Aegina (€7.35). Two companies operate the service on alternate days. You'll find departure times on the waterfront outside **Alasia Travel** (☎ 2298-074 098), which sells tickets. The **port police** (☎ 2298-072 245) are opposite the quay.

There are water taxis to Kosta, just 15 minutes away on the Peloponnese mainland and three buses daily from Kosta to Nafplio (€5, 2¼ hours).

There are up to nine Flying Dolphin services daily to Piraeus (€19.10). Most services travel via Hydra (€7.05, 30 minutes) and Poros (€10, 70 minutes) and take about 2½ hours. There are also daily connections to Leonidio (€7.35, one hour) and Monemvasia (€12.65, 1½ hours).

Getting Around
There are three or four buses daily from Plateia Agias Mamas in Spetses Town to Agioi Anargyri (€1.50) via Agia Marina and Xylokeriza. Departure times are displayed on a board by the bus stop. There are hourly buses to Ligoneri (€0.80), departing from in front of the Hotel Possidonion.

No cars are permitted on the island. Unfortunately this ban has not been extended to motorcycles, resulting in there being more motorbikes here than just about anywhere else.

The colourful horse-drawn carriages are a pleasant way of getting around. Prices are displayed on a board where the carriages gather by the port.

Water taxis (☎ 2298-072 072) go anywhere you care to nominate, departing from opposite the Flying Dolphin office at Dapia Harbour. Fares are displayed on a board, samples of which include €17.60 to Agia Marina and €35.20 to Agioi Anargyri. In summer there are caïques from the harbour to Agioi Anargyri (€5.30 return) and Zogheria (€3.55 return).

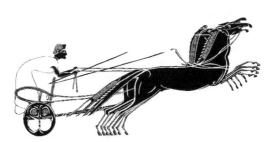

Language

The Greek language is probably the oldest European language, with an oral tradition of 4000 years and a written tradition of approximately 3000 years. Its evolution over the four millennia was characterised by its strength during the golden age of Athens and the Democracy (mid-5th century BC); its use as a lingua franca throughout the Middle Eastern world, spread by Alexander the Great and his successors as far as India during the Hellenistic period (330 BC to AD 100); its adaptation as the language of the new religion, Christianity; its use as the official language of the Eastern Roman Empire; and its eventual proclamation as the language of the Byzantine Empire (380–1453).

Greek maintained its status and prestige during the rise of the European Renaissance and was employed as the linguistic perspective for all contemporary sciences and terminologies during the period of Enlightenment. Today, Greek constitutes a large part of the vocabulary of any Indo-European language, and much of the lexicon of any scientific repertoire.

The modern Greek language is a southern Greek dialect which is now used by most Greek speakers both in Greece and abroad. It is the result of an intralinguistic influence and synthesis of the ancient vocabulary combined with words from Greek regional dialects, namely Cretan, Cypriot and Macedonian.

Pronunciation

All Greek words of two or more syllables have an acute accent which indicates where the stress falls. For instance, άγαλμα (statue) is pronounced *aghalma*, and αγάπη (love) is pronounced *aghapi*. In the following transliterations, bold lettering indicates where stress falls. Note also that **dh** is pronounced as 'th' in 'then'; **gh** is a softer, slightly guttural version of 'g'.

Greetings & Civilities

Hello.
*ya**sas***   Γειά σας.
*ya**su*** (informal)   Γειά σου.
Goodbye.
*an**dio***   Αντίο.

Good morning.
*kali**mera***   Καλημέρα.
Good afternoon.
***here**te*   Χαίρετε.
Good evening.
*kalis**pera***   Καλησπέρα.
Good night.
*kali**nihta***   Καληνύχτα.
Please.
*paraka**lo***   Παρακαλώ.
Thank you.
*efharis**to***   Ευχαριστώ.
Yes.
ne   Ναι.
No.
ohi   Οχι.
Sorry. (excuse me, forgive me)
*sigh**nomi***   Συγγνώμη.
How are you?
*ti **kanete**?*   Τι κάνετε;
*ti **kanis**?*   Τι κάνεις;
(informal)
I'm well, thanks.
*kala efharis**to***   Καλά ευχαριστώ.

Essentials

Do you speak English?
*milate angli**ka**?*   Μιλάτε Αγγλικά;
I understand.
*katala**veno***   Καταλαβαίνω.
I don't understand.
*dhen katala**veno***   Δεν καταλαβαίνω.
Where is ...?
*pou **ine** ...?*   Πού είναι ...;
How much?
***poso** kani?*   Πόσο κάνει;
When?
***pote**?*   Πότε;

Small Talk

What's your name?
*pos sas **lene**?*   Πώς σας λένε;
My name is ...
*me **lene** ...*   Με λένε ...
Where are you from?
*apo pou **iste**?*   Από πού είστε;

I'm from ...
ime apo ...   Είμαι από ...

The Greek Alphabet & Pronunciation

Greek	Pronunciation Guide		Example		
A α	a	as in 'father'	αγάπη	*aghapi*	love
B β	v	as in 'vine'	βήμα	*vima*	step
Γ γ	gh	like a rough 'g'	γάτα	*ghata*	cat
	y	as in 'yes'	για	*ya*	for
Δ δ	dh	as in 'there'	δέμα	*dhema*	parcel
E ε	e	as in 'egg'	ένας	*enas*	one (m)
Z ζ	z	as in 'zoo'	ζώο	*zoo*	animal
H η	i	as in 'police'	ήταν	*itan*	was
Θ θ	th	as in 'throw'	θέμα	*thema*	theme
I ι	i	as in 'police'	ίδιος	*idhyos*	same
K κ	k	as in 'kite'	καλά	*kala*	well
Λ λ	l	as in 'leg'	λάθος	*lathos*	mistake
M μ	m	as in 'man'	μαμά	*mama*	mother
N ν	n	as in 'net'	νερό	*nero*	water
Ξ ξ	x	as in 'ox'	ξύδι	*ksidhi*	vinegar
O o	o	as in 'hot'	όλα	*ola*	all
Π π	p	as in 'pup'	πάω	*pao*	I go
P ρ	r	as in 'road'	ρέμα	*rema*	stream
		a slightly trilled r	ρόδα	*rodha*	tyre
Σ σ, ς	s	as in 'sand'	σημάδι	*simadhi*	mark
T τ	t	as in 'tap'	τόπι	*topi*	ball
Υ υ	i	as in 'police'	ύστερα	*istera*	after
Φ φ	f	as in 'find'	φύλλο	*filo*	leaf
X χ	h	as the 'ch' in Scottish *loch*, or like a rough 'h'	χάνω	*hano*	I lose
			χέρι	*heri*	hand
Ψ ψ	ps	as in 'lapse'	ψωμί	*psomi*	bread
Ω ω	o	as in 'hot'	ώρα	*ora*	time

Combinations of Letters

The combinations of letters shown here are pronounced as follows:

Greek	Pronunciation Guide		Example		
ει	i	as in 'police'	είδα	*idha*	I saw
οι	i	as in 'police'	οικόπεδο	*ikopedho*	land
αι	e	as in 'bet'	αίμα	*ema*	blood
ου	u	as in 'mood'	πού	*pou*	who/what
μπ	b	as in 'beer'	μπάλα	*bala*	ball
	mb	as in 'amber'	κάμπος	*kambos*	forest
ντ	d	as in 'dot'	ντουλάπα	*doulapa*	wardrobe
	nd	as in 'bend'	πέντε	*pende*	five
γκ	g	as in 'God'	γκάζι	*gazi*	gas
γγ	ng	as in 'angle'	αγγελία	*angelia*	classified
γξ	ks	as in 'minks'	σφιγξ	*sfinks*	sphynx
τζ	dz	as in 'hands'	τζάκι	*dzaki*	fireplace

The pairs of vowels shown above are pronounced separately if the first has an acute accent, or the second a dieresis, as in the examples below:

γαϊδουράκι	*gaidhouraki*	little donkey
Κάιρο	*kairo*	Cairo

Some Greek consonant sounds have no English equivalent. The υ of the groups αυ, ευ and ηυ is generally pronounced 'v'. The Greek question mark is represented with the English equivalent of a semicolon ';'.

America
tin ameriki την Αμερική
Australia
tin afstralia την Αυστραλία
England
tin anglia την Αγγλία
Ireland
tin irlandhia την Ιρλανδία
New Zealand
ti nea zilandhia τη Νέα Ζηλανδία
Scotland
ti skotia τη Σκωτία

How old are you?
poson hronon iste? Πόσων χρονών είστε;
I'm ... years old.
ime ... hronon Είμαι ... χρονών.

Getting Around
What time does
the ... leave/arrive?
ti ora fevyi/ ftani to ...? Τι ώρα φεύγει/ φτάνει το ...;

plane	*aeroplano*	αεροπλάνο
boat	*karavi*	καράβι
bus (city)	*astiko*	αστικό
bus (intercity)	*leoforio*	λεωφορείο
train	*treno*	τραίνο

I'd like ...
tha ithela ... Θα ήθελα ...
a return ticket
isitirio me epistrofi εισιτήριο με επιστροφή
two tickets
dhio isitiria δυο εισιτήρια
a student's fare
fititiko isitirio φοιτητικό εισιτήριο
first class
proti thesi πρώτη θέση
economy
touristiki thesi τουριστική θέση

train station
sidhirodhro- mikos stathmos σιδηροδρομικός σταθμός
timetable
dhromologio δρομολόγιο
taxi
taxi ταξί

Where can I hire a car?
pou boro na nikyaso ena aftokinito? Πού μπορώ να νοικιάσω ένα αυτοκίνητο;

Signs

ΕΙΣΟΔΟΣ	**Entry**
ΕΞΟΔΟΣ	**Exit**
ΩΘΗΣΑΤΕ	**Push**
ΣΥΡΑΤΕ	**Pull**
ΓΥΝΑΙΚΩΝ	**Women (toilets)**
ΑΝΔΡΩΝ	**Men (toilets)**
ΝΟΣΟΚΟΜΕΙΟ	**Hospital**
ΑΣΤΥΝΟΜΙΑ	**Police**
ΑΠΑΓΟΡΕΥΕΤΑΙ	**Prohibited**
ΕΙΣΙΤΗΡΙΑ	**Tickets**

Directions
How do I get to ...?
pos tha pao sto/ sti ...? Πώς θα πάω στο/ στη ...;
Where is ...?
pou ine ...? Πού είναι...;
Is it near?
ine konda? Είναι κοντά;
Is it far?
ine makria? Είναι μακριά;

straight ahead	*efthia*	ευθεία
left	*aristera*	αριστερά
right	*dexia*	δεξιά
behind	*piso*	πίσω
far	*makria*	μακριά
near	*konda*	κοντά
opposite	*apenandi*	απέναντι

Can you show me on the map?
borite na mou to dhixete sto harti? Μπορείτε να μου το δείξετε στο χάρτη;

Around Town
I'm looking for (the) ...
psahno ya ... Ψάχνω για ...

bank	*trapeza*	τράπεζα
beach	*paralia*	παραλία
castle	*kastro*	κάστρο
church	*ekklisia*	εκκλησία
... embassy	*tin ... presvia*	την ... πρεσβεία
market	*aghora*	αγορά
museum	*musio*	μουσείο
police	*astynomia*	αστυνομία
post office	*tahydhromio*	ταχυδρομείο
ruins	*arhea*	αρχαία

I want to exchange some money.
  thelo na exaryiroso lefta
  Θέλω να εξαργυρώσω λεφτά.

Accommodation

Where is ...?
  pou ine ...?   Πού είναι ...;
I'd like ...
  thelo ena ...   Θέλω ένα ...

a cheap hotel
  ftino xenodohio   φτηνό ξενοδοχείο
a clean room
  *katharo dho-   καθαρό δωμάτιο
  matio*
a good hotel
  kalo xenodohio   καλό ξενοδοχείο
a camp site
  kamping   κάμπιγκ

single	*mono*	μονό
double	*dhiplo*	διπλό
room	*dhomatio*	δωμάτιο
with bathroom	*me banio*	με μπάνιο
key	*klidhi*	κλειδί

How much is it ...?
  poso kani ...?   Πόσο κάνει ...;
per night
  ti vradhya   τη βραδυά
for ... nights
  ya ... vradhyez   για ... βραδυές
Is breakfast included?
  *symberilamvani   Συμπεριλαμβάνει
  ke pro-ino?*   και πρωϊνό;
May I see it?
  boro na to dho?   Μπορώ να το δω;
Where is the bathroom?
  pou ine tobanio?   Πού είναι το
                         μπάνιο;
It's expensive.
  ine akrivo   Είναι ακριβό.
I'm leaving today.
  fevgho simera   Φεύγω σήμερα.

Food

breakfast	*pro-ino*	πρωϊνό
lunch	*mesimvrino*	μεσημβρινό
dinner	*vradhyno*	βραδυνό
beef	*vodhino*	βοδινό
bread	*psomi*	ψωμί
beer	*byra*	μπύρα
cheese	*tyri*	τυρί
chicken	*kotopoulo*	κοτόπουλο

Emergencies

Help!
  voithya!   Βοήθεια!
Police!
  astynomia!   Αστυνομία!
There's been an
accident.
  eyine atihima   Εγινε ατύχημα.
Call a doctor!
  *fonaxte ena   Φωνάξτε ένα
  yatro!*   ιατρό!
Call an ambulance!
  *tilefoniste ya   Τηλεφωνήστε για
  asthenoforo!*   ασθενοφόρο!
I'm ill.
  ime arostos (m)   Είμαι άρρωστος
  ime arosti (f)   Είμαι άρρωστη
I'm lost.
  eho hathi   Εχω χαθεί
Thief!
  klefti!   Κλέφτη!
Go away!
  fiye!   Φύγε!
I've been raped.
  me viase kapyos   Με βίασε
                         κάποιος.
I've been robbed.
  meklepse kapyos   Μ'έκλεψε
                         κάποιος.
Where are the toilets?
  *pou ine i   Πού είναι οι
  toualetez?*   τουαλέτες;

Greek coffee	*ellinikos kafes*	ελληνικός
		καφές
iced coffee	*frappe*	φραππέ
lamb	*arni*	αρνί
milk	*ghala*	γάλα
mineral	*metalliko*	μεταλλικό
water	*nero*	νερό
tea	*tsai*	τσάι
wine	*krasi*	κρασί

I'm a vegetarian.
  ime hortofaghos
  Είμαι χορτοφάγος.

Shopping

How much is it?
  poso kani?
  Πόσο κάνει;

I'm just looking.
aplos kitazo
Απλώς κοιτάζω.
I'd like to buy ...
thelo n'aghoraso ...
Θέλω ν΄αγοράσω ...
Do you accept credit cards?
pernete pistotikez kartez?
Παίρνετε πιστωτικές κάρτες;
Could you lower the price?
borite na mou kanete mya kaliteri timi?
Μπορείτε να μου κάνετε μια καλύτερη τιμή;

Time & Dates

What time is it?
ti ora ine?   Τι ώρα είναι;

It's ...	*ine ...*	είναι ...
1 o'clock	*mia i ora*	μία η ώρα
2 o'clock	*dhio i ora*	δύο η ώρα
7.30	*efta ke misi*	εφτά και μισή
am	*to pro-i*	το πρωί
pm	*to apoyevma*	το απόγευμα
today	*simera*	σήμερα
tonight	*apopse*	απόψε
now	*tora*	τώρα
yesterday	*hthes*	χθες
tomorrow	*avrio*	αύριο

Sunday	*kyriaki*	Κυριακή
Monday	*dheftera*	Δευτέρα
Tuesday	*triti*	Τρίτη
Wednesday	*tetarti*	Τετάρτη
Thursday	*pempti*	Πέμπτη
Friday	*paraskevi*	Παρασκευή
Saturday	*savato*	Σάββατο

January	*ianouarios*	Ιανουάριος
February	*fevrouarios*	Φεβρουάριος
March	*martios*	Μάρτιος
April	*aprilios*	Απρίλιος
May	*maios*	Μάιος
June	*iounios*	Ιούνιος
July	*ioulios*	Ιούλιος
August	*avghoustos*	Αύγουστος
September	*septemvrios*	Σεπτέμβριος
October	*oktovrios*	Οκτώβριος
November	*noemvrios*	Νοέμβριος
December	*dhekemvrios*	Δεκέμβριος

Health

I need a doctor.
hriazome yatro   Χρειάζομαι ιατρό.

Can you take me to hospital?
borite na me pate sto nosokomio?   Μπορείτε να με πάτε στο νοσοκομείο;
I want something for ...
thelo kati ya ...   Θέλω κάτι για ...
diarrhoea
dhiaria   διάρροια
insect bites
tsimbimata apo   τσιμπήματα από
endoma   έντομα
travel sickness
naftia taxidhiou   ναυτία ταξιδιού

aspirin
aspirini   ασπιρίνη
condoms
profylaktika   προφυλακτικά
(kapotez)   (καπότες)
contact lenses
faki epafis   φακοί επαφής
medical insurance
yatriki asfalya   ιατρική ασφάλεια

Numbers

0	*midhen*	μηδέν
1	*enas*	ένας (m)
	mia	μία (f)
	ena	ένα (n)
2	*dhio*	δύο
3	*tris*	τρεις (m & f)
	tria	τρία (n)
4	*teseris*	τέσσερεις (m & f)
	tesera	τέσσερα (n)
5	*pende*	πέντε
6	*exi*	έξη
7	*epta*	επτά
8	*ohto*	οχτώ
9	*enea*	εννέα
10	*dheka*	δέκα
20	*ikosi*	είκοσι
30	*trianda*	τριάντα
40	*saranda*	σαράντα
50	*peninda*	πενήντα
60	*exinda*	εξήντα
70	*evdhominda*	εβδομήντα
80	*oghdhonda*	ογδόντα
90	*eneninda*	ενενήντα
100	*ekato*	εκατό
1000	*hilii*	χίλιοι (m)
	hiliez	χίλιες (f)
	hilia	χίλια (n)

one million
ena ekatomyrio   ένα εκατομμύριο

Glossary

acropolis – highest point of an ancient city

agia (f), agios (m) – saint

agora – commercial area of an ancient city; shopping precinct in modern Greece

agioritiko – variety of grape that grows only in the wine-producing area around Nemea, Corinthia

akroceramica – a decorative tile at the edge of a roof

amphora – large two-handled vase in which wine or oil was kept

Archaic period – (800–480 BC), also known as the Middle Age; period in which the city-states emerged from the *'dark age'* and traded their way to wealth and power

Asia Minor – the Aegean littoral of Turkey centred around İzmir but also including İstanbul; formerly populated by Greeks

asklepion – shrine complex

basilica – early Christian church

bouleuterion – council building

bouzouki – stringed lute-like instrument associated with *rembetika* music

Byzantine Empire – characterised by the merging of Hellenistic culture and Christianity and named after Byzantium, the city on the Bosphorus which became the capital of the Roman Empire in AD 324; the Byzantine Empire dissolved after the fall of Constantinople to the Turks in 1453

caïque – small, sturdy fishing boat often used to carry passengers

capital – top of a column (in architecture)

cella – room in a temple where the cult statue stood

city-states – states comprising a sovereign city and its dependencies; the city-states of Athens and Sparta were famous rivals

classical Greece – period in which the city-states reached the height of their wealth and power after the defeat of the Persians in the 5th century BC

Corinthian – order of Greek architecture recognisable by columns with bell-shaped *capitals* with sculpted elaborate ornaments based on acanthus leaves

Cyclopes – mythical one-eyed giants

dark age – (1200–800 BC) period in which Greece was under *Dorian* rule

dolmades – stuffed vine leaves

domatio (s), domatia (pl) – room; a cheap accommodation option available in most tourist areas

Dorians – Hellenic warriors who invaded Greece around 1200 BC, demolishing the city-states and destroying the Mycenaean civilisation; heralded Greece's *'dark age'*, when the artistic and cultural advancements of the Mycenaeans and Minoans were abandoned; the Dorians later developed into land-holding aristocrats, encouraging the resurgence of independent city-states led by wealthy aristocrats

Doric – order of Greek architecture characterised by a column which has no base, a *fluted* shaft and a relatively plain *capital*, when compared with the flourishes evident on *Ionic* and *Corinthian* capitals

ELPA – Elliniki Leshi Periigiseon & Aftokinitou; Greek motoring and touring club

ELTA – Ellinika Tahydromia; Greek post office

EOS – Ellinikos Orivatikos Syndesmos or the Greek Alpine Club; Greece's main mountaineering and trekking organisation

EOT – Ellinikos Organismos Tourismou; national tourism organisation which has offices in most major towns

estiatorio – restaurant serving pre-cooked food as well as à la carte dishes

evzones – famous border guards from the northern Greek village of Evzoni; they also guard the Parliament building

fasolia – white haricot beans

fluted – (of a column) having vertical indentations on the shaft

frappé – iced coffee

frieze – part of a temple between the tops of the columns and the roof, usually decorated with sculpture

galaktopoleio (s), galaktopoleia (pl) – a shop which sells mainly dairy products

garides – shrimps

Geometric period – (1200–800 BC) period characterised by pottery decorated

with geometric designs; sometimes referred to as Greece's *'dark age'*
gigantes – lima beans
giouvetsi – casserole of meat and pasta
gyros – grilled meat wrapped in pitta bread with salad

Hellas, Ellas or Ellada – the Greek name for Greece
Hellenistic period – prosperous, influential period of Greek civilisation ushered in by Alexander the Great's empire-building and lasting until the Roman sacking of Corinth in 146 BC
hora – main town (usually on an island)

iconostasis – altar screen embellished with icons
Ionic – order of Greek architecture characterised by a column with truncated *flutes* and *capitals* with ornaments resembling scrolls

kafeneio (s), kafeneia (pl) – traditional (male-only) coffee house
kalamaria – squid
keftedes – meatballs
KKE – Kommounistiko Komma Elladas; Greek communist party
kolokythakia – deep-fried zucchini
KTEL – Kino Tamio Ispraxeon Leoforion; the national bus cooperative; runs all long-distance bus services

loukanika – sausages

maistros – light northwesterly wind
mavromatika – black-eyed beans
megaron – central reception hall of a Mycenaean palace
melitzana – deep-fried aubergine (eggplant)
melitzanosalata – aubergine (eggplant) dip
metope – the sculpted section of a *Doric frieze*
meze (s), mezedes (pl) – appetiser
moni – monastery or convent
Mycenaean civilisation – (1900–1100 BC) first great civilisation of the Greek mainland, characterised by powerful independent city-states ruled by kings

Nea Dimokratia – New Democracy; conservative political party

necropolis – literally 'city of the dead'; ancient cemetery
nomos (s), nomoi (pl) – prefectures into which the regions and island groups of Greece are divided
nymphaeum – in ancient Greece, building containing a fountain and often dedicated to nymphs
ohtapodi – octopus

OA – Olympiaki Aeroporia or Olympic Airways; Greece's national airline and major domestic air carrier
odeion – ancient Greek indoor theatre
odos – street
OSE – Organismos Sidirodromon Ellados; Greek railways organisation
OTE – Organismos Tilepikinonion Ellados; Greece's major telecommunications carrier
oud – a bulbous, stringed instrument with a sharply raked-back head
ouzeri – place which serves *ouzo* and light snacks
ouzo – a distilled spirit made from grapes and flavoured with aniseed

Panagia – Mother of God; name frequently used for churches
Pantokrator – painting or mosaic of Christ in the centre of the dome of a Byzantine church
paralia – waterfront
PASOK – Panellinio Sosialistiko Komma; Greek socialist party
pediment – triangular section (often filled with sculpture) above the columns, found at the front and back of a classical Greek temple
periptero (s), periptera (pl) – street kiosk
plateia – square
Politiki Anixi – Political Spring; centrist political party
propylon (s), propylaia (pl) – main entrance to an ancient city or sanctuary; a propylon had one gateway and a propylaia more than one
psarotaverna – taverna specialising in seafood
psistaria – restaurant serving grilled food

rembetika – blues songs commonly associated with the underworld of the 1920s
retsina – resinated white wine
saganaki – fried cheese

skyladika – literally 'dog songs'; popular, but not lyrically challenging, blues songs often sung in nightclubs

stele (s), stelae (pl) – grave stone which stands upright

stifado – stew

stoa – long colonnaded building, usually in an *agora*; used as a meeting place and shelter in ancient Greece

taverna – traditional restaurant which serves food and wine

tekedes (pl), tekes (sing) – hashish dens of the 1920s

tholos tomb – a beehive-shaped tomb used by the Mycenaeans between 1500 and 1200 BC

toumberleki – small lap drum played with the fingers

vaulted – having an arched roof, normally of brick or stone

zaharoplasteio (s), zaharoplasteia (pl) – patisserie; shop which sells cakes, chocolates, sweets and, sometimes, alcoholic drinks

LONELY PLANET

ON THE ROAD

Travel Guides explore cities, regions and countries, and supply information on transport, restaurants and accommodation, covering all budgets. They come with reliable, easy-to-use maps, practical advice, cultural and historical facts and a rundown on attractions both on and off the beaten track. There are over 200 titles in this classic series, covering nearly every country in the world.

Lonely Planet Upgrades extend the shelf life of existing travel guides by detailing any changes that may affect travel in a region since a book has been published. Upgrades can be downloaded for free from **www.lonelyplanet.com/upgrades**

For travellers with more time than money, **Shoestring** guides offer dependable, first-hand information with hundreds of detailed maps, plus insider tips for stretching money as far as possible. Covering entire continents in most cases, the six-volume shoestring guides are known around the world as 'backpackers bibles'.

For the discerning short-term visitor, **Condensed** guides highlight the best a destination has to offer in a full-colour, pocket-sized format designed for quick access. They include everything from top sights and walking tours to opinionated reviews of where to eat, stay, shop and have fun.

CitySync lets travellers use their Palm™ or Visor™ hand-held computers to guide them through a city with handy tips on transport, history, cultural life, major sights, and shopping and entertainment options. It can also quickly search and sort hundreds of reviews of hotels, restaurants and attractions, and pinpoint their location on scrollable street maps. CitySync can be downloaded from **www.citysync.com**

MAPS & ATLASES

Lonely Planet's **City Maps** feature downtown and metropolitan maps, as well as transit routes and walking tours. The maps come complete with an index of streets, a listing of sights and a plastic coat for extra durability.

Road Atlases are an essential navigation tool for serious travellers. Cross-referenced with the guidebooks, they also feature distance and climate charts and a complete site index.

ESSENTIALS

Read This First books help new travellers to hit the road with confidence. These invaluable predeparture guides give step-by-step advice on preparing for a trip, budgeting, arranging a visa, planning an itinerary and staying safe while still getting off the beaten track.

Healthy Travel pocket guides offer a regional rundown on disease hot spots and practical advice on predeparture health measures, staying well on the road and what to do in emergencies. The guides come with a user-friendly design and helpful diagrams and tables.

Lonely Planet's **Phrasebooks** cover the essential words and phrases travellers need when they're strangers in a strange land. They come in a pocket-sized format with colour tabs for quick reference, extensive vocabulary lists, easy-to-follow pronunciation keys and two-way dictionaries.

Miffed by blurry photos of the Taj Mahal? Tired of the classic 'top of the head cut off' shot? **Travel Photography: A Guide to Taking Better Pictures** will help you turn ordinary holiday snaps into striking images and give you the know-how to capture every scene, from frenetic festivals to peaceful beach sunrises.

Lonely Planet's **Travel Journal** is a lightweight but sturdy travel diary for jotting down all those on-the-road observations and significant travel moments. It comes with a handy time-zone wheel, a world map and useful travel information.

Lonely Planet's eKno is an all-in-one communication service developed especially for travellers. It offers low-cost international calls and free email and voicemail so that you can keep in touch while on the road. Check it out on **www.ekno.lonelyplanet.com**

FOOD & RESTAURANT GUIDES

Lonely Planet's **Out to Eat** guides recommend the brightest and best places to eat and drink in top international cities. These gourmet companions are arranged by neighbourhood, packed with dependable maps, garnished with scene-setting photos and served with quirky features.

For people who live to eat, drink and travel, **World Food** guides explore the culinary culture of each country. Entertaining and adventurous, each guide is packed with detail on staples and specialities, regional cuisine and local markets, as well as sumptuous recipes, comprehensive culinary dictionaries and lavish photos good enough to eat.

OUTDOOR GUIDES

For those who believe the best way to see the world is on foot, Lonely Planet's **Walking Guides** detail everything from family strolls to difficult treks, with 'when to go and how to do it' advice supplemented by reliable maps and essential travel information.

Cycling Guides map a destination's best bike tours, long and short, in day-by-day detail. They contain all the information a cyclist needs, including advice on bike maintenance, places to eat and stay, innovative maps with detailed cues to the rides, and elevation charts.

The **Watching Wildlife** series is perfect for travellers who want authoritative information but don't want to tote a heavy field guide. Packed with advice on where, when and how to view a region's wildlife, each title features photos of over 300 species and contains engaging comments on the local flora and fauna.

With underwater colour photos throughout, **Pisces Books** explore the world's best diving and snorkelling areas. Each book contains listings of diving services and dive resorts, detailed information on depth, visibility and difficulty of dives, and a roundup of the marine life you're likely to see through your mask.

LONELY PLANET

OFF THE ROAD

Journeys, the travel literature series written by renowned travel authors, capture the spirit of a place or illuminate a culture with a journalist's attention to detail and a novelist's flair for words. These are tales to soak up while you're actually on the road or dip into as an at-home armchair indulgence.

The range of lavishly illustrated **Pictorial** books is just the ticket for both travellers and dreamers. Off-beat tales and vivid photographs bring the adventure of travel to your doorstep long before the journey begins and long after it is over.

Lonely Planet **Videos** encourage the same independent, tough-minded approach as the guidebooks. Currently airing throughout the world, this award-winning series features innovative footage and an original soundtrack.

Yes, we know, work is tough, so do a little bit of deskside dreaming with the spiral-bound Lonely Planet **Diary** or a Lonely Planet **Wall Calendar**, filled with great photos from around the world.

TRAVELLERS NETWORK

Lonely Planet Online. Lonely Planet's award-winning Web site has insider information on hundreds of destinations, from Amsterdam to Zimbabwe, complete with interactive maps and relevant links. The site also offers the latest travel news, recent reports from travellers on the road, guidebook upgrades, a travel links site, an online book-buying option and a lively travellers bulletin board. It can be viewed at **www.lonelyplanet.com** or AOL keyword: lp.

Planet Talk is a quarterly print newsletter, full of gossip, advice, anecdotes and author articles. It provides an antidote to the being-at-home blues and lets you plan and dream for the next trip. Contact the nearest Lonely Planet office for your free copy.

Comet, the free Lonely Planet newsletter, comes via email once a month. It's loaded with travel news, advice, dispatches from authors, travel competitions and letters from readers. To subscribe, click on the Comet subscription link on the front page of the Web site.

LONELY PLANET

Guides by Region

L onely Planet is known worldwide for publishing practical, reliable and no-nonsense travel information in our guides and on our Web site. The Lonely Planet list covers just about every accessible part of the world. Currently there are 16 series: Travel guides, Shoestring guides, Condensed guides, Phrasebooks, Read This First, Healthy Travel, Walking guides, Cycling guides, Watching Wildlife guides, Pisces Diving & Snorkeling guides, City Maps, Road Atlases, Out to Eat, World Food, Journeys travel literature and Pictorials.

AFRICA Africa on a shoestring • Botswana • Cairo • Cairo City Map • Cape Town • Cape Town City Map • East Africa • Egypt • Egyptian Arabic phrasebook • Ethiopia, Eritrea & Djibouti • Ethiopian Amharic phrasebook • The Gambia & Senegal • Healthy Travel Africa • Kenya • Malawi • Morocco • Moroccan Arabic phrasebook • Mozambique • Namibia • Read This First: Africa • South Africa, Lesotho & Swaziland • Southern Africa • Southern Africa Road Atlas • Swahili phrasebook • Tanzania, Zanzibar & Pemba • Trekking in East Africa • Tunisia • Watching Wildlife East Africa • Watching Wildlife Southern Africa • West Africa • World Food Morocco • Zambia • Zimbabwe, Botswana & Namibia
Travel Literature: Mali Blues: Traveling to an African Beat • The Rainbird: A Central African Journey • Songs to an African Sunset: A Zimbabwean Story

AUSTRALIA & THE PACIFIC Aboriginal Australia & the Torres Strait Islands •Auckland • Australia • Australian phrasebook • Australia Road Atlas • Cycling Australia • Cycling New Zealand • Fiji • Fijian phrasebook • Healthy Travel Australia, NZ & the Pacific • Islands of Australia's Great Barrier Reef • Melbourne • Melbourne City Map • Micronesia • New Caledonia • New South Wales • New Zealand • Northern Territory • Outback Australia • Out to Eat – Melbourne • Out to Eat – Sydney • Papua New Guinea • Pidgin phrasebook • Queensland • Rarotonga & the Cook Islands • Samoa • Solomon Islands • South Australia • South Pacific • South Pacific phrasebook • Sydney • Sydney City Map • Sydney Condensed • Tahiti & French Polynesia • Tasmania • Tonga • Tramping in New Zealand • Vanuatu • Victoria • Walking in Australia • Watching Wildlife Australia • Western Australia
Travel Literature: Islands in the Clouds: Travels in the Highlands of New Guinea • Kiwi Tracks: A New Zealand Journey • Sean & David's Long Drive

CENTRAL AMERICA & THE CARIBBEAN Bahamas, Turks & Caicos • Baja California • Belize, Guatemala & Yucatán • Bermuda • Central America on a shoestring • Costa Rica • Costa Rica Spanish phrasebook • Cuba • Cycling Cuba • Dominican Republic & Haiti • Eastern Caribbean • Guatemala • Havana • Healthy Travel Central & South America • Jamaica • Mexico • Mexico City • Panama • Puerto Rico • Read This First: Central & South America • Virgin Islands • World Food Caribbean • World Food Mexico • Yucatán
Travel Literature: Green Dreams: Travels in Central America

EUROPE Amsterdam • Amsterdam City Map • Amsterdam Condensed • Andalucía • Athens • Austria • Baltic States phrasebook • Barcelona • Barcelona City Map • Belgium & Luxembourg • Berlin • Berlin City Map • Britain • British phrasebook • Brussels, Bruges & Antwerp • Brussels City Map • Budapest • Budapest City Map • Canary Islands • Catalunya & the Costa Brava • Central Europe • Central Europe phrasebook • Copenhagen • Corfu & the Ionians • Corsica • Crete • Crete Condensed • Croatia • Cycling Britain • Cycling France • Cyprus • Czech & Slovak Republics • Czech phrasebook • Denmark • Dublin • Dublin City Map • Dublin Condensed • Eastern Europe • Eastern Europe phrasebook • Edinburgh • Edinburgh City Map • England • Estonia, Latvia & Lithuania • Europe on a shoestring • Europe phrasebook • Finland • Florence • Florence City Map • France • Frankfurt City Map • Frankfurt Condensed • French phrasebook • Georgia, Armenia & Azerbaijan • Germany • German phrasebook • Greece • Greek Islands • Greek phrasebook • Hungary • Iceland, Greenland & the Faroe Islands • Ireland • Italian phrasebook • Italy • Kraków • Lisbon • The Loire • London • London City Map • London Condensed • Madrid • Madrid City Map • Malta • Mediterranean Europe • Milan, Turin & Genoa • Moscow • Munich • Netherlands • Normandy • Norway • Out to Eat – London • Out to Eat – Paris • Paris • Paris City Map • Paris Condensed • Poland • Polish phrasebook • Portugal • Portuguese phrasebook • Prague • Prague City Map • Provence & the Côte d'Azur • Read This First: Europe • Rhodes & the Dodecanese • Romania & Moldova • Rome • Rome City Map • Rome Condensed • Russia, Ukraine & Belarus • Russian phrasebook • Scandinavian & Baltic Europe • Scandinavian phrasebook • Scotland • Sicily • Slovenia • South-West France • Spain • Spanish phrasebook • Stockholm • St Petersburg • St Petersburg City Map • Sweden • Switzerland • Tuscany • Ukrainian phrasebook • Venice • Vienna • Wales • Walking in Britain • Walking in France • Walking in Ireland • Walking in Italy • Walking in Scotland • Walking in Spain • Walking in Switzerland • Western Europe • World Food France • World Food Greece • World Food Ireland • World Food Italy • World Food Spain **Travel Literature:** After Yugoslavia • Love and War in the Apennines • The Olive Grove: Travels in Greece • On the Shores of the Mediterranean • Round Ireland in Low Gear • A Small Place in Italy

LONELY PLANET

Mail Order

L onely Planet products are distributed worldwide. They are also available by mail order from Lonely Planet, so if you have difficulty finding a title please write to us. North and South American residents should write to 150 Linden St, Oakland, CA 94607, USA; European and African residents should write to 10a Spring Place, London NW5 3BH, UK; and residents of other countries to Locked Bag 1, Footscray, Victoria 3011, Australia.

INDIAN SUBCONTINENT & THE INDIAN OCEAN Bangladesh • Bengali phrasebook • Bhutan • Delhi • Goa • Healthy Travel Asia & India • Hindi & Urdu phrasebook • India • India & Bangladesh City Map • Indian Himalaya • Karakoram Highway • Kathmandu City Map • Kerala • Madagascar • Maldives • Mauritius, Réunion & Seychelles • Mumbai (Bombay) • Nepal • Nepali phrasebook • North India • Pakistan • Rajasthan • Read This First: Asia & India • South India • Sri Lanka • Sri Lanka phrasebook • Tibet • Tibetan phrasebook • Trekking in the Indian Himalaya • Trekking in the Karakoram & Hindukush • Trekking in the Nepal Himalaya • World Food India **Travel Literature**: The Age of Kali: Indian Travels and Encounters • Hello Goodnight: A Life of Goa • In Rajasthan • Maverick in Madagascar • A Season in Heaven: True Tales from the Road to Kathmandu • Shopping for Buddhas • A Short Walk in the Hindu Kush • Slowly Down the Ganges

MIDDLE EAST & CENTRAL ASIA Bahrain, Kuwait & Qatar • Central Asia • Central Asia phrasebook • Dubai • Farsi (Persian) phrasebook • Hebrew phrasebook • Iran • Israel & the Palestinian Territories • Istanbul • Istanbul City Map • Istanbul to Cairo • Istanbul to Kathmandu • Jerusalem • Jerusalem City Map • Jordan • Lebanon • Middle East • Oman & the United Arab Emirates • Syria • Turkey • Turkish phrasebook • World Food Turkey • Yemen **Travel Literature**: Black on Black: Iran Revisited • Breaking Ranks: Turbulent Travels in the Promised Land • The Gates of Damascus • Kingdom of the Film Stars: Journey into Jordan

NORTH AMERICA Alaska • Boston • Boston City Map • Boston Condensed • British Columbia • California & Nevada • California Condensed • Canada • Chicago • Chicago City Map • Chicago Condensed • Florida • Georgia & the Carolinas • Great Lakes • Hawaii • Hiking in Alaska • Hiking in the USA • Honolulu & Oahu City Map • Las Vegas • Los Angeles • Los Angeles City Map • Louisiana & the Deep South • Miami • Miami City Map • Montreal • New England • New Orleans • New Orleans City Map • New York City • New York City City Map • New York City Condensed • New York, New Jersey & Pennsylvania • Oahu • Out to Eat – San Francisco • Pacific Northwest • Rocky Mountains • San Diego & Tijuana • San Francisco • San Francisco City Map • Seattle • Seattle City Map • Southwest • Texas • Toronto • USA • USA phrasebook • Vancouver • Vancouver City Map • Virginia & the Capital Region • Washington, DC • Washington, DC City Map • World Food New Orleans **Travel Literature**: Caught Inside: A Surfer's Year on the California Coast • Drive Thru America

NORTH-EAST ASIA Beijing • Beijing City Map • Cantonese phrasebook • China • Hiking in Japan • Hong Kong & Macau • Hong Kong City Map • Hong Kong Condensed • Japan • Japanese phrasebook • Korea • Korean phrasebook • Kyoto • Mandarin phrasebook • Mongolia • Mongolian phrasebook • Seoul • Shanghai • South-West China • Taiwan • Tokyo • Tokyo Condensed • World Food Hong Kong • World Food Japan **Travel Literature**: In Xanadu: A Quest • Lost Japan

SOUTH AMERICA Argentina, Uruguay & Paraguay • Bolivia • Brazil • Brazilian phrasebook • Buenos Aires • Buenos Aires City Map • Chile & Easter Island • Colombia • Ecuador & the Galapagos Islands • Healthy Travel Central & South America • Latin American Spanish phrasebook • Peru • Quechua phrasebook • Read This First: Central & South America • Rio de Janeiro • Rio de Janeiro City Map • Santiago de Chile • South America on a shoestring • Trekking in the Patagonian Andes • Venezuela **Travel Literature**: Full Circle: A South American Journey

SOUTH-EAST ASIA Bali & Lombok • Bangkok • Bangkok City Map • Burmese phrasebook • Cambodia • Cycling Vietnam, Laos & Cambodia • East Timor phrasebook • Hanoi • Healthy Travel Asia & India • Hill Tribes phrasebook • Ho Chi Minh City (Saigon) • Indonesia • Indonesian phrasebook • Indonesia's Eastern Islands • Java • Lao phrasebook • Laos • Malay phrasebook • Malaysia, Singapore & Brunei • Myanmar (Burma) • Philippines • Pilipino (Tagalog) phrasebook • Read This First: Asia & India • Singapore • Singapore City Map • South-East Asia on a shoestring • South-East Asia phrasebook • Thailand • Thailand's Islands & Beaches • Thailand, Vietnam, Laos & Cambodia Road Atlas • Thai phrasebook • Vietnam • Vietnamese phrasebook • World Food Indonesia • World Food Thailand • World Food Vietnam

ALSO AVAILABLE: Antarctica • The Arctic • The Blue Man: Tales of Travel, Love and Coffee • Brief Encounters: Stories of Love, Sex & Travel • Buddhist Stupas in Asia: The Shape of Perfection • Chasing Rickshaws • The Last Grain Race • Lonely Planet ... On the Edge: Adventurous Escapades from Around the World • Lonely Planet Unpacked • Lonely Planet Unpacked Again • Not the Only Planet: Science Fiction Travel Stories • Ports of Call: A Journey by Sea • Sacred India • Travel Photography: A Guide to Taking Better Pictures • Travel with Children • Tuvalu: Portrait of an Island Nation

LONELY PLANET

You already know that Lonely Planet produces more than this one guidebook, but you might not be aware of the other products we have on this region. Here is a selection of titles that you may want to check out as well:

Athens map
ISBN 1 74059 320 0
US$5.99 • UK£3.99

Athens condensed
ISBN 1 74059 350 2
US$11.99 • UK£5.99

Greek phrasebook
ISBN 0 86442 683 6
US$7.99 • UK£4.50

Athens
ISBN 1 86450 295 9
US$12.99 • UK£8.99

Greece
ISBN 1 86450 334 3
US$19.99 • UK£12.99

World Food Greece
ISBN 1 86450 113 8
US$13.99 • UK£8.99

Greek Islands
ISBN 1 74059 050 3
US$19.99 • UK£11.99

Corfu & the Ionians
ISBN 1 74059 070 8
US$14.99 • UK£8.99

Rhodes & the Dodecanese
ISBN 1 86450 117 0
US$15.99 • UK£9.99

Mediterranean Europe
ISBN 1 74059 302 2
US$27.99 • UK£16.99

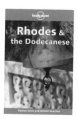

The Olive Grove:
Travels in Greece
ISBN 0 86442 459 0
US$12.95 • UK£6.99

Crete
ISBN 1 74059 049 X
US$15.99 • UK£9.99

Available wherever books are sold

Index

Bold indicates maps.

Bold indicates maps.